PARTICIPATION
— and the —
GOOD

PARTICIPATION
— *and the* —
GOOD

A Study in
Boethian Metaphysics

Siobhan Nash-Marshall

A Herder & Herder Book
The Crossroad Publishing Company
New York

The Crossroad Publishing Company
www.crossroadpublishing.com

Copyright © 2000 by Siobhan Nash-Marshall

All rights reserved. No part of this book may be reproduced, stored in a retrieval system, or transmitted, in any form or by any means, electronic, mechanical, photocopying, recording, or otherwise, without the written permission of The Crossroad Publishing Company.

Printed in the United States of America

Library of Congress Cataloging-in-Publication Data
Nash-Marshall, Siobhan.
 Participation and the good : a study in Boethian metaphysics / Siobhan Nash-Marshall; foreword by Joseph W. Koterski.
  p. cm.
 "A Herder & Herder book."
 Includes bibliographical references and index.
 ISBN 978-0-8245-1852-3 (alk. paper)
  1. Boethius, d. 524. De consolatione philosophiae. Boethius, d. 524. Quomodo substantiae. 3. Participation. 4. Good and evil. I. Title.
B659.D473 N37 2000
189–dc21
                                                                 99-050966

1 2 3 4 5 6 7 8 9 10   06 07 04 03 02 01 00

This printing: October 2017

To Antonia

Οὔτοι συνέχθειν, ἀλλὰ συμφιλεῖν ἔφυν

CONTENTS

Foreword ix

Preface xiii

Part One
THE BOETHIAN DOCTRINE OF PARTICIPATION: THE PROBLEM / 1

1. Participation in the *Quomodo Substantiae* 5

2. Participation in the *Consolatio Philosophiae* 10

3. A Survey of Possible Methodologies 18
   The Historical Problem   20
   The Boethian Corpus   24

4. The Direct Theoretical Approach: The Good 31
   The Metaphysics of the Good   31
   Boethius and the Good   37

Part Two
THE GOOD / 39

5. The Definitions of the Good 41
   The Teleological Good: The Nature of Objects   44
   The Teleological Good: The Relation between Subject
     and Object   46
   The Good as the Object of Desire   67

6. The Two Definitions of the Good and Their Paradoxes 69

7. The Foundations of a Solution 73
   Substantiality and Real Relations   76

8. The Elements of a Solution 98
   An Analysis of the Definitions   99
   A Deduction from the Definitions   101

9. Outline of the Solution 108
   The *Exitus* and the *Reditus* of the Good   109
   The Good   113

10. Conclusion 114

Part Three
BOETHIUS AND THE GOOD:
THE *QUOMODO SUBSTANTIAE* AND
CONSOLATIO PHILOSOPHIAE / 117

11. The *Exitus:* The *Quomodo Substantiae* 119
    - Interpretations of the Solution   121
    - The *Quomodo Substantiae:* The Problem   141
    - Preliminaries to the Solution   158
    - The Solution   164
    - Objections   178
    - The Good in the *Quomodo Substantiae*   183

12. The *Consolatio Philosophiae* 186
    - The *Consolatio*'s Object and Structure   191
    - The Good   198
    - Freedom and God   210
    - The *Consolatio*'s *Reditus*   219

Part Four
PARTICIPATION / 223

13. The *Quomodo Substantiae* 225
    - The *Quomodo* and the Causes of Complex Things' Substantial Goodness   226
    - The *Quomodo*'s Axioms: Interpretations   230
    - The *Quomodo*'s Axioms   246
    - The Axiom's Metaphysics and Doctrine of Participation   263
    - *Sed Contra*   265
    - Universals *Ante Rem*   271

14. The *Consolatio Philosophiae* 274
    - The *Consolatio* and the Causes of Complex Things' Perfection   275
    - Participation in the *Consolatio*   285

Part Five
CONCLUSION / 291

Bibliography 299

Index 305

FOREWORD

Studies in the history of philosophy profit not just from the painstaking archeology of manuscript research and the delicate sensibility of cultural hermeneutics but also from the critical yet sympathetic labors of philosophizing along with the source thinker. Each of these three aspects is crucial. Unless there are good texts, the effort will amount only to an interesting projection. Unless there is appreciation of the historical context, there looms the risk of misinterpreting the basal thinker as responding only to our modern questions rather than those actually afoot. And unless one thinks all the way through the matter for oneself, even while accompanying the original philosopher, one may well miss understanding the reasons for having set up the problem a certain way, not to mention missing an opportunity for bringing out implications genuinely within the position and reasoning of the source that the original thinker may not have seen. In *The Unity of Philosophical Experience*,[1] Etienne Gilson offers a wealth of examples in which the later figures in various schools of thought managed to make progress well beyond the source of their inspiration even while remaining loyal to the original insights in every respect.

The fruitfulness of such a three-pronged approach for understanding the medieval development of Neoplatonic philosophy has been richly evident in the scholarship produced over the past century. The establishment of a reliable text for Plotinus, for instance, was especially complicated beyond the normal difficulties of manuscript transmission because of the intrusive redactions of Porphyry, but increasing success in this area aided the scholarly considerations pertinent to the sociology of philosophical knowledge in that day as well as profited efforts to understand Plotinus's seminal metaphysics better. In turn, a deeper comprehension of the interworkings of elements within Neoplatonic metaphysics enabled textual scholars to make still better choices in their construction of critical texts.

---

1. New York: Charles Scribner's Sons, 1937.

In the study of the history of Neoplatonic philosophy in the three religious traditions of the middle ages (Judaism, Christianity, and Islam) that found Neoplatonism an attractive option, these three interlocked approaches have proven vital. For many of the figures, the textual work remains in process, and the appreciation of the interactions with other schools of thought is simply all the more difficult because religious commitments are in play besides strictly philosophical considerations. But equally indispensable is the effort to think through each metaphysical proposal, in much the fashion that David B. Burrell has attempted to do in *Freedom and Creation in Three Traditions*.[2] Neoplatonic emanation theory, he argues, struck thinkers in each of these religious traditions as an extremely plausible framework for articulating philosophically the doctrine of creation to which they were profoundly committed. But they also sensed a need somehow to adapt the basic idea received from Neoplatonic sources and to modify the necessity that strict Neoplatonic theory attributed to emanation so as to respect an equally important commitment to the sovereign freedom of God. The contemporary historian of medieval Neoplatonism cannot succeed without engaging in a sympathetic but critical re-thinking of the entire metaphysics of each thinker in order to appreciate the significance of what is adopted, what adapted, and what rejected from the main stream of Neoplatonism in each case.

For Boethius, the textual problems — although not yet fully resolved — are not as acute as for many of the other figures in Christian Neoplatonism. Studies of the various influences upon Boethius and the influences which Boethius has had upon others are numerous. But thinking through the issues in company with Boethius has proven the hardest task. The problems are numerous, including the problem of being sure of the author's own voice within a dialogue such as the *Consolation of Philosophy*, the pithy nature of the axioms and inferences of an explicitly metaphysical treatise like the *Quomodo Substantiae*, and the unfinished status of his proposed synthesis of Plato and Aristotle, given his untimely death. Yet, the application of a method that uses a directly theoretical approach has special likelihood for success, precisely because this source thinker was such a keen logician and such a profound metaphysician. Re-thinking any of the doctrines of Boethius from the perspective of the problems he claims to have been trying to solve permits a reconstruction of his thought at greater length and depth than the brief but dense *Quomodo* achieved and the ex-

---

2. Notre Dame, Ind.: University of Notre Dame Press, 1993.

pansive but elusive *Consolation* employed without always explaining thematically.

What Siobhan Nash-Marshall offers in this volume is a study in Boethian metaphysics by focusing on participation and the good. Neither doctrine is unambiguous in the texts of Boethius — in fact, the *prima facie* claims seem contradictory and relatively obvious problems appear to go unresolved. Boethius never explicitly employs any of his axioms (let alone those that mention participation) in his explanation of the ontological goodness of composite beings. Yet, he envisions participation as crucial for the resolution of the problem of how things can be good by virtue of their essences without thereby being substantial goodness (that is, God). The variety of definitions offered for the good in the *Consolation of Philosophy* sometimes invoke the notion of participation, for instance, in the claim that the human good resides in one's participation in the prime good, and yet the inclusion of such language seems directly at odds with other definitions, including the notion that the human good consists in the self-possession of one's own being, for this cannot involve participation in anything other than one's own nature.

By engaging in the thoughtful reconstruction of both of these key Boethian doctrines — participation and the good — Nash-Marshall proposes a credible and sustained case for better understanding the inner logic of Boethius. But in doing so she also offers an exceptional insight into the very problems that drew Boethius to begin to articulate his own views — whether so tersely in the succinct deductions of the *Quomodo* or so tantalizingly unreconciled a set of affirmations that undergird the conversations of the *Consolation*.

Central to her re-thinking of the issues is the assumption of the dialectic of *exitus* and *reditus* that Neoplatonists are always traversing, but to which they consciously advert as seldom as travelers do to the road itself when their minds are fixed on getting to their destination or getting back home. Yet, this simple distinction enables both the philosopher and the historian of philosophy to make better sense of the fragmentary comments in Boethius's texts about participation. From this distinction too one gains a stance by which to reconcile the apparently contradictory claims Boethius makes about the substantive and teleological definitions of the good for composite beings. On the basis of the difference between *exitus* and *reditus*, Boethius needs to assign analogous meanings to participation which in turn help us to grasp why composite beings must already be good in their essence and yet still need to acquire the perfections appropriate to their existence by their participation in God and in their own essences.

To grasp the inner logic of Boethius's reasoning on these issues entails a readiness to complete the articulation of a synthesis Boethius envisioned but was unable to provide. While some scholars have thought the project impossible, Nash-Marshall ventures a thoughtful reconstruction of the connections intrinsic to his positions.

JOSEPH W. KOTERSKI, S.J.
Fordham University

PREFACE

Why Boethian metaphysics? Why should one analyze the thought of a man who died with an empire, the echoes of whose mentality were drowned out by the many revolutions that stirred its ashes? What can the thought of a culture long dead have to tell us today? And more importantly why metaphysics, in a day and age in which philosophy has declared it a thing of the past?

The preface of a book is no place to answer these questions, which have as much to do with who and what we are, as they do with what and why we do anything at all. To preface a book with these questions is to preface a book with a book, and make of one's production an introduction to an introduction: a Hegelian circle.

But perhaps it is not out of place to preface a book with a question, and with an intent. Ours is a strange Janus-like mentality. Every age believes that its object, its mission, is to begin anew, to accomplish what past ages have not. Each age is convinced that it, unlike the age that preceded it, has the answers, or at least the proper questions and methods to obtain them. At the same time each age views itself as the prelude to the end, and the past as the haven of dreams unobtainable. Our age is no exception to either phenomenon. We have, it seems, distinguished ourselves from the dreaded past by deciding that the point is that there is no point, or at least that there is no unquestionable point: that the problem with ages past is that they thought they could make one. At the same time, we are so enamored with the past that we look upon it as the refuge for our restless hearts. Never has there been such an ample production of both history of philosophy and new speculation, and never has history and speculation seen so little communication. In our age, it seems, Janus's two faces have become separate heads.

Is this as it should be? Of course not. The risk of not having our culture's two faces communicate is to unknowingly keep the past present, to return unknowingly to the past, and unknowingly to repeat its errors. It is, as Kierkegaard put it, to have, "All of the plans I project fly straight back at me," so that "when I want to spit, I spit in my own face." It is also not to understand one's present: the real problems that one's age presents.

Two and a half millennia have passed since Aristotle formulated his categories, and despite the dialectical relation between each successive age, they still frame our questions, our answers, our *Weltanschauung*. Hume may have questioned the relation between cause and effect, but he nonetheless used it in order to formulate his epistemology. And as this is true of Hume and causation, so too is it true of Leibnitz and the category of relation, Descartes and the category of substance. Benedetto Croce once said that although Western culture has become increasingly less Christian, it has not and cannot abandon Christian categories. It is through the past that we define the present. To really take a step forward, to answer the questions that the past has left us, to counter its dreaded answers, entails knowing what we and our past are: to know the foundations that gird both us and them, and perhaps see if they are correct. It is to question the categories in their formation, at their roots: the problems they attempt to solve. This is why Boethius, and metaphysics: *vetera novis augere et perficere*.

New York
October 30, 1999

Part One

THE BOETHIAN DOCTRINE OF PARTICIPATION
The Problem

Our main object in this book is to determine and define the Boethian doctrine of participation: how Boethius conceived participation generally — what he thought participation meant — and how he conceived it in particular — how he thought it took place and what he thought it constituted. In brief, it is to understand why Boethius formulated a doctrine of participation, and how he understood participation itself.

Given the object, ours would seem to be primarily an historical project and to entail using the sort of methodology which one finds in many analyses of historically significant philosophers' metaphysical doctrines (such as analyses of Aristotle's notion of substance, of the Augustinian notion of time, or of the Thomist notion of participation): that is, identifying those passages in a specific author's works pertinent to a given doctrine and examining them, setting forth the doctrine contained therein, commenting on it, and arguing about it. It would be a pleasure to determine the Boethian doctrine of participation by using a methodology of this sort. The fact of the matter is, however, that those Boethian texts that deal with participation do not afford this luxury. For the historical exposition of a given doctrine presupposes that the author under examination has given at least one unambiguous definition of the matter being analyzed, and Boethius did no such thing with regards to participation.

There are two texts in which Boethius delineated his doctrine of participation: the *Quomodo Substantiae* — or *De Hebdomadibus*, as the third of the so-called *Theological Tractates*[1] was known in the

---

1. Luca Obertello rightly points out that calling the *Quomodo Substantiae* a "theological" tractate is somewhat of a misnomer, because the work does not deal with matters of faith, or with revelation, as Boethius's other *Theological Tractates* do, but with a metaphysical problem. Cf. Luca Obertello, *Boezio e dintorni: ricerche sulla cultura altomedievale*

Middle Ages — and the *Consolatio Philosophiae*. Both of these texts are metaphysical, and both attempt to elucidate what the good is. The more technical of these is the *Quomodo Substantiae*. It is an extremely brief work — 175 lines in modern critical editions — whose object is to define the nature of contingent things' ontological goodness: how things can be good in virtue of their essences without being substantially good (*quomodo substantiae in eo quod sint bonae sint cum non sint substantialia bona*),[2] or, to be more precise, without being God.[3] The *Consolatio Philosophiae*, on the other hand, is Boethius's swan song, a work whose object is, as its title suggests, to console a mind which is weary (and wary) of the evils of the world, by delineating and defining the true nature of man's goodness and its relation to God.[4]

(Florence: Nardini Editore, 1989) p. 43: "Quel trattatello che, sotto l'improprio nome di *De Hebdomadibus*, è impropriamente annoverato tra gli *Opuscoli teologici*....I problemi discussi non sono più quelli della predicazione o della significazione, ma dell'essere e della forma, dell'essere e della partecipazione. Bastano questi accenni per farci capire che ci muoviamo in un'atmosfera tipicamente metafisica e tipicamente neoplatonica." Thus, although the other *Theological Tractates* — the *De Fide Catholica*, the *De Trinitate*, the *Utrum Pater et Filius*, and the *Contra Eutychen* — are surely theological in nature, the one we are dealing with is not. See also, on this point, the introduction to Sancti Thomae de Aquino, *Opera Omnia* iussu Leonis XIII P.M. edita, tomus L, *Super Boetium De Trinitate — Expositio libri Boetii De Ebdomadibus* (Rome-Paris: Éditions du Cerf, 1992) p. 259: "S'il apparaît que le sujet du troisième opuscule de Boèce est essentiellement métaphysique, il n'en est pas moins sûr que Thomas...a traité l'opuscule en tant qu'oeuvre théologique."

2. This is the full title of the work as it is to be found in the Steward, Rand and Tester edition (Boethius, *The Theological Tractates and The Consolation of Philosophy*, Cambridge, Harvard University Press, 1973) and it is drawn from the first lines of the work itself. Cf. *Quomodo Substantiae*, 1–3: "Postulas, ut ex Hebdomadibus nostris eius quaestionis obscuritatem quae continet modum quo *substantiae in eo quod sint bonae sint, cum non sint substantialia bona*, digeram et paulo evidentius monstrem." There are variations on this title: *Quomodo substantiae bonae sint cum non sint substantialia bona, Liber an omne quod est bonum est*, and so forth. We will refer to the work as the *Quomodo Substantiae* (henceforth abbreviated as *Quomodo*), and will use the Steward, Rand and Tester edition of the text for our Latin quotations.

3. Boethius's premise is that God alone is technically speaking substantially good because God is the only being whose essence or substance (Boethius seems to have used the terms interchangeably), is his existence. Given the premise it would seem to follow that if beings other than God were substantially good they would have to be God, and it is precisely this conclusion that he is attempting to avoid. Cf. *Quomodo*, 72–80: "Sed si esse bonum est, ea quae sunt in eo quod sunt bona sunt idemque illis est esse quod boni esse; substantialia igitur bona sunt, quoniam non participant bonitatem. Quod si ipsum esse in eis bonum est, non est dubium quin substantialia cum sint bona, primo sint bono similia ac per hoc hoc ipsum bonum erunt; nihil enim illi praeter se ipsum simile est. Ex quo fit ut omnia quae sunt deus sint, quod dictu nefas est."

4. Cf. *Consolatio Philosophiae*, I, 4, 98–106: "Qua in re non ita sensus nostros maeror hebetavit ut impios scelerata contra virtutem querar molitos, sed quae speraverint effecisse vehementer admiror. Nam deteriora velle nostri fuerit fortasse defectus, posse contra innocentiam, quae sceleratus quisque conceperit inspectante deo, monstri simile est. Unde haud iniuria tuorum quidam familiarum quaesivit: 'Si quidem deus,' inquit, 'est, unde mala? Bona vero unde, si non est?'" This is Boethius's problem, the source of his "illness," and is thus disclosed after Philosophy asks him to lay bare his wound. See *Consolatio*, I, 4, 5ff. The matter is simplified a bit here. For as we shall see, the 'good' is at once an ontological, and a teleological term in the *Consolatio*.

Given the nature of the problems with which these two works deal, the fact that both attempt to define the nature of the 'good' and the relationship that subsists between contingent good things and God — that is, particular good things and the Absolute Good — it is no surprise that Boethius formulated and made use of a doctrine of participation. He was not the first, or the last, philosopher to resort to a doctrine of participation to solve the problem of the one and the many. What is surprising, however, is that his treatment of participation is as obscure as it is, despite the significant role the doctrine plays in his metaphysics. For the truth of the matter is that Boethius did not clearly define his doctrine of participation in either the *Quomodo Substantiae* or the *Consolatio Philosophiae*. In neither did he explicitly state whether he considered it a doctrine of creation or a means of explaining how contingent beings can acquire accidental properties; in neither did he characterize participation in causal terms; in neither did he delineate the metaphysical problems involved in participation; and to make matters worse, he filled both works with apparent contradictions. It is precisely for these reasons that one cannot simply lay out and discuss the Boethian doctrine of participation as something which is already clear in the texts.

Our first problem, as such, is to define the methodology we will use to determine the doctrine itself. That is the object of this first part of our book. We will begin by delineating the difficulties involved in Boethius's two metaphysical texts in order to illustrate what problems our methodology must solve. We will then analyze the possible methodologies that one can use to solve these problems, and the reasons why they can or cannot serve as our means. Once we have done that, we will outline the methodology we will use in the work: its difficulties and how we intend to solve them.

Chapter 1

PARTICIPATION IN THE *QUOMODO SUBSTANTIAE*

The *Quomodo Substantiae*, the first of Boethius's metaphysical works, has two main two sections. The first section is an extremely dense and abstract metaphysical *"summula"*[1] of nine axioms in which Boethius spells out the *"regulae"* with which he claims he will define contingent things' ontological goodness.[2] In the second section, he explains how particular things can be substantially good.[3] Of the nine axioms of the first part, the third and sixth deal directly with participation.[4]

It is here that we encounter our first problem. There seems to be a discrepancy in Boethius's treatment of participation in the two sections of the *Quomodo*. If we take the work's axioms as the basis for our interpretation of its content (as the text would seem to call us to do), then participation would seem both to be an essential part of what Boethius considers a complete metaphysics, and one of the means with

---

1. The term "summula" is Maioli's. Cf. Bruno Maioli, *Teoria dell'essere e dell'esistente e classificazione delle scienze in M. S. Boezio: una delucidazione* (Rome: Bulzoni, 1978) p. 14: "Le *regulae* del *De Hebdomadibus* costituiscono, nel loro stile estremamente conciso ed esoterico, un concentrato metafisico dove Boezio condensa in formule rigorosamente assiomatiche — ma non immuni da un certo alone oracolare ed enigmatico — la summula del suo cosmo ontologico." See also on this point, Carmelo Pandolfi in Tommaso d'Aquino, *L'essere e la partecipazione: commento al libro di Boezio de Hebdomadibus*, ed. Carmelo Pandolfi (Bologna: Edizioni Studio Domenicano, 1995) p. 15: "Non è possibile compendiare in alcun modo tali assiomi: la loro logica risulta già serrata in maniera non ulteriormente sintetizzabile... Diciamo soltanto che Boezio parte dall'essere, nell'essere rinviene l'*aliquid* (perché l'essere "vuoto" non esiste); vede perciò come *esse* e *aliquid* facciano *unum* (con le relative implicazioni)."
2. *Quomodo*, 14–17: "Ut igitur in mathematica fieri solet ceterisque etiam disciplinis, praeposui terminos regulasque quibus cuncta quae sequuntur efficiam."
3. *Quomodo*, 53–55: "Sufficiunt igitur quae praemisimus [i.e., termini et regulae]; a prudente vero rationis interprete suis unumquodque aptabitur argumentis."
4. *Quomodo*, III, 31–34: "Quod est participare aliquo potest, sed ipsum esse nullo modo participat. Fit enim participatio cum aliquid iam est; est autem aliquid, cum esse susciperit," and VI, 41–44: "Omne quod est participat eo quod est esse ut sit; alio vero participat ut aliquid sit. Ac per hoc id quod est participat eo quod est esse ut sit; est vero ut participet alio quolibet."

which he determines and defines the nature of the relation that subsists between (and the distinction between) the contingent universe's ontological goodness and the transcendent goodness of God: how things can be substantially good without being God.

The first point would seem to be proven by the inclusion of participation within the set of axioms themselves. For if the axioms are a *summula* of Boethian metaphysics, then the fact that participation plays a prominent role in them (two of the *Quomodo*'s eight metaphysical axioms deal with participation) would seem to imply that it plays a prominent role in Boethian metaphysics. As for the second point, if Boethius's axioms spell out the *regulae* with which he proposes to define the nature of contingent things' ontological goodness, and if two of these axioms deal with participation, then it stands to reason that participation must be at least one of the means with which he determines the nature of contingent things' goodness and the relation between that goodness and God.

The fact of the matter is, however, that the second section of the *Quomodo* makes what seem to be two simple deductions rather complicated. For not only does Boethius not explicitly employ any of his axioms (and specifically those regarding participation) in his explanation of the nature of things' ontological goodness — and thus ostensibly contradict or at least ignore his own claim that the axioms are the *regulae* of his solution — he makes no explicit positive reference to participation in his solution at all,[5] thus apparently gainsaying the very metaphysics that he outlines in the axioms. For participation does play a prominent role in that metaphysics. To make matters worse, his most important comment on participation in the second section, which is to be found in the preface to his definition of things' ontological goodness, is to the effect that participation cannot be called upon to explain how things are substantially good.[6]

This discrepancy in Boethius's treatment of participation clearly creates an interpretational dilemma. For if one takes the second part of the *Quomodo* as the basis for his interpretation of the work, as indeed

---

5. As McInerny puts it: "Neither Aquinas [in his commentary on the *Hebdomadibus*] nor Boethius uses the language of participation to speak of the goodness of creatures." Cf. Ralph McInerny, *Boethius and Aquinas* (Washington, D.C.: Catholic University of America Press, 1990) p. 227.

6. Cf. *Quomodo*, 60–68: "Sed quemadmodum bona sint, inquirendum est, utrumne participatione an substantia? Si participatione, per se ipsa nullo modo bona sunt; nam quod participatione album est, per se in eo quod ipsum est album non est. Et de ceteris qualitatibus eodem modo. Si igitur participatione sunt bona, ipsa per se nullo modo bona sunt: non igitur ad bonum tendunt. Sed concessum est. Non igitur participatione sunt bona."

many scholars have,[7] then participation would not seem to play a central role in Boethian metaphysics at all, nor serve as one of the means with which he defines contingent things' ontological goodness.[8] If, on the other hand, one takes the first part of the *Quomodo* as the foundation of his interpretation, as many other scholars have,[9] then the exact contrary would seem to be true.

How, then, is one to interpret the *Quomodo Substantiae*'s doctrine of participation? Is one to attend to it as it is delineated in either of the work's two sections alone, or is one to attempt to unravel the apparent inconsistency by finding a coherent doctrine in them both? The question is a rhetorical one. For since Boethius was a keen logician we can neither suppose that he did not understand the apparent contradictions in his text, nor believe that he intentionally contradicted himself. It stands to reason, as such, that there ought to be a non-contradictory way of understanding his doctrine of participation. The problem is determining how to do so. For Boethius himself does not give a clue as to what it could be. Hence the difficulty of the text.

Nor is solving the apparent textual discrepancy the only or even the principal difficulty involved in understanding the *Quomodo*'s doctrine of participation. Interpreting what Boethius meant by participation in either of the two sections of the *Quomodo* is no simple task. What we have seen regarding the second section shows that to determine what he meant by participation by analyzing it alone is a virtual impossibility.[10] For Boethius's own enigmatic definition of things' ontological goodness simply contains no positive reference to participation at all. It just dis-

---

7. Cf., e.g., Rudi A. te Velde, *Participation and Substantiality in Thomas Aquinas* (Leiden: E. J. Brill, 1996) pp. 6–20. Te Velde's interpretation of the *Quomodo Substantiae* does not even take the work's axioms into account.

8. This can be seen, once again, in te Velde's treatment of Boethius's solution to the problem of the good, where he claims that Boethius's solution hinges upon a comparative relation: the "relation in which the being of (created) things stands to the first good" rather than on participation. Cf. te Velde, pp. 17–20.

9. Cf., e.g., Maioli, on this point, p. 14: "La distinzione fra *esse* e *id quod est*, alla luce della esplicitazione offerta dagli altri assiomi gioca un ruolo fondamentale nella soluzione del problema del bene."

10. The risk involved in not attempting to find doctrine common to both sections of doctrine is to misunderstand the doctrine itself. This can be seen in te Velde's case. For te Velde's own interpretation of the Boethian doctrine of participation, grounded as it is in the second section of the work, is that it only accounts for accidental properties. Cf. e.g., te Velde, p. 19: "Boethius starts from an opposition between participation and substance. Because in his view participation implies an accidental addition, he resorts, for the goodness of substance, to the relation in which the being of (created) things stands to the first good."

Now, if te Velde is right, I fail to see how one is to interpret Boethius's third axiom: "Omne quod est participat eo quod est esse ut sit; alio vero participat ut aliquid sit. Ac per hoc id quod est participat eo quod est esse ut sit; est vero ut participet aliquid quolibet." For the axiom's explicit claim is that participation is substantial: "omne quod est participat eo quod est esse *ut sit*." This means that Boethius cannot simply have held participation to "imply accidental addition."

tinguishes three ways in which created things are good and leaves it to the reader to understand how one is to reconcile these three ways.[11]

As for understanding the doctrine of participation as Boethius delineated it in the first section of his work, it too is no simple matter. A brief glance at the first section's axioms shows that understanding what 'participation' means in them presupposes understanding what *'ipsum esse,' 'id quod est,'* and *'esse'* mean, and how Boethius distinguished *'esse'* and *'esse aliquid.'* And the fact of the matter is that the axioms at hand do not give us a clue as to what any of these terms mean: they simply do not define any of them. The texts are as follows:

> Quod est participare aliquo potest, sed ipsum esse nullo modo participat. Fit enim participatio cum aliquid iam est; est autem aliquid, cum esse susciperit (III, 31–34).

> Omne quod est participat eo quod est esse ut sit; alio vero participat ut aliquid sit. Ac per hoc id quod est participat eo quod est esse ut sit; est vero ut participet alio quolibet (VI, 41–44).

Nor, it would seem, did Boethius intend for these axioms (or for his concept of participation) to be self-evident.[12] He did not define any of the above terms in any of the *Quomodo Substantiae*'s other seven axioms. Indeed, the difficulty of the axioms in general is that none of

---

11. Boethius's solution to his problem — *quomodo substantiae in eo quod sint bonae sint cum non sint substantialia bona* — would seem to distinguish three ways in which a created thing can be good: things' existences are good because they are created by God (cf. *Quomodo* 115–18); things' essences are good because they are created by God (cf. *Quomodo*, 124–27); things' existences are good because their essences are good (cf. *Quomodo*, 130ff.). But what Boethius meant by this distinction, that is, how he actually solved his problem, is a matter of debate. Indeed, there are about as many different interpretations of Boethius's solution as there are of his axioms. Geiger, for instance, claims that the solution makes things' goodness contingent upon God's will. Aquinas interprets the point in a similar way. Obertello, on the other hand, claims that the solution shows that Boethius considered the good a transcendental property of being. We will naturally return to this point.

12. Since Boethius tells his readers to supply their own arguments for each of the axioms we must suppose that he intended for his readers to furnish their own arguments to understand his doctrine of participation too. Cf. *Quomodo*, 53–55: "A prudente vero rationis interprete suis unumquodque aptabitur argumentis."

That Boethius intends for the axioms not to be immediately self-evident can also be seen from the fact that his first axiom distinguishes a proposition which is immediately self-evident from one which is not, by claiming that the former makes use of terms whose meaning is known, whereas the latter does not. For given his distinction, the fact that he does not define his terms makes it more than clear that he had no intention of taking them as self-evident. Cf. *Quomodo*, 18–27: "Communis animi conceptio est enuntiatio quam quisque probat auditam. Harum duplex modus est. Nam una ita communis est, ut omnium sit hominum, veluti si hanc proponas: 'Si duobus aequalibus aequalia auferas, quae relinquantur aequalia esse,' nullus id intelligens neget. Alia vero est doctorum tantum, quae tamen ex talibus communibus animi conceptionibus venit, ut est: 'Quae incorporalia sunt, in loco non esse,' et cetera; quae non vulgus sed docti comprobant."

their technical terms is clear.[13] This has led many scholars to abandon the attempt to understand them directly.[14]

Given what we have seen about the work, it is clear that the *Quomodo Substantiae* affords no direct way of understanding the Boethian notion of participation. Nor is this surprising: the work at hand is intentionally abstruse.[15]

---

13. This abstruseness has engendered a myriad of interpretations of both the meanings of the axioms' terms and of the axioms themselves. We will deal with this matter in the fourth section of our book. To give an idea of the complexity of the problems they pose one need only realize that *'esse'* can mean: essence, existence or being—the substance (or act) of the entire cosmos; *'id quod est,'* on the other hand, can mean: a particular existing thing, a composite, an essence, or a form. This means that the axioms can regard essence and a particular existing thing, essence and a composite, essence and a form, existence and a composite, existence and essence, and existence and a form, being and a particular existing thing, being and the essence of a particular thing, and so on. There is at least one scholar who holds each of these positions.

14. Brosch makes this point quite clear in his analysis of the *Quomodo Substantiae*'s axioms: "Nach einer kurzen Einleitung für den Diakon Johannes, den Adressaten der Schrift 'Wie die Substanzen gut sind,' folgen neun Axiome, von denen sich acht mit dem Sein befassen. Es wäre, wie wir bereits angedeutet, eitles Bemühen, diese zuerst untersuchen zu wollen. Sie sind formell so vieldeutig und werden auch von den einzelnen Schulen so mannigfaltig interpretiert und den Sentenzen der eigenen Schule als Beweis *ex auctoritate* beigefügt." Cf. Hermann Josef Brosch, *Der Seinsbegriff bei Boethius. Mit besonderer Berücksichtigung der Beziehung von Sosein und Dasein* (Innsbruck: Felizian Rauch, 1931) pp. 38–39.

15. My use of "intentional" is intentional. Boethius himself says he wants to be obscure. Cf. *Quomodo Substantiae*, 8–14: "Hebdomadas vero ego mihi ipse commentor potiusque ad memoriam meam speculata conservo quam cuiquam participo quorum lascivia ac petulantia nihil a ioco risuque patitur esse seiunctum. Prohinc tu ne sis *obscuritatibus brevitatis adversus, quae cum sint arcani fida custodia tum id habent commodi, quod cum his solis qui digni sunt conloquuntur.*" This is in line with some of Boethius's other *Theological Tractates*. The *De Trinitate*'s preface, for instance, is much along the same lines. See *De Trinitate*, 16–22.

Chapter 2

PARTICIPATION IN THE CONSOLATIO PHILOSOPHIAE

As for the second work in which Boethius makes use of a doctrine of participation, that is, the *Consolatio Philosophiae*, it is a veritable *nœud de vipères*. Indeed, above and beyond its Christianity, a point which was a great source of contention among scholars until very recently,[1] it is not obvious how one is to reconcile its various doctrines concerning the good, or consequently how one is to interpret any one of its doctrines singly.

That the work as a whole is a progressive definition of the good, a sort of *itinerarium mentis in Deum*,[2] is more or less generally agreed

---

1. This is not the time to enter into this debate. It has been raging and lulling for roughly a thousand years, and has had many well known protagonists. But one need only compare statements such as Whittaker's and Barrett's to grasp its gist. In his introduction to Neoplatonic thought, Whittaker claims: "It was when he [Boethius] had fallen into disgrace that he wrote the *De Consolatione Philosophiae*; and the remarkable fact has often been noticed that, although certainly a nominal Christian, he turned in adversity wholly to heathen philosophy, not making the slightest allusion anywhere to the Christian revelation" (Thomas Whittaker, *The Neoplatonists*, Cambridge: Cambridge University Press, 1928, p. 186). Barrett, on the other hand, drawing upon Boethius's own sharp distinction between *fides* and *ratio*, claims that the book is the book of a Christian who is not relying on his *fides*: "There are in the *Consolation of Philosophy* one or two short passages, which, though they can bear another interpretation, support, I think, this view, and seem to show that the writer, while well aware that there is another approach to the subjects under discussion, is of deliberate purpose limiting himself to what he regards as able to be discovered by man's reason" (Helen M. Barrett, *Boethius*, New York: Russell and Russell, 1966, p. 161). Chadwick, to name another case, seems to have had a conversion, as regards Boethius's Christianity. For in his earlier works he does not think that the *Consolation* is the work of a Christian at all, whereas his later works claim that it is. Cf. *The Early Church* (London: Penguin, 1967) p. 251: "[The *Consolation* is] remarkable for its strictly classical and pagan character almost untouched by any Christian motifs." In his latest book, on the other hand, he not only defends Boethius's adherence to the faith but claims that the *Consolation* is wholly orthodox. Cf. Henry Chadwick, *Boethius: The Consolations of Music, Logic, Theology and Philosophy* (Oxford: Clarendon Paperbacks, 1981) p. 249.

For a good survey of the positions of the more recent (and noteworthy) protagonists of this debate and their arguments see Stephen Varvis, *The 'Consolation' of Boethius. An Analytical Inquiry into His Intellectual Processes and Goals*, San Francisco: Mellen Research University Press, 1991, 16–26.

2. Cf. *Consolatio Philosophiae*, IV, 1, 31–38: "Et quoniam verae formam beatitudinis me dudum monstrante vidisti, quo etiam sita sit agnovisti, decursus omnibus quae praemit-

upon.³ It is the details of the ascent that are a matter of debate. For aside from the question about what it is an ascent to — that is, whether it is an ascent to a God (a First Good) having those characteristics (such as transcendence, freedom, and personhood) that one would expect the God of Christianity to have, or whether it is an ascent to a God having those characteristics (such as lack of freedom, consubstantiality with creation, lack of personhood, and lack of transcendence) that the God of pagan philosophy might be expected to have⁴ — it is not altogether clear what kind of an ascent it is, or what kind of metaphysics it implies.

As for the type of ascent, there are those who contend that it is an ethical ascent,⁵ those who consider it a sort of mystical ascent,⁶ and those who hold that it is a metaphysical ascent.⁷ As for the metaphysical doctrines which the ascent implies, on the other hand, there are those who contend that the work's metaphysics is an odd potpourri of Neoplatonic doctrines.⁸ Some claim that its Neoplatonism is of an

---

tere necessarium puto, viam tibi quae te domum revehat ostendam. Pennas etiam tuae menti quibus se in altum tollere possit adfigam, ut perturbatione depulsa sospes in patriam meo ductu, mea semita, meis etiam vehiculis revertaris."

3. Cf., e.g., Henry Chadwick, introduction to *Boethius: His Life, Thought, and Influence*, ed. Margaret Gibson (Oxford: Basil Blackwell, 1981) p. 11: "The essential shape of the *Consolation* is a Neoplatonic thesis that the imperfections of this world are allowed to facilitate the return of the soul to its origin in God." Ferruccio Gastaldelli, *Boezio* (Rome: Edizioni Liturgiche, 1974) p. 51: "L'opera appare nel suo insieme ... [come] un *itinerarium mentis in Deum*."

4. My point here requires some clarification. I am not claiming that paganism is a univocal word or that it was a single coherent religious movement which had a determinate set of tenets. My list of characteristics does not mean to imply that there is or was such a thing as a "pagan" God, or consequently that the Neoplatonic "One" is to be identified with the gods of classical mythology, with Valentinus's plethora of gods, or so on. That would be absurd. Rather, I am using the word "pagan" in its original sense, i.e., to describe those various religious beliefs which are antithetical to Christian religious beliefs, and it is in this sense that I am listing a series of characteristics a "pagan" God might have.

5. Cf., e.g., Frederick Mayer, *A History of Ancient and Medieval Philosophy* (New York: American Book Company, 1950) p. 368: "In the *Consolation of Philosophy* we notice especially the influence of the Stoics, with their denial of the reality of evil. Like the Stoics, Boethius believed the main function of philosophy to lie in the realm of *ethics*. But we must not neglect the impact of Plato and Aristotle on Boethius, who all of his life was interested in these two Greek philosophers....Neo-Platonism also entered into the philosophy of Boethius, for he interpreted Plato in a religious and mystical manner. Like Plotinus he was intent upon finding the unity and oneness of the universe." See also Whittaker: "In philosophy Boethius represents an eclectic Neo-Platonism turned into an ethical account."

6. Cf. Gastaldelli, p. 46: "La *Consolatio* è pertanto una soteriologia umanistica, una specie di storia laica della salvezza, che si articola nella prima parte con motivi presi dalle antiche *consolationes* e nella seconda con una scelta di temi neplatonici, l'una e l'altra inserite in un dialogo che dapprima ha la mobilità talvolta aggressiva della diatriba, poi viene gradatamente a smorzarsi per assumere la composta cadenza del dialogo ciceroniano." See also footnote 25.

7. Cf., e.g., Alessandro Ghisalberti, "L'Ascesa boeziana a Dio nel libro III della *Consolatio*," in *Atti del Congresso Internazionale di Studi Boeziani* (Rome: Herder, 1981) pp. 183–92.

8. Cf., e.g., *Consolation*, p. xv: "Both the *Consolation* and the *opuscola* are pervaded

Alexandrian bent.[9] Other claim that it is of an Augustinian strand.[10] Some claim that the work's metaphysics is almost wholly Aristotelian.[11] Others contend that it is wholly Stoic.[12] Some assert that the gist of its argument is not Neoplatonic, Stoic, or Aristotelian but belongs to a school of its own.[13] Yet others claim that there is no systematic unity to its points[14] and imply, as such, that there is no point in looking for a systematic metaphysical doctrine in the *Consolatio*; others yet again distinguish its various metaphysical doctrines, without, however, attempting to draw the metaphysical implications from them.[15] Others focus on its single points, and so on.

---

by the teaching of Proclus and the Neoplatonists. Yet there is much in Proclus for which Boethius evidently finds little or no use. Boethius has woven out of the material with which Proclus had provided him, a fabric of alternating highly compressed argument and fine poetry, an account of the moral problem of evil in a good Creator's world and of the reconciliation of an all-knowing providence with human freedom in a world of apparent contingency." See also C. J. De Vogel, "The Problem of Philosophy and Christian Faith in Boethius' *Consolatio*," in *Romanitas and Christianitas*, ed. W. den Boer et al. (Amsterdam: North Holland Pub., 1973), p. 364.

9. See, e.g., Pierre Courcelle, *La Consolation de Philosophie dans la Tradition Littéraire: Antecedents et Posterité de Boèce* (Paris: Études Augustiniennes, 1967) and *Les lettres greques en Occident*. *De Macrobe à Cassiodore* (Paris: De Boccard, 1948). In Courcelle's view Boethius's whole philosophical production was strongly influenced by Ammonius, one of Proclus's followers.

10. I am thinking here of Silk who argues that model for the *Consolatio* were Augustine's *Soliloquies*. See E. T. Silk, "Boethius's *Consolatio* as a Sequel to Augustine's *Dialogues* and *Soliloquia*," in *Harvard Theological Review*, 32, 1939, 19–39.

11. The view is Hermann Usener's, who holds that the only original parts of the *Consolatio* are its verses and the autobiographical parts. He contends that most of the book is either a compilation or a translation of the lost *Protrepticus*. Cf. Hermann Usener, *Anecdoton Holderi. Ein Beitrag zur Geschichte Roms in Ostgothischer Zeit*, Bonn: Universitäts-Buchdrückerei, 1877, and "Vergessenes" in *Rheinisches Museum für Philologie*, XXVIII, 1873, pp. 400–403.

12. In his *Prolegomena* to the *Consolation*, Wilhelm Weinberger claims that there is not a single verse of the *Consolation* that cannot be found in Seneca. Cf. *Anicii Manlii Severini Boethii philosophiae consolationis libri quinque. Rudolfi Peiperi atque Georgii Schepssii copiis et Augusti Engelbrechti studiis usus ad fidem codicium recensuit Guglielmus Weinberger*, Corpus Scriptorum Ecclesiasticorum Latinorum 67 (Vienna: Hölder-Pichler-Tempsky, 1938) p. ix.

13. Cf. H. F. Steward and E. K. Rand, introduction to the Boethius, *The Theological Tractates and the Consolation of Philosophy*, p. xii: "The *Consolatio* is not, as has been maintained, a mere patchwork of translations from Aristotle and the Neoplatonists. Rather it is the supreme essay of one who throughout his life had found his highest solace in the dry light of reason. His chief source of refreshment, in the dungeon to which his beloved library had not accompanied him, was a memory well stocked with the poetry and thought of former days. The development of the argument is anything but Neoplatonic; it is all his own."

14. Cf. Gastaldelli, p. 42: "La riflessione di Boezio non si sviluppa in una sistematica trattazione filosofica, ma in una meditazione che è quasi una confessione."

15. I am thinking of Chadwick here. For in his book on Boethius, he does do us the wonderful service of distinguishing the various doctrines to be found in the various books of the *Consolation* and of showing their sources, but he does not attempt to explain why Boethius combines these different doctrines, or what metaphysics this combination implies.

What scholarly opinion indicates is that the *Consolatio* poses many of the same problems that the *Quomodo* does: that it is not altogether clear how one is to reconcile its various doctrines, or consequently how to interpret any one of them singly. For the text's ambiguity is in some sense the cause of the plethora of interpretations that one can find of it. This can be seen if one attempts to define the work's central doctrine. For although it is a relatively simple matter to determine that its aim is to define man's 'good' and its relation to God, it is no easy task to establish what Boethius meant by the term 'good' in the *Consolatio,* or consequently how he defined the relation between the 'good' and God. Indeed, there are at least three principal definitions of the 'good' in the *Consolatio:* (1) the second book's main definition claims that man's 'good' is his being *"sui compos"* (self-sufficient), that is, his possessing himself.[16] (2) The third book's primary definition states that man's 'good' is his participating in the First Good.[17] (3) To this one must add the fourth book's admonition that man must not seek external rewards for his virtuous behavior, for virtuous behavior is its own reward.[18] Indeed, that book's central claim is that man's 'good' is his virtuous behavior, for man's virtuous behavior is both his possession of himself,[19]

---

16. Cf. *Consolatio*, II, 4, 72–84: "Quid igitur o mortales extra petitis intra vos positam felicitatem? Error vos inscitiaque confundit. Ostendam breviter tibi summae cardinem felicitatis. Estne aliquid tibi te ipso pretiosius? Nihil inquies. Igitur si tui compos fueris, possidebis quod nec tu amittere umquam velis nec fortuna possit auferre. Atque ut agnoscas in his fortuitis rebus beatitudinem constare non posse, sic collige. Si beatitudo est summum naturae bonum ratione degentis nec est summum bonum quod eripi ullo modo potest, quoniam praecellit id quod nequeat auferri, manifestum est quoniam ad beatitudinem percipiendam fortunae instabilitas adspirare non possit."

17. Cf., e.g., *Consolatio*, III, 11, 22–23: " 'Omne quod bonum est boni participatione bonum esse concedis an minime?' 'Ita est.' "; *Consolatio,* III, 10, 83–90: "Nam quoniam beatitudinis adeptione fiunt homines beati, beatitudo vero est ipsa divinitas, divinitatis adeptione beatos fieri manifestum est: sed uti iustitiae adeptione iusti, sapientiae sapientes fiunt, ita divinitatem adeptos deos fieri simili ratione necesse est. Omnis igitur beatus deus, sed natura quidem unus; participatione vero nihil prohibet esse quam plurimos."

18. Cf., e.g., *Consolatio,* IV, 3, 4–14: "Rerum etenim quae geruntur illud propter quod unaquaeque res geritur, eiusdem rei praemium esse non iniuria videri potest, uti currendi in stadio propter quam curritur iacet praemium corona. Sed beatitudinem esse idem ipsum bonum propter quod omnia geruntur ostendimus. Est igitur humanis actibus ipsum bonum veluti praemium commune propositum. Atqui hoc a bonis non potest separari neque enim bonus ultra iure vocabitur qui careat bono; quare probos mores sua praemia non relinquunt."

19. The point is made negatively. Boethius claims that the good man's reward is reflected in an opposite manner in the evil man's punishment (*Consolatio,* IV, 3, 33–36) and the punishment of evil men is their loss of their humanity. See *Consolatio,* IV, 3, 44–50: "Omne namque quod sit unum esse ipsumque unum bonum esse paulo ante didicisti, cui consequens est ut omne quod sit etiam bonum esse videatur. Hoc igitur modo quidquid a bono deficit esse desistit; quo fit ut mali desinant esse quod fuerant, sed fuisse homines adhuc ipsa humani corporis reliqua species ostentat." This clearly means that the good man's reward is his possession of his humanity.

and his becoming a god,[20] where one supposes such a claim to mean man's participating in God.[21]

There are several apparent contradictions at play here. For if man's 'good' is his possession of himself, then it cannot be his possession of something other than himself, unless one wants to violate the principle of non-contradiction. Nor can man's 'good' simultaneously be his self-sufficiency — his not requiring anything other than himself — and his participating in something other than himself. Thus, it would not seem possible for man's 'good' at once to be his being *"sui compos"* and his participating in God, unless, of course, one wants to claim that man is God, which Boethius did not.[22] This means that the *Consolatio*'s second and the third books' definitions of the 'good' seem, at a first glance at least, to be contradictory. The temptation would be to conclude that the contradiction here arises from a misinterpretation of one or the other of the definitions of the good.

The problem is that we cannot do so. For the contradiction is reaffirmed in the fourth book's claim that man's 'good' is both his possession of himself and his participating in God. What one must do, as such, is understand what Boethius meant by that contradictory claim in order to understand the point of the *Consolatio*. Did he mean that man's possession of himself is his possession of God, and hence that man is God? For indeed that is what the text could seem to imply, both because of its definition of man's 'good,' and because of the activity that it claims yields the 'good.' Or did Boethius use the term 'good' in an ambiguous way, as meaning both man's perfection and his beatitude, and hence mean for the claim that man's 'good' is both his "possession of himself" and his "participation in God" to be understood as stating that man's good is both his natural and super-natural perfection? Both interpretations are clearly laden with difficulties. For if one were to accept the first interpretation, he would either have to explain

---

20. Cf., e.g., *Consolatio*, IV, 3, 21-31: "Postremo cum omne praemium idcirco appetatur quoniam bonum esse creditur, quis boni compotem praemii iudicet expertem? At cuius praemii? Omnium pulcherrimi maximique. Memento etenim corollarii illius quod paulo ante praecipuum dedi ac sic collige: cum ipsum bonum beatitudo sit, bonos omnes eo ipso quod boni sint fieri beatos liquet. Sed qui beati sint deos esse convenit. Est igitur praemium bonorum quod nullus deterat dies, nullius minuat potestas, nullius fuscet improbitas, deos fieri."

21. Lady Philosophy herself allows us to make this deduction. For the corollary she refers to in the passage quoted ("Memento etenim corollarii illius quod paulo ante praecipuum dedi") is that men become gods by participating in God, who is transcendent. Cf. *Consolatio*, III, 10, 80-90. See footnote 17.

22. The passage cited above, *Consolatio*, III, 10, 80-90 makes clear. For in it Lady Philosophy claims that although many can participate in God, there is only one God by nature: "Omnis igitur beatus deus, sed natura quidem unus; participatione vero nihil prohibet esse quam plurimos" (87-90).

why Boethius did affirm God's transcendence, or prove that he did not. Moreover, he would have to account for the very odd definition of 'participation' that the interpretation would entail. For if man is God, then it is not at all clear that he can participate in God. Can something participate in itself? If, on the other hand, one were to adhere to the second interpretation he would have to explain why Boethius held that man can attain a supernatural end with natural means, and that too is no mean problem.

What did Boethius mean by the 'good'? Once again the Boethian reader is forced to make a choice: is he to believe that as keen a logician as he was, Boethius did not understand that his various doctrines were (or could be construed as being) contradictory, and hence that there is no point in looking for a systematic doctrine of the 'good' in the *Consolatio*? Or is the very prowess of Boethius's mind proof enough of the fact that there is likely to be a non-contradictory way of reading the work, of reconciling its various doctrines, and of Boethius's own systematic intent? The question is once again rhetorical. For a carefully constructed work such as the *Consolatio* ought to contain a systematic metaphysical doctrine. The matter at hand, thus, is to search for such a doctrine.

What this consideration indicates is that a main challenge in reading the *Consolatio* is accounting for the unity underlying the multiplicity of its apparently contradictory doctrines. For unless one does this his interpretation of any one of the work's doctrines cannot but be simplistic, and the case of participation is no exception to the rule. In this sense, the text is very similar to the *Quomodo*.

Nor is this the only difficulty, for just as the *Consolatio* shares the *Quomodo*'s heterogeneous exposition of its doctrines, so too does it share its complexity. The *Consolatio* is a multifaceted work. Like the Platonic dialogues it is often ambiguous.[23] Like the Platonic dialogues

---

23. An excellent example of this is his play on the word 'exile.' When he was writing the work, Boethius was in exile at Pavia and was, as he himself tells us (cf., e.g., *Consolatio*, I, 3; II, 4), quite distressed at the fact. At the very outset of her consolation, however, Lady Philosophy comments on his distress by counterposing his physical exile in Pavia to his exile from his soul's true land, and stating that the latter rather than the former is Boethius's true exile and cause of despair (I, 5, 4–9). From that point on in the *Consolatio*, then, "exile" has both a symbolic and a literal meaning, and often it is difficult to determine the primary sense in which Boethius himself intended for it to be understood. A brief glance at some of the other passages in which "exile" appears demonstrates this rather plainly. Cf., e.g., *Consolatio* I, 6, 42–44: "Nam quoniam tui oblivione confunderis, et exsulem te et exspoliatum propriis bonis esse doluisti." Does "exile" refer to Boethius's exile to Pavia or to his spiritual exile? Lady Philosophy's specifying that Boethius has "lost all of his possessions," would seem to indicate the former. Yet, her stating that "you have forgotten what you are," would seem to point to the latter. See also *Consolatio* I, 5, 3–7: "Maestum lacrimantemque vidissem, ilico miserum exsulemque cognovi. Sed quam id longinquum esset exilium, nisi tua prodidisset oratio, nesciebam. Sed tu quam procul a

its metaphysics is presented on at least two different levels simultaneously: through the content of the dialogue between Lady Philosophy and Boethius, and through the scenario of the dialogue itself.[24] Like the Platonic dialogues it is a meticulous work, the order of whose arguments plays an integral part in the arguments being presented.[25] As is the case with the *Quomodo,* the intent behind its order is not an obvious one; and consequently its metaphysics, like the *Quomodo*'s is not easy to determine.

What this implies is that commenting on one of the *Consolatio*'s metaphysical doctrines requires more than simply identifying those passages which are pertinent to that doctrine, examining them, commenting on them and arguing with them.[26] The point, in other words, is that the *Consolatio* does not afford a direct way of understanding the Boethian doctrine of participation.

We are thus back to the point where we started our work: neither of Boethius's metaphysical works is clear enough to allow us to use classical methodology alone to determine and define his doctrine of participation, if by classical methodology one means that sort of

---

patria non quidem pulsus es sed aberrasti"; IV, 1m, 23–30: "Huc te si reducem referat via, / Quam nunc requires immemor: / 'Haec,' dices, 'memini, patria est mihi, / Hinc ortus, hic sistam gradum.' /Quod si terrarum placeat tibi / Noctem relictam visere, / Quos miseri torvos populi timent/ Cernes tyrannos exules."

Boethius's play on the word 'exile' is but one of many. Chadwick points out another example in Boethius's own description of his imprisonment in the first book: "He is encumbered with a heavy chain round his neck. This, however, is primarily a symbol of his earth-bound condition. It may be literal as well as symbolic; one cannot be sure, for his physical prison is simultaneously the counterpart of the Platonic prison of his soul from which he seeks liberation" (*Consolations*, p. 226). Cf. also, for the massive stratification of literary allusions in the *Consolation*, A. M. Crabbe, "Anamnesis and Mythology in the *De Consolatione Philosophiae*," in *Congresso Internazionale di Studi Boeziani,* p. 311ff.

24. Reiss makes this point in his work on Boethius. Cf. Edmund Reiss, *Boethius* (Boston: Twayne Publishers, 1982) pp. 104–30. Reiss also shows that the *Consolation* is not the first work in which Boethius uses an allegorical frame, for he also did so in his first commentary on Porphyry's *Isagoge.* See Reiss, pp. 28ff.

25. This is why the work is considered an *itinerarium mentis in Deum.*

26. Rapisarda makes a similar point when he indicates that one cannot prove that the *Consolatio* is a Christian work by showing that it contains some very Christian-sounding passages (or that it is a pagan work because it has some pagan-sounding passages). "Per esempio, non vedo l'utilità che si può trarre, per stabilire se Boezio abbia aderito o meno alle concezioni creazionistiche, dall'indagine dei termini che egli usa per menzionare Dio. Egli infatti fa uso di vari termini, come *auctor, princeps, pater, sator, conditor,* ma non già perché intenda con ciascuno di essi esprimere una sua concezione sul carattere della creazione, ma perché spinto da vari motivi, che un esame particolare potrebbe mettere in rilievo togliendo certamente quel valore, che ad essi si suole attribuire. *Sator,* per esempio, è usato per riflesso virgiliano; l'uso di *conditor* non può avere il significato di una adesione ad idee anticreazionistiche, come pensa lo Steward, perché esso era stato usato già da scrittori cristiani, presso i quali non è alcun sospetto di adesione a siffatte concezioni...Né d'altra parte si può considerare una prova per dimostrare l'adesione di Boezio alle concezioni creazionistiche l'uso di *creator,* perché tale termine è comune anche in scrittori pagani come Lucano...ed altri." Cf. Emanuele Rapisarda, *La crisi spirituale di Boezio* (Catania: Centro Studi di Letteratura Cristiana Antica, G. Reina, 1947, p. 29.

deductive methodology which is often used to determine a specific philosopher's metaphysical doctrine. What this means is that we must use an inductive method in order to determine the Boethian doctrine of participation. That is the alternative. That is, if we cannot deduce what Boethius meant by participation from a set of unequivocal passages drawn from either of the metaphysical works in which he discusses it, we have no choice but to reconstruct what participation meant for him, in order to define it.

Chapter 3

A SURVEY OF POSSIBLE METHODOLOGIES

To reconstruct a metaphysical doctrine, one must begin by discovering that doctrine's causes. In our case, this entails discovering the reason why Boethius made use of a doctrine of participation. There are a variety of ways in which this can be done, inasmuch as metaphysical doctrines can have a variety of different types of cause: historical causes, metaphysical causes, doctrinal causes, and so forth. Thus, one can reconstruct a doctrine by identifying its historical antecedents and determining the influence of these antecedents upon the formulation of the doctrine under examination. This is, for instance, the method Geiger uses in the first part of his analysis of the Thomist doctrine of participation,[1] and it is the method many Boethian scholars use to determine the meaning of *'esse'* in the *Quomodo Substantiae*'s axioms.[2] There are often very good reasons for taking this historical approach, as Geiger's own work shows.[3] In our case, it would entail understanding the Boethian doctrine of participation by finding its historical sources, and determining how these influenced Boethius's thought.

Then again, one can also reconstruct a given philosopher's meta-

---

1. Geiger's study begins with analyses of the Platonic and Boethian doctrines of participation and shows how they are the sources of Thomas's own doctrine. Cf. L.-B. Geiger, *La Participation dans la Philosophie de S. Thomas d'Aquin* (Paris: Librairie Philosophique J. Vrin, 1941) pp. 37–67.
2. Hadot, for instance, uses Porphyry's and Victorinus's metaphysics to understand Boethius's treatment of *esse*. Cf. Pierre Hadot, "La Distinction de l'être et de l'étant dans le *De Hebdomadibus* de Boèce," in *Die Metaphysik im Mittelalter. Miscellania Medievalia*, 2, ed. P. Wilpert (Berlin: De Gruyter, 1963), pp. 147–53; Maioli uses Themistius's distinction between ὕδωρ and ὕδατι εἶναι to interpret the Boethian *esse*. Cf. Maioli, p. 21.
3. The reason Geiger does begin his analysis of the Thomist doctrine of participation with Boethius is that Thomas did not make extensive use of the doctrine before he wrote his commentary on the *Quomodo Substantiae*. The beginning of this explicit reflection on participation can be pinpointed to the Commentary on the *De hebdomadibus* (1256–59). In Boethius's treatise *De hebdomadibus* the notion of participation plays an important but problematic role. Aquinas takes great interest in this work, as appears not only from his commentary but also from his discussion of the same problem of goodness and participation in *De Veritate*.

physical doctrine by examining its indirect theoretical antecedents: that philosopher's positions on those problems which are related to the doctrine under examination. Thus, he can analyze what Aristotle meant by ἴδια πάθη in the fifth book of the *Metaphysics* in order to understand why he claimed that the human intellect is receptive in the third book of the *De Anima*, and what he meant by that claim. This is the approach te Velde uses in the second part of his analysis of the Thomist doctrine of participation,[4] as it is also the approach several Boethian scholars use to determine the meaning of the *Quomodo Substantiae*'s axioms.[5] The basis of the Boethian scholars' methodology is the claim that Boethius's metaphysics is more explicit in works other than the one in question: that his *De Trinitate* gives a clear picture of his notion of being. In our case, then, it would call for analyzing Boethius's treatment of those metaphysical problems related to participation — such as his doctrines of creation, causality, or receptivity — in order to discover how he conceived of participation.

Lastly, one can reconstruct a metaphysical doctrine by examining its direct theoretical antecedents: the specific problems to which the particular doctrine arises as a solution. In the case of the νοῦς παθητικός, this would entail analyzing what human understanding is and seeing why it implies intellectual receptivity. This last approach seems to be the most philosophical in nature, insofar as its aim is to grasp a particular doctrine as a particular solution to a specific philosophical problem. It is the sort of approach that Ross uses in his analysis of the foundations of ethics,[6] and in our case it would call for understanding Boethius's doctrine of participation by analyzing the problem to which he thought participation was the solution.

In our work, we will use the last of these possible approaches, for it is the least inadequate. We are missing the prerequisites of both the historical approach and the indirect theoretical approach: exhaustive and precise historical data, and an unambiguous exposition of the main tenets of Boethian metaphysics, respectively.

---

4. Cf. te Velde, pp. 87-208. His analysis of the Thomist doctrine of participation proceeds from an analysis of his doctrine of creation.

5. Maioli's work is a good example of this approach, inasmuch as he uses the definition of the cause of *esse* in Boethius's *De Trinitate* to interpret the *Quomodo Substantiae*'s axioms. Cf. Maioli, p. 24: "La nostra convinzione è che il significato base di *esse* (sostanzialmente costante negli *Opuscola*) sia quello di 'struttura che fa essere,' *forma essendi*. Il postulato base di tutta la metafisica boeziana è la tesi del *De Trinitate*: *'omne esse ex forma est.'*" It is this definition that guides his approach to the Boethian notion of participation. Cf. Maioli, p. 31ff. See also Gangolf Schrimpf, *Die Axiomenschrift des Boethius als philosophisches Lehrbuch des Mittelalters* (Leiden: Brill, 1966) for this sort of approach.

6. Cf. Willam David Ross, *The Right and the Good* (Oxford: Clarendon Press, 1930).

The Historical Problem

As for our historical data, the fact of the matter is that our knowledge of sixth century Italy is really quite limited. Although we do know many things about that age's protagonists, about its religious problems, and so forth — insofar as we have a very glib primary source in Cassiodorus — there is much about the epoch that we do not know. One need only think about the ongoing discussion regarding the cause of Boethius's condemnation to see just how patchy sixth century Italian history can be.[7] Nor is our ignorance surprising since the Graeco-Gothic War was a particularly devastating one and was followed by a ruinous Lombardic invasion. For if the war left Italy a virtually barren peninsula, the invasion destroyed what was left of sixth century Roman culture: the Lombards were an illiterate people who had had no contact with Roman culture prior to their invasion.

But if our knowledge of Boethius's era is sketchy, our knowledge of Boethius himself is that much more so, and that not only with regards to his personal life — what he did, whom he associated with, who his friends and teachers were — but more importantly with regards to his scholarly life. As for our acquaintance with Boethius's personal life, there is nothing that points out its incompleteness more than the fact

---

7. Was it Boethius the Catholic defender of the faith, Boethius the politician with the enemies he inevitably made, Boethius the Roman nobleman who tried to defend the rights of other Romans, or Boethius the Eastern Emperor's man who attempted to re-unify the fractured Roman Empire, who was condemned to death by Theodoric (and the Senate)? The matter is not an easy one to determine, and indeed there have been a number of articles that claim one or the other of the above things. The best analysis of this matter to date is Obertello's. See Obertello, *Boezio*, pp. 40–151. In his detailed study, the Italian scholar points out that it is for all of the above reasons that Boethius was condemned, insofar as all of Boethius's activities had a common object: bridging the gap between East and West. Boethius, the defender of the faith, was a man who worked towards maintaining (and re-establishing) the unity of the Eastern and Western branches of the Church. Boethius the politician attempted to re-establish the Western Empire's glory and to re-establish Roman rule of Italy (and thus to re-unify the Empire). Obertello claims that even his philosophical program was a part of this attempt to restore the Empire. See *Boezio*, pp. 146ff. His theory is that Boethius's father-in-law, Symmachus, had established a circle of noblemen-scholars (of which Boethius was the most important member) who worked together in the attempt to restore the Empire and the unity of the faith. "L'azione del 'circolo di Simmaco' si sviluppò dunque su due direttive: assimilazione, da un lato, della cultura greca a quella latina, per mezzo di tradizioni o rifacimenti delle opere più autorevoli nei vari campi dello scibile; incoraggiamento, dall'altro a una reciproca conoscenza e a contatti di lavoro più serrati, che costituissero infine una cultura comune. Se la paternità di un simile programma si deve attribuire a Simmaco, la sua esecuzione fu affidata a Boezio, per la parte filosofica, e, a quanto pare, a Prisciano, per la parte grammaticale e retorica." Luca Obertello, *Severino Boezio* (Genoa: Accademia Ligure di Scienze e Lettere, Collana di Monografie, 1974) vol. 1, pp. 149–50.

that we do not know his mother's name,⁸ the exact date of his birth,⁹ or, for that matter, his genealogy.¹⁰ As far as our knowledge of his

---

8. All we know about Boethius's mother is that she belonged to the *gens Anicia* (Boethius's own name, *Anicius* Manlius Severinus, attests to this), and that the Anicii were an ancient, powerful, wealthy and very Catholic family. The first Anicius seems to have been a consul in the second century B.C.; the family seems to have gained its power and wealth in the fourth century A.D., and to have converted to Christianity in the early part of the fourth century. See *Boezio*, pp. 7–15.
9. Cf. on this point, *Boezio*, pp. 17–20.
10. Boethius wanted to be classified as a Roman patrician: *Consolatio*'s self-portrait is of a Roman patrician. His ruse was successful. It is canonical to claim that Boethius belonged to the *gens Anicia*. Roman patrician or not, there is a mysterious thing about Boethius, which his scholarly life highlights: his knowledge of Greek. In classical Rome it was not rare to be perfectly versed in Greek. Caesar was. This was not so in late antiquity. Victorinus, who translated part of Aristotle's *Organon* a century before Boethius, was not nearly as well versed in Greek as Boethius was. It has been a matter of some concern to scholars to establish why Boethius knew Greek as well as he did.

There is an obvious solution to the problem: Boethius's origins. Boethius, it is claimed, is a Greek name. Scholars hypothesize that it can be transcribed as Βοηθος and that it derives from Βοηθειν (to aid). They then justify its having been transcribed into the Roman alphabet as *Boetius* by claiming, that "Romans had problems with the Greek *theta*" (*Consolations*, p. 1). Boethius, the claim goes, was Greek.

These two claims are not easy to reconcile. One cannot very well belong to the *gens Anicia* and have a Greek father. "È abbastanza curioso che la Gens Boezia, cui Severino apparteneva, proprio con lui, suo massimo rappresentante, perda nome e memoria. Nella quasi totalità degli studi...si legge che egli era della Gens Anicia" (Milani, 23).

But Boethius's Greek heritage is also problematic. Chadwick to the contrary, Boethius's name is not usually spelt with a θη (Βοηθος) but with a τε (Βοετιος). Romans may well have had trouble with the Greek *theta*, but I doubt Procopius did. And Procopius spells the name with a τε (*De Bello Gothico*, ed. Haury, vol. II, pp. 9–11). This makes Boethius's very pat Greek origins dubious to say the least. For the problem with the latter transcription is that its meaning in Greek is not clear.

So what are Boethius's origins? He was not an *Anicius*. He may well not have been Greek. The key, I think, is Boethius's father. His name is to be found on an ivory diptych in Brescia which has the following inscription: "NAR MANL BOETHIUS V C ET IN EX P P P V SEC CONS ORD ET PATRI," which I have found interpreted in two ways: "*Narses Manlius Boethius Vir Clarissimus et Inlustris ex Praefecto Praetorio, Praefectus Urbi Secundo, Consul Ordinarius et Patricius*" and "*Nonius Arrius I Boethius...*" The prior interpretation is the more frequent and is Obertello's, among others (*Boezio*, p. 5); the latter is R. Delbrück's (as reported and followed by Chadwick, see *Consolations*, p. 286).

The interesting part of the name is clearly the "NAR," and for two reasons: (1) it is the part of the inscription on which the two interpretations differ; and (2) Narses is an Armenian name. As for the first point, I am no expert in late Roman epigraphy and cannot weigh Delbrück's arguments in favor of his claim (Chadwick's for following suit), or Obertello's. They are all indubitably good. Fortunately I do not have to, for the first interpretation is confirmed by the *Acta Ecclesiastica*, which reports that the consul in 487 was "Flavius Narses Manlius Boethius" (See *Boezio*, p. 5) and thus puts the validity of the first interpretation beyond doubt.

This brings us to the second point. Was the Boethius family Armenian? Possibly. Boethius's father's Armenian first name (a fact which scholars seem to have ignored altogether) seems to indicate that it was. As I understand things, Armenian first names were never common in Rome. And Narses, specifically, was virtually unheard of. The only other famous Narses in the history of the Italian peninsula, as far as I know, was Narses the Eunuch, whom Justinian sent to finish off the Graeco-Gothic War long after Boethius's father died. But if Armenian names were as rare as all of that, why would someone give his son an Armenian name? This point would also seem to be confirmed by the Boethian last name. For the name Boethius, or *Boetios* as Procopius reports it, does seem to mean something in Krapar (ancient Armenian) — "boet" means general.

scholarly life is concerned, on the other hand, although we know that Boethius made a reputation for himself very early on as a scholar[11] — he was consulted when Theodoric wanted to send a water clock and a sun dial to the king of the Burgundians[12] and when he wanted to send a musician to Clovis, the king of the Franks[13] — our knowledge of things which are more pertinent to our own study — such as what texts he actually had, who his teachers were, and so forth — is scanty. We certainly know that he had copies of Aristotle's *Organon, Metaphysics* and *Physics,* of Porphyry's *Isagoge,* of Plato's *Gorgias, Republic* and *Phaedo,* at least part of St. Augustine's corpus, and of Cicero's *Topics* — to mention a few of the philosophical works which he either translated, commented on, or quoted in one or another of his works. But we can only speculate as to what other works he had. One supposes that he had all of Plato's dialogues and at least as much of the Aristotelian corpus as we have, because his explicit intention was to translate all of both philosophers' works.[14] But we cannot be sure that he did, as we cannot be sure that he had the *Enneads,* or any other of the great classics, unless of course he quoted the works. This means that we can only speculate as to what texts he was influenced by.[15] Nor is our ignorance limited to the composition of his library or to the works that influenced his thought. We do not know who his teachers were,[16] or

---

What is more important than genealogies is that Boethius's *Armenian* heritage might cast an interesting, albeit tenuous, light on Boethius himself: on the motives behind his attack of Eutychus — Armenians were labeled as monophysites — and on his tremendous need to be identified with his mother's *gens.* Armenia had lost its independence at the end of the fourth century.

11. Cf. Ennodius, *Paraenensis didascalia,* 21 (ed. Vogel, pp. 314–15) and the *Epistula* 7, 13, 2. See also Cassiodorus, *Variae,* I, XLV and XLVI, and II, XL.

12. Cf. *Variae,* I, 45.

13. Cf. *Variae,* II, 40.

14. Cf. *In De interpretatione* II: "Ego omne Aristotelis opus, quodcumque in manus venerit, in Romanum stilum vertens eorum omnium commenta Latina oratione perscribam, ut si quid ex logicae artis subtilitate, ex moralis gravitate peritiae, ex naturalis acumine veritatis ab Aristotele conscriptum sit, id omne ordinatum transferam atque quodam lumine commentationis inlustrem omnesque Platonis dialogos vertendo vel etiam commentando in Latinam redigam formam."

15. Obertello makes this point very clearly: "Tracciare le linee che convergono, come loro consuntivo finale, nel pensiero di Boezio, sarebbe impresa impossibile. L'indagine filologica vi si è lodevolmente impegnata, e non ha mancato di conseguire soddisfacenti risultati critici...ma si è ancora lontani dall'avere esaurito le possibilità e le indicazioni che i testi stessi propongono. Anche i pensatori più originali raccolgono, come fiumi durante il corso, innumerevoli apporti della natura e della cultura...tanto più questo è vero per Boezio, che la voce popolare designa un eclettico." Cf. *Boezio,* p. 408.

16. Reiss sums this point up nicely: "How and where Boethius received the education that made him expert in Greek and knowledgeable in the sciences and philosophy available in this language are questions still being posed. Although because of the scarcity of extant records no definite answer is now possible, the questions themselves are worth asking if for no other reason than that they allow us to appreciate the unusualness of Boethius's accomplishment." See Reiss, p. 6.

A Survey of Possible Methodologies   23

where he learned his Greek, for that matter.[17] We do not even know for sure who the Deacon John to whom he dedicated the *Quomodo Substantiae* was.[18]

The fact is, then, that imperfect historical knowledge makes for an imperfect historical analysis of a given metaphysical doctrine.[19] To be precise, it makes for a contestable one, as the ongoing discussion regarding the historical sources of the *Consolatio* admirably points out. Hence, we will not attempt to explain what Boethius meant by participation by recurring to some of the possible sources of his doctrine.

This is clearly not to say that we will ignore the historical aspect of Boethian participation metaphysics altogether. For that would be impossible, since many scholars who deal with Boethius's thought attempt to find its historical roots, and we will have to respond to their arguments. It is to say the historical route will not provide the foundation of our analysis.

---

17. This is a matter of debate. For centuries scholars held that Boethius had studied in Athens, because the *De disciplina scholium*, a work which until quite recently was commonly held to have been by Boethius (it is even included in Migne's *opera omnia* of Boethius's works), seems to indicate that its author did study in Athens — "annis duobus de viginti Athenis convalui" (P.L. LXIV, vol 1232 B) — and one of Cassiodorus's letters to Boethius would seem to confirm this fact (cf. *Variae*, I, 45, 3: "sic enim Atheniensium scholas longe positus introisti, sic palliatorum choris miscuisti togam, ut Graecorum dogmata doctrinam feceris Romanam"). Rapisarda, for instance, is one of the scholars who held that Boethius had indeed studied in Athens (see Rapisarda, pp. 45, 51).

The fact is, however, that the *Disciplina scholium* has been proven to be spurious, and Cassiodorus's phrase is ambiguous. As such, the hypothesis has been abandoned. The newer hypothesis is that Boethius studied in Alexandria (see, e.g., Courcelle, *Les lettres greques en Occident*, pp. 299–300). There are a number of reasons why this hypothesis is plausible. The first is that the *Historia Ecclesiastica* mentions that a "Βοετιος" (who was presumably his father or one of his close relatives) was the Prefect of that city between 475-7 and because Boethius's own work is "heavily indebted to the teachings of the master of this school, Ammonius Hermiae; and his writings are very much in accord with those of Ammonius' disciples" (Reiss, p. 8). This latter hypothesis is also a matter of debate, for the evidence in its favor is not ironclad. Courcelle argues for it in various places (see the *Lettres Greques* and "Boèce et l'école d'Alexandrie," in *Mélanges d'Archéologie et d'Histoire de L'Ecole Française de Rome* 52, 1935, pp. 185–223). Obertello, on the other hand, finds the evidence in favor of the argument inconclusive (see *Severino Boezio,* pp. 28–29). De Vogel hypothesizes that Boethius spent time in both Athens and Alexandria. Cf. De Vogel, "Boethiana" in *Vivarium* 9 (1971), pp. 49–66 and *Vivarium* 10 (1972), pp. 1–40.

18. Some scholars claim that he may have been the man who became Pope John I in 523. Cf., e.g., Reiss, p. 66.

19. Maioli makes the same point: "Ogni tentativo di ricondurle [le tesi ontologiche del *De Trinitate*] a alle tesi originarie di questo o quell'autore (Porfirio, Vittorino, lo stesso Aristotele) oltre che estremamente difficile a documentarsi, rischia inevitabilmente di forzare e tradire — per amor di prova — l'inconfondibile sapore boeziano." Maioli, p. 21. So too does Varvis for the *Consolatio:* "The one who would take on the task of tracing the sources of the *Consolation* must content him or herself with stating in a general way for the reader of the work the general picture of the intellectual world with which Boethius was in contact." Varvis, p. 12.

The Boethian Corpus

Nor will we take the indirect theoretical approach, or attempt to understand the Boethian doctrine of participation by searching for clues in works other than the ones which deal with participation, or by analyzing Boethius's solutions to problems that are indirectly related to participation. For we seem to lack the basic prerequisite for this approach too: a clear statement of Boethius's positions on metaphysical doctrines that are indirectly related to participation.

There are several reasons for this. The most important regards the dearth of Boethius's metaphysical works. For the fact of the matter is that despite his rather conspicuous and variegated philosophical production,[20] only two of Boethius's works are truly metaphysical, and these are precisely the works which we propose to analyze. What this means, of course, is that most of his texts are of little or no direct relevance to our work at all. The point here is a contentious one, and it is thus best for us to address it more carefully.

There are a number of ways in which scholars have categorized Boethius's works. In his authoritative monograph, *Severino Boezio,* for instance, Obertello classifies Boethius's works in at least two different ways. The first way is chronological; the second is thematic. In his first classification he divides Boethius's works into three periods: the "Victorine-Nicomachean" period (500–509), the "Porphyrian" period (510–17), and the "Ciceronian" period (518–24).[21] His second classification,[22] whose aim is to show that the Boethian corpus is not that eclectic mass of works it is often taken to be but is rather a whole (whose intent is to lead its reader to contemplate eternal truth) of which each work is a part, elucidates the function each of Boethius's works' plays in his exposition of philosophy.[23] In this sense,

---

20. The Boethian corpus is astounding given his relatively early death. He translated and wrote commentaries on Aristotle's *Organon* and on Porphyry's *Isagoge*; he wrote a commentary on Cicero's *Topics*; we have his analyses of hypothetical and categorical syllogisms, a text on geometry (the *De institutione geometria*), one on music (*De institutione musica*), and another on arithmetic (*De institutione arithmetica*), five theological tractates, and the *Consolatio*. We also know that he wrote a text on astronomy (the *De institutione astronomica*). For a complete list and chronology of Boethius's texts see *Boezio*, pp. 157-379.

21. Cf. *Boezio*, p. 342.

22. Cf. the fourth section of Obertello's massive work (pp. 565–781), whose structure is analogous to the Italian scholar's own concept of Boethian philosophy: the progression of its chapters mirrors the Boethian "path to philosophy." Its first chapter deals with the 'degrees of knowledge' and draws out the relation and distinction between Boethius's 'introductory' works and his 'metaphysical works'; the second chapter of the section deals with the logical works; the third deals with the Boethian notion of being; while the fourth, fifth and sixth deal with God (His existence, the Divine Eternity, Fate and Providence respectively).

23. Cf. *Boezio*, p. 565: "Nonostante la natura specialistica delle opere di Boezio, ciascuna delle quali è consacrata a un determinato settore dello scibile...un'acuta e sempre

he divides the Boethian corpus into three different groups, which he draws from Boethius's own division of the sciences in the *De Trinitate:* the introductory works (the *quadrivium*), the logical works, and the metaphysical-theological works.[24]

If we take our cue from Obertello's second classification,[25] it will be noticed that there is very little of the Boethian corpus that is actually applicable to our own study. The bearing of his introductory works on arithmetic, geometry, and music upon our own work is clearly minor. For although these works are certainly of historical moment, inasmuch as they indicate what treatises were available in Rome in Boethius's time and also seem to have defined the mediaeval notion of science,[26] they are youthful works, closely modeled on the works of several Greek Neoplatonists and Pythagoreans,[27] and they do not deal with the problems with which we are concerned,[28] or with any other metaphysical problem for that matter. Indeed, Boethius himself seems to have held that their object was not, strictly speaking, philosophical, but pedagogical, insofar as they were to furnish their readers with the *means* to philosophize.[29]

---

presente consapevolezza del comune riferimento ad alcuni valori filosofici di fondo conferisce al loro complesso una struttura fondamentalmente unitaria. La concezione che Boezio ha della filosofia è quanto mai ampia ed elevata: studio e amore della sapienza, essa coincide, in quanto tale, con la conoscenza della Divinità."

24. Cf. *De Trinitate,* II, 5–21.

25. Chadwick's *Consolations* uses a similar classification of Boethius's works. After outlining the "educational" unity of the Boethian corpus in his introduction (which he claims Boethius draws from Plato, p. xii), he dedicates a chapter each to the "liberal arts" (i.e., the *quadrivium*), to logic, and to "Christian theology" (in which he deals with all of the *Theological Tractates,* and as such with both philosophy and theology). The final chapter deals with the *Consolatio.*

26. Boethius, it seems, was the direct source of the mediaeval *quadrivium,* and of its notion of knowing. See Obertello, *Boezio,* p. 567: "In Boezio, dunque, vige, codificato ed esposto in forma che rimarrà canonica per tutto il Medioevo, il principio che la scienza è un tutto unitario, in cui la distinzione degli elementi costitutivi non equivale a una scissione interna." He seems to have coined the very work '*quadrivium.*' "Boethius appears to have been the first writer to use the term to delineate these areas [arithmetic, music, geometry, and astronomy] existing in the timeless world of being. For these arts were seen not merely as isolated sources of skills and information, but as an indispensable path to abstract knowledge. The created world, Boethius says, appears to have been formed according to number, 'for this was the principal design in the mind of the Creator.'" Alison White, "Boethius in the Mediaeval Quadrivium," in *Boethius: His Life, Thought, and Influence,* p. 162.

27. Cassiodorus' comment on this point is telling: "By your translations Latin readers now have Pythagoras' music, Ptolemy's astronomy, Nicomachus' arithmetic, Plato's theology, Aristotle's logic, and Archimedes' mechanics" (*Variae* I, 45, 4).

28. There are parts of the works in question that do deal with problems that are related to ours. A noteworthy example is the final chapter of the first book of Boethius's arithmetic that deals with the good, claiming that there is a first Good, which the human mind can come to know and imitate; that evil strays from the Good, and is nonetheless controlled by Providence. The point is clearly reminiscent of the *Consolatio.* Cf. on this point, Chadwick, *Boethius,* p. 75.

29. Cf. *Boezio,* p. 566: "Boezio rileva ancora una volta il valore insieme strumentale, speculativo ed etico di queste scienze [the *quadrivium*]; esse non costituiscono infatti parte

As for the relevance of Boethius's logical works upon our study, it too is minor, inasmuch as Boethius does not respond to metaphysical questions in them.[30] This is not surprising, since he was Aristotelian enough to hold that logic is instrumental to philosophy[31] — or as Chadwick puts it that it is the "foothill of a massif whose summit is in heaven"[32] — and did not have the unfortunate habit of discussing the nature of his ends while he was elucidating the means with which to attend to them. Nor are Boethius's logical works original enough to enjoin us to analyze them in order to understand the means with which Boethius subsequently delineated his metaphysics, although they do seem to present some fine puzzles for the modern logician.[33] Boethius was not Hegel. This means that the works in question are not even indirectly pertinent to our work. There is, as such, no reason why we should expect either to find any clues regarding the Boethian notion of participation, or the means with which to infer what that doctrine may be, in his logical works.

This leaves us with the metaphysical-theological works, a category which includes the *Theological Tractates* and the *Consolatio Philosophiae*. Now, as the category itself indicates, it is generally taken for granted that Boethius's theological works (the *De Trinitate*, the *Utrum Pater et Filius*, and so forth) can (and do) clarify the content of Boethius's metaphysical works (the ones with which we will deal). This is especially true of the *De Trinitate*. Scholars often use its proposition

---

integrante ed essenziale della filosofia (o 'teoretica') che consiste nella contemplazione degli intelligibili, ma vi innalzano gradualmente lo spirito, affinandone e irrobustendone le capacità naturali"; or again p. 571: "le scienze del quadrivio disvelano per gradi alla mente un panorama unico eppur variato, il cui orizzonte lontano è illuminato da una luce che proviene da altra fonte," et *passim*.

30. Boethius was the source of the mediaeval problem of universals for precisely this reason. In his commentary on Porphyry's *Isagoge* he shows how Platonic and Aristotelian metaphysics differ — i.e., that the first hypostasizes the ideas and the latter claims they only exist *in re* — and their inherent problems, but refuses to claim allegiance to either one. On the mediaeval outcome of his commentary see Etienne Gilson, *La Philosophie au moyen âge* (Paris: 1952) p. 170ff.; David Knowles, *The Evolution of Mediaeval Thought* (New York: Image, 1962) p. 107ff.

31. Cf. Boethius, *In Categorias*, 161 D: "Qua re quoniam omnis ars logica de oratione est, et in hoc opere de vocibus principaliter tractatur, quamquam enim sit huius libri relatio ad ceteras philosophiae partes, principaliter tamen refertur ad logicam, de cuius quodammodo simplicibus elementis, id est, de sermonibus, in eo principaliter disputavi."

32. Chadwick, *Consolations*, p. 111.

33. Cf. Jonathan Barnes, "Boethius and the Study of Logic," in *Boethius: His Life, Thought, and Influence*, p. 84: "Boethius was not an original logician: he did not pretend to be. He saw himself as a translator, conveying Greek wisdom to a Greekless world; the insights which his works contain are not his own, his knowledge is tralatitious. From time to time we can, I believe, hear Boethius's own voice; and some at least of the disposition and organization of his material originated in his own head. But these touches of personality are relatively rare and relatively unimportant: the *summa logicae* which Boethius determined to present was traditional Peripatetic logic; and it is an error to speak of a Boethian logic." Barnes also points out that Boethius's treatise on hypothetical syllogisms, presents some problems which are a "challenge to philosophical interpreters." Barnes, pp. 83–84.

"Omne namque esse ex forma est" in order to clarify the content of the *Quomodo Substantiae*'s axioms.[34] There are at least three very sound reasons why they do so. The first is tradition: since the Middle Ages at least, all of Boethius's *Tractates* and the *Consolatio* have been considered theological works. The second is that Boethius's own division of the sciences seems to indicate that he considered theology a part of philosophy, or to be precise, the pinnacle of philosophy.[35] The third reason is a corollary of the second: the metaphysics in the *Quomodo Substantiae* (and thus the Boethian doctrine of participation) would seem to stem from a query regarding his own *De Trinitate*.[36]

Now, as for the first point, it is true that mediaevals tended to consider all of Boethius's *Tractates,* the *Quomodo Substantiae* included, theological works. Aquinas himself did.[37] This does not, however, mean that they were right in doing so. Indeed, if a theological work is one which has revelation as one of its premises, then by our present standards the *Quomodo* cannot be considered a theological work.[38] Nor can the *Consolatio*. Hence, although the mediaevals may have felt quite justified in using contents of one or the other of them to shed light on any of the others, we cannot.

As for the second point, Boethius's claim that *"studium sapientiae* [est] *studium divinitatis et purae mentis illius amicitia"*[39] is not an original one — Aristotle's *Metaphysics* has a similar definition of the πρώτη φιλοσοφία.[40] It is also not a controversial one, if one means by it, as

---

34. As we will see in the third part of this work, Maioli, Obertello, and Micaelli (*Studi sui Trattati Teologici di Boezio* (Naples: D'Auria, 1988) among others, all follow this path.

35. Boethius had a rather broad concept of philosophy — it seems that he interpreted the term rather literally — as that love of wisdom which is (and leads to) the study — and love — of God. Cf. *In Isagogen* I,17, 12–20, ed. Brandt: "Est enim philosophia amor et studium et amicitia quodammodo sapientiae, sapientiae vero non huius, quae in artibus quibusdam et in aliqua fabrili scientia notitiaque versatur, sed illius sapientiae, quae est nullius indigens, vivax mens et sola rerum primaeva ratio est. Est autem hic amor sapientiae intelligentis animi ab illa pura sapientia inluminatio et quodammodo ad se ipsam retractio atque advocatio, ut videatur studium sapientiae studium divinitatis et purae mentis illius amicitia."

36. See Rapisarda, p. 73: "Il terzo [opuscolo]... scaturisce anche da una delucidazione richiesta da Giovanni... Molto probabilmente il passo oscuro, su cui Giovanni aveva richiesto spiegazioni, è quello in cui, nell'Opuscolo sulla Trinità, Boezio, trattando delle varie categorie da riferire a Dio e agli uomini, afferma che la bontà e la giustizia in Dio si identificano con la sostanza, mentre negli uomini costituiscono un predicato *secundum rem*: Giovanni avrà allora formulato la sua obiezione a cui risponde il terzo trattato."

37. See footnote 1, pp. 1–2.
38. See footnote 1, pp. 1–2.
39. See footnote 36 above.
40. Cf., e.g., *Metaphysics*, E, 1026ª 18–23: "It follows that there must be three kinds of theoretical philosophy, mathematical, natural, and theological; for it is not hard to see that the divine is a constituent of nature of such a kind, if of anything. Of these the most estimable ought to deal with the most estimable genus. The theoretical are to be pre-

it seems Boethius did, that natural theology is the crowing point of metaphysics: that is, that the apex of philosophy is the study of being, and that the summit of the study of being is the study of the *Ens Primum,* or *Ipsum Esse Subsistens.* The claim would be controversial if it were to the effect that natural theology is the only theology, that there is no need for Revelation to understand God, or to the effect that one can equate natural theology with revealed theology. But Boethius's own rather sharp distinction between *ratio* and *fides*[41] would seem to obviate these latter interpretations of the statement.

This means that there is no technical reason why one cannot use those *Theological Tractates* (or those parts thereof) that deal with natural theology to understand his metaphysics, but that there is a grave impediment to using those *Tractates* (or parts thereof) that deal with Revelation (or have Revelation as one of their principal premises) to interpret his metaphysical works. For Boethius himself cannot have considered them as belonging to the same category. If this is so, however, then Boethius's *Tractates* other than the *Quomodo Substantiae* are largely inapplicable to our study. For they mostly deal with Revelation: the *De Fide Catholica* is a commentary on Scripture; the *Contra Eutychen* is a response to the Eutychan and Nestorian heresies regarding the person of Christ; the *Utrum Pater et Filius* is an attempt to understand the unity and plurality of the Trinity, as is the *De Trinitate.*

Be that as it may, there are parts of some of the *Tractates* that could theoretically serve to shed light on Boethius's metaphysics: most notably a large part of the first five sections of the *De Trinitate,* which deal variously with Aristotelian categories, predication, and the composition of matter and form, and the first three sections of the *Contra Eutychen,* which define the meaning of nature, personhood, and the relation between the two. For these sections deal with philosophical rather than theological matters. Now, it is precisely these sections of the texts that scholars sometimes use to elucidate the content of the *Quomodo.*

The fact of the matter is, however, that those philosophical sections of Boethius's theological works that could theoretically serve as the

---

ferred, then, among the other disciplines, and this among the theoretical" (translation is by Christopher Kirwan, Oxford: Clarendon Press, 1971, p. 68).

41. In the first two of his *Tractates* Boethius draws a rather sharp distinction between *fides* and *ratio.* Cf., e.g., *De Trinitate,* 23ff., VI, 30ff.; *Utrum Pater et Filius,* 68ff. The distinction sheds a great deal of doubt upon the soundness of applying any of Boethius's theology to his philosophy, that is, of using the former to understand the latter, especially if one takes the *De Fide Catholica*'s admonition that the human mind cannot fully grasp theological matters, and must thus rely upon the authority of Scripture, seriously: "qui sit tamen processionis istius modus ita non possumus evidenter dicere, quemadmodum generationem filii ex paterna substantia non potest humanus animus aestimare. Haec autem ut credantur vetus ac nova informat instructio." Cf. *De Fide Catholica,* 26–30.

foundation for our reconstruction of the Boethian doctrine of participation — most especially those in the *De Trinitate* — are not of any direct assistance in our work because they do not deal with participation or with problems that are directly related to it.

Indeed, the third point above (that is, Rapisarda's claim that the *Quomodo* responds to a query raised by Deacon John with regards to the *De Trinitate*) more than amply proves our point. For the Italian scholar points out that Boethius wrote the *Quomodo Substantiae* precisely because he had overlooked an important metaphysical problem in his *De Trinitate:* that is, he had not properly dealt with the matter of distinguishing the modes of contingent creation's goodness and Divine goodness.[42] What this means is that there is no reason to expect a response to our question concerning the Boethian distinction between Divine Goodness and the goodness of contingent things, or the means with which he distinguished them, in the *De Trinitate*. And indeed, the *De Trinitate* is silent on the matter. But it is precisely these means with which we are concerned. For these means are the doctrine of participation. Hence the *De Trinitate* can be of no direct service to our study.

Nor is this the only reason why the Boethian *De Trinitate* is of no direct assistance to us. For the fact of the matter is that the work is almost as obscure as the *Quomodo Substantiae*.[43] To use it to elucidate the content of the latter work, as such, is tantamount to explaining the cryptic by means of the abstruse. Thus, there would seem to be no good reason for attempting to reconstruct the Boethian doctrine of participation by recurring to it. This means that its role in one's attempt to determine the Boethian doctrine of participation can be marginal and indirect at best.

But if Boethius's theological works do not shed direct light on the metaphysical matters with which we are concerned, then there is no work of Boethius's which we can call upon to shed light upon matters directly related to his doctrine of participation. For we have excluded all of the texts in the Boethian corpus. What this means is that we cannot use the indirect theoretical approach in order to reconstruct the Boethian doctrine of participation.

This is not to say that our study will ignore all Boethian texts other than his metaphysical ones in our work. That would be impossible —

---

42. Cf. footnote 36 above.
43. The work contains a warning similar to the one to be found in the *Quomodo* with regards to its obscurity. Cf. *De Trinitate*, 16–22: "Idcirco stilum brevitate contraho et ex intimis sumpta philosophiae disciplinis novorum verborum significationibus velo, ut haec mihi tantum vobisque, si quando ad ea convertitis oculos, conloquantur; ceteros vero ita submovimus, ut qui capere intellectu nequiverint ad ea etiam legenda videantur indigni."

insofar as we will have to respond to those scholars who have used his theological works in their interpretations of his metaphysics — and counterproductive: we can use the works to confirm our interpretation of the terms whereby Boethius enunciates his two axioms regarding participation in the *Quomodo Substantiae* — of *'esse,' 'id quod est,'* and so forth. It is to say that we will not base our reconstruction on them.

Chapter 4

THE DIRECT THEORETICAL APPROACH: THE GOOD

Having discarded the historical and the indirect theoretical approach, we are left with the third of the methods we listed above: the direct theoretical approach. That is, the best way to begin our reconstruction of the Boethian doctrine of participation is to analyze the problem (or series of problems) to which participation arises as a solution.

That problem concerns the good: the nature of the good, what it means for things to be good, and why they are good. For Boethius uses his doctrine of participation in order to determine the nature of the ontological goodness of created things in both the *Consolatio* and in the *Quomodo Substantiae*. If this is so, then it stands to reason that if we are able to determine the Boethian conception of the good, we will be well on the way to understanding how he understood participation. If we understand the *definitum*, we can derive the *definiendum* from it. It is thus with the good that we will begin.

Beginning with the good is, however, problematic, and for two main reasons. The first, and most important, reason is metaphysical and regards the good itself. It is no easy thing to define the nature of the good. The second reason, on the other hand, is historical and regards the Boethian treatment of the good. As we have seen, both the *Quomodo Substantiae*'s and the *Consolatio*'s definitions of the 'good' are ambiguous and abstruse. And, what is more important, understanding them would seem to presuppose understanding his doctrine of participation.

The Metaphysics of the Good

The root of the metaphysical problem concerning the good seems to lie in the double definition of the good transmitted to us — and to Boethius — by ancient philosophy: the good is both a substantial property of all things and the object of their desire, that towards which all things tend.[1] For as these two definitions show, defining the nature of the good entails solving several of the most basic problems in metaphysics: explaining how universal terms can be predicated of different particular things and determining the ontological status of universals; solving the problem of the one and the many; and solving the problem of being and becoming.

Historically speaking, the problem of predication is related both to the matter of the ontological status of universals and to both definitions of the good. This is something of which Boethius seems to have been more than aware.[2] In the first book of the *Nicomachean Ethics,* after having stated that the good is the object which all things by nature desire, the end which they pursue, having claimed that there is a hierarchy of such ends (for the end pursued for its own sake is the highest good), and defined the highest good as happiness, Aristotle turns to the Platonic doctrine of the good in order to counterpose his doctrine to Plato's own. He delivers three objections to the Platonic 'Form of the Good,' claiming that there cannot be a universal Good, which makes all things good in themselves: (1) because 'good' is a term which is predicated in all categories;[3] (2) because there is no science of the 'good';[4]

---

1. Cf. *Quomodo Substantiae,* 56–60: "Ea quae sunt bona sunt; tenet enim communis sententia doctorum omne quod est ad bonum tendere, omne autem tendit ad simile. Quae igitur ad bonum tendunt bona ipsa sunt." The passage is, of course, a synthesis of both definitions. For in it Boethius claims both that the good is a property of all that is ("Ea quae sunt bona sunt"), and that it is the end of all things ("omne quod est ad bonum tendet"). Both definitions, then, could be either Platonic or Aristotelian in origin, for both philosophers claim both things, to one degree or another. We will analyze the Aristotelian doctrine of the good as it is to be found in the first book of the *Nicomachean Ethics* in the pages to follow. As for the Platonic position there can be no doubt that he held that there is an Idea of the Good that causes the goodness of particular things (cf., e.g., *Gorgias* 497^e), that the good is the "brightest region of being" (Rep. VII, 518^c 10), and that it is the object of desire (cf. *Gorgias* 506^{c}ff.). The origin of the Boethian doctrine is, however, debatable. For the source could be Augustine, insofar as the *Consolatio*'s query "'Si quidem deus,' inquit, 'est, unde mala? Bona vero unde, si non est?'" (I, 4, 8) sounds very Augustinian. Cf., e.g., *De doctrina christiana,* I, 32: "Quia Deus bonus est, nos sumus, et in quantum sumus, boni sumus." Then again it could be Plotinus, or some other philosopher, but it is of no real importance to determine who he was.

2. As we shall see in the third part of our work, Boethius's definition of the cause of contingent things' goodness is a reconciliation of the two classical definitions of the good which postulates the existence of universals *ante rem.*

3. Cf. *Nicomachean Ethics,* I, 4 1096^a 23–29: "Further, good is spoken of in as many ways as being is spoken of. For it is spoken of in [the category of] what-it-is, as god and mind; in quality, as the virtues; in quantity, as the measured amount; in relative, as the useful; in time, as the opportune moment; in place, and the [right] situation; and so on. Hence it is clear that the good cannot be some common [nature of good things] that is universal and single; for if it were, it would be spoken of in only one of the categories, not in them all." The translation is by Terence Irwin, Aristotle *Nicomachean Ethics* (Indianapolis: Hackett Publishing Company, 1985) p. 9. All of our quotations of the *Ethics* will be drawn from this text.

4. *Ethics,* 1096^a 30–35, p. 10: "Further, if a number of things have a single Idea, there

and (3) because a separate Good Form could not explain the goodness of particular good things.[5] Having dismissed the possibility of there being a universal good, however, he must have realized that there has to be some reason why different things are called 'good,' for he recants a bit. For in the lines that follow his rebuttal of the Platonic notion of the good, he claims that 'good' things are not homonymous by chance.[6]

What Aristotle meant by that claim is not exactly clear. He does not tell us why 'good' things are not homonymous by chance: what the cognitional and ontological grounds of our non-accidental predication of the 'good' is. He seems to skirt the question by claiming that these latter matters do not have to do with his current inquiry, which deals with that good which is the object of man's activity, and are better dealt with by another branch of philosophy, which one presumes is metaphysics.[7] Given, however, that he does claim that the homonymy of 'good' things is not accidental, one must assume that he held that there is some non-accidental cause — an ontological or cognitional cause — which grounds our use of the word. For the alternative to accidental homonymy of the 'good' is some sort of substantial homonymy: a homonymy in which each of one's uses of the word is dictated by the same cause. One assumes that Aristotle must have held that that cause is both ontological and cognitional: a common definition which holds for all good things.[8] But one can only speculate as to what he really meant by that claim.

The passage at hand is a fascinating one for many reasons. It

---

is also a single science of them; hence [if there were an Idea of Good] there would also be some single science of all goods. But in fact there are many sciences even of the goods under one category; for the science of the opportune moment, e.g., in war is generalship, in disease medicine. And similarly the science of the measured amount in food is medicine, in exertion is gymnastics."

5. Cf. *Ethics*, 1096ª 34ff., p. 10: "One might be puzzled about what [the believers in Ideas] really mean in speaking of The So-and-So Itself, since Man Itself and man have one and the same account of man; for in so far as each is man, they will not differ at all. If that is so, then [Good Itself and good have the same account of the good]; hence they also will not differ at all in so far as each is good, [hence there is no point in appealing to the Good Itself]."

6. *Ethics*, 1096ᵇ 25ff., pp. 11-12: "But how, after all, then, is good spoken of? For [these goods have different accounts, i.e., are homonymous, and yet] are seemingly not homonymous by chance. Perhaps they are homonymous by all being derived from a single source, or by all referring to a single focus. Or perhaps they are homonymous by analogy: for example, as sight is to body, so understanding is to soul, and so on for other cases."

7. *Ethics*, 1096ᵇ30ff., p. 12: "Presumably, though, we should leave these questions for now, since their exact treatment is more appropriate for another [branch of] philosophy. And the same is true about the Idea. For even if the good predicated in common is some single thing, or something separated, itself in itself, clearly it is not the sort of good a human being can pursue in action or possess, but that is just the sort of thing we are looking for in our present inquiry."

8. Cf. *Ethics*, V, 1, 1129ª 27: where Aristotle claims that things that are homonymous do not only share the same name but also have a common definition.

counterposes Plato's ontological view of the good and Aristotle's action-oriented one, and it shows just how bewildering the Platonic view must have been to Aristotle, who finds it remarkably difficult indeed to conceive of things as sharing a common good.[9] It betrays an ostensibly fragile Aristotle, who seems to be torn between his need to distinguish his own philosophy from the Platonic, and his need to explain why different things are called 'good,' are considered good, or are good. Indeed, the reasons he gives for rejecting the Platonic notion of the good are ones he himself would not accept in the *Metaphysics*.[10] What is closer to our point is that the passage exhibits Aristotle's own struggle with the 'good,' with the foundation which justifies our predicating goodness of different things and activities. Aristotle realizes that he cannot affirm that there is no such thing at all as a universal good. For if there were indeed no such thing, 'good' would just be an equivocal term, and that is something that he is not willing to accept. That is why he does affirm that 'good' things are not homonymous by chance — thus allowing us to assume that he held that there is such a thing as a universal idea of the 'good' — although he does not dare explain why they are or what the universal good may be. He realizes that his affirming that things are "homonymously" good would seem to indicate that there is some ontological foundation for our use of the word, but he does not indicate (or know) what that foundation is.[11] He understands that an ontological foundation for our use of the word 'good' implies that there must be a universal cause of things' goodness, but he does not risk defining the nature of that cause.[12]

Aristotle's struggle illustrates one of the basic metaphysical problems which the 'good' poses. Most of the universal terms we use to describe or define reality — 'tree,' 'dog,' 'human,' and so forth — have an ontological correlative which grounds our use of the term. Both Aristotle and Plato would have called that ontological correlative a form, in the case of the terms above. The fact is, however, that the ontological cor-

---

9. Cf. *Ethics*, 1096^b 17ff., p. 11: "Well what sorts of goods may be regarded as goods in themselves? (a) Perhaps they are those that are pursued even on their own, e.g., intelligence, seeing, some types of pleasures, and honors; for even if we also pursue these because of something else, they may still be regarded as goods in themselves. (b) Or perhaps nothing except the Idea is good in itself." It will be noticed that Aristotle's good in itself is an activity rather than a substance.

10. The *Metaphysics* responds to his first two objections. His first objection to there being such thing as a Good, i.e., that the term 'good' is used in all categories, is parallel to the objection regarding 'Being' to which he responds in the fourth book of the *Metaphysics* (Γ, 2, 1003^a 33ff.) by pointing out that the term is used analogously, and that this fact is no impediment to there being a primary sense in which 'being' is intended, and hence that the word's ambiguity is no impediment to there being a science of Being.

11. See footnote 6 above.

12. See footnote 7 above.

relative of the term 'good' is not an easy one to determine. For like 'being,' 'good' is, as Aristotle himself points out, a term which is predicated in all categories — it is predicated of substances as well as of accidents, of activities as well as of their objects — and it is predicated of all things — not just those that belong to a certain genus or species. As such, it cannot have a form as its ontological correlative. Unlike 'being,' on the other hand, 'good' would not seem to have a correlative act or substance to which one can pin its primary meaning. As such, there would not seem to be anything upon which to ground the claim that our use of the term in categories other than substance is analogous. Nor does the term seem to have any other quality which could serve as its primary referent. Our own use of the word makes this very point. For we say both that things are good insofar as they are — 'music is good' — and that they are good insofar as they are in a specific way — 'that is good music' — and these two uses would seem to be mutually exclusive. Our specifying that a particular thing is good would seem to imply that at least some of the particular things which belong to the same category or genus of things as that thing which we have called 'good' are not good. 'That music is good' would seem to imply that 'that stuff that they are playing over there is horrible.' *Omnis definitio est negatio* after all. If this is so, however, then that use of the word 'good' whereby we commend a specific thing would seem to contradict our more basic use. For our more basic use would seem to claim that all things that belong to a specific genus or category are good. As such, our own use of the term 'good' would seem to indicate that it has no primary referent at all. Were our use to have a primary referent, that referent would have to be a contradictory one. But this is tantamount to saying that the term 'good' has no ontological correlative at all.

What, then, do we mean by the word 'good,' and what justifies our use of the term? This is one of the primary problems an analysis of the 'good' must solve. It must determine the foundation of our use of the word: its ontological correlative.

As for the problem of the one and the many, it is, of course, one of the roots of the problem of predication. For if the term 'good' must have some ontological correlative, then it must be some sort of property which all of those things of which it is predicated share. This is why it has been claimed that the 'good' is a substantial property of all things, for the term is predicated (or predicable) of all things. The point of the first definition of the good, in other words, is to furnish the ontological correlative which our use of the word requires. The problem is determining how that ontological correlative can at once be common — can always denote the same thing — and present in a plurality of different things. The problem is determining the universal to which 'good' corresponds and the relation between that universal and particular things. As Aristotle's discussion shows, this entails discovering the cause of the 'good.' Indeed, it entails discovering how that cause can at once be 'one' and present in different things, in things belonging to different genera.[13]

The second definition of the good, on the other hand, makes the problem of the 'good' akin to the problem of being and becoming. For what Aristotle seems to have meant in his claim that the 'good' is the object all men desire by nature, is not merely that it is what men desire, but that it is their final cause: that activity which actualizes the desirer.[14] That is why he claims that man's highest good is wisdom. For wisdom is the actualization of what is most characteristic of man.[15] If this is so, then the 'good' must regard things' development, their actualization, or their becoming. The problem is, however, that the 'good' also has to do with things themselves as they are, simply insofar as they are. Indeed, if there is an ontological correlative to our use of the term, then the 'good' must also be a property which all things possess independently of the degree of their actualization. What this means is that 'good' must indicate both a property of all things, and a property all things can acquire. Explaining what the 'good' is, as such, must entail explaining how things can at once be good and become good: how things can both be and become.

Addressing that specific problem is no easy matter. Indeed, it is not at all clear that the problem of being and becoming implicit in the 'good' is anything more than a paradox. For claiming that the 'good' is both a substantial property of all things and their final cause is in

---

13. See footnote 5 above.
14. Cf. *Ethics*, 1098^a 20ff., p. 17: "(a) We have found, then, that the human function is the soul's activity that expresses reason [as itself having reason] or requires reason [as obeying reason]. (b) Now the function of F, e.g., of a harpist, is the same in kind, so we say, as the function of an excellent F, e.g., an excellent harpist. (c) The same is true unconditionally in every case, when we add to the function the superior achievement that expresses the virtue... (d) Now we take this human function to be a certain kind of life, and take this life to be the soul's activity and actions that express reason. (e) [Hence by (c) and (d)] the excellent man's function is to do this finely and well. (f) Each function is completed well when its completion expresses the proper virtue. (g) Therefore [by (d), (e) and (f)] the human good turns out to be the soul's activity that expresses virtue."
15. Cf. *Ethics*, 1177^a 10ff., p. 284: "If happiness, then, is activity expressing virtue, it is reasonable for it to express the supreme virtue, which will be the virtue of the best thing. The best is understanding, or whatever else seems to be the natural ruler and leader, and to understand what is fine and divine, by being itself either divine or the most divine element in us. Hence complete happiness will be its activity expressing its proper virtue; and we have said that this activity is the activity of study. This seems to agree with what has been said before, and also with the truth. For this activity is supreme, since understanding is the supreme element in us, and the objects of understanding are the supreme objects of knowledge."

some sense nonsensical. After all, since things only desire what they lack, the 'good' cannot be a substantial property of those things which desire it. But all things desire the good. It follows that the good cannot be a substantial property of all things, if it is their final cause. Nor is the point less paradoxical if one reverses its terms. For if the 'good' is a substantial property of all things, it is not at all clear how it can also be the object of all things' desire: things do not desire what they already have. What, then, is the 'good' and how is one to make sense of the metaphysical landscape it paints?

The metaphysical side of the problem of the good is at once challenging and perplexing. It entails more than just analyzing our use of the word 'good' and solving the problem of the one and the many. It entails finding an ontological correlative for a slippery word and explaining how that correlative can be universal. It entails addressing both the problem of being and becoming and the problem of the one and the many simultaneously. And this makes things very complicated. For it entails doing a cross section of the two great metaphysical problems: explaining why the problem of the one and the many implies the problem of being and becoming in the case of the good, and vice versa; and it entails correlating the problems, that is, determining the relation that subsists between the many's becoming and the One, the relation that subsists between the many's being and the One, and so forth.

Boethius and the Good

Boethius's treatment of the good is the second reason why starting with that problem is so troublesome. For the *Consolatio* has at least three different doctrines of the good,[16] and the *Quomodo Substantiae*'s delineation of the cause of contingent things' ontological goodness is a matter of debate.[17] Hence our attempt to avoid Boethian abstruseness would seem to be frustrated from the very start: there would simply seem to be no straightforward way of dealing with the Boethian notion of the good.

Were the ambiguity of Boethius's texts not enough of a stumbling block from the historical point of view, the fact that the Boethian notion of participation lies at the heart of both the *Consolatio*'s[18] and the *Quomodo Substantiae*'s definitions of created things' goodness seems

---

16. See footnotes 16–20, pp. 13–14.
17. Indeed, as McInerny puts it: "There is no scholarly consensus on the meaning of the Boethian tractate taken in itself." McInerny, p. 197.
18. Both the third and the fourth books' definitions of the good make use of the doctrine of participation.

to be enough to beware attempting to begin a discussion of the Boethian notion of participation with an analysis of his doctrine of the good. For if his doctrine does indeed rely upon participation, then to begin one's analysis of the Boethian doctrine of participation by examining his doctrine of the good is to presuppose that one has understood what he is attempting to define by analyzing the doctrine of the good.

We would thus seem to be at an *impasse* before even having begun our work. For the last point seems to leave us no place to start our examination of the Boethian doctrine of participation. We cannot begin with the doctrine itself, because it is obscure and presupposes understanding the context within which it arises. The fact of the matter is, however, that we cannot begin at that context either, because it presupposes understanding his doctrine of participation. Where does one begin, then?

Although there is a sense in which impasse is a real one, there is a way of avoiding the circularity which it would seem to make inevitable: and that is to examine the problems which the *good* poses, so as to establish the groundwork of the possible solutions to them; to determine how Boethius understood those problems, and how he conceived the foundation of his solution to them. It is, in other words, to retrace the steps that Boethius took in order to delineate his doctrine of the good: those steps that led him to the doctrine of participation. For this approach does not presuppose understanding either his doctrine of the good or his doctrine of participation. It simply entails coming to understand a problem, how he interpreted it, and noting how his interpretation of the problem in question made participation the inevitable solution. If the approach does presuppose something, it is the definitions of the good which Boethius himself had as his starting point. This, however, is a minor presupposition. For these definitions were in use long before Boethius was born. They are the classical definitions.

This is precisely what we will do. Therefore, rather than beginning with the Boethian doctrine of the good, our work will begin by analyzing the classical definitions of the good. It is only after we have done this that we will examine the Boethian doctrine of the good in the *Quomodo Substantiae* and the *Consolatio Philosophiae*. And it is only after we have dealt with the good both speculatively and in Boethius's case, that we will turn to participation and analyze the doctrine as it is to be found in both the *Quomodo Substantiae* and in the *Consolatio Philosophiae*.

Part Two

THE GOOD

The root of the metaphysical problem concerning the good lies in the term's equivocity. Since antiquity 'good' has been used to designate both a substantial property of all things — *ens et bonum convertuntur* — and the object of desire — that towards which all things tend.[1] And the fact of the matter is that pure equivocity and metaphysics are incompatible. Aristotle points this out.[2] This means, of course, that the metaphysician, who wants to deal with the good, must either prove that 'good' is not an equivocal term — show that (and how) its two definitions can be reduced to a single definition — or that the term is purely equivocal.[3] The former case is clearly the prerequisite of a metaphysical analysis of the good. The latter precludes one.

A logical analysis of the definitions indicates that the metaphysical *impasse* is not at all insurmountable. For if an equivocal term is one which does not have either an ontological or a cognitional referent — it is once again Aristotle who points this out[4] — then 'good' cannot be a purely equivocal term. If both definitions of 'good' are valid, then the term 'good' must have an ontological referent: one of the two definitions is unmistakably ontological. This means that the metaphysician, who wants to deal with the 'good' in an adequate manner, must necessarily attempt to reconcile its two definitions. Boethius seems to have been more than aware of this: both the *Consolatio*[5] and the

---

1. The reason I have chosen these definitions as my starting point, is not only historical, that is, because they seem to be the sort of definitions which Boethius uses. Cf., e.g., *Quomodo*, 56–60: "Ea quae sunt bona sunt; tenet enim communis sententia doctorum omne quod est ad bonum tendere, omne autem tendit ad simile. Quae igitur ad bonum tendunt bona ipsa sunt." It is also speculative. For the definitions seem to be the mutually exclusive alternatives of a dichotomy. If a thing is good it must be so either in itself or in relation to another.
2. *Nicomachean Ethics*, 1096ª 30–35.
3. *Tertium non datur*. Excluding one of the definitions is tantamount to presupposing that the term is equivocal.
4. Cf. *Nicomachean Ethics*, 1129ª 27ff.
5. *Consolatio*, III, 10, 43–62: "Ne hunc rerum omnium patrem illud summum bonum quo plenus esse perhibetur vel extrinsecus accepisse vel ita naturaliter habere praesumas, quasi habentis dei habitaeque beatitudinis diversam cogites esse substantiam. Nam si extrinsecus acceptum putes, praestantius id quod dederit ab eo quod acceperit existimare

Quomodo[6] define the good by means of a synthesis of the two classical definitions of the good.[7] This too is important, at least as far as we are concerned. For our analysis of the good is an introduction to our examination of the Boethian doctrine of the good.

But as clear as it is from a logical point of view that 'good' must have an ontological referent, it is not at all clear from the metaphysical point of view what one is to make of the term. As we saw above, both of the definitions of the 'good' are problematic. And what is more, they seem to be mutually exclusive.

It is our objective in this chapter to enucleate a metaphysics of the good, which will furnish the structure with which to begin to unravel the Boethian doctrine of participation. Our plan is to begin from the root of the problem and work our ways up. We will start by analyzing the two classical definitions of the good, aiming to determine the metaphysical problems they imply: what they claim the good is, and what metaphysical conditions must hold in order for their claims to be valid. Once we have done this, we will examine the problems involved in reconciling the two definitions, outline a possible way in which this can be done, and conclude with an attempt to define the 'good' itself.

---

possis. Sed hunc esse rerum omnium praecellentissimum dignissime confitemur. Quod si natura quidem inest, sed est ratione diversum, cum de rerum principe loquamur deo, fingat qui potest: quis haec diversa coniunxerit?...Omnino enim nullius rei natura suo principio melior poterit exsistere, quare quod omnium principium sit, id etiam sui substantia summum esse bonum verissima ratione concluserim."

6. *Quomodo*, 56–60.

7. Cf. on this point Pandolfi, pp. 17–18: "Notiamo: tre parti del *De Ebdomadibus*...assumono come loro tema (e smentiscono) rispettivamente le ontologie *platonizzante*, *equivocista* (che dissipa nominalisticamente il logo unitario nei "molti," alla maniera di Eraclito) e *univocista* (risalente ad Elea)."

Chapter 5

THE DEFINITIONS OF THE GOOD

The first definition of the good — *ens et bonum convertuntur* — is clearly an ontological one: its claim is that 'goodness' is a substantial property of all beings. It shows that our investigation must involve a metaphysical concern about both the ontological constitution of things and a substantial property that they all seem to share. In this sense, then, 'why are things good?' is a variation of the problem of the one and the many: a problem whose solution entails finding a way of justifying the attribution of a characteristic common to a plurality of things, without denying either the plurality of things or the unity of their characteristic. Let us call this interpretation of our problem the *ontological interpretation*.

As we saw above, the *ontological interpretation* is an unusually difficult variation of the problem of the one and the many. For although we do say that things are 'good' and mean by that that *goodness* is a characteristic which those things that we call 'good' have, it is not at all clear what we mean by that claim, or what kind of characteristic 'goodness' is. It cannot be a specific genus or species. For 'good' is predicated of all genera and species. It cannot be a specific act or a substance, because all acts and substances are called 'good.' Nor can it be a specific quality or quantity, a given time, a definite place, or any other determinate attribute that one can classify by means of one of Aristotle's categories. For 'good' can be predicated of all things in all categories, as Aristotle himself points out.[1]

These problems indicate that responding to the ontological version of our question entails three things: (1) determining what characteristic we predicate of beings when we say that the 'good' is a substantial property of being; (2) understanding why all beings have that characteristic and why it is a 'substantial' one; and (3) explaining how that characteristic can be the same in all things, although it is present in a multiplicity of different kinds of things.

---

1. Cf. *Nicomachean Ethics*, I, 4 1096ª 23–29.

The second definition of 'good' is teleological: it takes 'good' to mean the object of desire. If our question is formulated in terms of this second definition, 'why are things good?' seems to mean: 'why are things objects of desire?' In this second form the question can also be ontological. For just as asking why one likes Bach's *Chromatic Fantasy and Fugue* can be asking something about the work itself — about its construction, its modulations, its key, its passion, or what not — so too can asking why something is an object of desire be asking something about some specific thing one desires: about its properties, or, more specifically, that property that causes us to desire it.

If it is thus interpreted, the question at hand seems to be of much the same sort as the ontological interpretation of the question. For if there is a plurality of things which we all desire, and if it is some one property or characteristic of these things that makes us desire them, then to ask why things are good is tantamount to asking what that characteristic or property is, and why different things share it. Let us call this second interpretation of our question the *onto-teleological interpretation*.

The *onto-teleological interpretation* makes use of one of the classical interpretations of the teleological definition of the good, and there are obvious reasons why metaphysicians would want to revert to it. The primary is that it allows one to elude the discrepancies between the two classical definitions of the good. The fact of the matter is, however, that as valid as the *onto-teleological* interpretation is, it does not do justice to the definition of the 'good' whence it stems, and that for two main reasons. The first is that it answers our question by presupposing that an 'object of desire' is necessarily the efficient or moving cause of an act of desire. The second is that it would answer our question simply in terms of the *object*. Both of these points make it simplistic.

As for the first point, although it is certainly licit to presuppose that an 'object of desire' is the moving cause of an act of desire — we can and often do desire to eat because we smell appetizing food — the presupposition is incomplete. For it is not at all necessary for an 'object of desire' to be the efficient cause of an act of desire. Our desire to eat something need not at all be caused by that thing, as appetizing as it may smell. It can be caused by sheer gluttony, nervousness, or ten thousand things other than the ones which we actually do desire to eat. Thus, even though it is true that asking why something is an object of desire can be asking something about a specific characteristic, which those things which we actually do desire have, it is not necessarily — or exclusively — asking something about those things' characteristics. It might be asking something about the desirer.

The second point is related to the first. For since the *onto-teleological* interpretation views the 'good' simply as the efficient cause of desire, it overlooks the fact that desiring presupposes both a desirer and a relation between the desirer and his *desideratum*. And this too is simplistic: not just because there can be no desiring without a desirer, but more importantly because desiring seems to be contingent upon the desirer himself to some degree. We do not desire to eat good food that smells putrid if we do not know that there is a good taste hidden behind the smell. The point here is not just a technicality. In overlooking the fact that the teleological definition of the good presupposes some relation between a desirer and his *desideratum*, the *onto-teleological* interpretation would risk overlooking one of this definition's basic points: that there is a sense in which the desired object is (or actuates) the desirer's own τέλος, his final cause.

This point is best made negatively. Were a *desideratum* merely other than the desirer, in the sense that it causes his desire irrespectively of his needs and wants, then we would all necessarily desire all desirable things. Hungry or not, we would always have to want to eat everything edible that is presented to us; thirsty or not, we would always have to want to drink when we are in the presence of water; tired or not, we would always have to want to read our copies of the *Summa*. But this is simply not the case. One of the conditions of the normal person's wanting to eat in normal circumstances is hunger; thirst is a condition of a normal person's wanting to drink under normal circumstances; and intellectual curiosity is one of the conditions of picking up a book like the *Summa*. And the fact of the matter is that hunger is not just caused by food, thirst is not just caused by water, and curiosity is not just caused by the *Summa*. There are such things as empty stomachs and low blood sugar, thirst, and *docta ignorantia*.

But there is another sense in which a *desideratum* cannot simply be something other than the desirer: it isn't the term of the act of desire it causes insofar as it is other than the desirer. If it were, desiring would necessarily be the term of the activity elicited by all desirable things. And this is simply not the case.[2] Our relations with our heroes do not

---

2. I realize that this account of desire differs from the one Aristotle gives in the *Metaphysics*. For Aristotle seems to have held that the term of our desire is extrinsic to us. That is why those things which are moved by their desire for the Prime Mover *circle* around Him. Cf. *Metaphysics*, L, 1072^a 26ff.: "And the object of desire and the object of thought move in this way; they move without being moved...But since there is something which moves while itself unmoved, existing actually, this can in no way be otherwise than it is. For motion in space is the first of the kinds of change, and motion in a circle the first kind of spatial motion; and this the first mover *produces.*" [The translation is Richard McKeon's (New York: Random House, 1941) pp. 879–80, which will be used henceforth.] Our account is closer to Augustine's, for whom the good was an object of desire to be possessed. Cf., e.g., *Confesssions*, I, 5: "Who shall grant me to rest in Thee? By whose gift shalt Thou

end with our desire to look upon them from afar. Were they to, it would be very difficult to explain why throngs of people ask their heroes for autographs, attempt to meet them, emulate them, read as much about them as they can in gossip columns, and buy their memorabilia. Were desire to be the term of our relations with music, it would be very difficult to explain why we go to concerts, buy recordings, and play instruments. Were desire the term of our relations with food, there would be no need for us to eat.

Now, if no *desideratum* can simply be other than the desirer, then every *desideratum* must also be the desirer in some sense. For that is the alternative. That is, if a desirable thing cannot cause a person's desire irrespectively of his own needs, then the person's needs must also be the cause of his own desire. If, on the other hand, a desirable thing cannot be the term of a person's desire simply insofar as it is other than him, then the person himself must in some sense be the term of his own desire. This means that the desirer must in some sense be the *desideratum* for all of his acts of desire. After all, an object of desire is (or can be) the cause and term of desire. If this is so, however, it cannot be himself as he already is that he desires. Strictly speaking, one cannot desire what he already possesses. What he must therefore desire is himself as he can be: his completion, his fulfillment, his τέλος. There must therefore be a sense in which every *desideratum* effects the desirer's own actuation: his achieving his τέλος, his attaining his end. This would explain both why we actively seek things which cause our desire, and why we are never really satisfied by any of them.

The gist of the matter is that a *desideratum*'s eliciting an act of desire cannot simply be a matter of that *desideratum*'s properties. This means that the *onto-teleological* interpretation cannot be the most basic interpretation of the teleological definition of the good. What we must therefore do before we attempt to see if and how one can reconcile the two definitions of the good is analyze the teleological definition more carefully.

The Teleological Good: The Nature of Objects

The basic flaw in the *onto-teleological* interpretation is that it does not make use of an adequate notion of 'object.' For the object of an act need not necessarily be the efficient cause of an act. Nor is it the necessary cause of an act, in the event that it is. The object of an activity

---

enter into my heart and fill it so compellingly that I shall turn no more to my sins but embrace Thee, my only good?" [The translation is F. J. Sheed's (Indianapolis: Hackett, 1992) p. 5]

can technically speaking be one of two things: (1) the efficient or the moving cause of an activity,[3] or (2) the term of an activity which is caused by the agent himself.[4] In the prior sense, the *Chromatic Fantasy and Fugue* can be the object of an act of desire, that is, if it is the composition itself that causes a person to desire to listen to it. It is in the second sense, on the other hand, that writing a clear book is the object of my present activity. For my present activity does have an object: something towards which it tends. But this object clearly cannot be the efficient or the moving cause of my writing: it doesn't exist yet. It is the term of an activity which I myself, for better or worse, have caused.

One could raise an objection here. For although the *object* of an act need not be the act's efficient cause, it would nevertheless seem to have to be its term, no matter how the act is caused. We saw above that an object is the term of an agent's self-willed act. The fact is, however, that the same thing seems to hold for those acts which are caused by the object — efficiently caused. This is clear in the case of an act of desire.[5] For the term of an act of desire is not the desiring *per se* but the *desideratum*, no matter how the act of desire is caused.[6] We do not desire to listen to the *Chromatic Fantasy and Fugue* because we desire our desiring. Nor is our desire satisfied by our desire, unless we are maniacs. Rather, we desire to listen to the *Chromatic Fantasy and*

---

3. I am using the term efficient causality in the Aristotelian-Thomist sense in which it is not only a *principium motus*, but also a *principium agendi in aliud in quantum aliud*. That is why I have distinguished an efficient cause from a moving cause, which I take to mean a *principium motus* purely and simply. This distinction holds henceforth for this section of the work.

4. In order to provide an adequate metaphysical discussion of the good that will furnish us with the means to reconstruct the Boethian doctrine of the good, I am using the Thomist distinction between the object of an active potency and the object of a passive potency. Cf., e.g., *Summa Theologiae*, I, q. 77, a. 3 c: "Ratio autem actus diversificatur secundum diversam rationem obiecti. Omnis enim actio vel est potentiae activae vel passivae. Obiectum autem comparatur ad actum potentiae passivae sicut principium et causa movens; color enim in quantum movet visum, est principium visionis. Ad actum autem potentiae activae comparatur obiectum ut terminus et finis; sicut augmentativae virtutis obiectum est quantum perfectum, quod est finis augmenti."

5. This is not only true of an act of desiring. The same thing holds for an act of knowing, i.e., that the object can be both the cause and term of the act itself. This is why every concept is a *medium quo* as opposed to a *medium quod* to use Thomist terminology once again. Cf. *De Veritate*, q. 3, a. 2 c: "sicut in intellectu speculativo videmus quod species, qua intellectus informatur ut intelligat actu, est primum quo intelligitur; ex hoc autem quod est effectus in actu, per talem formam operari iam potest formando quidditates rerum et componendo et dividendo; unde ipsa quidditas formata in intellectu, vel etiam compositio et divisio, est quoddam operatum ipsius, per quod tamen intellectus venit in cognitionem rei exterioris; et sic est quasi secundum quo intelligitur."

6. Despite the definition above, Aquinas makes a similar point. Cf. *Summa Theologiae*, I, q. 5, a. 4c; *In I Ethica Nicomachea*, 1094ᵃ 1–2 §8. So too does Plato in the *Symposium*. See 204ᵃ 1ff.

Fugue because we desire the *Chromatic Fantasy and Fugue* and because it is in listening to the *Chromatic Fantasy and Fugue* that our desire is satisfied.

This means, of course, that we have distinguished the two possible meanings of 'object' through a term which is common to both. For precision's sake, thus, let us define the object of the first interpretation as the active cause and term of an act, and the object of the second interpretation as the desired effect of an act which originates in the agent.

The point here is clearly applicable to the 'good.' What it implies is that the teleological 'good' can be one of two things: (1) the active cause and term of an act of desire, or (2) the desired effect of a self-caused act of desiring.

The Teleological Good:
The Relation between Subject and Object

There is a second point to clarify with regards to objects. For 'object' in the metaphysical sense is necessarily a relational term. That is, if something is an object in the metaphysical sense insofar as it is the cause or term of an act, then an object must be such in relation to the act it causes, or whose term it is. This is especially clear in the case of desire. A *desideratum qua desideratum* is such only in relation to a desirer and to his act of desire. Were this not so, were for instance the *Chromatic Fantasy and Fugue* a *desideratum* independently of some act of desire, which it causes or by which it is caused, then not only would everyone have to desire the *Chromatic Fantasy and Fugue,* but we would all have to do so in the same way. As desirable as the first part of the implication may be, it is simply not the case. Nor is the point at hand only apparent in those cases in which the *desideratum* is some thing, some property of an already existing thing, or a group of things. It also holds for those *desiderata* which result from our own free acts. Some of us do not write poetry in our spare time.

The fact that an 'object' in the metaphysical sense is essentially a relational term implies three things regarding the teleological good: (1) that it is contingent upon an act of desire; and as such that (2) its nature is determined by the nature of the act of desire, and (3) ultimately by the desirer himself in some way. For if the teleological good implies a relation, then its specific nature must be contingent upon that relation, while the nature of the relation must be contingent upon the nature of the *relata*.

The Teleological Good Is Contingent upon an Act of Desire

This point is an obvious corollary of the teleological definition of the good. If an object must be either the efficient cause and term of an act, or the desired effect of a self-willed act, then something can be an object in the metaphysical sense if and only if there is an act whose object it is. This is evident in both cases.

Nothing can be the efficient cause — or term — of an act unless it actually causes that act. An efficient cause is such only when it attains its effect. It is only when something has actually been hit by a foot that the act of kicking takes place. Were one to miss what he intends to kick, he would simply swing his leg. This is why the mediaevals insisted that *actio est in passo* for all transient acts.[7] What this means is that an object, in the metaphysical sense, can be such — the efficient cause and term of an act — only when it has caused an act, or conversely, that it is in the act which it causes that something becomes an *object*. This clearly means that there is a sense in which an object in the metaphysical sense is contingent upon the act whose object it is.

The same thing holds for those objects which are the desired effects of self-willed acts. Nothing can be the effect of an act independently of the act that causes it. For there can be no effect of an act, if there is no act whose effect it is. My book, the effect of my present activity, cannot exist unless I write it, however much as I would love for it to write itself. But an object in the metaphysical sense can be the effect of a self-willed act. In this case too, as such, an object in the metaphysical sense must be contingent upon the act whose object it is.

The present point is more than apparent in the case of the *Chromatic Fantasy and Fugue*. For John Cage and Keats to the contrary, silence is not music, nor are unheard pipers painted on Grecian Urns. If there is such a thing as the "spirit ditty of no tone," it is not the spirit of music. Music is essentially a relational phenomenon, and in this it is no different from any other form of art: its object is to communicate, and it exists once some form of communication takes place. It is, as such, not scores and it is not sounds. For unread scores are nothing more than collections of black blotches scribbled on a piece of paper, and unheard sounds are nothing more than disturbances of the air. Scores and sounds are definitely components of music, but in themselves they have as much right to be called music as a compact disc without a stereo does, or as an unplayed piano does. Rather, scores become music in the

---

7. I am using the Aristotelian-Thomist notion in order to provide adequate metaphysical language for the point at hand. Cf., e.g., *De Anima*, 426^a 2-15, §592, 417^a 14-17, §356-57; 418^a 20-25, §393-94; 423^b-424^a 10, §547; 426^a 2-15, §590ff.

acts of being composed, read, performed, or listened to. The score of the *Chromatic Fantasy and Fugue* is music in relation to Bach, insofar as he improvised it; it is music in relation to a performer, insofar as he reads, understands, and performs the score; it is music in relation to a listener insofar as he hears the performance. Namely, it is in an act that scores become music; it is in an act that sounds become music. Were there no such acts, there would be no music.

The point is clearly applicable to the good. For the 'good' in the teleological sense is the object of desire. What it shows is that something's being teleologically good is contingent upon the act of desire it causes, or the act of desire by which it is caused. For it is only insofar as it is desired and in relation to that act of desire that it is an object.

The Nature of the Teleological Good Is Defined by the Nature of Desire

The second implication of the teleological definition of the good is more complex. For the claim that the nature of desire defines the good can be a modal corollary of the teleological definition of the good: if the good is the object of desire, and if an object of desire is such in relation to a desirer, then the quality of the desirer's relation to his object must determine the quality of the desired object's goodness. Thus, the specific manner in which someone actually desires something determines the specific manner in which that thing he desires is good. As such, if one desires something intensely, the object of his desire must be 'intensely' good; if his desire for that thing is barely perceptible, then the object of his desire must be minimally good, and so on.

The implication can, however, also be a metaphysical corollary of that definition: if the good is the object of desire, and if an object of desire is such because it is desired — its being an object of desire is contingent upon its being the object of an actual act of desire — then the nature of an act of desire must determine the nature of the good. But the nature of an act is determined by its cause. As such, the nature of the good must be determined by the cause of one's act of desire. That is, if goodness is a relational term, then its nature must be contingent upon the nature of the relation it implies. But the nature of a relation is determined by its cause. Hence, the cause of that relation which the good implies must determine the nature of the good.

Both interpretations of the point are licit. But since the first one presupposes the second — for it must needs presuppose that a subject's desire is caused in a specific way in order to claim that that specific way of desiring admits of different modalities — the second must be the more basic one. Hence before seeing if and how there are different modalities of the good, we must understand what the good is, and what its basic definitions are. We will therefore concentrate on the metaphysical interpretation of the matter.

That the nature of desire determines the nature of the good is actually a corollary of the first implication. The first implication showed two things: (1) that an object in the metaphysical sense can be such only in relation to an agent insofar as he acts, and as such that, (2) in order for any given thing to be an object, it must either cause an act, or be the effect of an act which constitutes it. What this means is that the act in relation to which an object is such can have one of two causes: (1) the object itself, or (2) the agent who constitutes the object. The act, therefore, can be of two different kinds: the effect of the object or the effect of the agent. The converse of this is crucial to our present point: if an object causes a agent to act, it must actualize the agent's potential. If an object is the effect of an agent's free act, on the other hand, it must be the effect of his actuality — *actiones non progrediuntur nisi ab existente in actu secundum quod est in actu*[8] — and his will.

This point is essential to elucidating the nature of an object. For if an object is such only in relation to an act, and if that act can either actualize an agent, or be the effect of his actuality, then an object can be such only insofar as it actualizes an agent or is the effect of the agent's actuality. This elucidates a basic point regarding objects. When we speak of objects in the metaphysical sense, we always speak of them in relation to agents and to their activity, and what we are describing thereby are real relations: the real relation between an agent and his object, or the real relation between an object and its efficient cause. For a real relation is one which actualizes the relater, and is the effect of the relatee's actuality.

The *Chromatic Fantasy and Fugue* is a helpful example with regard to this point too. For just as the score of the composition is music only in relation to an agent's acts — a performer's reading and playing it, and an audience's hearing and enjoying it — so too can it be music only insofar as it causes some change in a musician who learns it insofar as he learns it, or in a listener who hears it being performed insofar as he hears it being performed. That the composition causes some change in the listener — that it actualizes him in some sense — is too obvious to comment on. Music has been used throughout the centuries to elicit action of some sort: cure insanity, soothe rages, and what not. That is why every army has a band, a drummer, or a fife, why every nation has an anthem, and why every religion has its sacred hymns. The fact that

---

8. Cf. *De Veritate*, q. 8, a. 6 c.

one can like or dislike the *Chromatic Fantasy and Fugue* is a sure sign of the fact that it does cause a change in him: a reaction presupposes a real relation with the thing to which one reacts. And as the composition changes the listeners, so too does it change those who perform it. Were this not true, all performing musicians would be improvisers, and this is simply not the case. The point, as such, is that just as the score of the *Chromatic Fantasy and Fugue* is music only in relation to an act, so too is it music only insofar as it causes some change in the musicians, who perform it, and in audiences. Namely, the *Chromatic Fantasy and Fugue* is music insofar as its performer has a real relation with its score, or insofar an audience has a real relation with its performance.

Nor is the only relevant point that the score of the *Chromatic Fantasy and Fugue* is music when there is a real relation between a performer and its score, or between an audience and its performance. The converse is also true: there is also a real relation between the composition *qua* music and Bach, and a real relation between the composition *qua* music and a performer. The first of these real relations is the most basic one with regards to the composition. For none of the real relations above would be possible if there had been no real relation between the score and Bach, or (to be precise) if there had been no real relation between the music and Bach, and no real relation between the score and the audience, since Bach improvised the piece and several members of the audience transcribed it. But these real relations were clearly not of the same sort as those that an audience tends to have with the composition. The real relations here constituted the music as such and left it for posterity, rather than being real relations through which the composition *qua* music changes those who hear it. Nor does the reversal of the relation imply that the *Chromatic Fantasy and Fugue* was not music to Bach or to its transcribers. For music was the object of Bach's act of improvising, an object he attained gloriously in his improvisation, and it was the object of the transcribers' writing it down.

As there is a real relation between the composition and Bach, so too is there a real relation between the *Chromatic Fantasy and Fugue* as music and every pianist who performs the composition in his performance. For the performer transforms the score of the composition into music. His relation to the composition is one that constitutes music as such. That relation may not be tasteful, and one can object to it on the grounds that it does not fully express the depth of Bach's intention. The fact of the matter is, however, that objecting to the performance presupposes that the performer has transformed the score of the work into music, else there would be nothing to which to object.

Music therefore is constituted by real relations and constitutes real relations. That is why it is essentially a form of communication.

This point is clearly applicable to the good. What it indicates is that the teleological good can be one of two things: (1) a real relation between a desirer and some actually existing thing which causes him to become such; or (2) a real relation between a thing and an agent, who desires that thing. Indeed, it indicates that the precise nature of the teleological good is dependent upon whether it is a real relation between a *desideratum* and an agent, or a real relation between an agent and *desideratum*. The difference here is one of direction. In the first case, the good is something upon which the agent is in some sense contingent: it is something which causes the agent to change, to become. In the second case, on the other hand, the good is contingent upon the agent himself: it is something which the agent makes, forms, and so forth.

The point here can be made in another way. If the good is the object of desire, the nature of the 'good' must be contingent upon the nature of desire. Desiring, then, can be either an activity which is caused by something other than the desirer, or it can be an agent's own free activity. In the first case, it must be the actualization of the subject: it must make him a desirer of some thing which he had hitherto not possessed or desired to possess. In the second case, on the other hand, desiring cannot be the agent's actualization. For the agent himself is the cause of his own desire. His desire, in other words, is the act of a being who is actual, insofar as he is actual. What is actuated or changed by his act is the thing he desires. That thing must be formed, or changed in some way by his act, if he is to desire at all. After all, one cannot desire nothing, and it is *ex hypothesi* that the subject does not desire something that causes his own desire.

This can happen in two ways: the subject can either form (make or construct) the object of his desire, or he can cause himself to desire some actual thing that does not actually cause him to desire it. The first case is the more obvious one. It is the case of every artist and scientist, of every builder and inventor, of every person who feels the need to form, express, or change something. For what the person in question feels the need to form does not exist unless he makes it. This does not imply that the person actually needs to build, form, or change the object he desires *per se*. I do not have to finish writing this book in order for it to be the object of my present desire. It means that he has to conceive his object and plan it. After all, we cannot actually make all of those objects that are born of our desire: Leonardo certainly did not make his flying machine.

The second case, on the other hand, is the source of our more 'exotic' activities: genocides, slave-trading, and so forth. For the strange thing about our partaking in those less than human activities is that we have to redefine them and their objects in some way, as goods, or as desirable, in order to engage in them. The objects in question are by definition undesirable: they are not the sort of things that cause us to desire them for themselves. Thus, the Turks still do not acknowledge that they committed the first genocide of the century when they slaughtered approximately one and a half million Armenian men, women and children during World War I. They claim that they were engaged in skirmishes against the Armenians, that they were attempting to block Armenian collaboration with the Russians, or that they were creating a pan-Turkish nation. Nor do they admit that they are presently murdering the Kurds. They simply claim (among themselves) that they are executing the third stage in their creation of the pan-Turkish nation. Hitler did not convince Europe to murder the Jews. He convinced to liberate the world of the overbearing Jewish influence in worldwide economics, politics, arts and sciences. Slave traders don't sell human beings. They boost economics by providing them with a free labor force which, they claim, just happens to look and act human. In each of these cases, those who would perform these actions redefine the undesirable objects of their acts in order to make them seem desirable and to elicit action. In the case of each of these atrocities a 'good' was pursued; in each of these cases the 'good' pursued was defined by the instigators of the atrocities; in each of these cases the 'good' was defined through a real relation between an object and the subject who defined it. The 'good' in the metaphysical sense need not look anything like the ethical good.

The Teleological Good Is Contingent upon the Desirer

This brings us to the third implication of the teleological definition of the good: that its nature is in some sense contingent upon the desiring subject himself. This point can again be a modal corollary of the definition of the good with which we are dealing. For if desiring is an agent's free act, and if every act must "issue from a thing which is actually existing insofar as it is in act," then the modality of the agent's actuality — his habits, culture, and so forth — must determine the modality of his desire. This implies that it is the modality of the agent's actuality that determines the nature of the good that he desires. This is the point behind the Latin dictum *qualis quisque est talis finis videtur ei,* and would explain why some of us do not write poetry. Then again, this is not the most basic interpretation of the point at hand. For it presupposes that desiring is a free activity, and, as we have seen, this need not be the case. Desire can also be caused by the *desideratum*.

This means that there is a more fundamental distinction to be made here: a metaphysical one. Now, if desiring can be either one's free activity or an activity which is caused by something other than the desirer, then it can be the act of either the desirer's active potency, or his passive potency. If this is so, however, then it must also be the desirer's own potential with respect to his *desideratum* that determines the nature of his desire. This clearly means that it is also the desirer's potential with respect to that object that determines the nature of his teleological good: what the good he desires is. Thus teleological 'good' can be: (1) that which actualizes the desirer's passive potency, and in this sense be the cause and term of his desire, or (2) be what is actuated by the desirer's active potency, and in this sense be the term of his self-willed act of desire.

This point is the obverse of the second implication. For if the 'good' is that real relation whereby the subject becomes a desirer of some given thing, and if that which causes a subject to act must actualize his potential, then the *good* must be both that which actualizes the subject's potential and his actualization. Indeed, something seems to be good in this sense only insofar as it actualizes the subject: *actio est in passo* after all. We saw this above. What we did not see is that the potentiality that the good actualizes in this case must be a passive or a receptive one. Nor could it be otherwise, since the good is what the subject comes to desire through the object's agency. That is, if desiring in this present case is an instance in which *actio est in passo,* then it must be the desiring subject's *pati* that makes him a desirer and the object a desired one. But *pati* is the act of a passive potency. It is an activity which does not originate in the subject.

This picture clearly changes if the *good* is that relation between some given thing and the subject whereby the thing becomes desired and actuated. In this case the good must be the effect of the desirer's own actuality and accordingly be the effect of an act of his active potency. It is the creation or construction of some thing which the subject desires, and that creation or construction takes place because the subject is capable of creating, constructing, or somehow making his object, and not because the thing to be formed, made, or created impresses itself upon the subject in some way. Desire in this case, then, must indicate not only that the desiring subject possesses the power and capacity to form and to actuate his object in some way, but also that he is making use of that power and capacity in his act of desire. As such, both the subject's desire and the object he desires must be the effect of his active potency.

The *Chromatic Fantasy and Fugue* is helpful in this case too. For what distinguishes Bach's relation to the composition from that of the mass of his listeners is Bach's own genius: his capacity to compose music. The *Chromatic Fantasy and Fugue* is the fruit of that genius, of Bach's active potency. The composition was music for him insofar as he composed it: it was music to him because it was the product of his active potency. There are no romantic details one can relate concerning Bach's composition techniques. Composing was something of utmost ease to him, as the extraordinary variety of his composition techniques shows. Now, Bach's relation to the *Chromatic Fantasy and Fugue* is obviously very different from those which the mass of listeners have with it. For the composition is not the fruit of their genius, or of their active potency. It is music to them nonetheless. It is music to them because they can listen to it, understand it, and enjoy it. It is music to them because they are receptive to it, because their enjoyment is the act of their passive potencies. The intermediate case here are performers, who play both an active and a passive role with regards to the composition, and hence must relate to it through both their active and passive potencies. They must relate to it through their passive potency for they must learn the score, and one of the marks of a great performer is the depth with which he does so. So too, however, must they relate to the composition through their active potencies, or rather the composition must relate to them because of their active potencies. For were a performer not capable of performing the composition — were he not to have a good keyboard technique — there would be no *Chromatic Fantasy and Fugue* for listeners to enjoy.

The Degrees of the Good

There are two important corollaries to the third implication of the teleological definition of the good. Both imply that it admits of degrees. For the teleological good is a real relation, and relations admit of degrees, as does the realization of the term of a real relation.

The Degrees of Real Relations. That real relations admit of degrees is something which we all know by experience. It is the reason why we pursue those things that cause us to desire them, as it is also the reason why beautiful projects never quite satisfy us. For desiring is not possessing, and our desire for something is satisfied only when we possess it. But our possession of the objects of our desire is also a real relation with them — or theirs with us. Indeed, it is the completion of that real relation whereby they become the objects of our desire.

The point at hand thus calls us to distinguish the different senses in which something can be an object of desire: the different senses in which something can be said to be good in the teleological sense. For that good which is the object of an act of one's passive potency must also be the term of the act of desire that it causes, whereas the good which is the object of the act of one's active potency must admit of different degrees of realization.

This is especially clear when the good is the object of an act of a passive potency. For the activity of a passive potency is reception, and desiring *per se* cannot be the complete reception of the desired object, else desire could not be for what one lacks. Desire therefore calls for an additional act through which the desirer comes to possess what he desires. This additional act must be a reception, if the good is the active cause of desire. For in this present case, the subject cannot come to possess the *desideratum* by creating it, precisely because that *desideratum* is an actually existing thing. The thing must *ex hypothesi* exist in order for him to desire it, since it is the cause of his desire. As such, he can only come to possess that *desideratum* because he receives it. That is the alternative. If this is so, however, then the subject's possessing his *desideratum* must also be case in which *actio est in passo*. What this means, of course, is that we must distinguish the senses in which it is something can be said to be teleologically good. For an object is both the cause of one's desire, and it is the term of the act of desire which it causes, and the ways in which it actualizes the subject in either capacity are clearly different.

Now, it could be objected that our distinction is in principle false. For a difference in acts implies a difference in the objects of those acts. That is, since acts are differentiated by their objects, different acts must have different objects. If this is so, however, then desiring something and possessing it must have different objects, because desiring and possessing are very different acts. They have different presuppositions: we do not possess what we lack, but we do desire what we lack, and so forth. The corollary to this objection is that the good must be differentiated insofar as it is the active object of one's desire: the cause of the subject's desire, and the cause of the subject's possessing the object of his desire.

As convincing as the argument may sound, it has a flaw. For it does not take into account the fact that the acts of desiring and of possessing what one desires are intrinsically related. One's desire for something is not an acknowledgement of its desirability. It is not the recognition of an object as such. Desire is not an altruistic act. It is by nature the desire to possess that thing which one desires.[9] This means that possessing

---

9. Plato makes a similar point in the *Symposium*. Cf. 206^e 9ff. So too does Aristotle. See *Nicomachean Ethics*, 1139^b 1ff.

a *desideratum* is the completion of an act of desire, rather than an act which is completely different from it. It means that possessing a *desideratum* is the object of one's desiring it. The implication here is that desiring and possessing something cannot have different objects. It follows that the teleological good cannot be two different things insofar as it causes our desire, and insofar as it causes our possession of the cause of our desire.

The difference between the senses in which something can be the object of one's desire, therefore, must be of degree. For that is the alternative. That is, if the acts of desiring and possessing do not have different objects, and if they are nonetheless different acts, they can only differ in degree. The degrees in question pertain to the real relation which the desirer has with his *desideratum*. For he must have a real relation with the *desideratum* both in order to desire it, and in order to possess it. But the first act stands to the second as an overture does to the main acts of an opera, as an incomplete act does to its completion. The act of desiring is by nature an incomplete relation with the thing which one desires. That is why we can desire what we lack. The act of possessing the thing which one desires, on the other hand, is the completion of that relation: it is the fullness of the real relation between a subject and the thing which he desires.

The point here is perhaps best exemplified through our personal relations. We must know someone to some degree in order for him to pique our curiosity. We must, as such, have a real relation with him in order for him to pique our curiosity. Yet our real relation with that person cannot be complete at the stage in which he piques our curiosity. If it were, that person could not pique our curiosity. Curiosity implies incomplete knowledge: an incomplete real relation with the object of one's knowledge. Hence we do what we can in order to come to know that person more fully: in order to satisfy our desire to know him. When we do satisfy our curiosity, however, our relation to that person does not change in any basic way. It does not lose its cognitional basis, nor does it cease to be a real relation. It merely becomes more complete.

The difference between our desiring something and our possessing it, as such, is not that the prior is a real relation while the latter is not. Both are real relations. Nor do these two real relations have different objects. The object of desiring is possessing the object of one's desire. Their difference lies in the degree to which the real relation between the subject and the object of desire is established. When a subject desires something, his real relation to it is incomplete. When he possesses the object of his desire, his relation with that object is complete.

We must make a similar distinction in the case in which the good is the effect of the subject's desire. For in this case too, one must distinguish two different phases in the real relation between the object and the subject. The first phase is the ideation and conception of the thing which one desires to make, form, or re-define. The second is the actual making, forming, or re-defining of that thing. The *desideratum*, in the first phase, is an object which one desires but has not yet attained. There is a real relation between the object and the subject in this first phase, because the object must exist in some sense in order for it to be desired. The second phase is the completion of the first, the term of the first. In it the object acquires actual existence.

The Degrees of Actualization. The second corollary regards the degrees to which the term of a real relation can be actualized. For just as a real relation with a *desideratum* admits of degrees, so too do different *desiderata* actualize the desirer to different degrees. This too is something we know by experience. It is the reason why we are willing to pay more for a concert ticket than we are for a praline. We simply get more out of the concert. It is also the reason why we are more attached to some of our works than we are to others. Some of our constructive activities seem to be real births. They require a lot of time and effort, and we have to put a great deal of ourselves into them. And the truth of the matter is that we care much more for these works than we do for those which require less attention.

Now, if it is possible for different *desiderata* to actualize a desirer to different degrees — listening to the *Chromatic Fantasy and Fugue* definitely actualizes a person more so than eating a good praline does — then there must be an ultimate *desideratum* the possession of which would actualize the desirer completely. For degrees presuppose a standard, which all things with degrees approximate and from which they all differ. This standard must be the ultimate teleological good, which all other 'objects of desire' approximate. This good is the complete actualization of the subject: the subject's final cause.

But if the ultimate good is what effects the subject's complete actualization, his attaining his final cause, and if each object which causes the subject's desire approximates the ultimate good, then each object which causes the subject's desire must actualize the subject's final cause to a limited degree. What this means, of course, is that each object of desire must actualize the subject's final cause.

We must make a similar point with regard to the object's real relation to the subject whose object it is. For just as the subject can actuate an object of his free desire to different degrees, so too can he express his active potency in different things he produces. And as he can express his active potency in different products, so too can he express his active potency to a different degree in each of them. Bach's *St. Matthew's Passion* is a greater expression of his active potency than his *Coffee Cantata* is: it is more intricate, deeper, and technically more varied. This means that there must be such a thing as an ultimate good *qua* self-willed term of desire, an ultimate expression of the subject's active potency: his complete and perfect expression of himself. Degrees, once again, presuppose a standard which all things which have a determinate characteristic to different degrees approximate and from which they all differ. If this is so, however, then each good which is a self-willed term of desire other than the ultimate good must be an imperfect and incomplete expression of the active potency by which it is made. But a complete and perfect expression of the subject's active potency must reflect the subject's active potency perfectly and completely. Were it not to do so, it could not be a perfect and complete expression of that active potency. As such, each incomplete and imperfect expression must be an imperfect reflection of the subject's active potency.

The Third Implication's Paradoxes

Although the main lines of the third implication are not problematic, its first corollary contains what appear to be a couple of paradoxes. The first pertains to the object as both cause and term of desire; the second concerns the relation between the object and the subject's potency. The first paradox emerges from an apparent contradiction in our reasoning. We claimed that if the good is the cause of someone's desire — if it is the object of his passive potency — it must be the term of his desire, because the activity of a passive potency is reception. Now, nothing initially seems wrong with that claim aside from the apparent oxymoron in the phrase 'activity of a passive potency.' Our hunger for pralines is only satisfied by good pralines. The problem arises when one juxtaposes that claim with the facts that we can and do actively seek those things which cause our desire, and that our seeking those things is often the cause of our obtaining them. For these latter facts seem to make the possession of an object of desire the term of a free act — one which is caused by the agent — rather than one which is caused by the object of desire. After all, no one forces anyone who wants to eat a praline to look for a pastry shop where they sell good pralines; no one forces anyone to buy pralines once he has found the place; and above all no one forces the person who does find and buy pralines to eat them. Not even the praline, else we would all be overweight.

Now, if those acts through which we come to possess something we desire are free, then it would not seem possible for their term — the possession of the object — to be the term of an act which is caused by something other than ourselves. More specifically, their term cannot be the effect of an act of desire which is caused by the *desideratum*. For one and the same thing cannot be the term of two simultaneous acts which have mutually exclusive causes. My having to digest pralines cannot be the effect of both my having eaten them and of my not having eaten any. But if possessing an object of desire were the term of both a series of free acts and an act which is caused by the object of desire, then it would seem to be the term of two simultaneous acts which have mutually exclusive causes. A free act, after all, is one which originates in the subject as such, and an act which originates in the subject is not and cannot be one which has something other than the subject thimself as cause. Conversely, an act which is caused by something other than the subject is not and cannot be free. As such, if our possessing a *desideratum* is the term of an act which is caused by the *desideratum* itself, it would not seem possible for our possessing that *desideratum* to be the term of our free acts of seeking, obtaining, and possessing it.

Have we claimed something contradictory, then, by stating that the cause of our desire must also be its term, thereby implying that the *desideratum* itself causes us to possess it, if the acts through which we come to possess that *desideratum* are manifestly free?

Nor is this the only problem in the first corollary. Just as our claim seems to make the object of desire the term of two simultaneous but mutually exclusive acts, so too does it seem to call for the desiring subject to be simultaneously active and passive with respect to the same object in his act of possessing it. After all, we did claim both that the subject actively pursues and acquires those things which cause his desire in order to possess them, and that he must receive those things in order for his desire for them to be satisfied. But this sounds impossible. If someone possesses something because he actively acquires it, then his potential with respect to that thing must be active; if he possesses the thing because he receives it, on the other hand, his potential with respect to it must be passive. And the fact of the matter is that it is contradictory to claim that someone's potential with respect to the same thing is both active and passive at the same time. There are at least two reasons for this. The first regards the different sorts of relations which a subject can have with things insofar as his potency with regards to them is active or passive. The second regards the nature of real relations.

In most cases when one claims that someone's potential with respect to a given thing is active, it is because he has actually acquired, or possessed, that specific thing through his free activity, or can do so. Brahms's potential with respect to his first piano concerto, for instance, was active, as is a pianist's who knows the score. This is how we have used the term thus far. Alternatively, if someone's potential with respect to a given thing is passive, it is because he has not actually made that thing, or cannot possess it through his own free activity. That is why we go to concerts to hear the professionals playing Brahms's first piano concerto: to acquire what we cannot compose or perform on our own, or to hear a specific piece we have not composed, or a specific performance other than our own. What this means is that if someone does acquire something for which he does not have the active potential, it cannot be through his own free acts that he does so. If one cannot play the piano or read Brahms's score, then he can stare at a keyboard as much as he wants, but he will not play the first piano concerto. If, on the other hand, he acquires some given thing for which his potential is merely active, then he cannot possess that thing because he has received it from something other than himself. Brahms certainly did not go to concerts to learn the score of his first piano concerto. As such, it seems contradictory to affirm that a subject's potential with respect to a given thing is both active and passive, or that his possessing that thing is the term of acts of both his active and passive potencies.

Moreover, if someone's potential with respect to a given thing were both active and passive then he would have to come to possess that thing through a real relation, and his real relation with that thing would have to be actively caused both by himself and that thing. But this is impossible. A real relation is one of dependence: it is one in which the real relater is actualized by the thing to which he relates. If someone were therefore to be the active cause of his own real relation to some given thing, he would have to be capable of actualizing himself in the manner in which the thing does. In order to actualize himself in that specific way, however, he would have to be already actual in that way. For every effect requires an actual cause, and *omne agens agit sibi simile*. But this is impossible. Nothing can actualize itself in the specific manner in which it already is actual. As such, the subject cannot be the active cause of his real relations. The converse of this is just as absurd. Nothing can depend upon something other than itself in order to acquire what it already has. But if someone were already actual in the specific way in which he is to be actualized by the thing with which he has a real relation, then he would have to be so. As such, were someone the active cause of his own real relations, he could not have real relations with anything at all.

But if no one can be the active cause of his own real relations, then no one can be the active cause of his possessing something to which he is otherwise passive. For his possessing the thing in that case is a real relation. This means that possessing something can be the term of an act of an active potency, or it can be the term of an act of a passive potency, but it cannot simultaneously be both the term of an act of an active potency and the term of an act of a passive potency.

What this implies in our case is that the good cannot at once be the term of acts of one's active and passive potencies: it cannot at once be something which an agent can and cannot acquire through his own free activity. As such, if the good is the object of desire because it causes desire, it must be the object of an act of a passive potency, and the desirer must come to possess the object through the object's own agency. Thus, the desirer cannot acquire that *desideratum* through his own free acts. Alternatively, if the subject actively seeks the *desideratum*, and if it is his seeking that yields it, then his possessing that *desideratum* must be the term of an act which issues from his active potency. As such, the subject's desire for that *desideratum* cannot be caused by the *desideratum* itself, nor can his potency with respect to that thing be passive.

Have we not claimed something contradictory by stating that the cause of our desire must also be its term, if the acts through which we come to possess the objects of our desire are manifestly free?

Our two problems are the obverse and reverse of the same problem. Both concern the causes of our possessing something we desire. Their difference lies in the fact that the first formulates the problem in terms of the acts through which we acquire what we desire, whereas the second formulates the problem in terms of the desiring subject's potential. For a free act is an act of an active potency, and an act which is caused by something other than the agent is the act of a passive potency. As such, if we ask how any given thing can be the term of both a free act and an act which is caused by something other than the agent, we are asking how that thing can be the term of an act of both his active and his passive potencies. This means that we need only solve one of our problems in order to have the main lines for our solution of the other. We will begin with the first.

In order to solve our first problem, we have to explain how something other than an agent can cause his free acts, or alternatively how the agent himself can freely cause those acts of his which are caused by something other than himself. This is the root of our problem. For an act which has what appear to be contradictory effects must have what seem to be contradictory causes. As such, if possessing a *desideratum* is the term of both a free act and an act which is not free, then possessing a *desideratum* must be caused both by the subject who possesses the *desideratum* and the *desideratum* which he possesses.

Now, it does seem contradictory to claim that a free act can be caused by something other than the agent. A free act originates in the agent by definition. The same thing clearly holds for the converse to this. And yet, it is more than possible for an act to originate in both the agent and the object of his act. This is especially clear in the case of our acquiring what we desire. After all, we are not the efficient causes of all of the *desiderata* which we acquire. My acquiring pralines is not making them: I haven't the vaguest idea how to make them. Nor, however, is the *desideratum* the efficient cause of our acquiring it. No praline can hypnotize me. What this means is that there must be a sense in which an agent's free act of possessing a *desideratum* must be caused by the *desideratum* itself, or conversely that his reception of the *desideratum* must be due to his free acts.

The act must be caused by the *desideratum* because no one can be the moving cause of his desiring something which he does not make or define through his free acts. If the object of an act of desire can be either the efficient cause of one's desire or the term of one's self-willed act of desire, then any object which is not the term of one's self-willed desire must be the efficient cause of his desire. But if no one can cause himself to desire something which he himself does not make (or define in some way), then he cannot be the only cause of his possessing that thing. One's desire for something is, after all, a cause of his act of possessing it. Desire is by definition the desire to possess one's *desideratum*. If this is so, however, then if one's desire is caused by the *desideratum*, so too must his act of possessing that *desideratum* be. For the possession of the *desideratum* is the term of his act of desire: it is its effect.

The act of possessing the *desideratum* must be a free act, on the other hand, because no *desideratum* is the necessary cause of one's possessing it. That is, if one's possessing an object of desire is not the necessary effect of one's desiring it — or the necessary effect of the object's causing one to desire it — then it must be a possible effect of one's desiring it — or of the object's causing him to desire it. If this is so, however, then the actuality of that effect cannot be determined by the object. As such, the actuality of that effect must be contingent upon the agent, or more specifically upon his will. *Tertium non datur.* The alternative to necessity is freedom, in this case. If this is so, then we have that one's act of possessing something he desires can be both free and caused by something other than himself.[10]

---

10. Aquinas claimed that there was one exception to this: the case in which the object of one's desire is God. Cf. *De malo*, q. 6: "Si autem consideretur motus voluntatis *ex parte obiecti determinantis* actum voluntatis ad hoc vel illud volendum, considerandum est, quod obiectum movens voluntatem est bonum conveniens apprehensum; unde si aliquod bonum proponatur quod apprehendatur in ratione boni, non autem in ratione convenientis,

Granted that it is possible for the same act to have what seem to be mutually exclusive causes, the problem is determining why it is. The way to do so is to distinguish the senses in which the object and subject cause a free act of possessing something.

Now, the free act of possessing something presupposes a free act of seeking to obtain it, and the free act of seeking to obtain something presupposes both that the thing which one seeks to obtain exists in one way or another — ideally or really — and that the subject desires it. Were that thing not to exist in some way or other, the subject simply would not seek it. We cannot seek nothing or what we do not know. If the subject were not to desire that thing, on the other hand, he would not bother to seek it. We do not seek what we do not want in one way or other. This implies two things: that the *desideratum* one seeks must define one's act of seeking it, and that it must cause one's act of seeking it. It must define the act because it is its object and every act is defined by its object. It must cause the act, on the other hand, because one's desire is a cause of his acts. This does not mean that it is necessary for the thing which one seeks to be the ultimate cause of one's seeking it. That cause can be the subject if the thing he seeks is one which he himself made or defined. We can seek to put one of our thoughts in words. Nor does it mean that seeking is the necessary effect of that thing. We can always let thoughts fly by. As such, it is not to claim that the act of seeking is not free. It is to say that seeking presupposes something which is sought, and that what is sought is both the object of the act and one of its causes.

If the act of seeking something is both defined and caused by the thing which one seeks and if it is the presupposition of an act of possessing that thing, then the act of possessing something must also be defined and caused by what one possesses. What one possesses must define that act because it is its object. Possessing is always possessing something. It must cause the act, on the other hand, because the subject must want what he comes to possess in order to come to possess it, and desire is always a cause of those acts which regard the object of one's desire. This again is not to claim that that act through which a subject comes to possess what he seeks is not free. For there must be a sense in which that act is free too. Seeking something is not the necessary cause of one's possessing it even if one's search is successful. We often turn

---

non movebit voluntatem. Cum autem consilia et electiones sint circa particularia, quorum est actus, requiritur ut id quod apprehenditur ut bonum et conveniens, apprehendatur ut bonum et conveniens in particulari, et non in universali tantum. Si ergo apprehendatur aliquid ut bonum conveniens secundum omnia particularia quae considerari possunt, ex necessitate movebit voluntatem; et propter hoc homo ex necessitate appetit *beatitudinem*, quae, secundum Boëtium est status omnium bonorum congregatione perfectus."

down the pleasure of enjoying things which we have come to obtain for fear of losing them, of being disappointed by them, and so forth. It is to claim that there is a co-cause of one's coming to possess the objects of his desire: the object itself.

The distinction we need to make here, as such, is between the act of seeking to obtain the object of one's desire insofar as that act is free and that free act's presuppositions; it is between the act through which a subject actually comes to possess that object as a free act and the presuppositions of that free act. As free, then, the act of seeking to obtain an object of desire can have no cause other than the subject: his whims and will. In order for that free act to take place, however, the subject must both have something to seek and desire that thing which he seeks. In a similar way, the act of possessing an object of desire can have no cause other than the subject insofar as it is free. But in order for that free act to take place, there must be something for the subject to possess, and the subject must desire that thing which he is to possess.

These prior acts, that is, one's having something to seek to possess and his desiring that thing, are not and cannot be free acts in those cases in which that thing which the subject desires is some actually existing thing other than himself. For if they were free, then the subject could not desire anything other than himself or his products. If desire is a self-willed act, then its term must be self-willed too, as we have seen. But *ex hypothesi* it is not. For the claim that we are trying to justify here is one which concerns things other than the desiring subject and his products. Now, if these acts are caused by something other than the subject, and if they themselves define and cause the subject's free acts of seeking, obtaining, and possessing something, then a subject's free acts of seeking, obtaining, and possessing something must have an extrinsic cause. This extrinsic cause, then, is the thing which one seeks, obtains, and possesses: the object of the subject's desire. As such, the object of desire must be a cause of the subject's free acts of seeking, obtaining, and possessing that object.

This does not mean, however, that the object of desire is the efficient or moving cause of those free acts through which a subject does acquire it. We would have a real contradiction on our hands if it were. Efficient causality and freedom are mutually exclusive. The fact is, however, that it cannot be, insofar as the acts in question are not the necessary effects of the subject's desire for the object. I do not eat pralines because pralines have deprived me of my free will. If the efficient or moving cause of an act is that cause of which the act is a necessary effect, then the moving cause of these acts must be the subject himself. The object of desire is the final cause of the free acts through which the subject acquires it. The point here is one which we saw before. Our desire for something is by nature the desire to possess that thing. But if possessing the object of one's desire is the final cause of all of the acts which arise from one's desire, and if one's desire is caused by the object of desire, then all of those acts which one undertakes in order to possess that object must be caused by the object itself. As such, the solution to our problem is to distinguish the efficient or moving cause of those acts through which one seeks, obtains, and possesses the object of his desire, and the final cause of those acts. The moving cause of the acts is the subject; the final cause is the object of the subject's desire.

We are now in a position to solve the first of our paradoxes. For if an act can be caused both by the object of that act and the subject who acts, then it is not contradictory to claim that the effect of that act is caused by both the subject and the object. But the effect of the act in this present case is the term of the act. What this means is that the act of possessing an object of desire can be the term of both a series of free acts and an act which is caused by something other than the subject if the object one possesses is neither the subject nor his products. It must be the term of his free act of acquiring an object which he desires through the object's own agency. Thus is our first problem solved.

As for the second paradox, if it is not contradictory to claim that an act can be both free and caused by something other than the agent, then it cannot be contradictory to claim that the subject's potential with respect to the same object of desire can be both active and passive. For if his possessing the object is the term of a free act, then his potential with respect to the object must be active, and if his possessing the object is the term of an act which is caused by that object, then his potential with respect to that object must also be passive. Hence, our second paradox seems to be solved too.

The fact of the matter is, however, that we must make a distinction here in order truly to solve our problem. For what we have said thus far could be seen to imply that a subject's free act actualizes his own passive potency directly. That is, since we said both that the subject and object are the cause of his possessing the object of his desire and that his possessing that object is the actualization of his passive potency, it might seem to follow that a subject himself is one of the active causes of the actualization of his own his passive potency. Appearances seem to indicate that this is so. For our desire for pralines is satisfied by our eating them, and our eating them is a free act. Appearances to the contrary, however, this is strictly speaking not the case. It is metaphysically impossible for a subject to actualize his own passive potency through his free acts. Indeed, were a subject's free acts to actualize his own passive potency, he would have to be the active cause of his real relation to the object of his passive potency, and, as we saw above, this is impossible. The distinction we need to make here, then, is between the ways in which the subject's possessing a *desideratum* other than himself or his products is the effect of his free acts, and in which his possessing a *desideratum* actualizes his passive potency.

Now, if the *desideratum* one comes to possess is something other than himself or his products, then he cannot possess that *desideratum* through his free acts, by definition, as we have seen. For possessing in this case is a real relation between the possessor and the object he possesses, and the subject cannot be the active cause of his own real relations to things. This means that for all that we can and do to obtain objects through our free acts, it is not our free acts that constitute our possession of them. Appearances to the contrary, it is not our eating pralines *qua* free act which satisfies our desire for pralines, because our desire is for the pralines, and our act of eating is not the pralines and does not create them. Rather it is our reception of these objects — an act of our passive potencies — that constitutes our possession of them. This means two things: (1) we are basically receptive with respect to those objects which cause our desire; (2) our free acts are not necessarily acts which make, or form things, but can be acts which provide the means with which we can receive the object which causes our desire.[11] Indeed, in this present case they must be such. As such, although it is true that possessing a *desideratum* is the term of both a series of free acts and an act which is caused by the *desideratum,* our possessing the *desideratum* does not satisfy our desire for it insofar as it is the term of a free act. Rather, our desire for the *desideratum* is satisfied by our real relation with it: by an act of our passive potencies, which our free acts have made possible. Namely, our possessing the *desideratum* is the effect of our free acts, but it is constituted by an act of our passive potencies.

---

11. Knowing presents a parallel case. For we must be both active and passive with regards to the objects of our knowledge. We must be basically passive with respect to the objects of our knowledge because knowledge is a real relation. We do not create most of the objects we know. Were we to do so, we would not know reality. The fact of the matter is, however, that most of the objects of our knowledge cannot impress themselves directly upon our intellects because they are material and particular and our knowledge is immaterial and universal, initially at least. Hence the need for an active intellect which performs the act which makes the possible intellect's reception of the object of its knowledge possible: it abstracts from the material conditions in which the object of human knowledge is first known. For it is first known through the senses. The fact that we do need active intellects to understand things, however, does not and cannot mean that our knowledge is the act of our active intellects. For that is metaphysically impossible. Rather, it means that our active intellects provide the prerequisites for what is basically a passive act.

The Good as the Object of Desire

We began our analysis of the teleological definition of the good with a series of objections to the onto-teleological interpretation of the definition itself. In the objections we claimed that the good cannot simply be a property that causes us to desire things, because we do not desire things necessarily, no matter what their properties may be. We therefore suggested that the good must also concern the desirer and his relations to the object of his desire. Indeed, we pointed out that the good in the teleological sense is closely related to the desirer himself. For nothing can be an object of desire irrespectively of the desiring subject, of his needs and wants. Nor can something be an object of desire insofar as it is completely extrinsic to the desirer. We concluded that far from being merely a property which causes us to desire things, the good must be something which is closely related to the desirer's own final cause.

Our analysis showed that the teleological definition of the good is an ambiguous one. The definition's ambiguity is present in the word 'object.' For an object can be the efficient cause and term of one's activity, or the desired effect of one's self-willed activity. Ambiguity notwithstanding, the definition implies one basic thing: that goodness in the teleological sense is a real relation. That it is a relation is implicit in the term 'desire.' For we desire what we lack and we can only lack what we are not. As the object of our desire, the good must therefore regard our relations to what is other than ourselves. That it is a real relation, on the other hand, is implicit in the term 'object.' For an object can be either the cause and term of our desire or the term of our self-willed activity of desiring. This means that something can be an object of desire insofar as it causes a change in a desirer — insofar as it actualizes him — or insofar as it itself is changed by the desirer's activity — insofar as it is the effect of his free act. This real relation can be of two sorts, and this is where the ambiguity lies. It can be a real relation between the subject and his object, or a real relation between the object and its subject. The difference here is one of direction. In the first case the real relation is one which actualizes the subject; in the second case, on the other hand, the real relation is one through which the subject actuates something other than himself. This difference in real relation corresponds to a difference in the subject's potential with regards to the object of his desire. In the case in which the good is the real relation between the subject and an object other than himself, the good is the object of the subject's passive potency. It is therefore the active cause of his desire and the term of his desire. For the activity of passive potencies is reception. If the good is result of the real relation between an object and a subject, on the other hand, it is the object of his active potency. In this sense, then, it is the effect of his actuality and a reflection of his actuality. As such, the 'good' in the teleological sense can be either that real relation between a subject and object whereby the subject becomes a desirer and possessor of an object, that real relation whereby the subject's passive potency is actualized; or it can be that real relation between an object and a subject whereby an object becomes actualized, that is, the effect of a subject's active potency. Each of these real relations admits of degrees. For the 'good' which actualizes the subject does so both because it causes the subject's desire — actualizes him *qua* desirer — and because it causes the subject to possess it — actualizes him *qua* possessor of the 'good.' Moreover, different actualizing 'good' things actualize the subject to different degrees. The 'good' which is actuated by the subject, on the other hand, is actuated in different phases and reflects the subject's actuality to different degrees.

Chapter 6

THE TWO DEFINITIONS OF THE GOOD AND THEIR PARADOXES

Now that we have grasped the main lines of the teleological definition of the good, we can finally formulate our original question regarding the nature of the good properly. The obstacle to our doing so was the teleological definition itself. 'Why are things good?' seems to have two basic interpretations: one which asks what kind of property goodness is, and why it can be shared by a multiplicity of beings, and one which asks what kind of real relation the good entails: whether it is an actuation of the desiring subject or the effect of the subject's actuality.

It is this latter ambiguity, rather than the ambiguity of the teleological definition *per se,* that makes our question an uneasy one. For a comprehensive understanding of the good must attempt to reconcile the two definitions of the good, and doing so seems to be an impossible task. There are a number of reasons for this. The principal ones concern the equivocity of the 'good' in the teleological sense and the accidentality of something's being an object of desire. For if the 'good' in the teleological sense denotes a series of *different accidental properties,* it would not seem possible for the 'good' to be a *substantial property* which all things have in *common.*

The equivocity of the 'good' in the teleological sense does not only stem from the ambiguity of the term 'object.' It also stems from the fact that both of the different senses in which the good can be said to be the 'object of desire' allow for a series of different modalities, and these modalities seem to correspond to a number of different properties in the *desiderata.* That is, if a thing's goodness is its being the object of an act of one's active potency, then it must be the effect of one's desiring and producing it. The good in this sense must be the actuation of an object of desire. The fact of the matter is, however, that we can desire and produce a multitude of different things in a multitude of different ways. I can desire both to write this book and to paint the moldings in my apartment (in order to alleviate the pressure of writing it), and my desire to do so differs in each case, as do the acts through which I satisfy it. Writing is not painting. But this means that the products of our desire must differ too. As such, 'good' must refer to a series of different types of things which we actually desire and produce. But these different things have no common property other than the fact that we desire and produce them. My painted moldings have no characteristic in common with my book, other than their color: both the ink and the paint I use are black. They stem from different genera of acts, and different acts have different objects. They belong to different categories of acts: one of the acts is physical, the other mental; one of the acts is practical, the other is not immediately so, and so on. As such, they seem to have no common property to which we can refer as 'good.'

The same thing holds, it seems, if the good is the efficient cause and term of our desire. For if the good is the cause of our desire — if it is what actuates our passive potency — then the fact that we desire different things in different ways — I certainly do desire both the stillness of a winter night in the mountains and listening to music, and I clearly do not desire them in the same way — seems to indicate that the good cannot be a single property of those things that cause us to desire them. The point can be made in two ways. For if by the 'good' in this case one means the cause of subject's act of desire, then the fact that the subject can and does desire different things in different ways seems to indicate that the 'good' must have a variety of different meanings. Different acts have different causes. Thus, a variety of different types of acts of desire implies that there are a variety of different types of causes of one's desire. If this is so, then 'good' cannot denote a single thing or property which all of those things which cause our desire share. If we desire to listen to the *Chromatic Fantasy and Fugue* because of its passion and the stillness of a winter night in the mountains because of its peace, then the 'good' must refer to both passion and peace, and passion and peace are clearly different things.

One comes to the same conclusion if by the 'good' he means the cause of the actualization of the subject's passive potential. For as the point above seems to show, 'desire' must be an equivocal term, insofar as it refers to a variety of different types of acts. This must mean that 'actuation' is also an equivocal term when it is referred to the 'good,' insofar as it can refer to a number of different goods that the subject desires and acquires because of his desire. Thus if the 'good' is the cause of the actuation of a subject's passive potential, then the 'good' cannot but be a series of different things.

If, on the other hand, one argues that the 'good' is not merely the cause of the subject's actuation but is also the actuation itself since *actio est in passo,* he cannot but come to the same conclusion. For if the subject's passive potency can be actuated in different ways, then the subject himself cannot but be good in a number of different ways. Goodness must also refer to different properties in the desiring subject. That is, it must once again be an equivocal term.

The equivocity of the term 'good' in the teleological sense seems to go hand in hand with the accidentality of the property, or properties, to which we refer as 'good.' A thing apparently has to exist in order to be desired, since we cannot actively desire nothing at all. If this is so, however, then a desired thing must also be capable of existing without being desired. Thus, if a thing's goodness precisely is its being an object of desire — goodness is after all a relational term — then goodness cannot but be an accidental property of those things that we do desire.

But if goodness is an equivocal term and an accidental property of things, it cannot be a substantial property of all things. For one and the same property cannot be both accidental and substantial in the same thing. An accidental property is one without which a thing can exist, whereas a substantial property is one which is essential to a thing's existence and it is contradictory to affirm that a given property is both essential and non-essential to a thing's existence. As such, if the 'good' is the object of desire, it cannot be a substantial property of all things.

Moreover, the equivocity of both of the principal senses of the teleological definition of the 'good' indicates that goodness cannot be a single property that things which are desired have. If this is so, then it cannot be a property which all 'good' things share. Sharing presupposes something to be shared, after all. Nor can it be a substantial property which all things share. As such, if the 'good' is the object of desire, it cannot be a substantial property of all things.

The conclusion to be drawn from these various arguments is that the two definitions of the good are antithetical: that the good cannot be a substantial property of all things if it is the object of desire.

Nor are matters any simpler if one proceeds with the assumption that goodness is a substantial property of things. For if this is true, one naturally finds himself wondering how it is at all possible for the good also to be the object of desire. After all, since one only desires what he lacks — and that is why the good can be the actuation of the subject's passive potency and the effect of one's active potency — then the fact that one desires something must imply that he is not good. But goodness, we have assumed, is a substantial property of all things. It is something which all things must have in order to exist. If one is good, as such, it must be impossible for him to desire the good. Hence it seems impossible for goodness to be both a substantial property of things and the object of desire.

There is an even more basic contradiction at play. If the good is a substantial property of all things, then all things must be good. If all things are good, however, and if the good is also the object of desire, then all things would have to be the objects of their own desire. The fact of the matter is, however, that this would again seem to be a contradiction in terms because it would imply that a thing is the efficient cause of its desiring itself, and/or the product of its desiring itself, and neither of these cases is possible.

The first case is impossible for it presupposes that something is both in act and in potency with respect to the same thing in the same way. For if one desires what he lacks, then in order to desire the good one must lack the good: he must be in potential with respect to the good. But in order to be the efficient cause of his own desire, one has to be actually good: he must be good in act. Every effect requires an actual cause. Thus, if one were the object of his own desire — and if by 'object' one means the efficient cause and term of desire — he would have to possess what he lacks. But that is manifestly impossible. Therefore, the good cannot be the object of desire if it is a substantial property of things.

Nor can the good be the effect or product of one's free act of desire if it is a substantial property of all things. For if the good is the term or effect of an act of desiring, it must presuppose a real relation with the desirer. Thus if a thing were its own object of desire, its goodness would necessarily presuppose its own desiring, that is, a real relation with itself. But we have stipulated that goodness is one of that thing's substantial properties. It follows that in order for the thing to be the object of its desire, it would have to have a real relation with itself in order to exist. But this is impossible. Therefore the good cannot be the term of one's desire if it is the substantial property of all things. Since the good cannot be either the cause or the term of one's desire if it is a substantial property of all things, however, it clearly cannot be the object of one's desire if it is a substantial property of all things. As such, we see again that the two definitions cannot be reconciled.

We have no choice, then, but to return our original question: what is the good? Can the good be the substantial property of all things and the object of desire? Must one accept both definitions? If so, how does one reconcile them? More importantly, to what purpose should one attempt to do so? Is the problem at hand truly one that can tell us something about being, about reality? Or is ours just a logical game, a play on definitions, which is comparable to those lovely geometrical games whose only rules are the principle of non-contradiction and axioms?

Chapter 7

THE FOUNDATIONS OF A SOLUTION

There are two basic problems which we must solve in order to reconcile the two definitions of the good. The first one concerns the ontological correlative of the term 'good.' For if the 'good' is both a substantial property of all things and the object of their desire, then the term might have no ontological correlative at all. If the 'good' means the object of desire, then it seems to denote a series of different properties in different things. If the 'good' is a substantial property of all things, on the other hand, its referent must be a single property which is present in different things. Now, the ontological correlative of the term 'good' cannot be both a series of different but unrelated properties and a single property which is common to all things. The two options are mutually exclusive. As such, if both definitions of the 'good' are valid, then either the term must have no ontological correlative at all — the ontological correlative of a contradiction is, after all, nothing, or as logicians would have it, the empty set — or there must be a way of reconciling the equivocity of the term 'good' in the teleological sense and the univocity of the term in its substantial sense. The former of these possibilities is not a viable option. For if both of the definitions of the good are valid, then the term 'good' must have an ontological correlative. One of the definitions of the 'good' is unmistakably ontological: it claims that the 'good' is a substantial property of all things. We must therefore assume that there is a way of reconciling the definitions. What we must to do to solve this first problem, as such, is to discover the relation between the different properties and things which are 'good' in the teleological sense, and determine the relation between their common element and the substantiality of the good. What we require, in other words, is a *reductio ad unum*.

The second problem, on the other hand, is a matter of reconciling two different types of definitions of goodness: an intrinsic one, which views goodness as a substantial property of all things, and an extrinsic one, which views it as a real relation. For the two types of definitions seem to be mutually exclusive. If a substance, as te Velde puts it, "relates to what something is essentially and by itself,"[1] and if goodness is a property of one's substance, then a thing's goodness has to "relate to" what that thing is "essentially and by itself." This, in turn, seems to imply that goodness cannot be (and that it cannot imply) a real relation between two discrete things. For what is present in a thing both "essentially" and "by itself" is not and cannot be something which is present in the thing "by its relations to things other than itself."

This is especially true of what a thing possesses "essentially." For a being cannot acquire what it possesses "essentially" after it has already begun to exist. Whatever comes to exist must come to exist as a specific thing. Existence itself cannot come to exist. In order to come to exist as a specific thing, however, something must have an essence: essences are what define a being's specific mode of existence. Thus what a being possesses "essentially" is a prerequisite of its existing. If this is so, however, then no being can acquire an essence after it has begun to be, that is, if the acquisition is ontological, and if the being is to continue to be the same being it was before the acquisition. For if a being were to acquire an essence, it would have to be some essence other than its own. But to acquire an essence other than one's own is to cease to be the being one is, and begin to be another being. An essence is what defines a being's specific mode of existing. Thus, to acquire an essence (ontologically) is to acquire a specific mode of existing. But to acquire a specific mode of existing is to become a different being. Thus, a being cannot acquire an essence and continue to be what it was. The same thing clearly holds for the properties of one's essence. For one cannot acquire them either and for the same reason.

But if a being cannot acquire something it possesses essentially after it has begun to exist (and continue to be itself), then what a being possesses essentially cannot derive from its real relations. For a relation seems to presuppose the existence of both *relata* — a thing must be, after all, in order to relate to something — and would therefore seem necessarily to be subsequent to the constitution of those substances of which goodness is a property. Therefore, the substantiality of the good precludes its relationality (its deriving from a real relation). As such, if goodness is a property which a thing possesses in virtue of its substance, it cannot be a property which that substance possesses in virtue of its real relations.

We can take the argument one step further. For if the good were a

---

1. Te Velde, p. 6.

property which a thing possesses in virtue of both its substance and its real relations, and if relations presuppose the existence of both *relata*, then a thing would have to precede itself in time in order to be good. That is, if goodness is one of the substantial properties of all things, then nothing can exist without being good. If things are good in virtue of their real relations, on the other hand, they would have to exist without being good in order to establish a real relation which makes them good. But we have assumed that nothing can exist without being good because goodness is one of the substantial properties of all things. This means that things must be good before they establish those real relations which make them good. But this too is impossible because we have assumed that things are good in virtue of their real relations. Thus, either things can precede themselves in time — be before they are — or the cause of things' goodness cannot be both a substantial property which all things share and things' real relations. The former option is not a viable one. Hence, the good cannot be both a substantial property of all things and the object of desire: a real relation.

The real cause of the contradictions in this second problem is the apparent antinomy of being and acquiring. If something possesses a given property in virtue of its own essence or substance, then it cannot possess that property because it acquires it. The converse also seems to be impossible. For if something possesses a property because it acquires it — if it possesses it in virtue of something other than itself — then it cannot possess that property in virtue of its own essence or substance. It therefore seems contradictory to affirm that something possesses a given property both by acquisition and essentially.

The irreconcilability of the substantial and relational definitions of the good is related to the problem of the ontological correlative of the term 'good.' It is the root of that problem. For if it is not metaphysically clear how the good can be both a substantial property of all things and their real relations, then it stands to reason that the ontological correlative of the term 'good' — the element which the teleological and substantial definitions of the good share — cannot be evident. For the ontological correlative is precisely what allows the good to be both a substantial property of all things and the object of their desire. And as the problem of the ontological correlative of the term 'good' is related to the apparent irreconcilability of the two principal definitions of the good, so too are their solutions related. For the solution to the first problem is analogy, a *reductio ad unum,* and the solution to the second problem furnishes the primary referent, the ontological correlative for that analogy: an ontological definition of the good. As such, we will solve the second problem before tackling the first.

Substantiality and Real Relations

Despite the obvious obstacles, the second problem seems to be soluble. The trick to solving it is to avoid the real causes of the contradictions it presents. For although being and acquiring — that is, substantiality and relationality — seem to be antinomical, they are truly so if and only if: (1) all relations necessarily presuppose the existence of both *relata*, and (2) no being can acquire a property that it already has. That is, they are antinomical if and only if: (1) a real relation cannot be the cause of being, and (2) being must preclude becoming. The trick, then, is to show that the presuppositions of the antinomy are not necessary ones or that they are false. This can be done.

Real Relations and Existence

Although every real relation has two *relata*, it is not at all necessary for both *relata* to exist before the relation is established. As we saw earlier, an object can be the term of an activity which originates in an agent. If this is so, then it must be possible for the object of such an activity to begin to exist only once the agent acts. Should some change of heart ever inspire me write a poem, the poem I write will clearly begin to exist only once I write it. As such, the fact that an object does not exist prior to the agent's activity does not imply that it does not have a real relation with the agent. On the contrary, in those cases in which the object of desire is the product of an act of desire, it is precisely because the object did not exist before the agent produced it that the real relation is necessary to the object. For the real relation is the cause of the object's existence, and it is what defines the object.

What this means is that a real relation need not presuppose the existence of both *relata* if the relation is the cause of one of the *relata*'s existence. If it does presuppose a *relatum*, it is because it presupposes the active cause of the relation, although it does not presuppose the active cause *qua relatum*: the active cause is a *relatum* only once it has established a relation. It only presupposes a being who is capable of causing a relation: an actual being.

The point at hand is clearly applicable to our problem. For the good is the object of desire, and from what we have seen this means that it must be a real relation. One of its practical implications is that it shows that it is not impossible to reconcile the extrinsic and intrinsic definitions of the good. For the obstacle to that reconciliation was precisely the assumption that a real relation presupposes the existence of both relata. Thus, since that assumption is false, so too the consequence that

The Foundations of a Solution 77

it is impossible for the good to be both a real relation and a substantial property of things must be false.

There is a proviso. Our present point demonstrates that the good can be both a real relation and a substantial property of things, provided that the good which is a real relation is the cause of a thing's existence — that is, provided that a thing's existence is the term of a free act of desire. It does not explain how the good can be both a real relation and a substantial property of being if the real relation is not the cause of things' existence. As such, it makes no claim with regards to the way in which the two definitions of the good can be reconciled if both *relata* exist.

Nevertheless, the present correlation does show how we can reconcile the two definitions of the good. For on this basis it is possible for the good to be both a substantial property and a real relation if the good *qua* real relation is the cause of the good's being a substantial property of things. That is, if the good is by definition the object of desire, then what comes to exist because it is the object of one's desire — or through a real relation with a desirer — must be substantially good. After all, what exists because it is desired must be good (because the good is the term of a free act of desire) and its goodness must be substantial (because it could not exist if it were not the term of a free act of desire). To state the point syllogistically:

The good is the term of a free act of desire,

the term of a free act of desire is an existing thing,

therefore an existing thing (*which is the term of a free act of desire*) must be substantially good.

This formulation of the correlation of the two definitions of the good, however, is incomplete as it stands because it implies that goodness is only a real relation and that is problematic. It ultimately leads to positing a foundation for things' substantial goodness which is not substantially good, and therefore ultimately contradicts one of the two definitions of the good. The best way of seeing this is to draw out the implications of the present correlation of the two definitions.

If things are substantially good simply because they are constituted by a real relation with something that desires them, then in order for goodness to be the substantial property of all things, all things have to be constituted through a real relation with something that desires them. But if all good things were to exist because of their real relations with something other than themselves, then all good things would have to presuppose real *relatees* which cause their existences. But if all good existing things were to presuppose real *relatees* which cause their existences, then there would necessarily be an infinite regress of real *relatees* which cause good things' existences. But if there were an infinite regress of real *relatees,* then nothing would exist or be good.

What one must do to make this correlation of the two definitions of the good acceptable, as such, is to avoid an infinite regress of causes and effects. Doing this is not too terribly difficult. All one needs to do it is to posit a First Undesired Desirer, in relation to whom all things are good, a Desirer who, in other words, is either the only efficient cause of the existence and goodness of all things, or who is the efficient cause of the existence and goodness of the first desired desirer, who is in turn the efficient cause of the existence and goodness of the second desired desirer, and so forth. That is, the solution to our problem is to claim that since the foundation of things' goodness is a real relation whereby things are constituted, formed, or created, then: (1) all things are good precisely because they are desired and created by the First Undesired Desirer's act of desire; or (2) each thing is constituted by a real relation with a desired desirer, who in turn is constituted by his relation with a desired desirer, and so forth, where the first desired desirer is directly constituted by the First Undesired Desirer.

The two positions are substantially identical, as least for present purposes. Both solve the problem inherent in this present correlation of the two definitions of the good. And both have the added advantage of solving the problem of the one and the many implicit in the problem of the good. For on the prior of the two ways of avoiding an infinite regress — i.e., the claim that all things are the effects of the First Undesired Desirer's act of desire — 'desiring' must be a univocal term. But if 'desiring' is a univocal term, and if it is the foundation of all things' goodness, then 'good' must also be a univocal term: it must be that property which all things have because all things must be desired by the Undesired Desirer in order to exist. 'Good' would be an analogous term, on the other hand, on the latter of the two ways of avoiding an infinite regress. For on it 'desiring' is an analogous term insofar as it is the act of different desirers. But since 'desiring' is the foundation of things' goodness, 'goodness' too would have to be an analogous term.

The fact of the matter is, however, that even if the basic setup of this correlation of the two definitions of the good does not pose any major problems, its necessary proviso — i.e., the Undesired Desirer — does. For if one accepts this correlation's definition of the good, the Undesired Desirer cannot be good. That is, if the good is a real relation whereby things are constituted, and if the Undesired Desirer is the First Desirer precisely because He is not constituted by a real relation, then

He cannot be Good. Plotinus was more than aware of this implication.[2] Herein lies the real problem with the present formulation of this correlation of the two definitions of the good. For if the First Desirer is not good, then the good cannot be the substantial property of *all* things. But this clearly contradicts one of the definitions of the good.

Now, if the cause of the contradiction in the above formulation is the claim that the First Cause of things' existence is not good, then the First Undesired Desirer must also be good. But this means that goodness cannot simply be a real relation which causes things to exist, and consequently that things which are constituted by their real relations cannot be good simply because they are constituted by their real relations with something which desires them.

What our first formulation is missing, as such, is exemplarity. But exemplarity is actually implicit in the interpretation of the teleological definition of the good which is the foundation of the present correlation of the two definitions of the good. When we were outlining the implications of the teleological definition of the good, we saw that the term of a free act of desire must reflect the desirer. For the term of a free act of desire is caused by a desirer's active potency, and one can express his active potency to different degrees in different objects, and one's complete and perfect expression of his active potency must reflect his active potency completely and perfectly. What this means is that if the term of a free act of desire is substantially good in virtue of its real relation with its desirer, it must be so also because it is similar to the desirer, that is, presupposing that the desirer is 'good' and that by 'good' one means something more than the term of an act of desire.

We can now give a more complete formulation of the present correlation of the two definitions of the good. What we have is that goodness can be both a substantial property of being and a real relation if the real relation is the cause of the being's existence and its similarity to the real *relatee*, and if the real *relatee* is good. To put the claim in syllogistic form:

The good is the term of a free act of a good being's desire,

the term of a free act of desire is an existing thing,

therefore the existing thing (*which is the term of a free act of a good being's desire*) must be substantially good.

---

2. Cf., e.g., *Enneads* VI, ix, 6.

This is one of the elements of our solution: making the intrinsic definition of the good contingent upon the extrinsic definition of the good.

Objections

Are we not contradicting ourselves on this point? When we outlined the paradoxes that the two definitions of the good present, we claimed that our desire for something presupposes the object of our desire because we cannot desire nothing at all. But if an act of desire presupposes its object, then our present claim that an act of desire constitutes the desired object is impossible. Nothing can constitute what it presupposes. Hence, as neat as the first element of our solution might seem, it is not an acceptable one.

Moreover, if an act is defined by its object, then an act of desire must be defined by its object. But if an act is defined by its object, then it must presuppose an object. If this is so, then once again our present claim that an act of desire constitutes its object is impossible. Nothing can constitute what it presupposes. Once again, then, our proposed synthesis of the two definitions of the good seems to be unacceptable.

As for the first objection, it is, of course, true that we cannot desire nothing at all. As such, the fact that we do desire something does presuppose that there is something which we do desire. The fact of the matter is, however, that it does not presuppose that we desire some actually existing thing, or that the object of our desire exists *before* we desire it. Namely, the converse to the statement that we cannot desire nothing is not that we must desire an *ens*, a substance, something subsistent, or something which exists independently of our desiring it. The converse is that we must desire something other than nothing, and there are plenty of things other than nothing, yet things which do not exist independently of our desiring them: prince charmings, private jets that fly at Mach 8, perfectly efficient spell-checkers on our word processing programs. The primary characteristic of these non-subsistent things other than nothing which we do desire is that they are contingent upon something other than themselves in order to exist: they are not substances. They are contingent upon the act of desire which constitutes them: prince charmings are contingent upon Spring day dreamers, private jets which fly at Mach 8 are contingent upon harried people with jet lag, perfectly efficient spell-checkers are contingent upon people who wish they could see typos. Now, if it is true that such objects do exist, the first objection misses its mark. For we can desire what does not exist independently of our desire.

As for the second objection, although it is true that every act must have an object, and that an object must (in a sense) precede the act whose object it is, this does not mean that it is necessary for that object to exist as anything other than the object of the act, prior to the act. That is, it does not mean that the object must exist independently of the act before the act. The point here calls for a distinction between the object as the term of one's desire and the object as cause of one's desire. An object is, as we have seen, always the final cause of the act of which it is the object: it is the final cause of free acts as well as acts which are caused by something other than the subject. For every act is some kind of act, and the kind of act it is determined by its aim. Its aim, then, is its object. This clearly means that there is a sense in which an object must precede the act whose object it is. All causes must precede their effects. It does not mean, however, that the object of an act needs to precede the act whose term it is *qua* term of the act. For the only acts which must presuppose objects in that sense are acts which are efficiently caused by the objects themselves. And the fact of the matter is that there are plenty of acts which are not efficiently caused by their objects. My writing this book is one of them. It follows that there are some acts that do not presuppose the real existence of their objects *qua* their terms. My book is one of them. But if the object *qua* term of the act need not precede the act whose term it is, then the object as an actually existing thing need not precede the act whose object it is. For some objects *qua* terms of an act only acquire real existence once the act, whose objects they are, are performed. My book is one of them. This means that the object of an act of desire need not precede the act of desire as an existing thing, although it does need to precede it insofar as it is its cause. Therefore, our point stands.

Existence and Real Relations

This brings us to the second reason why the two definitions of the good seem to be irreconcilable: the presupposition that things cannot acquire a property which they already have. The presupposition is ostensibly self-evident. If the good is something which causes a subject's desire, if it is something which actualizes the desirer, then goodness must be a property which things can acquire after they have begun to exist. If goodness is a substantial property of all things, however, then it cannot be a property which things can acquire after they have begun to exist. Nothing can acquire a property which it already possesses. I cannot become American because I already am. This is especially true if the property which one is to acquire is substantial. For, as we have seen, a being cannot acquire a substantial property after it has begun to exist without ceasing to be the being it was before it acquired that property.

As such, if the good is a substantial property of all things, it cannot be the object of their desire: it cannot be a real relation between a good thing and something other than itself.

This does not mean that good things cannot desire the good. Desiring can be a productive activity. It means that they cannot desire the good if desiring is not a productive activity: if it is not the act of an active potency. For if desiring is not the act of an active potency, it must be the act of a passive potency. But the act of a passive potency is reception, and it presupposes that the recipient does not actually have what it receives. In order to have passive potency with respect to the good, as such, one must not be actually good. But if one is not actually good, then the good cannot be a substantial property of all things. It makes no sense, in other words, to claim that our potency with respect to the good is passive if we are good in some active way, as we must be if goodness is a substantial property of all things. Hence, if the good is a substantial property of all things, it cannot be a real relation between two existing things.

Now, appearances to the contrary, the presupposition that a being cannot acquire a property which it already possesses also seems to be one that can be questioned. For although it is certainly true that I cannot become an American since I already am American, it is nonetheless possible for me to become wealthier than I am, for me to be more productive than I am, to be thinner than I am, to be happier than I am, and so forth. The point is that there are some properties that admit of degrees. Having these properties, as such, does not necessarily mean having them to the highest possible degree. If this is so, however, then it must be possible for someone to 'acquire' these properties even if he already possesses them. If he can 'acquire' them, then he must have potential for these properties. If he has the potential for these properties, then he must actually not have them in some way. For those properties that admit of degrees, as such, having them does not preclude either lacking them in some sense or acquiring them.

There are a number of properties which admit of degrees, but what is important in our case is that they are not just accidental properties such as wealth and weight: they are not just properties which one can acquire through his active potency. Our own being seems to allow for degrees. Although it is certainly true that there is a sense in which no adult's being is greater than a zygote's, a sense in which no adult is 'more human' than a zygote is, a sense in which being human does not admit "differences of degree," as Descartes puts it,[3] because every

---

3. Cf. *Discourse on Method*, 1 as translated by Donald A. Cress (Indianapolis: Hack-

substance must have its own substantial form completely, there is also a sense in which a zygote is not as fully actualized as an adult is. For a zygote's intelligence and will are not actualized to the degree to which an adult's intelligence and will are. But the actuality of a human being's intelligence and will is also his being. For as Aristotle puts it in one of those memorable phrases of his, ἡ γὰρ νοῦ ἐνέργεια ζωή:[4] the exercise of intelligence is the actuality of life, and so too, we might add, is loving. Indeed, they are man's highest life, for "actuality is more perfect than potentiality,"[5] and the exercise of intelligence and the giving of oneself are the actuality of what is most characteristic of man: of the specific difference of humanity. If this is so, then there must be a sense in which a zygote is 'less' than it can be, in which it is 'not as human as it can be,' as dangerous as that sounds. And as a zygote is 'less' than it can be, or 'less human' than it can be, so too is every adult 'less' than he can be, and 'less' human too. For although adults' intelligences and wills are definitely more actualized than a zygote's, there is no adult in whom they are fully actualized. No adult is perfect.

The crucial factor here is potential. We all have potential to develop; we all have as yet fully to attain "the actuality of life" even though we already are: we can all mature. What this means is not only that there is a sense in which our being can be 'greater or less' than the next person's, a sense in which our potential can have been actualized to a greater or lesser degree than the next person's, but more importantly that there is a sense in which we can become even though we are, a sense in which we can become actualized even though we already exist. For if this is so, then there must be a sense in which we can 'acquire' being, even though we already have it.

This brings us to the second point: a being cannot 'acquire' what it only possesses potentially through a free act, an act of its active potency. *Actiones non progrediuntur nisi ab existente in actu, secundum quod est in actu.* As far as I know, we have as yet to decipher the Etruscan language, even though we have plenty of Etruscan inscriptions. Our knowledge of that language is only potential. As such, we cannot sit back and read Etruscan poetry — or teach ourselves to do so — simply because we have decided that we will: our learning to read that language cannot simply stem from acts which originate in ourselves. Were a being to be able to acquire what it possesses only potentially through an act

---

ett, 1993) p. 2: "In this belief I am following the standard opinion held by philosophers who say that there are differences of degree only among accidents, but not among forms or natures of individuals of the same species."

4. *Metaphysics*, Λ, 7, 1072^b 26.
5. Aquinas, *In XII Met.*, 1072^b 26 §2544.

which originates in itself, its possession of that thing would have to be actual, in some sense. We can only give what we have. Every act requires an actual cause, which is capable of producing it. But a being's possession of something cannot be actual, if it is only potential. Hence no being can acquire what it only possesses potentially through its own free acts. To be able to decipher Etruscan inscriptions, we would have to know that language in some active way: we would have to have heard it when it was spoken, or have some friend who was, or we would have to have invented the Etruscan language. But since there is no one around who was alive when Etruscan was spoken, since again Etruscan is clearly not the product of our minds, we have not been able to decipher Etruscan. Our knowledge of that language is only potential and no free act of ours can change that fact.

What this means, of course, is that whosoever acquires something which he possesses only potentially must do so by some other means than an activity which originates in himself. We will be able to decipher Etruscan once we find a Rosetta Stone for the Etruscan language. But activities other than those which originate in some being must originate in something other than that being. If these acts are what allow a being to acquire the thing it is to possess, then the being must be passive or receptive with respect to these acts, else it could not 'acquire' what it is to possess. As such, a thing's acquiring what it possesses only potentially must be the object of its passive potency.

If this is true of acquiring in general, it must be true with regards to our being. If our being is in some respect potential even though we already exist, then there must be a sense in which our potential for being is passive, even though we are already actual. And those acts through which we become or 'acquire' being must originate in something other than ourselves. *Quidquid movetur ab alio movetur.* As such, our being must also entail a real relation, else we could not become.

There is another step here. For we have been claiming that beings can 'acquire' being without having defined what 'acquire' means in this case. It clearly cannot mean the ontological acquisition of an essence other than the acquirer's own, or the ontological acquisition of a substantial property that a being does not already possess to some degree or have the potential to possess ontologically (in the strict sense of the term), else a being's acquisition of being would annihilate the acquiring being and be the creation of another being, as we have already seen. And that is not the sort of acquisition through which we attain the "actuality of our own lives."

Nor can 'acquiring' in this case mean the acquisition of an accidental property. For the "actuality of one's own life" cannot be counted as one of someone's accidental properties (at least not in the sense in which Aristotle meant for it to be understood). Moreover, we can acquire accidental properties through our own free acts, through acts which originate in our active potential. I can buy a painting and thereby become a proprietress of that painting through my own free act. But this is not possible in the case of the 'acquisition' which we are discussing here. For 'acquiring' in this present case cannot be the act of an active potency.

But if 'acquiring' in this present case does not mean the acquisition of an essence or of a substantial property other than the acquirer's own, or the acquisition of an accidental property, then it must mean a being's actually coming to possess itself: its own essence or substantial properties. For that is the alternative. That is, if what one comes to 'acquire' in this present case is not an accidental property, then it must be a substantial property or an essence. But if that substantial property or essence cannot be other than the acquirer's own, it must be the acquirer's own, or a property which the acquirer has the passive potential to receive. *Tertium non datur.* If, on the other hand, 'acquiring' in this case cannot derive from a subject's own active potency, then it must be the actualization of his passive potency. But the actual possession of oneself which is the actualization of one's passive potency is what we commonly refer to as a being's actualization, its maturation, development, growth, or perfection. This, then, is what 'acquire' means in the present context.

Now, the various points we made concerning being are applicable to the good. Firstly, if the good is a substantial property of all beings, then it must be a substantial property of beings which become. But the actuality of beings which become admits of degrees. Hence, their goodness must also admit of degrees.

Secondly, just as it is possible for an actual being to become or to 'acquire' being, so too must it be possible for a being to become good — or to 'acquire' the good — even though it already is good. For if we can 'acquire' being, and if goodness is a substantial property of being, as we have assumed it is, then to 'acquire' being must be to 'acquire' goodness too, precisely because goodness is a substantial property of being.

Thirdly, as what becomes must be passive with respect to being when it becomes and in order to become, so too must what becomes good be passive with respect to the good and in order to become good. That is, as a being's becoming presupposes that that being possesses passive potential with respect to being even though it is an actual being, so too then must a being's becoming good presuppose that its potential with respect to the good is passive even though that being is actually good.

This follows once again from the fact that the good is a substantial property of being. If we are passive with respect to being, we must be passive with respect to the good. 'Acquiring' the good is, in other words, no exception to the rule that whatever is in potential cannot actualize itself. As such, if a being becomes good, the cause of its becoming good must be something other than itself. In order for that cause to actualize the being, however, its act must be received: *actio est in passo*. In order for that act to be received, the recipient must have the passive potency for it.

Lastly, as 'acquiring' being is a being's development, then, so too must 'acquiring' the good be a being's development. For as 'acquiring' being cannot mean the ontological acquisition of an essence other than the acquirer's own, 'acquiring' goodness cannot mean the ontological acquisition of a substantial property other than the acquirer's own, or one which the acquirer does have the passive potency to receive. For if the good is a substantial property of being, then if a being were ontologically to 'acquire' goodness which is substantially other than its own — or which it does not have the passive potential to receive — it would either not have the passive potential to 'acquire' it, or it would be annihilated by its reception of it. If the being were not capable of 'acquiring' the good, however, then it could not become good. The same thing holds if it were to be annihilated by the good. Nothing can be good if it is annihilated. As such, if it is possible to 'acquire' the good, acquiring the good cannot mean the ontological 'acquisition' of a substantial property other than one's own. It must therefore mean the 'acquisition' of one's own goodness. For that is the alternative. One's 'acquisition' of his own goodness, then, is his maturation or his perfection.

What these various points spell out, then, is that it is not a logical impossibility for a being which is good to acquire the good if that being is one that becomes. If this is so, however, then it cannot be a logical impossibility for the good to be both a substantial property of being and a real relation if the good is the property of a being which becomes. For a real relation is one which constitutes its becoming.

Objections

There is a possible objection to this point. Granted that it is possible for a being to acquire the good, it does not seem necessary for its acquisition of the good to derive from a real relation. For the claim that nothing can acquire what it only possesses potentially through an act which originates in itself is one that can be questioned, because there are some ways in which a subject can come to possess what he only possesses potentially through his own free acts. If it is true, for instance, that my possession of a painting that I am going to buy is only potential, then it must be true that I am only potentially its proprietress. The fact is, however, that despite the fact that I am only potentially its proprietress, I can acquire that painting through an act which originates in myself: I can go to the auction house with my own two feet, make my bid, pull out a checkbook with my own two hands, write out a check with my own hand, and buy it. If this is so, then I can acquire what I only possess potentially through my own free acts. But if I can acquire what I only possess potentially through my own free acts, then I must be able to actualize my own potential. And if I can actualize my own potential, there is no reason to suppose that my actualization is caused by something other than myself. Even if my own goodness is potential, as such, there seems to be no need to call upon something other than myself to actualize my own goodness. If there is no need to call upon an extrinsic cause for the actualization of my goodness, however, then the good need not be a real relation subsequent to my creation, if it is my substantial property. As such, the point above seems to be based upon a false premise.

Now, there are two ways of responding to this objection because it has a false premise of its own, and because it is an objection to which we have already responded. The false premise stems from a misinterpretation of the clause 'only potential.' Now, in the strictly economic sense, which is the only sense in which the objection has some validity, it is not at all true that a potential buyer of a painting is 'only potential' with regards to the painting if all he needs to do to acquire that painting is to march over to an auction house and pay for it. For one has to possess the actual means with which to pay for that painting. But to possess the actual means with which to acquire something signifies that one is not 'only potential' with regards to what one acquires. Hence the objection does not hold.

One could, of course, retort that it is also true that we have claimed that a being is not 'only potential' with regards to the good either. For if goodness is a substantial property of all beings, then no being is 'only potential' with regards to the good. As such, the objection once again seems to be plausible, and once again it does not seem necessary for a being to acquire the good through his real relations.

This second formulation of the objection is also founded on a misinterpretation. It presupposes that a being's actualized potential is the means with which that being can actualize the rest of its potential, and this is simply not true. The fact that one's potential to know being is actualized when one knows the principle of non-contradiction does not imply that his knowledge of the principle of non-contradiction is a sufficient means for him to come to know the rest of reality. If it were, we would already have deciphered Etruscan inscriptions. This means that our knowledge of the principle of non-contradiction can at best be *one* of the means with which we come to understand reality. As this is true of our knowledge of the principle of non-contradiction, so too is it true of the rest of our knowledge, and for precisely the same reason. We require means other than our actual knowledge to come to know reality. This clearly means that our actualized potential to know is not enough of a means for us to actualize our own potential to know, and as such that our actual knowledge does not preclude our needing an extrinsic cause for our knowledge.

As this is true of knowing, so too is it true of our becoming in a more general way. Were our actualized potential a sufficient means for us to actualize our potential, each of us would sooner or later be beings who are fully actualized. The fact that there are no fully actualized human beings alive demonstrates that our actualized potential can at best be one of the means through which our potential is actualized. Hence, actualized potential does not preclude our needing an extrinsic cause to be actualized. As this holds for being, so too must it hold for the good. As such, the objection once again does not touch our point.

There is another way of seeing this point, and it is the example itself that allows us to do so. For there is a more basic reason why one cannot be 'only potential' with regards to his acquisition of a painting if he can march over to an auction house and buy it. One must desire to buy a painting in order to buy it, and his desire, one hopes, is caused by the painting he wants to buy. If this is so, then the future proprietor of the painting must already have a real relation with the painting which he intends to acquire. Two things follow: (1) his possession of that painting cannot be 'only potential,' and (2) his possession of that painting cannot merely (or primarily) be the effect of his economic solvency.

We saw these points when we replied to the objection to the third implication of the teleological definition of the good: although our possessing an object which causes us to desire it seems to derive from our own free activity, this is strictly speaking not possible. For since we are basically receptive with respect to what causes our desire, our possession of the objects of our desire must also be basically a reception. This is more than clear if one analyzes the nature of that actuality which seems to make a person the actualizer of his own potential possession of a painting. For that actuality is economic, and we can all spend money in a myriad of different ways. Money is a means, and as all means it can be used to obtain many ends. As no means, as such, can it determine the end to which it will be put. But if money cannot determine the end to which it will be put, then money cannot be the real cause of one's possessing a painting. If money is not the real cause of one's possessing a painting, then that actuality which permits the subject to be the cause of his possessing a painting cannot be the primary cause of his possessing a painting.

What this means is that buying a painting cannot be the primary sense in which we 'acquire' a painting which we desire to possess. Rather, the possession of a work of art, which causes us to desire it, is a real relation with that work of art: it is allowing that work of art to change us. This real relation can cause us to become the material proprietors of a painting. But being the material possessor of a painting is neither a necessary effect of that real relation, or the completion of that real relation. For the real relation at hand is cognitional and one's owning what one knows does not alter his knowledge in any basic way. We do not need to be the material proprietors of a painting in order for us to know it. Were the material possession of art one of the primary ways of possessing art, we would have no museums. As this is true of art, it is also true of any other good thing we come to possess if the thing is an actually existing thing which we ourselves have not produced.

This brings us to the most basic point which the objection misinterprets. Being the material proprietor of a painting is an accidental property of the proprietor. The possession of a work of art which is the true term of one's desire for it — that is, knowing the work of art — is not an accidental property of the knower: it is the actuality of the knower's own being. For the latter possession is a real relation between the subject and the work of art. As the first possession is accidental, it can result from a subject's own active potency; the second possession, on the other hand, cannot. But possessing the good in the sense which we were discussing is not an accidental property of being. As such the objection misses its mark. Therefore our point stands. We cannot actualize our own potential for the good even though we must actually be good in order to exist.

The Substantial and Teleological Good

Our deduction of the properties of the good from its substantial definition is complementary to our deduction of the properties of the good from its teleological definition. It mirrors the teleological deduction. In the prior analysis we deduced that the good can be a real relation from the fact that it is a substantial property of beings who become. In the latter, on the other hand, we deduced that the good is the actualization of the subject's final cause — that it is the "actuality of a being's life" — from the fact that it is a real relation. That is, we claimed that if the good is the cause of desire, it must actualize the desirer, and that in order to do so it must be a real relation between the desirer and a *desideratum*. But the prerequisite of being actualized by the good is passive potential, which is actualized by one's desiring and possessing the object of his desire. It was this latter fact that explained why the cause of one's desire is also the term of his desire: for the act of passive potencies is reception, and reception only truly takes place when one possesses the object that causes his desire. This led us to indicate that the good is something which actualizes the desirer by degrees, both because the object *qua* cause of one's desire actualizes the desirer to a different degree than that to which the object *qua* term of one's desire actualizes him and because different objects actualize the desirer to different degrees. It was this latter point that demonstrated that the good *qua* object of desire actualizes the desirer's final cause. For if something can be actualized to different degrees, it must have an ultimate actualization. But the subject's ultimate actualization is his final cause. We therefore concluded that if each *desideratum* actualizes the subject to a limited degree, then each *desideratum* must actualize his final cause to a limited degree. If the good is the actualization of a subject's final cause, however, it must be a property of his actuality as well as a real relation which actualizes him. But a subject's actuality is his being. As such, the true conclusion of the teleological deduction is that the good must be a substantial property of being if it is a real relation.

What we have, then, is that the substantial deduction shows that the good must be a real relation if it is a substantial property of beings who become, whereas the teleological deduction shows that the good must be a substantial property of being if it is a real relation between a desirer and a *desideratum*. What this means is that each of the two deductions furnishes the other's premises.

This is most clear in the case of the teleological deduction. A thing's teleological goodness, we saw above, is contingent upon its causing some existing thing to have a real relation with it. But a thing causes a real relation if it actualizes something's potential. *Pati* is the act of a being who is in potential insofar as he is in potential. What this means is that something can be teleologically good if it actualizes a being's potential. What the substantial deduction elucidates is the reason why beings have potential, and why their actualization is good. For that reason is that goodness is a substantial property of beings who become. Were a being perfect, the good could not be both one of its substantial properties and its own real relations even if it were one of that being's substantial properties, precisely because that being could not become. The point here is that something can be good in the teleological sense because it perfects what is substantially good.

This is a point we made at the very beginning of this section when we were outlining the reasons why the onto-teleological interpretation of the good was incomplete. We saw there that since an object of desire cannot be such irrespectively of a subject's needs, and as extrinsic to the desiring subject, there must be a sense in which the subject desires himself — his perfection — in all of his acts of desire. The substantial deduction gives the positive reasons for a point which we made negatively there. For the good can be the cause and term of desire if what causes the subject's desire causes the subject's own development: that is, if the object of desire is related to the subject's final cause.

Nor does the teleological deduction merely presuppose the substantial goodness of the desirer — of the being to be perfected by his *desideratum*. It also presupposes that the *desideratum* itself, the perfecting being, is substantially good. For in order for a *desideratum* to actualize a desirer's goodness, it must actually be what it causes the desirer to become. *Actiones non progrediuntur nisi ab existente in actu secundum quod est in actu.* This means that a *desideratum* must be substantially good, in order to be a *desideratum*.[6] This is why the acquisition of the good can be the actuation of one's passive potential.

The point at hand, however, is also one of the prerequisites of the substantial deduction. For if beings must be actualized in order to attain the fullness of their being, then they must be actualized by something which is actually what they are not. Things therefore require a real relation with what is actually what they are not in order to become what they are not yet. Thus, if the good is a substantial property of beings which become, it must also be a real relation between beings which become good and beings which are so, if the beings which become are to become good. As such, the teleological deduction must in a sense furnish one of the premises of the substantial deduction.

As the two deductions furnish each other's premises, so too do they clarify each other's conclusions. The teleological deduction clarifies the conclusion of the substantial deduction: it spells out what a being's

---

6. Cf. *De Veritate*, q. 21, a. 1 c: "Ens est perfectivum alterius non solum secundum rationem speciei, sed etiam secundum esse quod habet in rerum natura. Et per hunc modum est perfectivum *bonum*. Bonum enim in rebus est, ut Philosophus dicit in VI *Metaphys*. In quantum autem unum ens est secundum esse suum perfectivum alterius et conservativum, habet rationem finis respectu illius quod ab eo perficitur; et inde est quod omne recte definientes bonum ponunt in ratione eius aliquid quod pertineat ad habitudinem finis; unde Philosophus dicit in I *Ethicorum* quod *bonum optime definiunt dicentes, quod bonum est quod omnia appetunt*."

development, what its 'acquisition' of the good entails. It specifies that that development is a real relation which a being has with something which is the cause and term of its desire: that it is a real relation which a being has with what it lacks — for we only desire what we lack — and which fulfills its lack because that real relation actualizes the being's final cause.

The substantial deduction, on the other hand, clarifies the conclusion to the teleological deduction's definition of the properties of the good: that the good is a substantial property of things' actuality if it is a real relation between a desirer and the object of his desire. Indeed, it clarifies both why the good is the final cause of the desirer and why the desirer's attaining that final cause entails his real relations to what is other than himself. For if the good is a substantial property of beings which become, and if the final cause of beings which become is the complete actuality of their being, then the final cause of beings must also entail the complete actuality of their goodness. That is, it is because the good is a substantial property of beings which become that the good is a property that beings which become must 'acquire' in order to become, in order to develop, mature, or be perfected. Or to put the point in Aristotelian terms: the good is things' final cause because it is in some sense their formal cause. The actuality of what only potentially good must derive from a real relation, on the other hand, precisely because beings can become actual. For what is potential cannot actualize itself. And that real relation must actualize their goodness because it actualizes their being. Hence, the reason why the good *qua* real relation can actualize the subject's final cause is that the good is a substantial property of beings which become, and it is because it is a substantial property of beings which become that it is a real relation.

Thus, the good must be a real relation if it is a substantial property of beings which become, and it must be a substantial property of beings which become if it is a real relation between two existing *relata*. It is here that we see the real reason why the two deductions mirror one another.

Objections

Now, one can raise a serious objection to our claiming that there is a mirror-like correlation between our teleological and substantial deductions of the properties of the good and that each of the deductions furnishes the premises of the other. For if the good is a real relation whereby things are actualized, then it must be a subject's possession of something other than himself. We saw this point repeatedly when we were discussing the teleological definition of the good. The otherness

The Foundations of a Solution 93

of the object of desire with respect to the desiring subject played an essential part in our deduction of the properties of the good from the teleological definition of the good. For, we claimed, the good can be a real relation between a subject and an object if a subject is potential, since what is potential cannot actualize itself. But then the object with which the subject has a real relation must be actual in a way in which the subject is not. But in order for the object to be actual in a way in which the subject is not, it must be other than the subject. This clearly means that the good *qua* real relation is the subject's possession of something other than himself. The fact of the matter is, however, that the good *qua* real relation is also the actualization of the subject's final cause, and the actualization of the subject's final cause is the actuality of his being. It follows then that the actuality of a subject's being is his real relation with a being other than himself.

Now, there is something paradoxical about this claim because it is not at all clear how the actuality of a subject's own goodness can be his real relation with something other than himself. This paradox is especially clear if one juxtaposes (1) the claim that the actuality of a subject's goodness is his real relation with something other than himself, with (2) the conclusion of the substantial deduction: that the actuality of the subject's goodness is a subject's possession of himself. There are two reasons why this juxtaposition is paradoxical. The first is that it seems to equate a subject's possession of himself with his possession of something other than himself. That is, if a subject's goodness is both his possessing something other than himself and his possessing himself, then his possessing himself must be his possessing something other than himself. But this sounds contradictory. For it seems to imply that the subject is what is other than himself. This identity is especially problematic here because in this present case the acquired object cannot be the acquiring subject, as we saw above, else the subject who is potential would have to be able to actualize himself.

But correlation is also paradoxical because we have also claimed that it is impossible for the subject to acquire anything other than himself, especially if what he acquires is an essence or a substantial property of being. For if a subject cannot acquire the essence or substantial properties of what is other than himself, he clearly cannot possess what is other than himself. If he cannot possess what is other than himself, however, he cannot have real relation with what is other than himself. But if he cannot have real relations with things other than himself, he cannot have real relations at all. For one cannot have real relations with himself by definition. It he cannot have real relations at all, however, then the good cannot be a real relation: it cannot be the object of desire. But this makes the subject's becoming good problematic. If the good cannot be a real relation, how can a subject become good? And if he cannot become good, is our correlation of the two deductions of the properties of the good built upon sand? How, then, can we have claimed that the good *qua* real relation is a subject's possessing something other than himself?

Now, there are two problems we must solve here. The first one concerns the apparent contradiction involved in claiming that a subject's actuality is a real relation; the second one concerns the apparent impossibility of one's coming to possess something other than himself.

We must make a distinction between different ways of acquiring something in order to solve the second problem. For the claim that no being can acquire an essence or a substantial property other than its own and continue to be the same being it was before the acquisition has a proviso: that its acquisition of that essence, or substantial properties, is ontological. It is only the ontological acquisition of a substantial form, or of a substantial property other than one's own, that entails the annihilation of a given substance. The fact of the matter is, however, that it is not at all necessary for one's acquisition of a given thing to be the ontological acquisition of its substantial form or properties. It can be an intentional acquisition of its substantial form or properties. As my having a friend does not imply that I am my friend, my acquiring a new friend does not imply that I become my new friend. If I were to become that new friend, he could not be my friend: a person must be other than I in order to be my friend. As it can be intentional, the acquisition of a thing need not be the subsumption of its properties. The fact that I do not become my friends does not imply that I cannot have friends, that I cannot acquire them, or that I cannot desire to acquire them. It simply means that acquiring and possessing friends does not entail the subsumption of their essences.

Nor does the intentionality of the acquisition not entail the perfection of the acquirer. If one of the presuppositions of friendship is the otherness of the two friends, then friendship must be a relation between two different people. That relation must be a real one. For if it were not a real relation, it would have to be a conceptual one. But a conceptual relation does not presuppose the existence of two subsistent *relata*, while friendship does. To be precise, friendship is in most cases two real relations whereby two people change each other: whereby I am changed by my friend and my friend is changed by me.

We are changed by our friends because we know them and receive their love. Both of the means whereby our friendship is established, as such, entail our reception of another's activity. In the case of love this is obvious. But it is also evident in the case of our knowledge. We do not create a person in order know him; we do not redefine him; we do not change him. Were we to change or redefine a person in order to know him, we would never know him: we would know our changes and definitions, and our changes and definitions are not our friends. If this is so, then people must change us if we are to know them. That is the alternative. But in order for something to change us, we must be the recipients of its activity, and that activity must actualize our passive potential. What we have is that friendship is a real relation which is constituted by one's reception of another person's activity, which is the actuation of his own potential. But the reception of another person's activity is the intentional reception of his essence. For a person's free acts are the expression of his essence: *omne agens agit sibi simile*.

Putting these points together, we have that the actuation of one's potential is the intentional reception of another's essence. But the actuation of one's potential is his possession of himself, as we have seen. The reception of another's essence, as intentional as it may be, on the other hand, is the possession of the other. As such, friendship must be our possession of ourselves which takes place through our possession of another.

If friendship illustrates the nature of our real relations, then our real relations cannot be our ontological subsumption of another being's essence, but are our intentional reception of another being's activity. As such, they do not entail our annihilation. But if this is true of all of our real relations, then it must also be true of that real relation which is our reception of the good. As such, as convincing as the objection may sound, it does not affect our deduction of the properties of the good from the two definitions of the good.

This brings us to the first problem: the apparent contradiction involved in claiming that our real relations are our actuality, or that our possession of another is the possession of ourselves. Here again we must make a distinction. For this point is paradoxical if and only if one assumes that a subject must be an object in order for his possession of that object to entail his possession of himself. This is simply not true, as we saw in the case of friendship. For as friendship is not the subsumption of another person's essence, but is one's being changed by another person's activity, so too is no other real relation the relater's subsumption of another being's essence, but is rather his being changed by the activity of a being other than himself. But one's reception of another being's activity is his being actualized by it: *actio est in passo* and *pati* is the *act* of a passive potency. Being actualized, as such, means one's coming to possess his own being. Now, if this coming to possess one's own being is caused by one's reception of another being's activity, and if one's reception of another being's activity is one's intentional reception of that being's essence, then it follows that one's possession of his own being must be the intentional reception of another's essence. But the intentional reception of another being's essence is the possession of that being's essence. What we have, as such, is that one possesses himself because he possesses another, as paradoxical as that may sound. More precisely, the conclusion to be drawn here is that our possessing ourselves is possessing another, since both of our acts of possession take place through the same act of reception. This is what the mediaevals meant when they claimed that transient acts are the perfection of the recipients of the acts.

A Second Synthesis of the Two Definitions of the Good

Our object was to show that the good can be a real relation if it is a substantial property of being. The various points we made above — most notably the mirror-like relation between the substantial and teleological deductions of the properties of the good — showed that it is not only possible for the good to be both a substantial property of being and a real relation, but that it is necessary for it to be both, if there are beings who become and if the good is one of their substantial properties.

This clearly means that there is a second way of reconciling the two definitions of the good to be added to the one we saw above, which made a thing's substantial goodness contingent upon a real relation which constitutes it. Here again there is a proviso. For we have seen that the good can be a real relation and a substantial property of things, provided: (1) that goodness is a property that desiring things have by degrees, (2) that the real relation in question is the actualization of the desiring thing's own substantial goodness, and (3) that it is with a good thing.

Thus, the second element in our reconciliation of the two definitions of the good is to make the extrinsic definition of the good contingent upon the intrinsic one: it is to make the fact that the good is a substantial property of being the cause of goodness' being a real relation. That is, it is to make the fact that a thing is good the cause of its desiring those things that cause its desire.

In this case there is a second reconciliation of the two definitions at hand. For our point also shows that a good thing's goodness is contingent upon its having its desire caused and fulfilled by something good. Thus, our present synthesis must also make the intrinsic definition of the good contingent upon the extrinsic definition in some fashion.

The Foundations of a Solution

Now, this second synthesis of the two definitions of the good also seems to satisfy both criteria of the solution. For it implies that a thing can be an object of desire both because the subject in whom it causes desire is good, and because it itself is good. It makes the substantial goodness of both *relata* the prerequisite of that real relation which is the good. If something is the object of desire because it is good, this clearly presupposes that it is good independently of its being desired. Nor need the object be the only good *relatum*. For if the real relation between that object and the subject is good and can actualize the subject's own goodness, the subject himself must be good independently of his desiring the good. What this means is that the finality of the good must presuppose that goodness is a substantial property of all that is desired, of all desirers, and of the real relations between desirers and objects that cause their desire.

Chapter 8

THE ELEMENTS OF A SOLUTION

We have seen that both of the presuppositions, which seem to make the synthesis of two definitions of the good impossible, are not necessary ones. For real relations need not presuppose the existence of both *relata*, nor does having a property preclude acquiring it. What this means is that the two definitions of the good can be reconciled: that the good can be both a real relation and the object of desire.

We have seen two ways of reconciling the two definitions. The first way correlates the good as the term of a free act of desire and the good as a substantial property of being by making the latter definition contingent upon the prior: it basically claims that the activity of desiring can be the cause of the existence and goodness of a desired thing, if the desirer is good. The second way, on the other hand, correlates the good as the cause and term of the desire of existing things and the good as a substantial property of being (1) by making the prior contingent upon the latter in the case of those things that cause desire — it claims that things can cause desire if they are good — and (2) by making the latter definition contingent upon the prior, in the case of the subject whose desire is caused — it claims that things become good by having a real relation with what is good.

These two ways of reconciling the two definitions of the good are the elements with which we can understand what the good is. The reason why they are elements through which we can understand what the good is, rather than solutions to the problem of the good, is that neither one of them completely reconciles the two definitions of the good. What this means is that each synthesis of the two definitions of the good needs to be complemented by the other in order to draw a complete picture of what the good is.

The point here is one that can be made in two ways: deductively or by principle.

An Analysis of the Definitions

To start with the definitions because it is always the quickest way to make a point, each of the two ways of reconciling the good makes use of one of the possible interpretations of the teleological definition of the good. The fact of the matter is, however, that neither way correlates both possible interpretations of the teleological definition and things' substantial goodness. As neat as the first synthesis is, it does not take both definitions of the object of desire into account when it claims that the good can be both a real relation and a substantial property of being if the real relation is the cause of one of the *relata*'s being. It reconciles the two definitions by overlooking the fact that the object of desire can also be something which causes one's desire. And the fact that it can be muddles things for its synthesis of the two definitions.

As suggestive as the second synthesis is, on the other hand, it too does not take both interpretations of the teleological definition into consideration: it simply considers the good to be the cause of an existing thing's desire and actualization, and does not account for its being the term of a free act of desire. But a complete synthesis of the two definitions of the good must needs correlate both interpretations of the teleological definition of the good and the substantial definition. It follows that a complete synthesis of the two definitions of the good must make use of both of the syntheses of the two definitions of the good, for each correlates one of the interpretations of the teleological definition of the good and the substantiality of the good.

The Incompleteness of the First Correlation

Nor could it be otherwise. To complete the first correlation of the two definitions of the good, one must explain why the good can be the cause and term of existing things' desire. Now, if the good is the cause and term of desire, it must actualize a desirer's goodness. As such, the good *qua* actualization of a desirer's goodness cannot derive from (1) another being's free act of desire, (2) the desirer's own free act of desire, or (3) from his causing desire in something other than himself. This leaves us with one final possibility, and that is to claim that the actuality of a thing's goodness is contingent upon its own real relations. But this final possibility is accounted for by the second correlation of the two definitions of the good. It follows that one can only complete the first correlation of the two definitions of the good through the second.

The actualization of an existing thing's goodness cannot derive from another being's free act of desire, for a free act of desire can only confer goodness upon the desired object if it constitutes that object, as the correlation we are trying to complete shows. But the free act cannot constitute the object in this case because *ex hypothesi* the being already exists. Nor can the desire whereby a desirer's goodness is actualized be his own free act of desire. If it were, it would have to be the act of the desirer's active potency, and (as we have already seen) a being cannot actualize his own potential through the acts of his active potency. If, on the other hand, one were to claim that the actuality of a thing's goodness is contingent upon its causing desire in something other than itself — upon some desirer's having a real relation with it — he would, of course, be both begging the principle and making an untenable claim. For the successful causal correlation of the good as a real relation and the good as a substantial property of all things must hold either: (1) that the relation confers a good existence upon a thing, or (2) that it actualizes its goodness. As such, it must either: (1) not presuppose the existence of both terms of a real relation, or (2) hold that a thing's goodness is potential and can be actualized by its real relation with something other than itself, and which causes its desire precisely because its goodness is potential. But neither of these two cases is applicable to this correlation of the two definitions of the good. For in order for something to cause desire, it must cause it in something other than itself. As such, this correlation must presuppose the existence of both terms of the relation. (That is why Aristotle posits the eternity of matter.) Nor can one claim that the desire which a being causes in something other than itself actualizes its own goodness. For desire in this case would be the effect of that being who causes desire insofar as that being is actual, and it cannot as such be the cause of its own actualization. What is actualized in this case, as such, is the desirer, and not the being who causes desire.

Thus, the attempt to complete the first synthesis of the two definitions of the good must either beg the principle or it must make use of the second synthesis of the two definitions of the good. As such, the complete solution to the problem of the good must needs be a synthesis of both of the proposed correlations of the definitions of the good.

The Incompleteness of the Second Correlation

To complete the second synthesis of the two definitions of the good, one must explain how something's goodness can be the term of a being's free act of desire. Now, if a thing's goodness is the term of a free act of desire, then the act of desire itself must confer goodness upon it. But if goodness is also a substantial property of being, it cannot be conferred upon something which already exists. No existing thing can acquire a substantial property other than its own and continue to be the same being it was before its acquisition. Thus, that act through which goodness is conferred upon something (as a substantial property) must also be the act through which existence is conferred upon that thing. This is to say that if goodness is the term of a free act of desire, it must be a property of a being whose existence is the term of that very same act of desire. This means that the only possible way of completing the second correlation of the two definitions of the good is through the first correlation.

A Deduction from the Definitions

What we have is that neither of the two suggested ways of reconciling the two definitions of the good correlates both interpretations of the teleological definition of the good and the substantial goodness of all things. And neither of the syntheses can correlate both interpretations of the teleological definition and the substantial definition without recurring to the other synthesis of the two definitions of the good. A complete synthesis of the two definitions of the good therefore needs both correlations.

The deductive proof makes the point even more clearly. Indeed, it shows precisely what is at stake in attempting to derive the solution to the problem of the good from just one of the two syntheses of the two definitions of the good. For the attempt to draw a complete synthesis of the two definitions of the good from the first correlation alone is the attempt to claim that beings can actualize their own potential through the acts of their active potency, and this ultimately leads to denying the finality of the good. The attempt to draw a complete synthesis of the two definitions from the second correlation, on the other hand, ultimately begs the question. For it cannot explain why the good is a substantial property of different things, or how different things can share the same property: it cannot explain why things are in fact good. As such, the attempt to draw a complete synthesis of the two definitions of the good from one of the two ways of reconciling the two definitions of the good leads into a contradiction at worst, or it begs the principle, at best.

The Incompleteness of the First Correlation

To begin with the first synthesis, its point is that the good can be a substantial property of all things because it is a real relation between an object and a desirer who constitutes the object. The incompleteness of this first correlation stems from its complete disregard for the fact that the good is the final cause of all existing things, including those who become. As such, if one were to want to claim that this point is the sole element of the synthesis of the two definitions of the good — that is, if he were to want to claim that goodness is essentially a real relation which is the cause of things' existences — he would have to explain how it accounts for the finality of the good. He would have to explain why the good is the object of desire for *all* things. For it must be. It is by definition that the good is both a substantial property of all things and all things' object of desire.

Now, one could claim that the present synthesis's correlation of the two definitions of the good is a sufficient means to explain why the good is the final cause of all things. For since it holds that the good is a substantial property of things because the good is a real relation which constitutes the *desideratum,* on its basis one can claim that the good is the object of all things' desire very simply because it is the object of all things' free acts of desire. After all, the object of a free act of desire must be good for at least two different reasons: (1) because it is by definition that the good is the object of desire, and (2) because *omne agens agit sibi simile,* which implies that all desired objects must be good if the desirer is.

The problem with this attempt to complete the first correlation of the two definitions of the good — aside from its outrageous implication that all beings are capable of free acts — is that it does not explain why those desirers who become desire their own good. That is, it does not explain why a desirer's own actualization can be the object of his desire. And it must be if the good is to be a substantial property of being. For if the final cause of a being which becomes is its complete actuality, and if that actuality must be good, insofar as the good is a substantial property of being, then the final cause of a being which becomes must also be the actuality of its own goodness.

It is this point which is so difficult to account for on the basis of the present correlation of the two definitions of the good. For the present correlation shows that the good is the product of a good being's active potency, and does not, as such, explain why good beings become good, or why they desire to do so. One could, of course, claim that the act of a being's active potency is the cause of its becoming. But this claim, we have seen, is problematic: it presupposes that a being can actualize its own potential. This is impossible. For the sake of the argument, however, let us analyze the claim more carefully.

Assuming that it is possible for a being to actualize its own potential, its actualization can either entail its relating with beings other than itself or not entail its relating with things other than itself. Now, if it does not entail its relating with beings other than itself, then the being which is to actualize itself would have to be the cause and term of its own desire. But in order to cause its own desire, a being would have both to be what it desires — every effect requires an actual cause — and not be what it desires — since one can only desire what he lacks. But this is clearly impossible. As such, if a being's actualization were not to entail its relating to anything other than itself, no being could be actualized, or desire any existing thing at all. This is, of course, to deny the finality of the good, and therefore contradict the teleological definition of the good.

If, on the other hand, one claims that a being's actualization does entail its relating with things other than itself, then *ex hypothesi* these relations must be caused by the relater rather than by the *relatee*. For the claim we are analyzing is that beings have the means to actualize their own potential. Thus, if beings can actualize their own potential, and if that actualization entails their relating with things other than themselves, then the beings must be able to cause their own relations with these things. The problem with this claim is that it is contradictory to affirm that beings can actualize their potential through relations which they themselves cause.

There are two things we must bear in mind as far as this scenario is concerned: (1) the *medium relationis,* and (2) the *relatees* with which a being can relate. As for the *medium,* all relations require a *medium* through which the *relata* can relate. For if two things were to have nothing in common, they could not relate. Now, this *medium* can be furnished by either the relater or the *relatee,* if one admits that the relater is passive. In this present case, however, since the relater is *ex hypothesi* the active cause of his own actualization, it must be furnished by the relater. What this means is that the relater can only relate to what is similar to himself, insofar as it is similar to him. If this is so, however, then he can only relate to what he produces or to what is ontologically similar to himself, insofar as it is similar to him. As for the *relatees,* on the other hand, they can be either the Undesired Desirer, or some other "desired" good thing which is produced by the Undesired Desirer. For both exist according to this first correlation.

Now, if the good to which a being relates in order to be actualized is a "desired" good, then it can be the relater's own product or some other good thing which is not his product. If it is the relater's own product, the relater can clearly relate to it. He does so by producing the product. The problem is, however, that the product cannot actualize the relater's potential goodness. For to actualize his potential goodness, the product would have to be good in a way in which the producer is not. But this cannot be. An effect cannot be actual in a way in which its cause is not.

If the desired good thing is not the relater's product, on the other hand, then the relater can only relate to it insofar as it is similar to him. As such, the relater cannot be actualized by his relation with the thing. For he would have to relate to that good thing insofar as it is other than himself in order to be actualized by it. But this cannot be, in this case, since through his own free activity the relater cannot receive a *medium relationis* which would permit him to relate to that good thing insofar as it is other than himself, and *ex hypothesi* his actualization takes place through his own free activity. As such, the relater cannot be actualized by his relations with good things which he does not produce.

If the relater cannot be actualized by his products or by desired good things which he does not produce, however, then he cannot be actualized by any "desired" good. This leaves us with one last possibility: the Undesired Desirer. Now, in order for a *desired* desirer to establish a relation with the Undesired Desirer insofar as He is other than the desirer, he must either produce the Undesired Desirer or have something in common with Him. But by definition nothing can produce the Undesired Desirer. Were something to do so, the Undesired Desirer would have to be a *desired* good thing. But this is impossible according to the present correlation. It holds that the Undesired Desirer is such precisely because there is no active cause of its goodness. This leaves us with the second option: a *desired* good can relate to the Undesired Desirer (insofar as He is other than the desirer) because they have something in common. This option, however, is no easier than the first one is. In order for a *desired* desirer to have something in common with the Undesired Desirer insofar as it is other than he, the *desired* desirer would have to be an undesired good, or the Undesired Desirer would have to be a desired good. The second option is impossible, as we saw above. But so too is the first. For if the desirer were an undesired good thing, he would either not exist (according to this present correlation), or he would have to be the Undesired Desirer. What this implies is that a *desired* desirer cannot even relate to the Undesired Desirer insofar as it is other than he, and much less so be actualized by his relations with it.

The gist of the matter, as such, is that if the good is only the term of a free act of a good being's free act of desire, no good being's potential goodness can be actualized. This means that this present correlation of the two definitions of the good cannot account for the finality of the good. It is precisely for this reason that it cannot explain why the good is the cause and term of existing things' desire.

The Incompleteness of the Second Correlation

As for the second correlation of the two definitions of the good, it too is incomplete. Actually, its incompleteness is even more obvious than the first correlation's. For this second correlation presupposes that things are substantially good. It merely claims that there is no contradiction involved in the good's being the cause of good things' desire because the good is a property that admits of degrees. It claims that things' substantial goodness is a prerequisite of their causing desire in good things and that substantial goodness is a prerequisite for having one's desire caused by a good thing. The fact of the matter is, however, that it does not attempt to explain why things are substantially good or what causes all things to be substantially good.

Now, one could claim that the fact that the good is a property that admits of degrees is a sufficient means to explain why things are substantially good. There are, after all, two prerequisites to something's having degrees: a standard and different things which approximate that standard with more or less success. As such, if goodness is indeed a property that admits of degrees, there must be an ultimate good — the Good — in relation to which all things good things are good, and from which all things which approximate the good differ. And this ultimate good must be that which all things which approximate the good lack to some degree or another. As such, the ultimate good must also be the ultimate object which causes our desire, an ultimate actualization for all beings who desire the good.

The fact that things approximate the standard proves that none of these is either the standard itself or the cause of its approximating the standard. That is, it proves that what approximates the standard cannot be the cause of either the standard itself, or of its own relation to the standard. An approximation cannot be the cause of the standard precisely because it only approximates it. And it cannot be the cause of its approximating the standard precisely because it is not the standard. I am not and cannot be the cause of humanity because I am not humanity itself, just as I cannot be the cause of my approximating humanity precisely because I am not humanity itself. What this means is that if all things are good, and if the good admits of degrees, the cause and principle of those things which do have goodness by degrees must be something other than themselves. It is precisely for this reason that the desire of those things which approximate the good can be caused by something other than themselves.[1]

---

1. The point here is one that Aristotle makes in the *Metaphysics*, II, 1, 993^b 23–31: "Now, we do not know a truth without its cause; and a thing has a quality in a higher

The beauty of this point is that it shows how the good can be a property of all things desired and of all desirers. In a different way than the first solution, it can account for the universality of goodness, and it would seem to be a real solution to the problem of the one and the many. As true as this is, however, it does not tell us whether the standard itself, the Good, is real or whether it is simply ideal, and as such it cannot tell us whether the relation between a being and that standard is real or merely ideal. That is, the fact that a specific property admits of degrees does not indicate whether the standard of that property is the efficient cause of all approximations — in the sense that it causes all approximations to have that property — or if it is merely the ideal cause of all approximations: if it is merely that in relation to which something can be said to be incomplete. And one cannot simply infer that the standard is subsistent from the fact that things do have a specific property by degrees, that is, unless he wants to run the risk of hypostasizing an idea. So too, can one not assume that the standard is the efficient cause of objects' having a property unless he wants to run the risk of positing real relations. I cannot assume that humanity *per se* has a separate existence simply because different things mature in their humanity by degrees, unless of course I were to be an unrepentant Platonist. And as I cannot assume that humanity exists, I cannot assume that it is the efficient cause of my humanity.

The same thing holds for the good. For there is no apparent reason for assuming that goodness must be any different from humanity, even if it is a property that belongs to beings of all genera and species. Therefore, one cannot assume either that the Good is a real standard, or that it is because things have a real relation to it that they exist as good things — that the Good is the efficient cause of things' goodness — simply because the degrees of goodness indicate that there must be a standard of goodness.[2] This ultimately means that the fact that there

---

degree than other things if in virtue of it the similar quality belongs to the other things as well (e.g., fire is the hottest of things; for it is the cause of the heat of all other things); so that that which causes the derivative truths to be true is most true. Hence the principles of eternal things must be always most true (for they are not merely sometimes true, nor is there any cause of their being, but they themselves are the cause of the being of other things), so that as each thing is in respect of being, so is it in respect of truth."

2. I am grateful to W. Norris Clarke for this point. For it is his critique of Aquinas's fourth way: "The basic flaw [in the fourth way] is the order: the argument as presented tries to pass immediately from the fact of degrees of perfection to the real existence of a maximum, and only later, in a second step, does it bring in causality. But merely from the fact of degrees of perfection it seems one can conclude only to an *ideal* maximum as a point of reference, not immediately to a real maximum, since there is no appeal to efficient causality here. Only after he has posited a real maximum does he [Aquinas] argue that such must be the cause of all beings possessing the perfection in question in limited degrees. And here too the argument is dubious. It is not clear why the highest in a genus need be the

is a standard of goodness does not get us any closer to understanding why the standard and its approximations relate, how they relate, or why there are approximations at all. Namely, it does not explain why all of those approximations are good, or why good things are approximations. As such, as suggestive as the point is, it cannot be a complete solution to the problem of the good.

---

cause of all others in the genus." Clarke proceeds by pointing out that elsewhere St. Thomas reverses the order of the argument, and when its order is reversed the argument is indeed valid. The quote is taken from Clarke's personal notes.

Chapter 9

OUTLINE OF THE SOLUTION

We are therefore back to the point which we made through our analysis of the definitions: neither of the proposed syntheses of the two definitions of the good is or can furnish a complete synthesis of the two definitions of the good. As such, the only way to define the good completely is to use them both. What we must do now is briefly outline how to correlate these two syntheses in order to explain why the good is both a substantial property of all things and the object of desire.

Now, it does not take much to see that the two syntheses complement each other. We saw as much in both of our proofs of their incompleteness. This complementarity is of two sorts. In the first proof we saw that they were complementary insofar as each one correlated a different interpretation of the teleological definition of the good and the substantial goodness of all things: the first correlation explains why the good is the term of a free act of desire and the second correlation explains why the good is the cause and term of existing things' desire; the first correlation accounts for the substantiality of the good, whereas the second can account for the finality of the good.

Secondly, the syntheses are complementary because it is only when one bears both in mind that he can understand what the substantiality of the good entails. For although the first correlation can explain why goodness is a substantial property of things, it is the second correlation that spells out the nature of the exemplarity which the first correlation implies. As such, we need both correlations in order to explain why the good is a substantial property of being. So too, however, do we need both correlations in order to explain why the good is the cause of existing things' desire. For one of the presuppositions of the good's being the cause of desire is that there are good things. Thus, since neither of the correlations alone can explain why things are good, we must need both in order to explain why the good is the object of desire.

The *Exitus* and the *Reditus* of the Good

The point of the basic complementarity of the correlations is clear: a complete account of things' goodness requires two real relations. The real relations are of different sorts. The first one is the cause of things' substantial goodness; the second is the cause of a good thing's becoming good. This can again be inferred from our two syntheses and from the interpretations of the teleological definition which they correlate with the substantial definition of the good. The first synthesis has to do with a real relation which causes things' existence and their substantial goodness. It correlates the good as the term of a free act of desire and the substantiality of the good and claims that if the good is both the term of free act of desire and a substantial property, it must be the term of an act which constitutes the desired thing, else existing things would have to be able to acquire substantial properties other than their own. This synthesis explains why things exist and are substantially good. The second synthesis, on the other hand, has to do with a real relation which accounts for things' actualization — the actuality of their goodness. It correlates the good as the cause and term of desire and the substantiality of the good and claims that if the good both is the cause and term of things' desire and a substantial property, it must be what actualizes an existing being's potential goodness. This synthesis explains why things desire the good and why the good is their actualization.

A Neoplatonist would say that we need two real relations to explain what the good is because we need to account for both things' *exitus* and their *reditus*. That is, he would claim that in order to explain what the good is, we need to spell out the real relation between creation and God which accounts for creation's existence and substantial goodness, and the real relation between creatures and God whereby creatures return to Him and attain their happiness.

The second form of complementarity between our two correlations of the definitions of the good elucidates the specific nature of these two real relations. For the fact that neither one of our syntheses of the two definitions of the good can explain why things are substantially good demonstrates that we must correlate both syntheses in order to define the nature of the *exitus:* the real relation whereby things come to exist and the good comes to be their substantial property. As a result, we also need to correlate our two syntheses of the good in order to define the nature of things' *reditus*, the real relation whereby things become good. For the *reditus* presupposes the *exitus* and mirrors it.

The Exitus

Now, as for the nature of the *exitus,* that real relation whereby things exist and the good comes to be their substantial property, the first correlation showed that it must be a real relation which is efficiently caused by a good being's *free act of desire*. The point of the first correlation was to show that the good can be both a substantial property of being and the object of desire, if the object of desire is constituted by a free act of desire. That it must be a real relation with a *good* being, on the other hand, was a point which the first correlation did not expound upon. It merely showed that the real relation which causes a being's existence cannot be with a being that is not good, else the foundation of things' goodness could not be good and goodness could not be a substantial property of all things. Hence it called upon exemplarity to complete the picture.

The nature of exemplarity was clarified by the second correlation, which showed that that being in relation to which good things are good must not only be good but must be the Good itself. For if the good is a property which beings have by degrees there must be a standard of goodness — the Good — in relation to which all things that are good by degrees are good. That standard, the Good, must be one which all desirers and desired things approximate in order to be able to desire and to be desired. For the presupposition of desiring, in the sense of having one's desire caused by something, is the substantial goodness of the desirer, and the presupposition of causing desire is the substantial goodness of the *desideratum*. The first correlation therefore delineates the causal relation between the First Desirer and other good things that accounts for the substantiality of things' goodness, and the second correlation elucidates the universal foundation of things' goodness.

Thus, the nature of the *exitus* can be defined by correlating our two syntheses. For if the real relation which makes goodness a substantial property of things must be one which causes their existence and if all things that are substantially good must be so in relation to the Good, then good things must exist because of their real relations to the Good. The *exitus* must therefore be that real relation which is caused by a free act of the Good's desire, whereby things come to exist and are good.

The fact that the *exitus* is a real relation with the Good makes the Good the exemplary cause of things' goodness as well as their efficient cause. This follows from both correlations. The first correlation allows us to claim that the cause of the existence and goodness of things is both efficient and good. For the products of one's active potency must reflect their producer: *omne agens agit sibi simile*. The second correlation, on the other hand, makes this exemplarity explicit. It claims that the cause of things' goodness is their real relation to the Good.

There is one last point to be made with regards to the *exitus*. For if all things exist and are substantially good because of their relations with the Good, there is no need to posit a chain of desirers each of whom is the cause and effect of another in order to explain why the good is a substantial property of all things. Rather, the cause of all things' existence and goodness must be the Good itself. For as the second correlation shows that real relation between a desirer and the object which causes his desire — that relation which actualizes the desirer — must presuppose that the desirer and the object have a real common property, a property which is the actuality of both things. But in order for things to possess that common property, that property must not only have a common standard, it must also have a common cause. Since that property is substantial, the beings who possess it must also have a common cause of their existence. For what confers a substantial property must confer existence. Hence all things must be and be good through their direct relations to the Good.

The Reditus

This brings us to the *reditus*. As the second correlation shows, the *reditus* is the actualization of an existing being's potential goodness which takes place through that being's real relation with something other than itself. This real relation is established when a being's desire is caused and fulfilled by something other than itself, and it admits of degrees, as does the actualization of the being itself. For some objects of desire actualize a being's potential more than others do. This means that a being must have an ultimate good, an ultimate object of desire, which is the complete actualization of its potential, or its attaining its final cause. This ultimate good is its real relation with the Good and it makes that being similar to the Good. It is this attaining the ultimate Good, that is, the actualization of a being's final cause, which is the goal of the *reditus*. It is the being's complete possession of itself through its possession of the Good.

Now, that a being's actualization takes place through its real relations is the point of the second correlation which showed that the good could be a substantial property and the object of desire because there are beings which become. That that actualization can take place by degrees is a corollary of the second correlation, as is the conclusion that there is an ultimate Good which is that being's complete actualization. The fact of the matter is, however, that it is the first correlation that justifies these corollaries. For it is the first correlation that shows why there can be degrees of goodness among different things, because it is the first correlation that allows us to claim that the Good is the efficient and exemplary cause of all good things.

One's being actualized by an object of desire has two main presuppositions: (1) that things are substantially good, and (2) that what actualizes them — what causes their desire — is substantially good. This means that both desirers and their *desiderata* must have real relations with the Good. For it is their real relations which account for their substantial goodness. The first correlation showed that this real relation is the effect of an act of the Good's efficient causality. But since the real relation which makes things exist and be good is the effect of an act of efficient causality, good things must be similar to the Good. *Omne agens agit sibi simile*. It is this similarity that has degrees. We saw this point when we were outlining the corollaries to the third implication of the teleological definition of the good. It is precisely because this similarity has degrees that one can claim that the substantial goodness of different things admits of degrees. And it is precisely because the substantial goodness of different things admits of degrees that they can actualize what desires them to different degrees. What this implies, of course, is that a thing's ultimate actualization must be its real relation to the Good itself. This real relation is the goal of the *reditus*.

Nor is this all the *reditus* is. For if desirers become good when their potential is actualized by good things, they must also become more similar to the Good. Here again there must be an ultimate similarity: one's being most similar to the Good. Now, the degree to which a desired object can cause a desirer to be similar to the Good must be contingent upon its own similarity to the Good: *actiones non progrediuntur nisi ab existente in actu, secundum quod est in actu*. It follows that one's ultimate similarity to the Good must be caused by what is most similar to the Good. But what is most similar to the Good is the Good itself. As such, one's ultimate similarity to the Good must be caused by the Good itself. What this means is that the complete actualization of existing things' potential by the Good must make them ultimately similar to the Good itself. As such, the goal of the *reditus* must also be one's likeness to the Good itself.

The *reditus*, as such, mirrors the *exitus*. For just as the good is a substantial property of being because all things are the effects of the Good's efficient causality, so too is the good a being's complete actuality because the Good is the cause of its ultimate actualization. As the Good's being the cause of one's being makes the Good the Exemplar of good things, so too the Good's being the cause of one's actualization makes good things like it.

The Good

What then is the good? It is by putting all of our points together that we can come close to defining the outline of the solution to the problem that the term poses. That solution is to distinguish two causes of the goodness of all created things and to distinguish two meanings of created things' goodness. As for the double cause, we have seen that things are good both because they are created and actualized by real relations, and because their real relations are to the Good. That is, things are good: (1) because their existence is the effect of an act of causal efficiency and their actuality is the effect of a being's causing them to desire and possess it, and (2) because they are similar to the Good, which is the Exemplary Cause of goodness. This means that the 'good,' as referred to created being, must be that aspect of being which implies both a real relation, which is the cause of actuality, and a logical one, a being's similarity to the cause of his actuality.

Now, the duality here clearly stems from the two definitions of the good which we have been attempting to reconcile. For the teleological definition is relational and the substantial definition is exemplary. What is more important, however, is that the duality seems to be one that can be broken down. For one must be able to trace the duality of created things' goodness back to the First Good if the First Good is the Exemplar of all created things' goodness. The move here is to claim that if goodness is that aspect of actuality which implies a relation, it must be that aspect of His Being which makes Him the Creator: it is, in other words, that aspect that brings Him to establish real relations between other things and Himself. For since the First Good cannot have passive potential, He cannot be actuated by anything other than Himself. Thus, His relations to things other than Himself cannot be real. As such, if goodness is that aspect of being which implies relation, the First Good must be good because He establishes relations, or is capable of doing so.[1] This seems to be the reason why the Neoplatonists claimed that *Bonum est diffusivum sui.*

---

1. Cf. *Summa Theol.*, I, q. 6, a. 2 c.: "Sic enim bonum Deo attribuitur, ut dictum est, in quantum omnes perfectiones desideratae effluunt ab eo, sicut a prima causa."

Chapter 10

CONCLUSION

We began this section by stating that since there are two definitions of the good, 'good' must either be an equivocal term, or its two definitions must be reconcilable. We opted for the latter possibility both because our analysis of the good is an introduction to our analysis of Boethius's metaphysics of the good, and because 'good' cannot be an equivocal term if both of its classical definitions are valid. After having drawn out the characteristics of the good from the teleological definition, our analysis showed that there are two real problems that one must solve in order to understand what the good is. Both stem from the fact that engaging with the good involves reconciling a relational and a substantial definition. The duality, on the other hand, derives from the fact that the teleological definition admits of two basic interpretations — an object of desire can be either the cause and term of one's desire or the term of a free act of desire. Thus, understanding what the good is entails effecting a double reconciliation which must show: (1) how the good can be the term of a free act of desire if it is the substantial property of being, and (2) how it can be the cause and term of desire if it is a substantial property of being.

Our analysis showed that effecting these reconciliations was tantamount to demonstrating how the substantiality of the good can be contingent upon the relationality of the good, and how the relationality of the good can be contingent upon the substantiality of the good. We claimed that this could be done through two real relations: one, which we called the *exitus*, which is a real relation between all things and the Good — or what we called the Undesired Desirer — which is His free act of desire, whereby things come to exist and are good both by exemplarity and because they are the terms of an act of desire; and one, which we called the *reditus,* which is a real relation between things and the Good, through which existing things' potential and likeness to the Good are actualized. We then attempted to see if either of the two possible correlations of the two definitions of the good could account for the both definitions of the good in their entirety. We saw that they could not. We therefore concluded that both were necessary to explain what the good is.

Our final move was to attempt to define the good itself: to break down the duality in the term, to discover why the Good is the Exemplar of all good things, and we suggested that if the good is that property of being which implies relations, it must be that property of the Undesired Desirer that makes Him the cause of creation.

Ours is clearly just the outline of a solution to the problem of the good: a definition of the problem, of the conditions which a solution to the problem must meet, and of a possible way of meeting those conditions. Nor does it intend to be more than that, at least as far as the metaphysical problem is concerned. For the outline's intent is to furnish a framework with which to understand a particular solution to the problem of the good without presupposing any particular metaphysical account of the relations between creation and God, without presupposing a doctrine of participation. The outline's intent is to furnish a structure with which to understand Boethius's doctrine of the good.

The most important aspect of that outline, as far as understanding the Boethian doctrine of the good is concerned, is understanding that the problem the good poses is at once metaphysical and logical. From a metaphysical point of view it entails understanding how the good can be a real relation which actualizes a being if it is a substantial property of being, and entails two real relations. There is also a logical side to the problem. For explaining why things are good also entails correlating the two classical definitions of the good. Both of these points are extremely important in our case: Boethius is unintelligible if one does not bear them in mind.

Part Three

BOETHIUS AND THE GOOD
The *Quomodo Substantiae* and *Consolatio Philosophiae*

Boethius's is an attempt to give a complete account of the good. His two metaphysical works each delineate one of the two real relations which a complete explanation of the nature of the good requires. The *Quomodo Substantiae*, which deals with the *exitus* of good things, defines the nature of that real relation which causes their substantial goodness; the *Consolatio Philosophiae*, on the other hand, deals with the *reditus* of good things and defines the nature of that real relation which they must have with the Good in order to be completely actualized. It is, however, not altogether obvious that the Boethian accounts of the *exitus* and *reditus* of creation delineate real relations. This is especially true of the *Quomodo Substantiae*'s abstruse account of the *exitus*. But it is also true of the *Consolatio Philosophiae*'s *reditus*. This is why our analysis of the good is useful. It gives us a key with which to understand the core of the Boethian doctrine of the good.

As for the *exitus*, there are many contrasting interpretations of the *Quomodo Substantiae*'s definition of the cause of contingent things' goodness. As we shall see below, some scholars claim that Boethius's account of the *exitus* makes goodness an accidental property of created things, others claim that it accounts for the substantial goodness of created things; some claim that Boethius's account uses a relation to explain why things are good, others claim that it uses a real relation to explain why things are good; some hold that his account makes good things consubstantial with God, others claim that it draws a real distinction between divine Goodness and created goodness. There is, in other words, no consensus with regards to the Boethian *exitus*.

As for the *reditus*, we saw how varied the scholarly interpretations of the *Consolatio Philosophiae* are in the first part of our work. Some scholars claim that the work is an odd *pastiche* of unrelated doctrines; others claim that it is a wholly Stoic work; others yet hold that it is an Aristotelian work; there are some who claim it is a Neoplatonic work, and so forth. The source of this plethora of interpretations is the work's three principal and apparently unrelated definitions of man's good. For in the *Consolatio*'s second book Boethius defines man's happiness — his highest good — as his possession of himself. In the third book he claims that happiness is something which man acquires by participating in the Highest Good: God. In the fourth book he claims that man's highest good is his possession of himself, which is his possession of God. What scholars typically do when they interpret the *Consolatio*'s doctrine of the good is to concentrate on one or another of these doctrines, find its historical sources and claim that it is core of the *Consolatio*'s doctrine of the good. They therefore propose radically different readings of the *Consolatio*'s *reditus*.

It is this section's object to analyze the details of the Boethian accounts of the *exitus* and *reditus* of creation insofar as they delineate the real relations between the Good and good things which are central to understanding his doctrine of participation. It will have two parts. In the first part we will examine the *Quomodo*'s definition of the goodness of contingent things; in the second part we will analyze the *Consolatio*'s definition of man's happiness. Our analyses of both the *exitus* and *reditus* will have four sections each. (1) We will delineate the problem Boethius intends to solve in each of his two metaphysical works; (2) we will review the most important scholarly interpretations of his solution to that problem; (3) we will give our own interpretation of the solution; and (4) and we will conclude by outlining the real relation between the Good and good things which Boethius's solution to that problem delineates. Our exposition will begin with the *Quomodo* both because it is the earlier of the two works, and because the *reditus* presupposes the *exitus* metaphysically.

Chapter 11

THE *EXITUS*:
THE *QUOMODO SUBSTANTIAE*

That the *Quomodo Substantiae*'s object is to delineate the *exitus* of creation can be seen in the very first lines in the work where Boethius claims that his intent is to determine how things can be essentially good without being substantial goods:

> You ask me to state and explain somewhat more clearly that obscure question in my *Hebdomads* concerning the manner in which substances are good in virtue of their essence (*in eo quod sint bonae sint*) without being substantial goods (1–4).[1]

---

1. All of my Latin quotations of *Quomodo Substantiae* will be taken from the edition of H. F. Steward, E. K. Rand, and S. J. Tester. I have, however, changed their translation somewhat.
   The Steward/Rand/Tester translation is liberal and even poetic at times — as can be seen from their translating "Ipsum esse nondum est" as "Simple being awaits manifestation," rather than as "Being itself is not yet." More often than not, however, it is simply confusing. This can be seen in their translation of the lines at hand. For they translate *"in eo quod sint bonae sint"* as "are good in virtue of their existence." This is their standard translation of the clause, and it is a contestable one for two reasons: (1) it does not respect Boethius's own definition of the clause in the fifth axiom; and (2) it makes Boethius's problem confusing.
   As for the first point, since Boethius defines substance as *"aliquid esse in eo quod est"* in the fifth axiom, I think it is rather clear that *"in eo quod sint bonae sint"* means "are good in virtue of their substance," or more simply, "in virtue of their essence" since 'substance' in Boethius's lexicon is a cause of being rather than an actually existing thing.
   As for the second point, Boethius's problem is determining how composite good things can be the cause of their own substantial goodness without being substantial goods. Now, that problem cannot be determining how composite things are good in virtue of their existences. For even if the existences of composite things were the cause of their goodness, composite things would not be substantial goods. Boethius himself states this quite clearly (*Cf. Quomodo*, 100ff.). On the other hand, composite things could be substantial goods if their essences were the cause of their goodness. For if good things are good in virtue of their essences, then their essences could seem to be the cause of their own existences. It is for this reason that Boethius will later say that if things are substantially good they are like God. In light of this, I think it evident that Steward, Rand, and Tester introduce "existence" into the picture. By doing so, they seem to misconstrue Boethius's problem.
   Their translation not only muddles the problem; it makes Boethius's solution incoherent. For when Boethius finally gives his solution to the problem of created things' goodness, he claims that although contingent things are good *in eo quod sunt* they are not similar to God who is the Good — i.e., whose essence is His goodness because His essence is His existence and His essence is the Good: "Qua in re soluta quaestio est. Idcirco enim licet

119

What Boethius means by a substantial good is a being whose essence or substance — the words are synonymous in the *Quomodo Substantiae*[2] — is its own goodness, or whose goodness does not have an extrinsic cause.[3] He explicitly claims that there is only one substantial good: God.[4] Hence when he states that he intends to show how things are substantially good without being substantial goods, his object is to prove that things are good in virtue of their essences, but that their essential goodness does not entail their consubstantiality with God.[5]

Boethius's statement of his problem shows two things (1) that he does consider contingent things to be essentially good, and (2) that he

---

in eo quod sint bona sint non sunt tamen similia primo bono... *Illud enim quoquo modo sit bonum est in eo quod est; non aliud est praeterquam bonum.*" And translating this as "For though they are good in virtue of their existence, they are not therefore like the first good... For that is good in any conditions in virtue of its existence; for it is nothing else but good" just does not make the *resolutio* clear. For all of these reasons, then, I have changed their translation of *in eo quod sunt/sint*.

Nor is this my only change. For Steward, Rand and Tester tend to translate *"esse"* as "existence," especially in the latter part of the work. I find this interpretation incorrect at times and have substituted it with "essence" where I saw fit. To make a long story short, I have interpreted the more technical terminology in accordance with Boethius's use or definition of it in the axioms, which their translation has not. I will always quote the Latin text in the footnotes when the text is not absolutely clear. For *"tradurre e tradire,"* the Italians say, and Boethius is certainly the test of one's patience. For since his terminology is often ambiguous, not to say polysemic, any translation of his works must be firstly and foremostly an interpretation. As such I am quite sure that my own translation is contestable.

As a final note, I am not the only person to have noticed the failings in the Steward/Rand/Tester translation. Scholars have found it "shocking." Cf. Lambert M. De Rijk, "Boece logicien et philosophe: ses positions sémantiques et sa métaphysique de l'être" in *Atti del Congresso Internazionale di Studi Boeziani*, p. 153 footnote 20: "L'interprétation de ce traité impliquée dans la traduction de Steward et Rand est défectueuse d'une manière tout à fait déconcertante."

2. Cf. *Quomodo*, V, 38–40: "Diversum est tantum esse aliquid et esse aliquid in eo quod est: illic enim accidens hic substantia significatur." Roughly translated this axiom states: "To be something and to be something in that which is are different; the prior is an accident, the latter signifies substance." Given this definition, 'substance' does not mean in this tractate what it meant, say, for St. Thomas. Aquinas defines a substance as "A thing to which it belongs to exist not in a subject," or as "That which has a *quiddity* to which it belongs to exist not in another" (*Contra Gentiles*, I, 25 §10). The Boethian definition of the term here defines 'substance' as what Aquinas would have considered an 'essence.' I will therefore treat substance and essence as equivalent terms in this section of the text.

3. Cf. *Quomodo*, 72–75: "Sed si esse bonum est, ea quae sunt in eo quod sunt bona sunt idemque illis est esse quod boni esse; substantialia igitur bona sunt, quoniam non participant bonitatem."

4. Cf. *Quomodo*, 75–80: "Quod si ipsum esse in eis bonum est, non est dubium quin substantialia cum sint bona, primo sint bono similia ac per hoc hoc ipsum bonum erunt; nihil enim illi praeter se ipsum simile est. Ex quo fit ut omnia quae sunt deus sint, quod dictu nefas est."

5. Cf., e.g., Geiger, pp. 36–37: "Mais si c'est la substance elle-même qui est bonne — et par substance entendez l'*essence*, ce qui *définit* un être et le constitue en sa nature propre — il suit nécessairement que la substance est identique à la bonté. En d'autres termes, la bonté de la substance est son essence même. Accorder une telle conclusion c'est supprimer toute multiplicité et toute diversité substantielles. C'est réduire toutes les substances à l'essence de la bonté, puisque toutes les substances sont bonnes. C'est les identifier toutes à la Bonté Première qui est Dieu, car il n'existe et il ne peut exister qu'*une* Bonté par essence."

distinguishes the goodness of contingent things from the Good, or God. The prior point demonstrates that he believes goodness to be a substantial property of all things. For if he holds that things are good "in virtue of their essences," then he cannot consider goodness to be something which things only 'acquire' after they have begun to exist. Nothing can 'acquire' an essence, or a substantial property, after it has begun to exist without becoming something other than it was. The latter point, on the other hand, demonstrates that he does not consider their goodness to be self-caused. For the only self-caused good by definition is the Good itself.

Now, if contingent things are essentially good and if their goodness is not self-caused, then their goodness must be caused by something other than themselves. But whatever causes contingent things to be essentially good must also cause their being — their existence — and vice versa. Thus, since the *Quomodo Substantiae*'s problem is to show how things are essentially good, its object must be to demonstrate how things are good in virtue of their creation. As such, Boethius's own statement of the problem which he intends to solve in the *Quomodo* shows that his work's object is to spell out the *exitus* of creation.[6]

Interpretations of the Solution

How then does Boethius delineate good things' *exitus*? There are many different interpretations of his definition of the cause of things' substantial goodness, and they fall into two main groups. The first group, whose adherents are all Thomists who follow Aquinas's own cue, holds that Boethius claims that things exist because God willed them and that they are good in relation to the Good.[7] The second group, on the other

---

6. This point also seems to explain why the work is called *de Hebdomadibus*. For the seven to which the title refers may just be the seven days of creation. That is, if the work's object is to spell out the *exitus* of creation, and how things are good in virtue of their creation, it may be a metaphysical explanation of the first chapter of the *Genesis*.

7. For the heart of Thomas's interpretation of the solution, see *In de Hebdomadibus*, IV: "Redit ergo eius solutio ad hoc quod esse primi est secundum propriam rationem bonum, quia natura et essentia primi boni nihil aliud est quam bonitas; esse autem secundi boni est quidem bonum, non secundum rationem propriae essentiae quia essentia eius non est ipsa bonitas, sed vel humanitas vel aliquid aliud huiusmodi, sed esse eius habet quod sit bonum et habitudine ad primum bonum quod est eius causa, ad quod quidem comparatur sicut ad primum principium et ad ultimum finem per modum quo aliquid dicitur sanum quo aliquid ordinatur ad finem sanitatis et dicitur medicinale secundum quod est a principio effectivo artis medicinae. Est igitur considerandum secundum praemissa quod in bonis creatis est duplex bonitas, una quidem secundum quod dicuntur bona per relationem ad primum bonum, et secundum hoc et esse eorum et quidquid in eis est a primo bono est bonum; alia vero bonitas consideratur in eis absolute, prout scilicet unumquodque dicitur bonum in quantum est perfectum in esse et in operari, et haec quidem perfectio non competit bonis creatis secundum ipsum esse essentiale eorum, sed secundum aliquid super-

hand, includes scholars from many different schools who claim that Boethius's *exitus* holds that things are good because they participate in God.

The Thomists

Thomists tend to base their interpretation of the *Quomodo Substantiae* on St. Thomas's own commentary on the work. Their reasons for doing so are diverse. McInerny follows Aquinas's suit because he maintains that St. Thomas's interpretation of the *Quomodo* is by far the best interpretation of the text.[8] He backs this claim by comparing Aquinas's interpretation of the axioms which precede Boethius's account of the *exitus* with the interpretations of this century's most important scholars.[9]

Geiger is not quite so authoritative. Boethius's problem, he claims, is finding a way of distinguishing Divine Goodness and created goodness, which does not deny that the good is a universal property of being,[10] or affirm that the Good is the essence itself of all things: something that all things have in common.[11] Boethius solves his problem, Geiger claims, through the logical category of relation. He affirms that things exist because God created them,[12] and they are good in relation to the Good, or God:

---

additum quod dicitur virtus eorum ut supra dictum est; et secundum hoc ipsum esse sorum non est bonum, sed primum horum habet omnimodam perfectionem in ipso suo esse, et ideo esse eius est secundum se et absolute bonum."

8. McInerny, p. 249: "The thesis of this book is that Boethius taught what Thomas said he taught and that the Thomistic commentaries on Boethius are without question the best commentaries ever written on the tractates." McInerny's purest expression of this thesis is the slogan which he uses as the title of the epilogue to his book: *"Sine Thoma Boethius mutus esset."*

9. McInerny, p. 161, where he outlines the methodology with which he will demonstrate that Aquinas's interpretation of the *Hebdomadibus* is the best yet: "This part is devoted to three things. First, a rapid survey of scholarly opinion on the third Boethian tractate which the medievals called *De Hebdomadibus*. Second, a look at the tractate through the eyes of St. Thomas Aquinas. Third, a brief indication of discussions of the good by Boethius and St. Thomas in other places. The deficiencies of the other interpretations will become clear and we will see that better than anyone else St. Thomas enables us (a) to understand the Boethian tractate in itself and (b) to place the solution the tractate reaches in a broader context, as an element of the comprehensive view Thomas constructs from Boethian and other sources."

10. Geiger, p. 41: "L'universalité absolue du bien est donc le centre de la difficulté. Elle s'oppose radicalement à toute explication de la multiplicité au moyen de la *composition*. Car l'universalité absolue implique que la propriété absolument universelle se retrouve en tous les principes du composé, antérieurement à toute composition."

11. Geiger, p. 42: "Pour maintenir simultanément l'universalité du bien et la multiplicité des substances, il faudrait trouver un moyen qui permît d'attribuer le bien à la substance en elle-meme, sans pour autant faire de la bonté la substance ou essence même des êtres."

12. Geiger, p. 40: "La solution de Boèce est donc la suivante: Une substance qui existerait sans être sortie du Premier Bien ne pourrait être bonne que par participation,

> Si on pouvait admettre, pour le bien, une nature telle qu'elle n'en fasse ni l'essence même des substances qu'elle affecte, ni une donnée absolue qui en soit formellement distincte, on pourrait du même coup admettre un type d'attribution qui ne serait ni par identité simple, ni par participation. Or cette forme d'être existe. C'est la *relation*. Et voilà pourquoi, croyons-nous, Boèce fait de la bonté des créatures la relation à la Bonté Première dont elles dépendent. La bonté des substances n'est ainsi, ni identique à la substance, ni différente d'elle, au sens où les données *absolues* sont identiques ou diverses. Elle n'est que la substance elle-même dans sa relation à la Bonté Première.[13]

The problem with Boethius's solution, in Geiger's view, is that it sacrifices the reality of goodness in order to salvage the universality of goodness.[14] For if things are good in relation to the First Good, they can only be good by extrinsic denomination, and not in themselves.[15]

In his more recent study, te Velde comes to more or less the same conclusion:

> Two phases can be distinguished in Boethius's solution. First he thinks away the presence of the first Good. The consequence is that a non-identity must be assumed between being and being good. Being good is accidental, like being white and other accidental properties of the substance. Next, he restores the relation with the first Good and on this account a certain goodness must be attributed to the being of things: the substantial being is good, too, though not in virtue of its essence, but in virtue of the relation to the first Good.[16]

---

c'est-à-dire, en recevant la bonté à la manière d'une propriété accidentelle. Une substance, par contre, qui est sortie du Premier Bien, et c'est le cas nécessairement de toute substance distincte du Premier Bien, peut être bonne dans sa substance même, sans qu'une telle manière d'être bon entraîne l'identité entre la substance et la bonté. La bonté appartient à la substance *en elle-même* sans *être* la substance, puisqu'elle dit non pas la substance en elle-même, mais sa *dépendence* à l'égard du Premier Bien. On dirait volontiers que la bonté est attribuée à la substance non pas *essentialiter* mais *per causalitatem*."

13. Geiger, pp. 43–44.

14. Geiger, p. 44: "En voulant sauver *l'universalité* du bien, Boèce semble en avoir sacrifié la *réalité*. La solution qu'il propose, quelqu'ingénieuse qu'elle soit, demeure incomplète, tant que n'aura pas été précisé le mode selon lequel la bonté, tout en étant réelle, peut être identique à la substance qu'elle qualifie, sans se confondre avec elle — et finalement avec la Bonté Première —, sans y être ajoutée, d'autre part, à la manière d'un accident."

15. Geiger, p. 44: "La bonté introduite par Boèce sous les espèces d'une relation ressemble fort à ce qui l'École appellera une *dénomination extrinsèque*. Si elle est telle, on ne voit pas comment, par elle, la substance est *réellement* bonne. Si elle ne l'est pas, si la bonté est *intrinsèque* à la substance, elle le sera, ou par identité avec la substance ou par inhérence accidentelle."

16. Te Velde, p. 18.

Although his conclusion is similar to Geiger's, his reasoning is not. For the crux of Boethius's problem, as far as te Velde is concerned, is the *opposition between participation and substance:*

> Boethius proceeds from an opposition between the two alternatives "substance" and "participation." Whatever something is by substance it is not by participation and vice versa. "Substance" relates to what something is essentially and by itself; the substance is what a thing possesses by itself, not derived by participation from something else.[17]

For the Boethian notion of participation, in te Velde's reading, only applies to accidental properties.[18] Hence in order to account for the substantial goodness of things Boethius has to "take recourse in" the substances of things. But things' substances cannot be the cause of their own goodness, else things would be God. As such, Boethius "resorts, for the goodness of the substance, to the relation in which the being of (created) things stands to the first Good."[19]

Now, if these Thomists are right, the *Quomodo*'s is not an *exitus* of good things, but is rather one of things which exist because of their real relations to the Good, and which are accidentally good in reference to Him. If this is so, it naturally means that Boethius has not solved the problem which he intends to solve in the *Quomodo*. For he means to explain why things are essentially good without being God. The Thomists' case is certainly strong. Since each of them uses Aquinas's interpretation in one way or another, they cannot be dismissed lightly.[20] Nor is their evidence limited to Aquinas's authority. For (as we shall see) Boethius does not explicitly claim that things are substantially good because they have real relations with the Good, and his two explicit references to participation would seem to dismiss it as a possible means of explaining why things are substantially good.[21]

---

17. Te Velde, p. 6.
18. Te Velde, p. 14: "Boethius, he [St. Thomas] notes further on in the commentary, speaks of 'participation' in the sense in which a subject is said to participate in an accident. An accident is an additional property of the subject and presupposes it in its essential content. That is why there exists for Boethius an opposition between 'to be something substantially' and 'to be something by participation.' Because 'participation' refers to an accidental property of a substance, Boethius cannot apply it to common properties which are consequent upon being as such." See also pp. 11, 16, 19, *passim*.
19. Te Velde, p. 19.
20. Cf. McInerny, p. 233: "Thomas seems to be spelling out here our worst fears about Boethius's solution. It looks as though the creature is known to be good only with reference to God and this is denominated good from the goodness of God." McInerny continues by showing how Thomas completes the Boethian solution.
21. Cf. *Quomodo*, 62–68: "Si participatione, per se ipsa nullo modo bona sunt; nam quod participatione album est, per se in eo quod ipsum est album non est. Et de ceteris

As strong as the Thomists' case is, however, their interpretation of the *Quomodo Substantiae*'s *exitus* is not necessarily the correct one. *Amicus Thomas, sed magis amica veritas.* The object of Aquinas's commentaries is often not to expound upon the specific thought contained in the works upon which he comments, but to comment on the problems that those works attempt to solve and on the means that they use to solve them. This would seem to be true of his commentary on the *Quomodo Substantiae*.[22] This is clearly not a point which all Thomists will readily accept.[23] But the fact of the matter is that Aquinas also commented on the *Quomodo* in his *De Veritate,* and in the latter work he does not claim that Boethius's account of the *exitus* asserts that things are substantially good in virtue of a logical relation. He claims that Boethius asserts that things are good because they participate in God.[24]

We clearly have a dilemma here. For Aquinas would have been inconsistent to have held that Boethius accounts for things' substantial goodness by means of both a logical relation and a real relation. Nor can one justify the discrepancy between the two accounts of the Boethian *exitus* in the same way in which he can justify the discrepancy between the *Summa Theologiae*'s claim that Boethius asserts that things are substantially good because they participate in God[25] and his interpretation of the Boethian *exitus* in his commentary on the work. For although the *Summa* is clearly a more mature work than the *In de*

---

qualitatibus eodem modo. Si igitur participatione sunt bona, ipsa per se nullo modo bona sunt: non igitur ad bonum tendunt. Sed concessum est. Non igitur participatione sunt bona sed substantia." See also *Quomodo,* 138.

22. Cf. on this point, e.g., Pandolfi, p. 35: "Fra i Commenti di Tommaso quello ad *De Ebdomadibus* risulta — per così dire — una *expositio-summa,* un lavoro tutto teoretico e personale, che s'avvale del testo d'una *auctoritas* soltanto come d'un'occasione per continuare il 'breve discorso sull'essere' iniziato da Parmenide e subito interrotto."

23. McInerny certainly does not — see footnotes 8 and 9 in this chapter — and neither does te Velde, who claims that "In his commentary Thomas closely follows the text of *De Hebdomadibus* and carefully analyzes Boethius's terse and sometimes difficult argumentation. He strictly keeps to his aim of giving an 'expositio' of the text" (p. 8). Pandolfi, however, does. See the footnote above. So too does Fabro. Cf., e. g., *La nozione metafisica di partecipazione secondo S. Tommaso d'Aquino* (Turin: Società Editrice Internazionale, 1950) p. 25: "S. Tommaso nel Commento al testo di Boezio ci ha dato, tutta di un getto, l'esposizione della nozione metafisica di partecipazione, e fra i testi tomistici ch'io conosco questo resta il più completo e sistematico. Le implicazioni dottrinali seguono l'una all'altra in modo serrato, senz'alcun riferimento d'ordine storico, onde è il pensiero personale dell'Aquinate che qui viene espresso."

24. Cf. *De Veritate,* q. 21, a. 5 c.: "Dato igitur quod creatura esset ipsum suum esse, sicut et Deus, adhuc tamen esse creaturae non haberet rationem boni, nisi praesupposito ordine ad creatorem; et pro tanto adhuc diceretur bona per participationem, et non absolute in eo quod est. Sed esse divinum, quod habet rationem boni non praesupposito aliquo, habet rationem boni per seipsum; et haec videtur esse intentio Boëtii in lib. *de Hebd.*"

25. Cf. *Summa Theologiae,* I, q. 6, a. 3 c.: "Sed contra est quod dicit Boetius in libro *de Hebdom.,* quod alia omnia a Deo sunt bona per participationem. Non igitur per essentiam."

Hebdomadibus, the *De Veritate* and the latter work would seem to be coeval.[26]

This is clearly not the proper place to discuss the nature of Aquinas's works. Our topic is Boethius. The point, however, is an important one because it casts some doubt upon one of the premises of the Thomist interpretation of the Boethian *exitus*. For if St. Thomas himself gives different accounts of the content of the *Quomodo Substantiae*'s *exitus*, then his interpretation of the work as it is to be found in his commentary need not be a precise account of what he considered to be the work's doctrine of the good. As such, although Aquinas's authority should bear some weight upon one's interpretation of the *Quomodo Substantiae*, one must establish what his interpretation of the text is before using it as the foundation of his own interpretation of the *Quomodo*. And establishing Aquinas's position entails more than simply understanding his *In de Hebdomadibus*.[27]

Nor is this the only reason why the Thomists' case is not as strong as it seems. For if there is one thing upon which all scholars — including the Thomists — agree, it is that the *Quomodo* is an abstruse work. Hence the fact that it does not explicitly state that the cause of things' substantial goodness is a real relation does not necessarily imply that Boethius does not consider real relations to be the cause of things' substantial goodness. But both Geiger and te Velde do seem to rely upon a literal reading of the text.[28] What this means is that, despite contrary evidence, Boethius's solution may well be more successful than the Thomists claim it is. That is, the solution may include a doctrine of real relations which account for contingent things' goodness, despite the fact that that doctrine is not explicit.

---

26. Both the *De Veritate* and the *In de Hebdomadibus* seem to have been written during St. Thomas's first regency in Paris, and that is, at some time between 1256 and 1259.

27. Te Velde does discuss the *De Veritate*'s interpretation of the *Hebdomadibus*. Cf. te Velde, p. 23ff. In his view, however, there is no discrepancy between its interpretation of the Boethian *exitus* and the *In de Hebdomadibus*'s interpretation. Indeed, he doesn't even seem to notice that the texts seem to contradict each other.

28. Both Geiger and te Velde interpret Boethius's denying that participation can explain why things are substantially good literally. Cf. te Velde, p. 6: "Boethius proceeds from an opposition between the two alternatives 'substance' and 'participation.' Whatever something is by substance it is not by participation and vice versa. 'Substance' relates to what something is essentially and by itself; the substance is what a thing possesses by itself, not derived by participation from something else." This passage is a literal interpretation of the first lines of Boethius's solution to the problem which the essential goodness of things poses. Cf. *Quomodo*, 56–85. The same thing can be said of Geiger's interpretation. Cf. Geiger, p. 37. In te Velde's case, then, his literal interpretation of Boethius's denying that participation can explain why things are essentially good stems from his having decided to ignore the content of the axioms that precede the solution. In Geiger's case, on the other hand, it stems from his having overlooked the content of the sixth axiom. For Geiger bases his claim that Boethius holds that things' goodness cannot derive from participation upon the fourth axiom.

The Participationists

There are several scholars who claim that his solution rests upon a doctrine of participation. One of these is Chadwick, who seems to hold that Boethius's solution claims that things exist and are good because they participate in God:

> Boethius lays down the axiom that everything existent is good, since everything tends to what is its good and to what is its like... But is this goodness so essential to all these good entities that it cannot be mentally abstracted, i.e., so that without goodness they would cease to be? The consensus of all men, of whatever race or education or culture, affirms that there is a primal Good. From this primal Good it is impossible mentally to subtract the notion of goodness. But in the case of things which derive their existence from it, it is one thing to be, another thing to be good. Their goodness is received by participation in the primal Good. To say that all things are God would be blasphemous (*dictu nefas*). So the goodness in creatures is neither substance nor mere accident, but attaches to their *esse* which tends to God who is their good. Remove their relation to God, and the goodness then becomes accidental.[29]

The problem with this interpretation, however, is that it is not clear what Chadwick thinks Boethius means by participation. For Chadwick claims both (1) that things' "goodness is received by participation in the primal Good" and (2) that if we were to "remove their relation to God, and the goodness then becomes accidental" and these two claims seem to be at odds with each other. The prior statement seems to indicate that Chadwick believes participation to be the cause of things' essential goodness. The latter statement, on the other hand, seems to indicate that he believes participation to be a logical rather than a real relation.

Now, if the *Quomodo*'s doctrine of participation does delineate a logical, as opposed to a real, relation, then it is not at all clear how it can account for things' essential goodness. For a logical, as opposed to a real, relation does presuppose the existence of both *relata*. As such, it can at best be the means whereby a thing acquires an accidental property. Therefore, were the *Quomodo*'s doctrine of participation to delineate a logical relation, Boethius would have to hold either that goodness is just an accidental property, or that a logical relation is truly the means whereby things acquire substantial properties. But we know that he does not consider goodness an accidental property of

---
29. Chadwick, *Consolations*, p. 207.

things, else his problem would not be to explain how things can be essentially good without being God. This leaves us with the second alternative: that he considers participation to be a logical relation. I gather that this is why Chadwick claims that if we "Remove their relation to God, and the goodness then becomes accidental." If this interpretation is the correct one, however, then as various Thomists have pointed out, Boethius's *exitus* cannot be an *exitus* of good things. Hence although Chadwick's claim that Boethius affirms that things are substantially good by participation implies that the Boethian *exitus* can account for things' substantial goodness, his interpretation of the *exitus* itself implies the contrary.

The ambiguity of Chadwick's understanding of the Boethian notion of participation is just a symptom of a deeper ambiguity in his interpretation of the Boethian *exitus*. For just as it is not clear what he thinks participation means, so too it is not clear what he thinks participation confers upon things. He claims that it does not confer either a substantial property or an accidental one, but "attaches" goodness to things' *esse*. Now, aside from the obscurity of the latter turn of phrase — I am not quite sure what "attaching" goodness to something's *esse* means — it is not quite evident what kind of property Chadwick thinks goodness is. For a property which is neither accidental nor substantial would not seem to be a property of any existing thing. That is, if a property must be either necessary to a given being — in the sense that a being must have it if it is to exist and be a specific thing — or not necessary to that being — in the sense that it is not necessary for a being to have that property in order to exist, or be a specific thing — then a property must be either substantial or accidental. *Tertium non datur.* Hence by claiming that goodness is neither a substantial nor an accidental property of being, Chadwick would seem to be claiming that it is no property at all of any being. I doubt that this is what Boethius means by the good.

The difficulty here can also be seen in Chadwick's affirming that "it is one thing to be, another to be good" for all beings other than the primal Good. For this statement too could seem to imply that goodness is not a substantial property of being. If it is one thing to be, and another to be good, it would seem possible for things to be without being good. If goodness is not a substantial property, however, then it must be an accidental one. Hence Chadwick would seem to hold that goodness is an accidental property of things for Boethius. If this is so, however, then it is very difficult to explain why Chadwick's closing remark claims that to "Remove their relation to God...goodness then becomes accidental." For this latter remark would imply that goodness is not an accidental property of things at all. That is, if goodness becomes an accidental property upon the removal of the "relation between things and the primal Good," then it cannot be an accidental property if that "relation" is not "removed." What we have once again is that goodness cannot be either an accidental or a substantial property of things, and hence that it cannot be any property at all. Given the ambiguity of Chadwick's interpretation of the Boethian *exitus,* therefore, it cannot be a viable alternative to the interpretations proposed by the Thomists.

One could object that Chadwick believes Boethius to hold that the good is a transcendental property of being, and hence that *tertium datur* in this case. He would have a valid point, of course, at least as far as the first part of the claim is concerned. The problem with the objection is, however, that transcendental properties are not a third category of properties over and above accidental and substantial properties. They are substantial properties whose specific difference is that all beings have them. Hence once cannot claim both that goodness is a transcendental property of being and that it is not a substantial property of being. But Chadwick does claim that goodness is not a substantial property of being. Hence our point still holds.

Moreover, if Chadwick does believe Boethius to hold that goodness is a transcendental property of being — a substantial property of all beings — and if that is the point of his claim that the good is neither a substantial nor an accidental property of being, then there would seem to be no explaining why he claims that "it is one thing to be, another to be good" for all beings other than the primal Good. For if goodness is a transcendental property of being, all beings must be good in virtue of their being. As such, no being could exist which is not good.

Gastaldelli's interpretation of the Boethian *exitus* is a bit clearer than Chadwick's. He too holds that Boethius's solution makes use of a doctrine of participation. Boethius's problem, he claims, is finding a way of distinguishing Divine Goodness and the goodness of created things. For God is absolutely and necessarily Good, whereas created things are not necessarily good.[30] He solves his problem, Gastaldelli claims then, through participation:

> Il nodo della difficoltà sta nell'assolutezza del bene in Dio che non può ammettere altro bene al di fuori di sé. Boezio lo risolve con il concetto di partecipazione: la "bontà delle sostanze create non è identica alla sostanza né differente da essa, ma è la sostanza stessa

---

30. Gastaldelli, p. 36: "La bontà divina è tale perché la sua essenza è di essere buona; le sostanze create sono invece buone senza esserlo necessariamente per la loro natura."

nella sua relazione con la bontà assoluta di Dio," e cioè la bontà relativa delle creature partecipa della bontà del Creatore.[31]

Although the passage is definitely clearer than Chadwick's, it is nonetheless not quite evident what Gastaldelli thinks Boethius means by 'participation.' For the brief account seems to indicate that Gastaldelli believes Boethius to make use of a doctrine of substantial participation in order to explain why things are essentially good — "la bontà relativa delle creature partecipa della bontà del Creatore...è la sostanza stessa nella sua relazione con la bontà assoluta di Dio." The fact of the matter is, however, that Gastaldelli does not explain why he believes Boethius to use a doctrine of participation. To make matters worse, he quotes Geiger's interpretation of Boethius's solution to back his own, and Geiger's interpretation of Boethius's solution, as we have seen, does not claim that it lies in a doctrine of substantial participation. Hence it is once again not too terribly clear what we are to make of Boethius's solution.

This brings us to Obertello, who gives two different interpretations of the *Hebdomadibus*'s solution to the problem of the good. In his first, which is to be found in his magisterial two volume analysis of Boethius's thought, he claims that Boethius does not envision goodness as either a substantial or an accidental property of being, but as being itself.[32] Hence, he can claim that things are substantially good, or that their essence is good, because being itself is goodness:

> Gli esistenti...sono sostanzialmente buoni, perché il loro essere è determinato dall'Essere primo che è il primo Bene. L'identità dell'essere e del bene nell'Essere primo fonda l'identità dell'essere e del bene negli esistenti.[33]

The identity of being and goodness, however, is only half of the explanation. It does not solve the other half of Boethius's problem, which is to explain how God's Goodness and the goodness of contingent things differ. As far as this latter problem is concerned, Obertello claims that Boethius's solution affirms that:

---

31. Gastaldelli, p. 36. His quotation is drawn from Geiger's text.
32. Obertello, *Boezio*, p. 646: "La distinzione tra l'essere e l'esistente costituisce il fulcro del *De Hebdomadibus* di Boezio. Gli esistenti sono buoni, ma la loro bontà non è qualche cosa che si aggiungerebbe all'essere come un accidente, o sia pure come un attributo sostanziale, che apparterrebbe allora all'esistente in tanto che *quell* 'esistente particolare."
33. Obertello, *Boezio*, p. 646.

> essa [l'identità dell'essere e del bene] non comporta l'identità di questi con l'Essere primo. In effetti questo è identico a se stesso (in lui l'esistente è identico all'essere), mentre gli esistenti non sono identici al proprio essere. L'essere degli esistenti è dunque buono prima di ogni determinazione, perché deriva dal primo Bene che è il proprio Essere.[34]

The passage here is a bit obscure. In the first part Obertello claims that the ground of Boethius's distinction between things' goodness and Divine Goodness is the fact that contingent things are not identical to their own being, whereas God is identical both to Himself and to Being: "[l'identità dell'essere e del bene] non comporta l'identità di questi con l'Essere primo... questo è identico a se stesso... mentre gli esistenti non sono identici al proprio essere." In the second part, on the other hand, he claims that the being of things is good "before it becomes determinate" because it "derives from the First Good who is His Being" — "l'essere degli esistenti è... buono prima di ogni determinazione perché deriva dal Primo Bene che è il proprio Essere."

The first part seems to be a syllogism. Its conclusion is clearly that contingent things are not identical to God; its major premise is that God is identical to Himself and to Being; its minor premise is that things are not identical to their own being. The problem with the syllogism is determining its middle term. For that middle term can be either (1) one's identity with his own being — the identity of a being's essence and existence — or (2) Being, depending upon whether one interprets the major premise to claim that (1) God is identical to His own Being or (2) that God is identical to Being itself.[35] On the first reading, the syllogism is a simple one:

> God is identical to His own Being (*God's Essence is His Existence*),
>
> contingent things are not identical to their own being (*their existences are not their essences*)
>
> therefore, contingent things are not God.

The problem with this first interpretation, however, is that it contradicts Obertello's exposition of the main tenets of Boethian metaphysics. For

---

34. Obertello, *Boezio*, p. 646.
35. The passage at hand is ambiguous. For Obertello claims (1) that God is identical to himself, (2) that He is Being, and (3) that He is his own Being and does not specify how these claims are related.

Obertello's claim is that Boethius believes God, or the First Being "not to be yet":

> L'Essere è ciò che vi è di più originale e più universale, ciò che è libero da ogni forma.... l'Essere è dunque agire puro, non limitato né da un soggetto né da un oggetto. Ogni forma, ogni determinazione intelligibile appare come un effetto dell'atto d'essere originario e fondante, e non può che essere posteriore all'Essere perché introduce una composizione. Vi sono, in sintesi, due modi d'essere: l'Essere trascendente che è superiore a ogni forma, e l'essere che deriva da esso. All'infuori dell'Essere assoluto non vi sono che forme di essere determinate che corrispondono a soggetti determinati. È questa, sostanzialmente... la dottrina di Boezio. L'Essere primo trascende ogni forma. Esso non è ancora, cioè non è ancora sostanza... è infatti anteriore alla sostanza e all'esistente, poiché è la loro causa. L'*id quod est* è l'esistente. Esso è e sussiste, cioè diviene sostanza, nel momento in cui riceve una forma del suo essere.[36]

Now, if God is "not yet," I fail to see how His essence can be identical to His existence. But if God's essence is not identical to His existence then the major premise of the syllogism above cannot be that God's essence is identical to His existence. Hence, if we accept Obertello's interpretation of the main tenets of Boethian metaphysics, the ground of Boethius's distinction between the goodness of contingent things and God's goodness cannot be the non-identity of the contingent things' essences and their existences and the identity of God's essence and existence.

This leaves us with the second interpretation. The problem with the second interpretation, however, is that it seems to have no middle term. For the terms of the major premise are God and 'Being,' and the terms of the minor premise are contingent things and their 'being,' and none of these terms would seem to qualify as a middle term. 'God' and 'contingent things' cannot be the middle term because they are the syllogism's extremes. This leaves us with 'Being' and 'contingent being.' Now, the middle term definitely cannot be 'contingent being.' If it were, God would have to be identical to contingent being — we must suppose that the major premise states that God is identical to the middle term — and if God were identical to what issues from Him, there would be no grounds upon which distinguish Divine Goodness and the goodness of contingent things. This leaves us with one last possible middle term: 'Being.'

---

36. Obertello, *Boezio*, p. 644.

If 'Being' is the middle term, however, then the syllogism begs the principle, insofar as its minor premise states what its conclusion intends to prove. That is, if the syllogism's middle term is 'Being,' then the minor premise must read: "created things are not identical to Being." But that is the conclusion the syllogism is attempting to prove. Hence, the syllogism begs the principle.

Secondly, if 'Being' is the middle term of the syllogism, then the only possible way to distinguish the goodness of contingent things from Divine Goodness is to claim that the goodness of contingent things is just a partial determination of Divine Goodness, whereas God Himself is identical to Goodness. Now, this would seem to be exactly what Obertello claims in the second part of the passage above where he claims that things' being is good "before it becomes determinate" because it "derives from the First Good who is His Being" — "l'essere degli esistenti è dunque buono prima di ogni determinazione perché deriva dal Primo Bene che è il proprio Essere." For if the being of contingent things is good before it becomes determinate (as Obertello claims it is), then it must exist before it becomes determinate. Nothing itself cannot become determinate. Moreover, that being must be indeterminate. For nothing can be determinate before it is determined. But indeterminate being is Being itself, as Obertello himself claims in the passage quoted above. Thus, things' indeterminate being must be Being itself. But if things' indeterminate being is Being itself, then things must be determinations of Being. As such, Obertello's claim that things are substantially good because they derive from the Good means that they are good because they are determinations of Being, which is Good. Therefore, on Obertello's reading the only reason why Boethius holds that things are not the Good is that they are partial determinations (or manifestations) of the Good.

This reading of Obertello's distinction between created things' goodness and Divine Goodness is corroborated by his definition of 'determination' in the passage we quoted above. For Obertello claims that the Boethian doctrine of being holds both that things exist because they are determinations of Being, and that they derive from Being insofar as they are determinations of Being.[37] This can be seen in his two claims that "the first Being... is not yet, that is it is not yet a substance" ("L'Essere primo... non è ancora, cioè non è ancora sostanza")

---

37. The position here is substantially identical to Pierre Hadot's. Hadot maintains that the central distinction in Boethius's metaphysics is between *esse*, which is to be understood Neoplatonically as meaning pure indeterminate activity (*agir pur*), and *id quod est*, which is to be interpreted as meaning the limitation of the *esse* in a concrete thing, which exists according to a certain form. This clearly makes all beings determinations of a primordial *Esse*. Cf. Hadot, *Distinction*, pp. 147–53.

and that Being "becomes a substance when it receives the form of its being" ("Esso è e sussiste, cioè diviene sostanza, nel momento in cui riceve una forma del suo essere"). For if Being itself becomes a substance when it receives a form, Being itself must be made determinate in every substance. This means that every substance must be a determination of Being. If Being is the Good, then, as we saw above, what we have is that things' essences are good because they are determinations of God's Being, which is identical to His Goodness.

The problem with this latter conclusion is that it contradicts Obertello's claim that Boethius holds that God's essence is identical to His existence: "In effetti questo è identico a se stesso (in lui l'esistente è identico all'essere)." For if Being becomes determinate in substances, and if God is Being, then God must in some sense be all substances. But if God is all substances, then His essence cannot be identical to His existence.

The gist of the matter is that Obertello's account of Boethius's *exitus* is contradictory, and begs the principle. If it is the correct one, as such, then Boethius has not only not solved the problem which he intends to solve in the *Quomodo,* but was also a very poor logician. Hence although Obertello's claim is that the Boethian *exitus* does account for things' substantial goodness, his account of the *exitus* itself implies the contrary.

Obertello's second interpretation of Boethius's doctrine of the good in the *Hebdomadibus* is very different from his first. In his first interpretation he claims (1) that Boethius believes that Goodness and Being are an identity[38] and (2) that Boethius believes created things to be substantially good because they derive from God whose Being is the Good. But where his first interpretation claims that Boethius affirms that the being of contingent things is a determination of Being itself — of God — his second interpretation claims that Boethius believes the being of contingent things to derive from a diffusion *ad extra* of Being itself:

Boezio discute a lungo il problema nel *De hebdomadibus*... ponendosi dal punto di vista del bene, che è da un lato un analogato dell'essere, e dall'altro ha forse una maggiore efficacia dell'essere stesso nel mettere in evidenza la derivazione del contingente dall'Assoluto: si tratta infatti di un atto di donazione, e

---

38. Cf. Obertello, *Dintorni,* p. 55: "Come è ben noto, la tradizione platonica e neoplatonica preferisce parlare più in termini di bene che di essere. Questa particolarità terminologica non deve trarre in inganno. Al fondo del bene sta l'essere, come nel cuore dell'essere sta il bene. La loro identità reale, e insieme la loro diversità concettuale, appaiono anche nell'uso linguistico fattone da Boezio in vari passi... del *De Hebdomadibus.*"

dunque di diffusione *ad extra* di bene da parte di Colui che è bene per essenza, così come è essere per essenza.³⁹

He also claims that Boethius holds that created things are the products of God's free will:

> La trascendenza divina è condizione della creazione; e questa è fondata sull'onnisciente e onnipotente (e libera perché onnipotente) scelta della volontà divina. Boezio ripete varie volte che le realtà composite "non avrebbero neppure potuto essere, se l'unico bene non avesse voluto che fossero. Per questo" aggiunge "sono dette buone, poiché il loro essere è scaturito dalla volontà del bene."⁴⁰

Indeed, he emphasizes the difference between his two interpretations by claiming that Boethius does not have a pagan *forma mentis*, which holds that God and the cosmos are consubstantial.⁴¹

Obertello's different perspective leads him to recast the details of his interpretation of the Boethian *exitus*. Thus, where his first reading claims that Boethius holds things to be substantially good because Being is the Good, and because the indeterminate being of contingent things is Being itself, his second reading claims that Boethius believes things to be substantially good because they participate in a transcendent God, whose Being is Good:

> Che cosa si intende per partecipazione? Dio è l'essere autosussistente, in cui non v'è distinzione reale tra essenza ed esistenza. La sua trascendenza rispetto alle creature è dunque assoluta: il che significa anche la sua diversità o alterità. E tuttavia, pur nella radicale differenza di natura, tra Dio e la sua creazione vi deve essere un legame ontologico, posto che è proprio il legame ontologico con Dio che costituisce e fonda la realtà totale delle creature.⁴²

Boethius's problem, he claims, is understanding whether things are good in virtue of participation or in virtue of their substances. Both alternatives are problematic. For if things are good in virtue of participation, their goodness seems to be accidental; if they are good in virtue of their substances, on the other hand, they seem to be God.⁴³

---

39. Obertello, *Dintorni*, p. 53.
40. Obertello, *Dintorni*, p. 59.
41. Obertello, *Dintorni*, p. 63: "Boezio non condivide in alcun modo questa visione necessaristica che — conviene ricordarlo — discende direttamente dall'identificazione tra Divinità e cosmo propria della *forma mentis* pagana."
42. Obertello, *Dintorni*, p. 53.
43. Obertello, *Dintorni*, p. 55: "La '*quaestio*' che ne provoca la stesura [i.e., del *De hebdomadibus*] è nota: posto che tutto ciò che è, è buono (in quanto tende al bene e perciò

Now, Obertello claims, the fact that Boethius formulates the problem in this way is a clear sign of the fact that he considers goodness to be a substantial property of all things.[44] How, then, does he define the cause of things' substantial goodness? Obertello asserts that we must reformulate our question in order to understand how he does so. For the heart of Boethius's solution lies in the counterposition between God's Absolute and Simple Being and creatures' limited and complex being.[45] Indeed, Obertello seems to think that it is this very counterposition that demonstrates that Boethius believes things to exist and be good because they participate in God:

> Il dilemma va letto secondo una chiave che ce ne fornisce la retta interpretazione... Da un lato, l'Essere-Bene assoluto, in cui sono identici l'essere e l'essere buono (ossia in cui l'essere è identico a se stesso); dall'altro, gli esseri-beni relativi e compositi, che non sono buoni in ciò che sono e di per se stessi (ossia che non sono in ciò che sono)... Della condizione specifica degli esseri compositi abbiamo... un'assai larga esperienza... Siamo, ma non siamo pienamente; abbiamo l'essere, ma non lo possediamo senza ... limitazioni. Diciamo che ne partecipiamo; purché sia d'altra parte chiaro che ne partecipiamo non come ad una qualità accessoria ed accidentale... ma come al fondamento di ciò che siamo. Proprio perché riceviamo da lui l'essere, a lui tendiamo per mantenere e incrementare ciò che siamo.[46]

But, Obertello indicates, it is problematic to assert that things are good because they participate in God. Participation, he claims, seems to presuppose the existence of the participant, and to confer accidental properties upon things. Hence, it does not seem to be the means with which we can explain why things exist. Being is not an acciden-

---

deve essere a lui simile), si chiede se sia tale per partecipazione o sostanzialmente. Ma se lo è per partecipazione, non possiede il bene come proprio principio costitutivo, e dunque non è buono; se per sostanza, è identico al bene, e dunque è Dio stesso."

44. Obertello, *Dintorni*, p. 55: "Il riferimento esclusivo al bene può far nascere notevoli difficoltà di comprensione. Boezio afferma che, se una data realtà è buona per partecipazione, non è buona di per se stessa 'in ciò che è,' ossia nella propria individua natura. Si potrebbe obiettargli che ciò è irrilevante, e che la bontà, come la bianchezza, potrebbe ben essere una qualità accidentale. Ma riflettiamo: il fatto che Boezio neghi recisamente questa ipotesi è indice chiarissimo di un presupposto della massima importanza: egli ritiene che la bontà *non* sia una qualità accidentale."

45. Cf. *Dintorni*, p. 59: "Tale, il corso della discussione boeziana. Il punto di partenza è chiaramente la consapevolezza profonda della contingenza universale, ossia della dipendenza dell'universo nell'essere stesso da Dio. Gli sviluppi successivi e le conclusioni tratte da questa fondamentale premessa sono in linea con essa."

46. Obertello, *Dintorni*, pp. 56–57.

tal property of existing things.[47] He claims that this is the very reason why Boethius states that participation cannot explain why things are substantially good.[48] In order to solve his problem, as such, Obertello distinguishes two different senses in which things can be said to participate in something: they can either participate *in* it, or participate *of* it. Things participate *of* something when they already exist, whereas they participate *in* something in order to exist.[49] The fact that created things must participate in something in order to exist is clear, he says, if we ask ourselves why composite things exist.[50] For the answer to that question is that they are created by God:

> E tuttavia, pur nella radicale differenza di natura, tra Dio e la sua creazione vi deve essere un legame ontologico, posto che è proprio il legame ontologico con Dio che costituisce e fonda la realtà totale delle creature.[51]

Since things must participate *in* God in order to exist, however, so too must they be substantially good because they participate *in* God. For God's Being is the Good. Creation thus makes things similar to God. It does not, however, make them similar to Him in all ways, because the goodness of created things is relative, whereas God's goodness is absolute:

> Interpretando queste peraltro esplicite asserzioni, diremo che, mentre Dio è Bene assoluto, le realtà che da lui derivano sono sì beni, ma relativi.[52]

As such, Obertello concludes that:

> La soluzione esposta da Boezio sta in una sola formula: la partecipazione si fonda sull'analogia. Anche se egli non usa il nome, possiede il concetto.[53]

Now, according to Obertello's second interpretation, the *Quomodo*'s *exitus* is not as glaringly incomplete as his first interpretation

---

47. Obertello, *Dintorni*, p. 57: "Sembra naturale pensare che chi 'prende parte' a qualche cosa sia già costituito in una sua sussistenza autonoma, e che dunque chi partecipa all'essere sussista di già per suo conto, ed *in sovrappiù* accolga in sé anche la qualità dell'essere. Ciò è manifestamente contraddittorio. L'essere non è accessorio, bensì radicale, essenziale."
48. Obertello, *Dintorni*, p. 57.
49. Obertello, *Dintorni*, p. 57: "Non si partecipa, dunque, *all*'essere, ma semmai *nell*'essere; e qui giova allora rifarsi al termine greco che i latini tradussero con 'participatio,' ossia μετοχή ο μέθεξις l'aver insieme, il partecipare inteso come l'avere in comune?"
50. Obertello, *Dintorni*, pp. 58–59.
51. Obertello, *Dintorni*, p. 53.
52. Obertello, *Dintorni*, pp. 58–59.
53. Obertello, *Dintorni*, p. 59.

makes it out to be. If the *exitus* claims that things exist because they are freely created by God, then Boethius does have the means to distinguish Divine Goodness from creatures' goodness. For if things are freely created by God, their being (as Obertello himself points out) must be completely dependent upon God's Being, whereas God's Being does not depend upon anything. If this is true of being, it must also be true of the good. For Obertello claims that Boethius considers being and the good to be an identity. The identity of being and goodness also justifies Boethius's claim that things are substantially good. For if things' being is their participating *in* God and if God's Being is Goodness, contingent things must be substantially good.

The main problem with Obertello's second interpretation is that it does not explain why Boethius uses a doctrine of participation in order to explain why things are substantially good, or what he means by that doctrine. As for the first point, Obertello indicates that Boethius is aware of the universe's complete dependence upon God. This is a point upon which all commentators agree. Even Thomists claim that Boethius believes things to be contingent upon God. The problem is, however, that the fact that Boethius asserts that God gives contingent things their existence does not necessarily imply that he uses a doctrine of participation to explain why things exist. If it were to do so, there would not be such a variety of interpretations of the *Quomodo*'s *exitus*. Hence, there is something gratuitous about Obertello's deducing that Boethius uses a doctrine of participation in order to explain why things exist from the fact that Boethius believes things to be completely dependent upon God for their existence.

As for the second point, Obertello's distinction between participating *in* something and participating *of* something is very suggestive. But he does not show his readers either where this distinction is to be found in the *Quomodo*, or why it is implied by the text. Hence, he would once again seem to be gratuitously asserting something about the *Quomodo*'s *exitus*. And *quod gratis asseritur gratis negatur*. This is not to say that Obertello's second interpretation is not a viable one. It is merely to say that it does not necessarily disprove the other interpretations of the Boethian *exitus*.

The most interesting recent account of Boethius's *exitus* is Pandolfi's. Pandolfi claims that the *Quomodo*'s aim is to synthesize the 'univocizing' and 'equivocizing' metaphysics of the schools that preceded him:

> le tre parti del *De Ebdomadibus*... assumono come loro tema (e smentiscono) rispettivamente le ontologie *platonizzante, equivo-*

cista (che dissipa nominalisticamente il logo unitario nei "molti," alla maniera di Eraclito) e *univocista* (risalente ad Elea). Esse potrebbero allora venire interpretate come un rapidissimo compendio della dottrina prearistotelica intorno all'essere, che Boezio corregge aristotelicamente.[54]

As for the way in which Boethius spells out the *exitus,* in Pandolfi's view it is divided into three distinct parts. In the first part Boethius defines his problem, which is to understand why things are substantially good, and then outlines two possible ways of solving that problem, i.e., explaining why things are substantially good. Both of these possible explanations make goodness an equivocal property of being. Thus, Boethius concludes that they cannot be the means with which to explain why goodness is a substantial property of all things.[55] In the second part Boethius defines the conditions which a monistic or univocal understanding of 'good' must meet and refutes the monistic understanding of the 'good.'[56] In the third part Boethius cuts a middle road between these two ways of defining the nature of things' goodness and claims that:

> le cose sono sì buone (contro la teoria *equivocista*), ma non sono simili al Primo Bene (contro l'accezione *univoca* e *monistica* di *bonum*). In dettaglio: (1) le cose sono buone in ciò che sono...il bene converge con l'essere (non si può dire lo stesso...del 'bianco' ...perché infratrascendentale, e neppure...del 'giusto' — perché solo in Dio essere e operare si identificano —). A ben guardare la pretesa *equivocista* di negare radicalmente la bontà delle cose è già stata confutata da Boezio...quando...egli ha fatto capire che alle varie realtà non può essere negato almeno il 'bene' di 'tendere al bene'; (2) Ora tale 'tensione'...mostra anche l'eccedenza del

---

54. Pandolfi, pp. 17–18.
55. Pandolfi, pp. 16–17: "L'alternativa logica è: o sono buone per partecipazione, oppure lo sono in sé (sostanzialmente). Le conseguenze della prima ipotesi: se le cose sono buone per partecipazione, non lo sono in sé (la prima ipotesi sembra escludere l'altra)...Ecco invece i risultati della seconda ipotesi: se le cose sono buone per sé, lo sono in virtù di 'ciò che sono,' quindi del loro 'essere'; ma se sono buone in coincidenza con il loro 'essere,' le cose 'sono' il bene (in senso assoluto) — sono Dio — e, invece, consta la loro pluralità, finitudine, privazione ecc., che ne attesta la bontà relativa; quindi non sono buone in sé. La conclusione: le cose non sono buone in nessun modo (si potrebbe dire: la bontà, nelle cose, ha un significato del tutto *equivoco*)." Cf. also Pandolfi, pp. 20–21.
56. Pandolfi, p. 17: "Boezio muove dall'ipotetica esclusione di ogni nesso fra le cose buone di quaggiù e il Primo assoluto Bene. La conseguenza, in termini semplici, risulta questa: a voler 'rimuovere' il Primo Bene, quello che resta sarebbe 'solo,' cioè assoluto; esso stesso si configurerebbe identico all'Assoluto (e invece, di fatto così non è: le cose risultano composte, carenti, diversificate, ecc.). Si può sostenere che in questa parte del *De Ebdomadibus,* Boezio utilizzi l'accezione *univoca* di bontà, confutandola subito (insieme alle coessenziali implicazioni monistiche)." Cf. also, Pandolfi, pp. 21–22.

Bene totale rispetto alle realtà immanenti, ossia la parzialità o partecipatività del loro 'esser bene' (contro la teoria *univocista*).[57]

According to Pandolfi's interpretation, Boethius's procedure is very scholastic. He begins by analyzing opposing attempts to explain the cause of things' substantial goodness; he proves that neither of these explanations is valid, and then he concludes that one must find a middle ground between the two. Moreover, his analysis is at once logical and metaphysical. For he analyzes both the univocal and the equivocal interpretations of the meaning of the 'good,' and refutes them on metaphysical grounds. That is, he claims that since 'good' cannot be a univocal term, there must be a common cause of 'good' things. As such, absolute pluralism is not a viable way of defining the cause of things' goodness. Nor is its extreme alternative. For 'good' cannot be an equivocal term either. Hence, the monistic view of the universe is not a viable way of explaining the cause of things' substantial goodness. Having refuted the univocal and equivocal interpretations of the 'good' Boethius has cleared the road which allows him to claim that 'good' is an analogous term and that the cause of things' substantial goodness must be participation:

> La "sintesi" boeziana del *De Ebdomadibus* conclude affermando la bontà relativa o partecipata delle cose del mondo.[58]

Pandolfi also claims that Boethius's middle road combines the most interesting elements of Platonism and Aristotelianism. He believes Boethian metaphysics to be an original Neoplatonic synthesis of the main tenets of Platonic and Aristotelian metaphysics (although admittedly he considers 'Neoplatonism' to be a *vox aequivoca*). For Boethius seems to claim that universals only exist *in re,* and hence sides with Aristotle on that point.[59] However, he also claims that universals exist *in re* because things participate in them,[60] and thus sides with Plato on that point:

> È possibile considerare l'opera boeziana come un abbozzo della successiva sintesi tomista, ossia come l'originale *traditio* degli aspetti in certo senso migliori di Platonismo ed Aristotelismo?

---

57. Pandolfi, p. 17.
58. Pandolfi, p. 31.
59. Pandolfi, p. 25: "Nelle *Ebdomades* Boezio si 'decide' e sceglie nettamente la logica realistico-moderata d'origine aristotelica, presuppone la distinzione reale fra potenza e atto, cioè la 'vera' compresanza della molteplicità potenziale e della forma unitaria 'attualizzante.' "
60. Pandolfi, p. 25: "Boezio sostiene che l'essere astratto ideale' non esiste; però l'essere esiste — realmente distinto — nel sinolo *id quod est,* in cui l'*id quod* riceve sopra sé ('subbietto') la *essendi forma,* cioè partecipa all'essere."

E, se "sintesi" fra le metafisiche dell'Ateniese e dello Stagirita è l'ontologia neoplatonica, in qual modo Boezio è "neoplatonico"? . . . Il testo delle *Ebdomades* induce a sostenere che realmente Boezio fu autore d'una propria originale "sintesi."[61]

Now, Pandolfi clearly believes that Boethius can and does demonstrate that contingent things are substantially good and that they are distinct from God, as his summary of the structure of the Boethian *exitus* more than amply demonstrates. The beauty of his interpretation is that it outlines just the sort of procedure which one would expect of a mind as logical as Boethius's, and it discloses an intent which would match the one which is to be found in Boethius's earlier works: i.e., to make both Aristotle's and Plato's philosophies available to the Latin speaking world and to understand the nature of universals.[62] Its shortcoming, if one can call it such, is that it is incomplete. Pandolfi simply does not give a detailed analysis of the *Quomodo*'s proof of things' substantial goodness. It is beyond his scope, which is to write an introduction to Aquinas's commentary on the *Quomodo*.

The *Quomodo Substantiae*: The Problem

As our brief review of the most important interpretations of the *Quomodo Substantiae*'s *exitus* shows, scholarly opinion regarding Boethius's definition of the cause of things' substantial goodness is split. Thomists generally believe it to claim that things are products of God's free will and that they are good in relation to Him. Boethian scholars, on the other hand, claim that Boethius's proof involves a doctrine of participation. The problem with the accounts the Boethian scholars give, however, is that they do not present a philosophical/textual case which is as strong as the Thomists' case is. The exception to this is Pandolfi, who is a Thomist who and yet sides with the Boethians. What we must do now, then, is to analyze the *exitus* ourselves in order to determine its content.

Boethius's explanation of the cause of things' substantial goodness has five parts. In the first part he defines his problem; in the second part he examines two contradictory explanations of things' substantial goodness; in the third part he outlines the preliminaries of his own solution; in the fourth part he spells out his solution; in the fifth part he counterposes his explanation of the cause of things' goodness and

---

61. Pandolfi, pp. 24–25.
62. I am thinking of the intent which Boethius mentions in his commentary on the *Isagoge*. Cf. *In Isagoge*, 64, col. 82–6.

the causes of their being white and just. The specific difference of his *modus operandi* can be seen in his definition of the problem in the first part of his solution, where he shows that his intent is to synthesize the two classical definitions of the good (i.e., the good is a substantial property of all things and is the object of all things' desire) or to demonstrate that goodness must at once be a real relation and a substantial property of being. This definition of the problem leads him to delineate the paradoxes involved in claiming that the good is both a real relation and a substantial property of being, in the second part of his solution. In the third part he demonstrates that the good can be a real relation if the real relation is the cause of being. In the fourth part he explains why things are substantially good; and in the fifth part he counters two possible objections to his proof. This is the scheme of Boethius's argument.

The Definition of the Problem

Boethius's problem is explaining how things can be substantially good without being God. We gathered as much from the work's first lines. The fact of the matter is, however, that immediately after having listed that battery of vicious axioms for which the work is best known, Boethius re-introduces the problem he intends to solve. His re-introduction is a proof of things' substantial goodness:

> Existing things are good. For the common opinion of the learned holds that everything that is tends to the good, and everything tends to its like. Therefore things which tend to the good are good. (56–60)

The proof here involves a synthesis of the two classical definitions of the good which is very similar to the ones upon which we were working in the second part of this book. It is a syllogism which deduces that things are ontologically good from the fact that the good is the final cause of all things. Its major premise is the teleological definition of the good: "everything that is tends to the good." Its minor premise, on the other hand, is ontological. It claims that a 'tender's' nature is the cause of its tending to the good: "everything tends towards its like." This minor premise can be interpreted in two ways, depending upon how one interprets the meaning of 'tending.' 'Tending' can be an activity which originates in the 'tender' or it can be an activity which is caused by that towards which the 'tender' tends. Accordingly, the minor premise can be read to the effect that since one's nature is the source of his activity, *omne agens agit sibi simile*. Thus, since 'tending' is an activity, "everything tends towards its like." We have seen this point before.

On the other hand, its point can also be that since one's 'tending' is caused by that towards which one 'tends,' it must be the actualization of the 'tender.' But in order for something to be actualized by that towards which it 'tends,' both it and the cause of its 'tending' must have a common property and a common cause. Therefore, "everything tends towards its like." We have seen this point before too. If one bases his interpretation of this minor premise upon the axioms which precede it, which seems to be the most warranted thing to do, then the latter of these two interpretations seems to be the more plausible one.[63] As such, the minor premise seems to be an ontological one to the effect that things desire and are actualized by what is similar to themselves. As the minor premise is ontological, so too is the conclusion that things must be substantially good, because they tend towards the good: "Therefore things which tend to the good are good." Boethius's point is that the good must be a substantial property of all things if it is everything's object of desire.

Now, the syllogism is clearly one that can be questioned. One can especially challenge its minor premise, because it is abstruse — that is, because Boethius does not qualify it. And indeed Boethius most likely meant for it to be challenged, precisely because it is his introduction to the problem of the good.[64] But that is not presently our intention. It would be beside the point. At present we are concerned with Boethius's own definition of the problem which the good poses rather than with his solution to that problem.

What the syllogism demonstrates as far as the problem is concerned, then, is two things: (1) that Boethius accepts both of the classical definitions of the good — i.e., that he does believe things to be substantially good and that the good is the final cause of all things — and (2) that Boethius views the problem of the 'good' in terms of both of the classical definitions of the good. That is, it demonstrates that he thinks that we need both definitions of the good in order to understand what the good is. Both points are more than amply proven by the syllogism itself. The first point is proven by the fact that the major and minor premises state the teleological definition and a version of the ontological definition of the good respectively. The second point is

---

63. The ninth axiom has bearing on this point, for it claims that: "Omnis diversitas discors, similitudo vero appetenda est; et quod appetit aliud, tale ipsum esse naturaliter ostenditur quale est illud hoc ipsum quod appetit" (IX, 49–52).

64. That this is so can be deduced from the fact that Boethius's last axiom — see the footnote above — has to do with the minor premise, and we know that Boethius's precise intention is for his reader to furnish his own arguments to understand the axioms. Cf. *Quomodo*, 53–55: "Sufficiunt igitur quae praemisimus; a prudente vero rationis interprete suis unumquodque aptabitur argumentis."

proven by the conclusion. For Boethius uses both the ontological and the teleological definitions of the good in order to prove that things are substantially good.

The reason why these points are important is that they show the true nature of Boethius's problem and what one should expect from his solution. As for the nature of the problem, it is not determining whether things are substantially good, or if the good is the final cause of all things. Boethius does not question that it is both. Rather, it is determining why things are substantially good if the good is the final cause of all things. That is, his problem is determining how the good can be both a substantial property of all things and a real relation. For on the teleological definition of the good, goodness is a real relation. As such, the syllogism demonstrates that Boethius does what one would expect a good logician to do when he is trying to discover the response to a metaphysical problem — what the good is — and that is to begin by making some sense of the opposing definitions of the good which tradition passed on to him.

As for the solution, the syllogism shows that Boethius thinks that the two definitions must be correlated in order to demonstrate that things are substantially good, that is, in order to answer the question to which the work as a whole sets out to respond. For Boethius's proof of things' substantial goodness is his introduction to the problem of the good, and it is a synthesis of two classical definitions of the good. Hence what one should expect in his solution is an attempt to show why the good is both a substantial property of all things and a real relation.

An Exposition of the Difficulties Involved in the Solution

Having shown that understanding why things are substantially good entails correlating the two classical definitions of the good, Boethius's next step is to demonstrate that it is difficult to explain why the good is both a substantial property of all things and a real relation, and that it is necessary to do so if one wants to understand why things are substantially good.

Correlating the two definitions of the good is difficult both if one assumes that the good is a real relation — participation — and if one assumes that it is a substantial property of all things, because the two definitions of the good seem to be mutually exclusive. For if the cause of things' goodness is a real relation — as the teleological definition implies — then the good cannot be a substantial property of all things. After all, in order to be substantially good, things must in some sense be the cause of their own goodness. But things cannot be the cause of their own goodness if that cause is a real relation. Things cannot have real relations with themselves. Moreover, the properties which things acquire through their real relations must, it seems, be accidental ones. For real relations seem to presuppose the existence of both *relata*. As such, it seems contradictory to claim that things are substantially good if a real relation is the cause of their goodness. Hence, the relational definition of the good would contradict the substantial definition of the good.

The same thing holds if things' essences are the cause of their goodness, as the substantial definition implies. For if things are the cause of their own goodness, that cause cannot be something other than themselves. If this is so, then the cause of things' goodness cannot be a real relation. Nothing can have a real relation with itself. Hence, the substantial definition of the good would contradict the relational definition of the good.

The reason why correlating the two definitions of the good is so important in Boethius's view is that the cause of the goodness of things cannot be their real relations alone, or their essences alone. This naturally means that things cannot be good at all if the only two possible causes of their goodness are their essences and their real relations, and if these two causes are mutually exclusive. This is Boethius's explicit conclusion. His implicit conclusion, on the other hand, is that things' goodness must be caused both by participation and things' essences and as such that one must find a way of correlating the two definitions of the good in order to explain why things are substantially good.

The second section of Boethius's argument, thus, has three parts. In the first part he lists the possible causes of things' substantial goodness; in the second part he demonstrates that neither of these two possible causes of things' goodness can account for their substantial goodness. In the third part he draws his conclusion: things cannot be substantially good if their goodness is not caused by both possible causes of goodness.

Boethius begins by claiming that there are two possible causes of things' substantial goodness, participation and things' own essences, and asks which is correct one:

> We must, however, ask whether things are good by participation or through their essences?[65]

---

65. Cf. *Quomodo*, 60–61: "Sed quemadmodum bona sint, inquirendum est, utrumne participatione an substantia?"

Boethius's formulation of his query is a bit misleading. For it might lead one to believe that he thinks participation and things' essences to be mutually exclusive causes of things' goodness, and hence to conclude that his object is to determine which of the two causes is the correct one.[66] After all, there is no mistaking that *"utrum"* means one of two. Hence the fact that Boethius asks *"utrumne participatione an substantia"* might seem to imply that he holds that the cause of things' goodness must be either participation or things' essences, but not both things' essences and participation and as such that his object is to determine which of the two possible causes is the correct one.

The fact of the matter is, however, that Boethius draws the two possible causes which he lists here from the major and minor premises of his opening syllogism respectively, and his opening syllogism proves that he does not believe these two causes of things' goodness to be mutually exclusive. It demonstrates that things are substantially good because the good is a real relation. That is, if the good is the object of all things' desire, as the major premise of Boethius's opening syllogism states, then the good must be (or imply) a real relation between a desirer and the object of his desire, else the desirer could not desire it. Since it is a real relation, the good must make the desirer good. If this is so, however, then a real relation must in some sense be the cause of things' goodness. But participation is a real relation. Thus, participation must be the cause of things' goodness, if the good is the object of desire. The good's being the object of desire, however, has a presupposition: the desirer's substantial goodness. This is the point of the minor premise. This means that things' own essences must also be the cause of their goodness. For a substantial property is one which a being possesses insofar as it is what it is, and what a being is is determined by its essence. What we have, then, is that the implicit claims of the major and minor premises of Boethius's opening syllogism are that the causes of things' goodness are participation and things' own essences respectively. This means that Boethius's object here cannot be to determine which of the two causes of things' goodness is the correct one, and thus that one must not interpret the formulation of his query as implying that participation and substantiality are mutually exclusive causes of things' goodness.

If we are right, the objectives of this second section of his argument must be: (1) to show that both participation and substantiality are nec-

---

66. Te Velde, for instance, would seem to interpret his query in this way. Cf. te Velde, p. 6: "Boethius proceeds from an opposition between the two alternatives 'substance' and 'participation.' Whatever something is by substance it is not by participation and vice versa. 'Substance' relates to what something is essentially and by itself; the substance is what a thing possesses by itself, not derived by participation from something else."

essary causes of things' goodness; (2) to outline the difficulties involved in reconciling these two causes of things' goodness, and (3) to delineate the conditions that a reconciliation of these two causes must meet. His problem, in other words, is finding a way of avoiding the paradoxes which the 'good' implies. After all, one can draw any number of paradoxical conclusions from the fact that the good is both something that things can acquire and a substantial property of all things: one can claim that things exist before they are, that beings have real relations with themselves, that an accidental property can be a substantial one, and so forth. And it is precisely these paradoxes which Boethius is trying to avoid.

In the second part of his argument, therefore, Boethius examines whether it is possible to account for things' substantial goodness on the basis of either of the two possible causes of things' goodness alone. His response is that it is not. For if one assumes that things can acquire the good through a real relation — through participation — then it would seem impossible for the good to be a substantial property of all things. No existing thing can acquire a substantial property after it has begun to exist: it cannot acquire its own substantial properties, because it must possess these in order to exist; and it cannot acquire the substantial properties of something other than itself, else it would be annihilated. What this means is that if things can acquire the good, goodness must be an accidental property of things. But an accidental property is not a substantial one. Hence, if the cause of things' goodness is a real relation, goodness cannot be a substantial property of things: things cannot be "good in themselves."[67]

> If [things are good] by participation, they are in no wise good in themselves; for a thing which is white by participation does not have an existence which is white in itself. So it is with all other qualities. If then things are good by participation, they are in no way good in themselves.[68]

But this is contrary to the initial hypothesis which claims that things must be substantially good in order for the good to be an object of desire:

---

67. Our interpretation of this point is similar to Pandolfi's. For Pandolfi holds that Boethius's claims here is that if participation were the cause of things' goodness, goodness would be an equivocal term. Cf. Pandolfi, p. 16.
68. *Quomodo*, 62–66: "Si participatione, per se ipsa nullo modo bona sunt; nam quod participatione album est, per se in eo quod ipsum est album non est. Et de ceteris qualitatibus eodem modo. Si igitur participatione sunt bona, ipsa per se nullo modo bona sunt."

Therefore they do not tend to the good.[69]

Hence, the good cannot be both a real relation and a substantial property of all things. Thus, he concludes, since it must be a substantial property of all things, it cannot be a real relation:

> But we have agreed that they do [tend to the good]. Therefore they are good not by participation but by substance.[70]

But if the good is a substantial property of all things, then things' essences must be the cause of their goodness:

> Whatsoever's essence is good must also have a good existence. But things acquire their existence from Him who is being. Their essence is therefore good; therefore the indeterminate essence (*ipsum esse*) of all things is good. But if the essence [of all things] is good, then things' existences are good in themselves. As such, their essence is the same as the essence of the good. It follows that they must be substantial goods, because they do not participate in goodness.[71]

Now, if things' essences are the cause of their own goodness, then things must be their essences in order to be good. Indeed, they must be the *indeterminate essence* of all things in order to be good.[72] As such, things'

---

69. *Quomodo*, 66–67: "Non igitur ad bonum tendunt."
70. *Quomodo*, 67–68: "Sed concessum est. Non igitur participatione sunt bona sed substantia."
71. *Quomodo*, 68–74: "Quorum vero substantia bona est, id quod sunt bona sunt; id quod sunt autem habent ex eo quod est esse. Esse igitur ipsorum bonum est; omnium igitur rerum ipsum esse bonum est. Sed si esse bonum est, ea quae sunt in eo quod sunt bona sunt idemque illis est esse quod boni esse."

The passage is a bit ambiguous, and my translation requires some clarification, I think, and that for two main reasons. The first regards the meaning of *esse* and its variant *ipsum esse*; the second regards the meaning of *id quod est*. To begin with the first point, then, it is not immediately clear what Boethius meant by *esse*, or *ipsum esse*. An analysis of the axioms, however, shows that the first term can mean either an actualized essence — the essence of a particular thing — or a thing's existence; the second term, on the other hand, means the indeterminate essence of things, or more specifically a sort of universal *ante rem*. As for *id quod est*, it is an actually existing particular thing. But an analysis of the axioms demonstrates that it also means a thing's existence as opposed to its essence.

72. The point here is that if things' essences were the cause of their goodness, then were things not to have the same essence, goodness would be an equivocal property. But this cannot be *ex hypothesi*. Hence things must share an essence. That essence cannot be the essence of a specific thing, else things of different natures could not share it. Hence, that common essence must be an indeterminate essence.

The point here is parallel to the one Pandolfi makes, pp. 16–17: "Ecco invece i risultati della seconda ipotesi: se le cose sono buone per sé, lo sono in virtù di 'ciò che sono,' quindi del loro 'essere'; ma se sono buone in coincidenza con il loro 'essere,' le cose 'sono' il bene (in senso assoluto) — sono Dio — e, invece, consta la loro pluralità, finitudine, privazione ecc., che ne attesta la bontà relativa; quindi non sono buone in sé. La conclusione: le cose non sono buone in nessun modo (si potrebbe dire: la bontà, nelle cose, ha un significato del tutto *equivoco*)."

goodness cannot be caused by a real relation, even though their existences are. For if it were caused by a real relation, that real relation would have to be one which things have with themselves — with their own essences — since *ex hypothesi* it is things' own essences which are the cause of their goodness. More precisely, it would have to be a real relation which things have with an essence which they share with all things — with the *indeterminate essence* of all things. But things cannot have real relations with their essences if they are those essences. Hence if things' essences — or their indeterminate essence — are the cause of their goodness, then a real relation cannot be the cause of their goodness. But if the cause of their goodness is not a real relation, then things' goodness must be self-caused:

> It follows that they must be substantial goods, because they do not participate in goodness.[73]

The problem is, Boethius points out then, that if things are substantially good, and if substantial goodness precludes goodness' being a real relation, then the good cannot be a substantial property of things at all:

> But if their indeterminate essence (*ipsum esse*) is good, then there is no doubt that since they are substantial goods, they must be like the first good. And for this very reason they would have to be the first good, for there is nothing like Him other than Himself. Therefore, all existing things are God. This is an impious assertion. Therefore they are not substantial goods, and for this reason their indeterminate essence (*esse*) cannot be good; as such, their essences cannot be good.[74]

The reasoning behind this is clear. As we saw above, if things are substantially good, their essences have to be the cause of their own goodness, and as such they cannot be good by participation. Now, if things' essences were the cause of their goodness, then all things would have to have the same essence, since all things are good. We saw this point too. The fact of the matter is, however, that if all good things were to have the same essence, then all things would have to be like God. For God too is, and God too is good:

---

73. Cf. *Quomodo*, 74–75: "Substantialia igitur bona sunt, quoniam non participant bonitatem."
74. *Quomodo*, 75–83: "Quod si ipsum esse in eis bonum est, non est dubium quin substantialia cum sint bona, primo sint bono similia. Ac per hoc hoc ipsum bonum erunt; nihil enim illi praeter se ipsum simile est. Ex quo fit ut omnia quae sunt deus sint. Quod dictu nefas est. Non sunt igitur substantialia bona ac per hoc non in his est esse bonum. Non sunt igitur in eo quod sunt bona."

But if their indeterminate essence (*ipsum esse*) is good, then there is no doubt that since they are substantial goods, they must be like the first good.[75]

That is, if an indeterminate essence were the cause of all things' goodness, then God would have to share things' indeterminate essence, since God Himself is good. What this means is that all good things would have to be God, if their essences were the cause of their goodness. For there is nothing like God other than God Himself:

> And for this very reason they would have to be the first good, for there is nothing like Him other than Himself. Therefore, all existing things are God.[76]

But this is impossible:

> This [that all existing things are God] is an impious assertion.[77]

It follows that things cannot be good at all if their essences — their indeterminate essence — are the cause of their goodness.

But if things' essences cannot be the cause of their goodness, then goodness cannot be a substantial property of all things:

> Therefore they are not substantial goods, and for this reason their indeterminate essence [*esse*] cannot be good; as such, their essences cannot be good.[78]

This too is contrary to the opening hypothesis, which claims that things are substantially good.

In the third part of his argument, Boethius thus draws the obvious conclusion of the second part of his argument: that if the good were just a substantial property of things, it could not be a substantial property of all things:

> Their essences are therefore not good.[79]

The fact of the matter is, however, that it cannot be a real relation if it is a substantial property of being, as we saw above:

---

75. *Quomodo*, 75–77: "Quod si ipsum esse in eis bonum est, non est dubium quin substantialia cum sint bona, primo sint bono similia."
76. *Quomodo*, 78–80: "Ac per hoc hoc ipsum bonum erunt; nihil enim illi praeter se ipsum simile est. Ex quo fit ut omnia quae sunt deus sint."
77. *Quomodo*, 80: "Quod dictu [omnia quae sunt deus sunt] nefas est."
78. *Quomodo*, 80–82: "Non sunt igitur substantialia bona ac per hoc non in his est esse bonum."
79. *Quomodo*, 82–83: "Non sunt igitur in eo quod sunt bona."

But nor do they participate in goodness.[80]

It follows that the good cannot be a substantial property of things at all:

They could therefore not tend to the good in any way. As such, they can in no wise be good.[81]

Now, Boethius's conclusion at this point is contrary to his opening hypothesis: that things are substantially good. We must therefore assume that his point is not to show that things cannot be good. Rather, it must be that the cause of the substantial goodness of things cannot be participation alone or things' essences alone. If this is so, then his implicit conclusion must be that the cause of the substantial goodness of things is both participation and the essences of things, and as such that one must discover how to reconcile the two classical definitions of the good if he is to explain why things are substantially good. After all, Boethius's implicit premise is that there are only two possible causes of the substantial goodness of things. Thus, if neither of these two possible causes can account for the substantial goodness of things, then things' substantial goodness must either have no cause at all, or it must be caused by both of these two possible causes. The fact of the matter is that Boethius cannot hold that things' substantial goodness is not caused. He himself tells us that the object of his work is to determine how the substantial goodness of things can be caused by their essences. As such, we are left with the second possibility: since the cause of things' goodness cannot be things essences alone, or participation alone, the cause of things' substantial goodness must be both things' essences and participation.

The Conditions a Solution Must Meet

We can draw a bit more from the second section of Boethius's argument than the implicit conclusion that the substantial goodness of things must be caused by both participation and things' essences. A closer look at his argument regarding participation shows that he believes a proper definition of things' substantial goodness to show that a real relation is the cause of the existences of things. And a closer look at his argument regarding things' essences shows that he believes a proper definition of things' substantial goodness to claim that things' essences can be the cause of their goodness, as long as they are neither God, nor the cause of their existences.

---

80. *Quomodo*, 83: "Sed nec participant bonitatem."
81. *Quomodo*, 83–85: "Nullo enim modo ad bonum tenderent. Nullo modo igitur sunt bona."

The point here is that the second section of Boethius's argument is a negative delineation of the conditions which a proper definition of the cause of things' substantial goodness must satisfy. For just as it demonstrates that both participation and things' essences must be the causes of the substantial goodness of things — since neither participation alone nor things' essences alone can account for their goodness — so too does it negatively delineate how both participation and things' essences can be the causes of things' goodness. For just as Boethius's conclusion contradicts his opening syllogism, so too do the conclusions of each of his two arguments in this second section contradict his opening syllogism. Thus, just as we know that Boethius's implicit conclusion must be that both participation and things' essences are the causes of their goodness since: (1) his explicit conclusion is that things cannot be good if the cause of their goodness is participation alone or their essences alone, and (2) his explicit conclusion contradicts his premise that things are substantially good, so too can we deduce that he believes participation to be the cause of things' existences from the facts that: (1) the conclusion of his argument regarding participation contradicts his opening syllogism, and (2) the definition of participation which he refutes presupposes the existence of both *relata*. Again, we can deduce that he believes that things' essences cannot be either the cause of their existence or identical to God's essence from the facts that: (1) the conclusion of his argument concerning things' essences contradicts his opening syllogism, and (2) that the view which he refutes considers things' essences to be both the cause of their existence and identical to God's own essence.

As for participation, Boethius states quite explicitly that he cannot accept the relational definition because it precludes things' being substantially good. The reason he gives for this is that real relations presuppose the existence of both *relata* and cannot as such confer substantial goodness upon things. That this is his reason can be inferred from his example. For he justifies his claim that participation precludes things' being substantially good by showing that a thing which possesses an accidental property through participation cannot be said to possess that property substantially:

> For a thing which is white by participation does not have an existence which is white in itself. So it is with all other qualities. If then things are good by participation, they are in no way good in themselves. (63–66)

The fact of the matter is, however, that the distinguishing characteristic of accidental properties is that they presuppose the existence of that thing in which they subsist. This means that if they are acquired through a real relation, that real relation cannot but presuppose the existence of both *relata*. Thus, if the example illustrates the reason why Boethius claims that goodness cannot be a substantial property of things if it is acquired through a real relation (as we must suppose it does) then he must hold that a real relation cannot be the cause of the substantial goodness of things *if* it presupposes the existence of both *relata*, or more specifically if it presupposes the existence of the *relatum* which becomes good through the real relation.

What this means is that a real relation can be the cause of things' goodness if it does not presuppose the existence of the *relatum* which becomes good through that real relation. Hence, if the cause of the substantial goodness of things must be both a real relation and things' own essences (as Boethius's conclusion implies), then Boethius's solution must entail proving that real relations need not presuppose the existence of both *relata*. But those real relations which do not presuppose both *relata* are those which constitute a *relatum*. Hence, if things are good (as we must assume Boethius thinks they are) and if the good is a real relation (as again we must assume that Boethius thinks it is) then (he must also think that) things are constituted by a real relation: participation.

As for things' essences, Boethius claims that if they were the cause of their goodness, the substantial goodness of things would have to have an intrinsic cause:

> But if the essence [of all things] is good, then things' existences are good in themselves. (72–73)

But if their substantial goodness has an intrinsic cause, it cannot be caused by a real relation:

> It follows that they must be substantial goods, because they do not participate in goodness. (74–75)

Boethius believes this to be a problematic conclusion, insofar as it implies that things are similar to God, or indeed that they are God. He gives two reasons for this. The claim that something is substantially good implies that its essence is the cause of its goodness, and this in turn implies that: (1) all good things (created and divine) must have the same essence — "their essence must be identical with the essence of the good" — and hence that (2) a thing's essence must be the cause of its existence — "But if their indeterminate essence (*ipsum esse*) is good, then there is no doubt that...they are substantial goods." His conclusion, as such, is that the essences of things cannot be the cause of their goodness:

> Whatsoever's essence is good must also have a good existence. But things acquire their existence from Him who is being. Their essence is therefore good; therefore the indeterminate essence (*ipsum esse*) of all things is good. But if the essence [of all things] is good, then things' existences are good in themselves. As such, their essence must be identical with the essence of the good. It follows that they must be substantial goods, because they do not participate in goodness. But if their indeterminate essence (*ipsum esse*) is good, then there is no doubt that since they are substantial goods, they must be like the first good. And for this very reason they would have to be the first good, for there is nothing like Him other than Himself. Therefore, all existing things are God, and this is an impious assertion. Therefore they are not substantial goods, and for this reason their indeterminate essence (*esse*) cannot be good; as such, their essences cannot be good. (68–83)

We saw the first point in our synopsis of the argument. It is a syllogism: all good things have the same essence; but God is good; therefore God must have the same essence as all good things. The point here is that the goodness of the existence of a thing must have a cause, and that cause is *ex hypothesi* its essence. As such, the cause of the goodness of all things must be an *indeterminate essence* which all things share. For if goodness were a property which individual things have in virtue of their own determinate essences, goodness could not be a universal property. If all things have the same *indeterminate essence,* however, then this *indeterminate essence* must also be God's essence. Were it not to be, God could not be good. It follows that all things share God's essence. This is what Boethius vehemently denies: *quod dictu nefas.*[82]

There is a second and more important reason why things would be like God if their essences were the cause of their substantial goodness. For the claim that things' essences are the cause of their substantial goodness implies that they are the cause of their existences. After all, if all existing things are good, then nothing can exist without being good.

---

[82]. Given this point, I find it very difficult to accept Obertello's first reading of the *Quomodo*'s *exitus*. For it claims that things are substantially good because their being is a determination of God's Being and that God's Being is the Good. The point also makes it very difficult to accept the reading of the *Quomodo*'s axioms upon which Obertello bases his reading of the *exitus:* Hadot's. Cf. Obertello, *Boezio*, p. 646. Cf. Hadot, *Distinction*, pp. 147–53.

As such, the cause of something's existence must also be the cause of its goodness. By the converse, the cause of something's goodness must also be the cause of its existence. Thus, if things' essences are the cause of their goodness, they must be the cause of their existences. As such, all things must be substantial goods:

> It follows that they must be substantial goods, because they do not participate in goodness. (74–75)

There are at least two reasons why Boethius could construe this point as implying that things are God. The first is that he explicitly states that God is the cause of things' existences:

> But things acquire their existence from Him who is being. (70)

Thus, if things' essences were the cause of their existences, they would have to be God. This is tantamount to claiming that things are God. The second reason, on the other hand, is that there is only one being whose essence is the cause of His existence: God, *id quod est esse*.[83] For all beings other than God, on the other hand, their essences cannot be or cause their existences.[84] As such, if the essences of things were their existences or the cause of their existences, they would have to be God. This is precisely what Boethius vehemently denies: *quod dictu nefas*.

Now, if Boethius believes that the essences of things cannot be the cause of their goodness if this implies: (1) that things' essences are identical to God's, (2) that they are identical to their existences, or (3) are the cause of their existences, then since he does indeed believe things' essences to be the cause of their goodness (as the opening syllogism shows) we must suppose that he believes that they can be so if: (1) they are not identical to God's essence, (2) they are not identical to their own existences, and (3) they are not the cause of their existences. But if things' essences are good, but aren't God's essence, and if God is the *primum bonum* (77), then they must in some sense be caused by God. If things' existences aren't identical to their essences, or caused by them, then they must be caused by something other than they. This means that Boethius must believe that things' essences can be the cause of their goodness if participation is too. The point, in other words, is that the

---

83. The point here is one that Boethius makes in the axioms: "Omne simplex esse suum et id quod est unum habet" (VII, 45–46). It is a point which will come up in his solution to the problem of the good.
84. The distinction is again one that Boethius makes in the axioms, most specifically in the eighth axiom: "Omni composito aliud est esse, aliud ipsum est" (VIII, 47–48). It is this distinction which he will also insist upon in his solution to the problem of the good, i.e., in his reconciliation of the definitions. Cf. *Quomodo*, 100ff.

very reasons why Boethius rejects an intrinsic cause of things' goodness illustrate the reasons why an intrinsic cause precludes an extrinsic one.

Putting our points together we have that participation can be the cause of the goodness of things if it is also the cause of the existences of things. The essences of things, on the other hand, can be the cause of their goodness if they are not the cause of their existences: if they are not identical to the existences of things and if they are not God. These two points are complementary, and imply that the next sections of Boethius's argument will show: (1) that God is the cause of things' existences — or that things exist because they participate in God; (2) that things' essences are not the cause of their existences or identical to their existences; and (3) that the goodness of things is analogous to God's.

Objections

Before we analyze the third section of Boethius's *exitus* we must respond to a possible objection to our interpretation. For one might claim that we are reading something into the *Quomodo* by stating that its object is to correlate the two definitions of the good, since Boethius does not explicitly link his proof of the substantial goodness of things in his opening syllogism with his two mutually exclusive attempts to explain why things are good.

This may be true. If it were, however, it would be difficult to explain: (1) why Boethius lists only two possible causes of the substantial goodness of things in his examination of the possible ways to explain why things are substantially good, and why these two possible causes of the substantial goodness of things happen to be a real relation and the essences of things; (2) why the doctrine of participation which he examines happens to presuppose the existence of both *relata*; and (3) why Boethius concludes both of his arguments (i.e., his proofs that the cause of things' goodness cannot be participation or things' essences) by showing that they are unacceptable insofar as they contradict his opening syllogism. For this latter point implies that his explicit intention is for his arguments to draw out the implications of his opening syllogism.

As for the first point, there are many more than two possible causes of things' substantial goodness and many ways to reduce the problem of explaining why things are substantially good to two mutually exclusive alternatives. One can determine the cause of things' substantial goodness by using Aristotle's four causes. As such, Boethius could have examined the possible causes of things' goodness by asking whether things are good because of their matter, their form, their efficient cause, or their final cause. And he could have made the two mutually exclusive causes things' matter or their form; their form or their efficient cause; their form or their final cause. Again, one can determine the cause of the substantial goodness of things by asking what the ontological correlative of the word 'good' is, and hence by examining our uses of the word 'good.' Boethius could thus have counterposed that use of the word 'good' whereby we commend an extraordinary exemplar of a specific genus of things — "that is good music" — with that use of the word whereby we define an entire genus of things — "music is good" — and he would thereby have shown that we have two mutually exclusive ways of attributing 'goodness' to things. He could then have shown that 'good' seems to be both an equivocal term and a univocal term, and so forth. We know that Boethius was capable of examining the problem in all of these ways. For he wrote commentaries on Aristotle's *Organon* and had more than a passing acquaintance with Aristotelian metaphysics.[85] This naturally forces us to ask ourselves why Boethius does claim that there are only two causes of things' goodness, and why those two causes are participation and substantiality.

The point becomes even more poignant if one asks why he lists these causes immediately after having proven that things are substantially good through a syllogism which correlates two definitions of the good, which are a relational and a substantial definition respectively. For the proximity of the opening syllogism and Boethius's two causes of things' goodness naturally makes one think that Boethius holds that the syllogism and the two causes of things' goodness are related.

This brings us to the second point. The specific doctrine of participation which Boethius examines in the second part of his argument presupposes the existence of both *relata*. Now, participation need not presuppose the existence of both *relata*, and Boethius was more than aware of this.[86] What this means is that the object of the second part of Boethius's argument cannot be to examine whether it is possible for any sort of participation to be the cause of the substantial goodness of things. Its object must therefore be to examine whether a specific sort of participation can be the cause of the substantial goodness of things. That specific sort of participation, then, is exactly of the sort which Boethius delineates in his opening syllogism. For if the good is the object of desire, it must also be a real relation. Indeed, it must be

---

85. That Boethius was more than capable of using any of these methods can be seen in his *De Trinitate*, where he uses both Aristotle's categories and his metaphysics to understand why God is a Trinity. For the first point see *De Trinitate*, IIIff. For the second point see *De Trinitate* II.

86. Cf. *Quomodo*, VI, 41–44: "Omne quod est participat eo quod est esse ut sit; alio vero participat ut aliquid sit. Ac per hoc id quod est participat eo quod est esse ut sit; est vero ut participet alio quolibet."

a real relation which presupposes the existence of both *relata* — the desired object and the desirer — and which makes one of the *relata* 'good': the object itself is by definition good, and a real relation with something good must make the real relater good. But participation is a real relation. Hence, when a real relater participates in the object of his desire, or in the good, he becomes good thereby. What we must assume, then, is that Boethius's object is to determine whether the sort of participation which he delineates in his opening syllogism can be the cause of things' substantial goodness.

As for the third point, the conclusions of both of Boethius's arguments in the second section of his *exitus* contain references to his opening syllogism. At the end of his argument regarding participation, he claims that:

> If then things are good by participation, they are in no way good in themselves. Therefore they do not tend to the good. But we have agreed that they do. (65–67)

And at the end of his argument regarding things' essences, he claims that:

> They could therefore not tend to the good in any way. As such, they can in no wise be good. (83–85)

These references clearly indicate that Boethius's arguments are related to his opening syllogism.

But if both of Boethius's arguments are related to the opening syllogism, if the major and minor premises of that syllogism present a relational and a substantial definition of the good respectively, and if the arguments regard a relational and a substantial cause of things' goodness respectively, then our interpretation would seem to stand on rather firm ground.

Preliminaries to the Solution

Having negatively delineated the conditions which a definition of the cause of things' goodness must satisfy, Boethius begins to outline his solution by demonstrating why things' essences cannot cause their existences, or the goodness of their existences. His argument is a *reductio ad absurdum* which was foreshadowed in his claim that if contingent things were the cause of their own goodness, they would have to be God. For the point of that claim was to show that things' substantial goodness must be caused by a real relation, and so too is this the point of the argument at hand.

The argument has two parts. In the first part, Boethius demonstrates that the essences of contingent things must be distinct from their existences and consequently that they cannot be the cause of either their substantial goodness, or their existences. In the second part, on the other hand, he shows that the essences of contingent things cannot be the cause of their substantial goodness because contingent things are complex. The implicit conclusion of the third part of Boethius's *exitus,* as such, is that things' substantial goodness must be caused by a real relation.

The argument begins with an abstraction. There are many things, Boethius tells us, whose components can be distinguished *in mente,* although they cannot be distinguished *in re.* A triangle, for instance, cannot be distinguished from its substrate — matter — *in re,* although we can mentally distinguish it from matter. This mental distinction is important, for it allows us to analyze the properties of things.[87] What we must do is to perform a similar abstraction with regards to things' goodness in order to understand what its cause is. Let us, thus, abstract from the First Good whose existence is known by all people, both ignorant and cultured alike, posit that all things are good, and ask ourselves how they can be good if their goodness is not caused by the First Good.[88]

Now, if things' substantial goodness were not caused by the First Good, it would have to be caused by their own essences. But in order for things' essences to be the cause of their substantial goodness *that things are* would have to be *what things are:*[89] things' existences would have to be identical to their essences. This is, however, impossible:

> This leads me to perceive that it is one thing for things to be good, another for them to be [things' good essences are distinct from their existence].[90]

For if the existences of all good things were identical to their essences, then the existences of complex things would have to be identical to

---

87. *Quomodo,* 87–91: "Multa sunt quae cum separari actu non possunt, animo tamen et cogitatione separantur; ut cum triangulum vel cetera a subiecta materia nullus actu separat, mente tamen segregans ipsum triangulum proprietatemque eius praeter materiam speculatur."

88. *Quomodo,* 92–98: "Amoveamus igitur primi boni praesentiam paulisper ex animo, quod esse quidem constat idque ex omnium doctorum indoctorumque sententia barbarumque gentium religionibus cognosci potest. Hoc igitur paulisper amoto ponamus omnia esse quae sunt bona atque ea consideremus quemadmodum bona esse possent, si a primo bono minime defluxissent."

89. To use Boethian terminology, "quod sunt" would have to be "esse in eis."

90. *Quomodo,* 98–100: "Hinc intueor aliud in eis esse quod bona sunt, aliud quod sunt."

their essences. But if the existences of complex things were identical to their essences, then all of the properties of complex things would have to be identical to each other. This is clearly impossible:

> Let us suppose that one and the same good substance is white, heavy and round. Thus the substance itself must be different from its roundness, its color, and its goodness. For if any one of these properties were one and the same as its substance, then weight would be the same thing as color, color would be goodness, goodness would be weight, all of which is contrary to nature.[91]

Therefore, the existences of complex things must be distinct from their essences.[92]

But if the existences of complex things are distinct from their essences, Boethius continues, then they could not be good even if their essences were good:

> Thus, in this case their essences would be one thing and their existing as something another, as such, and even if they were good, their existence would not be good at all.[93]

He gives two reasons for this. (1) Their existences would not be good because they would not derive from the good:

> Therefore, even if they were in some way to exist, their existences would not derive from the good, and be good, as such.[94]

---

91. *Quomodo*, 100–106: "Ponatur enim una eademque substantia bona esse alba, gravis, rotunda. Tunc aliud esset ipsa illa substantia, aliud eius rotunditas, aliud color, aliud bonitas; nam si haec singula idem essent quod ipsa substantia, idem esset gravitas quod color, [color] quod bonum et bonum quod gravitas — quod fieri natura non sinit."

92. There is a problem with the word *'substantia'* here. For the context indicates that it is an existing thing, an *'id quod est'* to use Boethian terminology, because Boethius posits that it is 'round,' 'heavy,' and 'white.' The reason why this is perplexing is that Boethius himself defines *'substantia'* as an essence in the *Quomodo* — cf. the fifth axiom — and his use of the word throughout the *Quomodo*, with the exception of this one passage and the first line of the work, conforms with his definition.

This means that we have a philological problem here. For if one were to abide by Boethius's own definition of the term, he would have to read this passage as claiming that complex things' essences are distinct from their accidental properties. The fact of the matter, is however, that the opening line of the passage does not allow this reading. For that fact that it is a *'substantia'* which has these properties and is distinct from them demonstrates that it cannot be an essence. That is, since we can distinguish the *'substantia'* from its 'heaviness,' 'whiteness,' and 'roundness,' these properties must be accidental. But only an *'id quod est'* can have accidental properties, as Boethius's third axiom shows. "*Quod est participare aliquo potest... Fit enim participatio cum aliquid iam est.*" As such, *'substantia'* here cannot mean an essence. We have therefore interpreted *'substantia'* as meaning an existing thing, an *'id quod est.'*

93. *Quomodo*, 106–8: "Aliud igitur tunc in eis esset esse, aliud aliquid esse, ac tunc bona quidem essent, esse tamen ipsum minime haberent bonum."

94. *Quomodo*, 108–9: "Igitur si ullo modo essent, non a bono ac bona essent."

And (2) their existences would not be their good essences:

> Nor would their existences be identical to [their] good essences. Rather their existence would be one thing, and their being good another.[95]

The second of these reasons is a corollary of Boethius's distinction between essence and existence in complex things. His point is that the existences of complex things could not be good if their essences were, because they are distinct from their essences. The first reason, on the other hand, is a bit more complex. For it is not altogether clear what that 'good' is from which Boethius tells us things do not derive. The gist of the argument suggests that it could either be God, or the essences of complex things. For we have abstracted from God, and are questioning whether the essences of complex things can be the cause of their goodness. Thus, Boethius's point could be that the existences of complex things would not be good even if their essences were, for their existences are not caused by God *ex hypothesi*. Or it could be that the existences of complex things could not be good even if their essences were, because they cannot derive from their essences.

Now, each of these interpretations is plausible. The evidence in favor of the first is linguistic. For Boethius's claim here is not that complex things' existences would not be good even if their essences were, because their existences would not derive from good things: 'a bonis.' Nor does he claim that they would not derive from some good thing: 'a quo bono.' His claim is that they would not be good because they would not derive from the good: "a bono." Now, since God is the Good, one is tempted to claim that 'good' in this case must mean God.

Evidence in favor of the second interpretation, on the other hand, is clearly the statement's context. For Boethius is questioning whether things' essences can be the cause of their existence in the absence of God, and hence his mentioning God when he has abstracted from Him would seem odd, to say the least. The problem with this second interpretation, however, is clearly Boethius's language. For there is no getting around the facts that his qualification of the source of things' existences is singular, and that different contingent things have different essences.

As I see the issue, evidence in favor of the second interpretation is stronger than the evidence in favor of the first, precisely because of the claim's context. Boethius's calling upon God when he has abstracted

---

95. *Quomodo*, 109–11: "Ac non idem essent quod bona, sed eis aliud esset esse aliud bonis esse."

from Him would be odd, indeed. Hence, his claim here seems to be that things' existences would not be good even if their essences were, because they cannot derive from their essences. The reason why he qualifies things' essences as "the good," then, seems to be that he has things' indeterminate essence in mind. He has already claimed the source of things' goodness to be the common indeterminate essence of contingent being.[96] The point of the first half of Boethius's *reductio*, as such, is that the claim that things' essences are the cause of their substantial goodness must ultimately contradict itself.

In the second half of his argument Boethius emphasizes his point and shows that even if one were to go as far as to suppose that the essences of contingent things were simple — that is, that they only had one property and were simply good — he still could not claim that those things which possess that property are good. For even in this extreme case the essences of contingent things could not be their existences, or cause their existences.

As for the first point, if things were their essences, and if their essences were only to have one property, then those things which possess that property would not be 'things' at all. Rather, they would have to be goodness itself, the principle of their goodness. But goodness itself cannot be different things. Hence if things were their essences, and their essences were goodness, there could be no 'things' at all:

> But if they were in no way anything other than good, if they were neither heavy nor colored, and if they were in no way extended in a spatial dimension, and if no other quality existed in them other than being good, in this case they would seem not to be things, but the principle of things; nor could it be said that 'they would seem' for in this case we would have to say 'it would seem.' For there is only one thing like this, which is only good and nothing else.[97]

But there is another point here. For Boethius's claim that there would be 'no things' at all if complex things were identical to their essences also implies that things' essences cannot cause their existences. This is obvious. In order to be the cause of their existence, goodness would have to be a subsistent thing — it would have to be an existing thing —

---

96. See footnotes 71 and 72 above.
97. *Quomodo*, 111–17: "Quod si nihil omnino aliud essent nisi bona neque gravia neque colorata neque spatii dimensione distenta nec ulla in eis qualitas esset, nisi tantum bona essent, tunc non res sed rerum viderentur esse principium nec potius vederentur, sed videretur; unum enum solumque est huiusmodi, quod tantum bonum aliudque nihil sit."

since it is *ex hypothesi* the sole cause of their existence. But goodness cannot be a subsistent thing. If it were, it could not be an essence. This clearly also means that things' essences cannot be identical to their existences or to the cause of their existences even if their essences were only good.

Now, the latter half of Boethius's argument clearly complements the first part. For it shows that we must not only distinguish all things' essences from their existences — all things, that is, excepting God, because we have abstracted from Him — and realize that this distinction implies that things' essences cannot be the cause of their existences, we must also understand that the reason why things' existences cannot derive from their essences is that contingent things are necessarily complex. And what complexity means in this case is not that contingent things have many different properties, but that they are a composite of essence and existence: that their essence is not their existence.[98]

The third section of Boethius's *exitus*, as such, has a negative point: we cannot abstract from the First Good in order to understand why things are good. For if we do, there is no explaining either why things exist or how their existences relate to their own essences. Like the conclusion of the second section of his *exitus*, however, this negative point has a positive consequence: that God must be the cause of both things' existences and of their relations to their essences. For if it is abstracting from the First Good that leads one to posit that things are good in virtue of their own essences alone, and if it is positing that things are good in virtue of their essences leaves things' existences and the relations between their essences and existences unaccounted for, then it stands to reason that restoring the First Good into the picture must show that: (1) things' existences are caused by God, and (2) that the relation between essences and existences in complex things is also caused by God. Indeed, it must show that both things' existences and the relation between their essences and their existences are real relations. For if complex things' existences do not have an intrinsic cause, then they can only have an extrinsic cause, inasmuch as intrinsic and extrinsic causality are the two alternatives of a dichotomy. If their existences must have an extrinsic cause, however, then their existences must be a real relation with that cause. That cause, then, must be the only being which does not require an extrinsic cause in order to exist: the First Good. As such, things' existences must be their real relations with the First Good.

The same thing holds for the relation between complex things' existences and their essences. For that too can either have an intrinsic

---

98. *Quomodo*, VIII, 47–48: "Omni composito aliud est esse, aliud ipsum est."

or an extrinsic cause. But that cause cannot be intrinsic. For Boethius has shown that things' essences cannot be the cause of the relation between complex things' essences and their existences, and we must suppose that their existences cannot be the cause of the relation with their essences, since every complex things' existence actuates an essence. Hence, the relation between complex things' existences and their essences also requires an extrinsic cause and must be a real relation with that cause. As both things' existences and the relation between their essences and their existences are real relations, then so too must their goodness be.

The Solution

Boethius has thus far shown: (1) that one needs both of the two classical definitions of the good in order to explain why things are substantially good; (2) that the implications of the two definitions ostensibly make them mutually exclusive definitions; (3) that neither of the definitions alone can account for the substantial goodness of things: that the good cannot be only a real relation, or only a substantial property of things; (4) that the good can be both a real relation and a substantial property of all things if the real relation is the cause of things' existences and if things' essences are not God (the cause of their existences) or identical to their existences; (5) that complex things' substantial goodness seems to entail two real relations: one which accounts for their existence, and one which accounts for the relation between their essences and their existences. One would expect his next move to be to show why things' substantial goodness entails two real relations. And that is exactly what he does. His solution to the problem of contingent things' substantial goodness is that there must be a First Good who is the cause of the goodness of things' essences and existences and of the relations between their essences and their existences, and that it is therefore because of their real relations to the First Good and to their essences that things are substantially good.

Boethius proves these points separately. Nor is this surprising, since he distinguished them in the third section of his *exitus*. He begins by proving that the existences of complex things are good because they are willed by God, who is good. He then proves that the indeterminate essence of things is good because it is both willed by God and like Him. Lastly, he proves that things are good in virtue of their essences because they are created by God. The fourth section of his *exitus* thus has three parts.

The Goodness of Things' Existences

Things other than God must have an extrinsic cause of their existences. This can be gathered from the third section of Boethius's *exitus*, where he proved that complex things cannot be the cause of their own existences. Boethius thus claims that God, or He who is Good, is the efficient cause of their existences.

> But since they are not simple, they could not even exist at all unless that whose existence is only good had willed them to [wanted them to].[99]

But, if contingent things exist because God wills them to — because God is the efficient cause of their existences — and if their essences are not God (*quod dictu nefas*) then what Boethius is claiming here is that complex things are created by God. He claims as much in his recapitulation of his solution.[100] This means, of course, that things' existences must be their real relations with God.

If God is the efficient cause of the existences of complex things, however, then He must also be the cause of their goodness. For since all things are necessarily good (as the syllogism in the first part of Boethius's *exitus* shows), then that which causes the existences of complex things must also be the cause of their goodness. It would be absurd to think that something could cause existence without causing one of the necessary properties of existence. I can't cook dinner if I don't have food. Thus, Boethius completes his first point by claiming that God causes the goodness of the existences of things:

> Thus, since their existence flowed from the will of the good (*a boni voluntate*), they are called good.[101]

---

99. *Quomodo*, 117–19: "Quae quoniam non sunt simplicia, nec esse omnino poterant, nisi ea id quod solum bonum est esse voluisset."

100. *Quomodo*, 140–50: "Igitur sublato ab his bono primo mente et cogitatione, ista licet essent bona, tamen in eo quod essent bona esse non possent, et quoniam *actu non potuere exsistere, nisi illud ea quod vere bonum est* **produxisset**, idcirco et esse eorum bonum est et non est simile substantiali bono id quod ab eo fluxit; et nisi ab eo fluxissent, licet essent bona, tamen in eo quod sunt bona esse non possent, quoniam et praeter bonum et non ex bono essent, cum illud ipsum bonum primum [est] et ipsum esse sit et ipsum bonum et ipsum esse bonum." See also on this same note, *Quomodo*, 150–55 where Boethius claims both that contingent things "flow" from God's will and that God creates them: "At non etiam alba in eo quod sunt alba esse oportebit ea quae alba sunt, *quoniam ex voluntate dei fluxerunt ut essent alba? Minime. Aliud est enim esse, aliud albis esse; hoc ideo, quoniam qui ea ut essent* **effecit** *bonus quidem est, minime vero albus.*"

101. *Quomodo*, 119–21: "Idcirco quoniam esse eorum a boni voluntate defluxit, bona esse dicuntur."

Now, Boethius seems to attribute a double cause to the goodness of things' existences: (1) their being willed and (2) their being willed by the Good. If the first cause of their goodness is an act of efficient causality, the second seems to be exemplarity. The first cause is one we have seen before. For if things' existences are the object of God's free act of will, they must be good. That is, if the good is the object of desire, and if an object can be the term of a free act of desire, then the term of a free act of desire must by definition be good. Hence, since things' existences are the terms of God's free act of will, things' existences must be good. Their goodness must as such be their real relation with God.

Nor is this the only reason why Boethius claims that things' existences are good. Were it to be, then the goodness of the existences of things would merely be a real relation. But if the goodness of the existences of things were merely a real relation, then goodness itself would have to be merely a real relation, and God could not be Good. This is, of course, contrary to Boethius's premise. He explicitly claims that God is good: "they could not even exist at all unless *that whose existence is only good* had wanted them to" (118–19).

Moreover, if things' existences were good only insofar as they are the terms of God's free act of will, then as Geiger points out,[102] things' existences would only be good by extrinsic denomination. As such, Boethius's definition of the cause of the goodness of the existences of things would not satisfy the conditions which he outlined in the first and second sections of his *exitus*. For he showed there that things' goodness must have both an intrinsic and an extrinsic cause.[103] As this holds for things in general, so too must it hold for things' existences specifically.

Boethius therefore specifies that things' existences are good because things are willed by the *First Good*. His specification implies that God's goodness is also a cause of the goodness of the existences of things. But if God's goodness is also a cause of the goodness of things' existences, then exemplarity must also be a cause of the goodness of things' existences. The point here is that since *omne agens agit sibi simile*, the effects of all of God's free acts must be similar to Him. Thus, since God is good, the effects of his free acts must be good: similar to Him. But things' existences are the effects of God's free acts of will. Hence, things' existences must be good because God is, that is, because they are similar to God:

---

102. Geiger, p. 44. See footnote 15.
103. The implicit point of both the first and second sections of Boethius's *exitus* is that things' goodness must be caused both by participation and substantiality.

For the first good, because it is, is substantially good; the second good, on the other hand, because it flows from Him whose very essence is good, is itself also good.[104]

The Goodness of Things' Indeterminate Essences

Having established that things' existences are good because they are both created by God and like God, Boethius's next move is to prove that their essences are good.

> But the indeterminate essence of all things flowed from Him who is the first good, and who is good in such a way that He is rightly said to be good in virtue of His substance. Their own indeterminate essence must therefore be good, because in this case it is in Him.[105]

The point here does not concern things' essences *per se*, but the indeterminate essence of all things: *ipsum esse omnium rerum*. Now, an indeterminate essence in Boethian metaphysics, as we have seen, is a universal *ante rem*.[106] His point here, as such, is that that God is the cause of things' *indeterminate* essence — *ipsum esse omnium rerum* "flows from Him who is good in virtue of His Substance" (124–25) — and that it is therefore good before it becomes determinate in particular things. Its goodness, then, would seem to have two causes: God's causality and its being like God: *ipsum esse omnium rerum* is good because it is "in Him" (127). Now, neither of these points is exactly clear. For Boethius's language is a bit elusive. Let us therefore analyze the passage more carefully.

An opening point is, I believe, in order. For appearances to the contrary, Boethius is not claiming in this passage that the indeterminate essence of all things is God. And there are at least two reasons why this is so. The first is that he explicitly claims that *ipsum esse* is not God in the second section of his *exitus*.[107] The second reason is a negative one: had Boethius wanted to claim that *ipsum esse* is God, there would have

---

104. *Quomodo*, 121–24: "Primum enim bonum, quoniam est, in eo quod est bonum est; secundum vero bonum, quoniam ex eo fluxit cuius ipsum esse bonum est, ipsum quoque bonum est."

105. *Quomodo*, 124–27: "Sed ipsum esse omnium rerum ex eo fluxit quod est primum bonum et quod bonum tale est ut recte dicatur in eo quod est esse bonum. Ipsum igitur eorum esse bonum est; tunc enim in eo."

106. Cf. footnote 71 above.

107. *Quomodo*, 75–83: "Quod si ipsum esse in eis bonum est, non est dubium quin substantialia cum sint bona, primo sint bono similia. Ac per hoc hoc ipsum bonum erunt; nihil enim illi praeter se ipsum simile est. Ex quo fit ut omnia quae sunt deus sint. Quod dictu nefas est. Non sunt igitur substantialia bona ac per hoc non in his est esse bonum. Non sunt igitur in eo quod sunt bona."

been no need for him to have used the preposition "in" in his definition of the cause of its goodness: "Their own indeterminate essence must therefore be good, because in this case it is in Him" (126–27). He could have stated that *ipsum esse* is good because it is God. This would have had the added advantage of making the passage a great deal clearer. The fact that he did not put it this way is, I take it, a sign of the fact that he did not believe *ipsum esse* to be consubstantial with God.

Now, if *ipsum esse* is not God, and if everything other than God must have an extrinsic cause for its existence (as the third part of Boethius's *exitus* proved) then *ipsum esse* too must have an extrinsic cause for its existence. Nor need we prove the point by extrapolation. In the third part of his *exitus* Boethius explicitly claims that if one abstracts from God, complex things' essences would not be essences at all: they would simply be principles of being.[108] By the converse we have that an essence can be such if and only if one does not abstract from God.[109] But abstracting from God in this case means abstracting from Him as a cause. As such, *ipsum esse* can be the essence of all things if we do not abstract from God as cause. But if *ipsum esse* is not an essence it is nothing at all, as the first metaphysical axiom in the *Quomodo* points out: *"Ipsum esse nondum est."*[110] Therefore, in order for *ipsum esse* to be, God must be its cause:

> But the indeterminate essence of all things flowed from Him who is the first good, and who is good in such a way that He is rightly said to be good in virtue of His substance. (124–26)

As for *ipsum esse*'s goodness, its causes (it seems) must be similar to those which Boethius adduces to account for the goodness of things' existences: it must be good both because it "flows" from God's will and because it is like God, in some sense. For if Boethius tells us that things' existences are good because they "flow from God's will," then since *ipsum esse* also "flows" from God, it would seem logical for it too to be good because it is the effect of God's will. It would also seem logical for it to be good because it is like God. After all, if things' existences are good, insofar as they are created by God, and are therefore like God, who is good — *omne agens agit sibi simile* — it seems to follow that *ipsum esse* must be good for the same reason. This deduction

---

108. *Quomodo*, 106–11: "Aliud igitur tunc in eis esset esse, aliud aliquid esse, ac tunc bona quidem essent, esse tamen ipsum minime haberent bonum. Igitur si ullo modo essent, non a bono ac bona essent. Ac non idem essent quod bona, sed eis aliud esset esse aliud bonis esse."

109. Boethius will make this very point in the lines to come. Cf. *Quomodo*, 131–33: "non potest esse ipsum esse rerum, nisi a primo esse defluxerit."

110. Cf. *Quomodo*, II, 28–29.

has textual support. For just as Boethius specifies that the goodness of things' existences stems from God's own goodness — "they could not even exist at all unless that whose existence is only good had willed them to" (118–19) — he also claims that "the indeterminate essence of all things flowed from Him who is the first good" (123). Hence, just as God's goodness is a cause of things' existences' goodness, so too must it be a cause of *ipsum esse*'s goodness.

The fact of the matter is, however, that Boethius does not state either of these reasons when he delineates the cause of *ipsum esse*'s goodness. For the *explicit cause* of the goodness of the indeterminate essence of things in his account is that is "in God":

> Their own indeterminate essence must therefore be good, because in this case it is in Him. (126–27)

What does he mean by that curious turn of phrase?

Now, in order to grasp the meaning of the clause we must: (1) examine the context of the clause and (2) understand what *ipsum esse omnium rerum* is. The clause's context is an attempt to characterize the cause of *ipsum esse*'s goodness. Boethius both vehemently denies that *ipsum esse* is God and claims that *ipsum esse omnium rerum* "flows" from Him, or is caused by Him. We took this to mean that God is the efficient cause of *ipsum esse*. There is, however, something problematic about claiming that God is the efficient cause of *ipsum esse*. For things' indeterminate essence does not exist in its own right: it is the unactualized essence of things, after all.[111] But the fact that *ipsum esse* does not exist in the strict sense of the word means that strictly speaking it cannot 'receive' anything. As such, not even its being can be a reception. This is what makes it so very difficult to speak of *ipsum esse* as the product of God's efficient causality. For if *actio est in passo* for all acts of efficient causality, then an act of efficient causality requires reception. How, then, is one to define the manner in which God causes *ipsum esse* to be?

Boethius came across a similar problem when he defined the cause of the existences of contingent things. For contingent things' existences are also the effects of God's efficient causality,[112] and it is also difficult to qualify them as the effects of God's efficient causality. He solved

---

111. Boethius claims that "ipsum esse nondum est" in the first of his metaphysical axioms. *Quomodo*, II, 28–29.

112. *Quomodo*, 140–50: "Igitur sublato ab his bono primo mente et cogitatione, ista licet essent bona, tamen in eo quod essent bona esse non possent, et quoniam actu non potuere exsistere, nisi illud ea quod vere bonum est produxisset, idcirco et esse eorum bonum est et non est simile substantiali bono id quod ab eo fluxit; et nisi ab eo fluxissent, licet essent bona, tamen in eo quod sunt bona esse non possent, quoniam et praeter bonum

that problem by using emanationist language, rather than Aristotelian terminology, in order to explain how things' existences come to be:

> Thus, since their existence flowed from the will of the good (*a boni voluntate*), they are called good. (119–21)

Using emanationist language to characterize creation, however, is also problematic. For it can imply that those things which emanate from God are consubstantial with Him and this is something which Boethius denies. Hence, emanationist language requires certain clear provisos if one wants to claim (as Boethius does) that emanations differ substantially from that which causes them to be. Thus, Boethius qualifies his claim that contingent things' existences flow from God by adding that they "flowed from the will of the good," rather than from God Himself.

Boethius's way of defining the creation of contingent things' existences gives us the key with which to understand what the clause "in God" means. For like the clause "from the will of the good" it is a clause which qualifies God's emanation of *ipsum esse*.[113] If this so, then the claim that *ipsum esse* is good because it is "in God" must be comparable to his claim that things' existences are good because they "flowed from the will of the good" (120). Like the analogous proviso "from the will of the good," as such, the clause "in God" must show why Boethius holds that things' indeterminate essence is good in virtue of its emanating from God. If this is so, then contrasting these two provisos must show why *ipsum esse* specifically is good in virtue of its being efficiently caused by God.

Now, we saw that Boethius claims that things' existences are good because they are willed by God, and what we took this to mean is that the act of causal efficiency whereby things' existences are produced makes them good because things' existences are the objects of God's free act of desire to create: the terms of God's desire to create. If this is so, then *ipsum esse omnium rerum* cannot be good because it is the object of God's free act of will to create. *Ipsum esse omnium rerum* is not an existing thing. It is not a 'final product.' *Ipsum esse omnium rerum* is what becomes actualized in existing things. Thus, Boethius does not claim that it is good because it "flows from" God's will. Rather, he claims that it is good because it is "in God," and what he means by that

---

et non ex bono essent, cum illud ipsum bonum primum [est] et ipsum esse sit et ipsum bonum et ipsum esse bonum."

113. The problem here is determining the nature of God's ideas of creation. It will be problematic for Aquinas just as it is for Boethius. We will deal with this point in the next chapter.

is that it is good because it is efficiently caused by God but does not exist in its own right. That is, he means that *ipsum esse* is good because it is something which God made, and through which He creates particular existing things.

Boethius, however, seems to mean more by the clause "in Him" than this. Were he not to, *ipsum esse* would only be good by extrinsic denomination, and this is contrary to both his premises, and contradictory. More importantly, were it the only meaning of the clause, the passage would make no sense. For the clause is part of a comparison: God is substantially Good because His substance is the Good, whereas *ipsum esse* is good because it is "in God."

Now, if Boethius's comparison between God's goodness and *ipsum esse*'s goodness is to work, the clause "in Him" must tell us why *ipsum esse* is intrinsically good, and it must define that cause intrinsically. For Boethius claims that God is intrinsically good and defines the cause of God's goodness intrinsically:

> But the indeterminate essence of all things flowed from Him who is the first good, and who is good in such a way that He is rightly said to be good in virtue of His substance. (124–26)

The intrinsic cause of *ipsum esse*'s goodness cannot be God Himself. For if God were the intrinsic cause of *ipsum esse*'s goodness, then *ipsum esse* would have to be God, which Boethius vehemently denies. Nor can the intrinsic cause of things' goodness be God *qua* the efficient cause of *ipsum esse*. For God is the extrinsic cause of *ipsum esse*'s goodness. What is left, it seems then, is exemplarity. For if something's goodness has an intrinsic cause — as it would seem *ipsum esse*'s must — and if that intrinsic cause is related to an extrinsic cause — as the intrinsic cause of *ipsum esse*'s goodness must be since *ipsum esse* is created — and if the relation between the intrinsic and extrinsic causes is not one of identity — as the intrinsic cause of *ipsum esse*'s goodness cannot be, else it would be God — then that relation must be one of likeness or difference. But the difference between *ipsum esse* and God cannot be the cause of *ipsum esse*'s goodness. For since God is the Good, what is different from Him cannot be good insofar as it is different from Him. Hence we are left with likeness. If this is so, however, then Boethius's point would seem to be that *ipsum esse* is good because it is similar to God. As such, the clause "in Him" must also mean "like Him." The second cause of *ipsum esse*'s goodness must therefore be exemplarity.

If we are right, our analysis of the clause "in Him" shows that *ipsum esse* is good because it is both created by the Good because it is like Him in some way. Hence, the causes of its goodness are similar to those which Boethius adduces for the goodness of things' existences. For he claims that they too are good because they are created by God, and are like God.

Objections

It may be objected that our interpretation is mistaken. For although Boethius's emanationist language can be interpreted as meaning that things are created by God, our claim that Boethius also calls upon exemplarity to explain why contingent things are good is not substantiated in the text. Boethius never claims that contingent things' existences or *ipsum esse* are like God. Hence, although one can accept that Boethius adduces an extrinsic cause of things' goodness, he does not show that that goodness has an intrinsic cause.

Now, it is true that Boethius never uses *'similis,'* or some variant of it, when he defines the causes of created things' goodness. Nor does he formulate an explicit doctrine of exemplarity. But in the second section of his *exitus,* Boethius does make clear the reason why he does not use the term *'similis.'* He states that nothing can be 'like' God other than God Himself:

> But if their indeterminate essence is good, then there is no doubt that since they are substantial goods, they must be like the first good. And for this very reason they would have to be the first good; for there is nothing like Him other than Himself. Therefore, all existing things are God, and this is an impious assertion. (75–80)[114]

The point here is, as such, negative: the fact that Boethius does not use terms such as *'similis'* or its variants when he defines the cause of created things' goodness must not be taken as proof of the fact that he does not believe things to be similar to God. His reticence is also in line with the problem his work sets out to solve: that things are substantially good without being God. For in the *Quomodo* he wants to distinguish Divine Goodness from the goodness of created things, and when one wants to distinguish things, he does not concentrate on their likenesses.

The fact that Boethius is reticent in his use of the word *'similis'* also justifies the fact that he does not formulate an explicit doctrine of exemplarity. One cannot very well formulate a doctrine of exemplarity without claiming that God is an Exemplar, or that things are like Him.

---

114. To compare two things, they must have something in common: some middle term. Thus the very attempt to compare God's goodness and the created good implies that they have something in common. That they have something in common might be construed as implying that created goodness is Divine goodness. And it is precisely this point that Boethius is trying to avoid.

If this is so, then just as the fact that he does not use the word *'similis'* is not an indication of the fact that he does not believe things to be like God, then so too must the fact that he does not formulate an explicit doctrine of exemplarity in his account of the cause of things' goodness not be taken as proof of the fact that he does not use exemplarity to explain why things are good.

There is also a positive point to be made in favor of our interpretation. For when Boethius explains why things' existences and *ipsum esse* are good, he asserts that one of these causes is God's own goodness:

> Thus, since their existence flowed from the will of the good, they are called good. (119–21)

> But the indeterminate essence of all things flowed from Him who is the first good... their own indeterminate essence must therefore be good. (124–27)

Now, the fact that Boethius explicitly claims that one of the causes of created things' goodness is God's own goodness would seem to be very good grounds for the argument that he does use a doctrine of exemplarity. For there is very little else that such a claim can be interpreted to mean, as we saw above.

Moreover, as can be seen from his claim that God is good, Boethius is aware of the consequences of not claiming that God's goodness is a cause of creation's goodness and that goodness is merely a real relation. The claim implies that God is not Good. But if one accepts that goodness cannot merely be a real relation, he must also accept that the cause of contingent things' goodness cannot merely be a real relation. As such, exemplarity must also play a role in things' goodness.

Things' Substantial Goodness

In his solution thus far Boethius has shown that (1) things' existences are good because they are willed by the Good and are in some way like Him, and (2) that their indeterminate essence is good because it is efficiently caused by God and like Him. This is the crux of his definition of the cause of contingent things' substantial goodness. For if things' existences are good, then things themselves must be good; if their indeterminate essence is good, on the other hand, they must be substantially good. This is, of course, half of the problem he is attempting to solve. The other half is distinguishing God from contingent things. But he has done this too. For if both things' existences and their essences are efficiently caused by God, they must be other than God. God cannot be his own efficient cause. Hence, the problem would seem to be solved. Boethius himself tells us that it is:

> Thereby the problem is solved. For although things are good in virtue of their substances, they are not like the first good thereby, not simply because they are not necessarily things whose indeterminate essence is good, but also because it could not be the indeterminate essence of all things unless it flowed from the first being, that is from the good; therefore although the indeterminate essence of all things is good, it is not similar to Him from whom it comes to be. He is necessarily good insofar as He is substantially good; for He is nothing other than good. But if it [the former] were not to exist through Him it could perhaps be good, but it could not be substantially good. For in that case it could perhaps participate in the good; but since they would not have had their indeterminate essence from the good, they could not possess this goodness.[115]

There is, however, one last matter to clarify. For although Boethius has shown that things' existences are good and that their indeterminate essence is good, he has not really shown that things are substantially good: that they are good in virtue of their essences. This is the main point with which Boethius deals in this passage, where he explains how *ipsum esse* is actualized in particular good things and hence why things are good in virtue of their essences. There is, however, a secondary point in the passage. It regards *ipsum esse*'s goodness and how it differs from God's.

To begin with *ipsum esse*'s goodness, Boethius not only corroborates that it is not God's — he tells us that it is not unconditionally good, while God is — and hence indicate that *ipsum esse* is efficiently caused by God. More importantly, he makes his repugnance for comparing contingent things' goodness and divine goodness explicit. For the passage indicates that Boethius considers similarity with the First Good to mean ontological similarity. That is, if he claims that things' goodness is not similar to the First Good's because it is not unconditionally good, by the converse he must consider something to be similar

---

115. *Quomodo*, 128–40: "Qua in re soluta quaestio est. Idcirco enim licet in eo quod sint bona sint, non sunt tamen similia primo bono, quoniam non quoquo modo sint res ipsum esse earum bonum est, sed quoniam non potest esse ipsum esse rerum, nisi a primo esse defluxerit, id est bono; idcirco ipsum esse bonum est nec est simile ei a quo est. Illud enim quoquo modo sit bonum est in eo quod est; non enim aliud est praeterquam bonum. Hoc autem nisi ab illo esset, bonum fortasse esse posset, sed bonum in eo quod est esse non posset. Tunc enim participaret forsitan bono; ipsum vero esse quod non haberent a bono, bonum habere non possent."

to God if its being is unconditional. This explains why he is so reticent to formulate an explicit doctrine of exemplarity or openly to claim that God's goodness is a cause of creation's goodness.

With both of these points in mind, we can confirm our own interpretation of Boethius' explanation of *ipsum esse*'s goodness. Like the goodness of things' existence, it has a double cause: its being efficiently caused by God, and its being efficiently caused by God insofar as He is the Good. If the first cause of its goodness is an act of causal efficiency, the second is exemplarity. What one must understand by exemplarity, however, is that it does not entail that things which are like God have a mode of being similar to God's. God's goodness is transcendent, and contingent things' goodness is not.

This brings us to the main point of the passage: that things are substantially good because they are actualizations of their good essence (*ipsum esse*). The point has two provisos. For Boethius claims that things can actualize their good essence (*ipsum esse*): (1) if their existences are efficiently caused by God, and (2) if their essence is caused by God.

Boethius makes his main point in the first lines of the passage:

Things are good in virtue of their substances. (129)

He states the first proviso in the last lines of the passage, where he claims that if things had not received their essences from God their goodness would be only accidental:

For in that case it could perhaps participate in the good; but since they would not have had their indeterminate essence from the good, they could not possess this goodness. (138–40)

And he states the second proviso in the central lines of the passage, where he claims that *ipsum esse:*

Could not be the indeterminate essence of all things unless it flowed from the first being, that is from the good. (131–33)

The reason for the provisos is that Boethius considers a complex thing's actualization of its essence a real relation between that thing and its essence, and he considers its real relation with its essence to be contingent upon that real relation between the thing and God which bestows existence upon it. Boethius makes the latter point in the central lines of his solution. For if he claims that things would not be substantially good if they were not efficiently caused by God — if things "were not to exist through Him they could perhaps be good, but they would not be substantially good" (136–38) — by the converse we have that a thing can be substantially good if its existence does derive from God.[116]

But something is substantially good because its good essence is actualized in it,[117] and its good essence is actualized in it if it has a real relation with that essence. For, as the third section of Boethius's *exitus* showed, a thing cannot be identical to its essence, or the cause of its actualizing that essence. But if something actualizes its essence, is not identical to that essence, and cannot be the cause of its actualizing that essence, then its actualization of that essence must be a real relation with that essence. (The point here is actually an extension of the distinction Boethius draws between the essence and existence of complex things.) As such, a thing can be good in virtue of its essence (*ipsum esse*) if its essence (*ipsum esse*) is good and if it is an actualization (or determination) of its essence (*ipsum esse*): if it has a real relation with its essence. The presupposition of a given thing's being an actualization or determination of its essence (*ipsum esse*), however, is its being efficiently caused by God, or having a real relation with God.

There are therefore three causes of the goodness of complex things. (1) Basically, things are substantially good because they actuate their essences. (2) In order for their actuating their essences to make them substantially good, however, their essences must be good. Thus Boethius tells us that *ipsum esse omnium rerum* is good because it is caused by God and is in some sense like Him. (3) In order for contingent things to be able to actuate their essences (*ipsum esse*) their existences must be efficiently caused by God. For Boethius claims that contingent things can only have real relations with their essences if they have real relations with God.

Boethius's recapitulation of his argument in the lines that follow corroborates our interpretation of his solution:

> Therefore, if the first good is removed from these things by a mind and thought, these things, though they might be good, could not be good in virtue of their essences, and since they could not actually have existed unless that which is truly good had produced them, their existence is as such good. And yet that which has derived from the substantial good is not like its source; and unless

---

116. Boethius actually made this point in the third part of his *exitus* where he pointed out that if we abstract from God, there is no accounting for complex things' existences, since they cannot be caused by their essences.

117. This point is actually the converse of the third part of Boethius's *exitus* where he claims that things' essences and existences would be completely distinct if one were to abstract from God. For the converse of that affirmation is that things' essences and their existences are not completely distinct if one does not abstract from God, or alternatively, that the relation between things' essences and their existences is contingent upon God.

they had derived from it they could not be good in virtue of their essence since they would be both apart from the good and not derived from it, while that very first good is existence itself and good itself, and good existence itself. (140–50)[118]

His first point is a negative confirmation: if there were no God, things could not be good in virtue of their essences: "if the first good is removed from these things by a mind and thought, these things, though they might be good, could not be good in virtue of their essences" (140–42). For things must be efficiently caused by God in order to be able to actuate *ipsum esse*. His second point is a confirmation of the real relation at the root of things' existences. He claims that had God not created them, they could not have existed: "they could not actually have existed unless that which is truly good had produced them" (143–44). Since He did, however, their existences must be good: "their existence is as such good" (144–45).

The heart of the matter, however, lies in the final sentence. For in it Boethius specifies that unless things derived from God, they could not be good in virtue of their substances because in that case "they would be both apart from the good and not derived from it" (148–49). What I take this obscure phrase to mean is that if things' existences were not efficiently caused by God, they could not actualize their own essences. For since this phrase is the explication of reasons for which a thing which does not exist in virtue of God's will cannot be good in virtue of its essence, the obverse must be an explication of the reasons for which those things which are created by God can be good in virtue of their essences. But the obverse of "they would be both apart from the good and not derived from it" is that for those things whose existences are efficiently caused by God the good is not apart from them, and they do derive from it. The question is, then, what is that 'good' from which things must not be apart and from which they must derive?

The answer to these question lies in the first passage we quoted above (128–40), where Boethius tells us that things are good in virtue of their essence: *ipsum esse*. For if things are good in virtue of their essence — *ipsum esse* — the good from which they must not be apart is their own essence. The fact of the matter is, however, that contingent things

---

118. *Quomodo*, 140–50: "Igitur sublato ab his bono primo mente et cogitatione, ista licet essent bona, tamen in eo quod essent bona esse non possent, et quoniam actu non potuere exsistere, nisi illud ea quod vere bonum est produxisset, idcirco et esse eorum bonum est et non est simile substantiali bono id quod ab eo fluxit; et nisi ab eo fluxissent, licet essent bona, tamen in eo quod sunt bona esse non possent, quoniam et praeter bonum et non ex bono essent, cum illud ipsum bonum primum [est] et ipsum esse sit et ipsum bonum et ipsum esse bonum."

cannot actualize their good essence (*ipsum esse*) unless their existences are efficiently caused by God. What this means, as such, is that the good from which contingent things must derive in order to be substantially good is both their essence (*ipsum esse*) and God.

What we have, then, is that things are substantially good: (1) if their existences are efficiently caused by God, and (2) formally caused by their essences: if they are not apart from their essences. But if a thing's existence is not apart from its essence, it must actualize its essence: it must have a real relation with it. If an essence cannot be the cause of existence, as we have seen countless times, but is nonetheless both actualized in an existing thing, it must be actualized in an existing thing by something other than itself. As such, if things do indeed actualize their essences, they must do so because they have a real relation with God. Thus, their goodness can derive from their essences if they are created by God.

The point here is that things' substantial goodness is contingent upon two real relations and an act of efficient causality: (1) the real relation between things and God, whereby God bestows existence upon things; (2) God's having produced *ipsum esse*; (3) the real relation between things' existences and *ipsum esse* whereby things actuate *ipsum esse*, and *ipsum esse* becomes their formal cause.

Objections

The last part of Boethius's *exitus* deals with two objections. Both concern exemplarity. For since Boethius has not explicitly called upon a doctrine of exemplarity to explain why things are substantially good, one could assume that he claims that things are substantially good only because God wills their existences: that is, after all, the only cause which he does explicitly call upon to account for their goodness.[119] Boethius's first objection specifies that he does use exemplarity to explain why things are good. The second objection, on the other hand, delimits the scope of exemplarity.

Exemplarity

If things were substantially good merely because God wills them to be, then all of their properties — including the accidental ones — would

---

119. There are many varied interpretations of the point of this last section of the *Quomodo*. Aquinas, for instance, identifies it for what it is: a series of two objections. Cf. *In de Hebdomadibus*, V. Chadwick, on the other hand, seems to think that the last section is essentially unrelated to the main body of the text. Cf. Chadwick, *Consolations*, p. 207: "Boethius ends the tractate by some incomplete, exploratory aphorisms about the relation of created existences to their divine Creator."

have to be substantial. For God willed them all. But, Boethius points out, this is absurd. Hence things cannot be good simply because they are willed by God. Rather, he claims, they are good because they are willed by a Good God:

> But will not those things which are white also have to be white in virtue of their substances' being white, since they have flowed from the will of God in order to be white? Not at all. For existing is one thing, and being white is another. And the reason for that is that He who produced them in order for them to exist is indeed good, but is certainly not white. It is therefore in accordance with the will of the good that they should be good in virtue of their substances; but it is not in accordance with the will of Him who is not white, that it should be white in virtue of its substance. Nor did they flow from the will of a white thing. Therefore, they are white simply because one was not white willed them to be white; but it is also true that since He who willed them to be good who was good, they are good in virtue of their substance.[120]

In the contrast here Boethius finally makes explicit the fact that he considers exemplarity to be a cause of things' goodness. Were things to be good simply because God wills them to be good, one could claim that things are white simply because God wills them to be. But whiteness and goodness are clearly different kinds of properties. Whiteness is more often than not an accidental property of things — white skin becomes tan, white cups can be painted, and so forth — and Boethius himself claims as much: "For existing is one thing, and being white is another" (153–54). Goodness, on the other hand, is not an accidental property. For things are good in "virtue of their substances" (163). Boethius's response thus distinguishes things' accidental properties from their substantial ones, and makes God's own Being the cause of the difference between them. "And the reason for that is that He who produced them in order for them to exist is indeed good, but is certainly not white" (154–55). His claim is that it is God's own being that determines which contingent properties are substantial and which are accidental. Thus, since God is not white, whiteness is not one of

---

120. *Quomodo*, 150–62: "At non etiam alba in eo quod sunt alba esse oportebit ea quae alba sunt, quoniam ex voluntate dei fluxerunt ut essent alba? Minime. Aliud est enim esse, aliud albis esse; hoc ideo, quoniam qui ea ut essent effecit bonus quidem est, minime vero albus. Voluntatem igitur boni comitatum est ut essent bona in eo quod sunt; voluntatem vero non albi non est comitata talis eius quod est proprietas ut esset album in eo quod est; neque enim ex albi voluntate defluxerunt. Itaque quia voluit esse ea alba qui erat non albus, sunt alba tantum; quia vero voluit ea esse bona qui erat bonus, sunt bona in eo quod sunt."

created things' substantial properties. But since God is good, goodness is one of created things' substantial properties.

There is a second point here. For whiteness is not a universal property of being. God is not white, nor are tomatoes, or tigers. "He who produced them in order for them to exist is indeed good, but is certainly not white" (154–55). Goodness, on the other hand, is a universal property of being, as Boethius's opening syllogism points out. As such, the causes of things' whiteness and their goodness — of their particular properties and their universal properties — must differ. Thus, if things' particular properties can and do stem from God's will alone, things' universal properties cannot stem from God's will alone.

Boethius's objection, as such, has two points: (1) the good is a substantial property of contingent things because it is a substantial property of God's Being; and (2) that all of those properties which are not God's substantial properties cannot be substantial properties of contingent things.

The first point clearly offers a confirmation of the fact that Boethius does use exemplarity to define the cause of things' goodness. For he expressly states that things are substantially good because God is. "It is therefore in accordance with the will of the good that they should be good in virtue of their substances" (155–57). His point also shows that he does not believe the good simply to be a real relation. The fact that he feels that it is necessary to specify that goodness is a substantial property of things because it is a substantial property of God's, although he has already made this point implicitly, shows that he is more than aware of the difficulties that emerge when one claims that the good is merely a real relation, and that he is attempting to obviate those difficulties. For if the good were just a real relation, as he claims whiteness is, God would not be good — just as he claims that God is not white. The argument implies that those properties which are merely real relations are merely real relations because God does not have them; and they are accidental properties precisely because God does not have them. By the converse, then, those properties which are substantial cannot be just real relations, precisely because God does have them.

The second point seems problematic. For if the only substantial properties which created things can have are those properties which God Himself has, then humanity cannot be a substantial property of human beings. God is definitely not human. Hence, Boethius's point would seem to be a bit extreme. This would be true if it were not for the fact that Boethius's work does not deal with particular types of created things, or particular contingent essences and their relations to particular existences. Rather, he is attempting to understand why all created things have a universal property, or what the mediaevals would call a transcendental property: goodness. That is why he explains how *ipsum esse,* or the indeterminate essence of all created things, can be good, but he never attempts to explain why humanity, dogginess or mammals are good. For were specific genera to be the cause of things' substantial goodness, 'good' would be an equivocal term. This clearly means that Boethius's work does not deal with the particular substantial properties of particular types of created beings. If this is so, however, then when Boethius does make God's own Being what distinguishes things' accidental properties from their substantial ones, the substantial properties he has in mind are not particular substantial properties such as humanity, dogginess, or treehood. The properties which he has in mind are those substantial properties which all beings have: transcendental properties. His point, then, is not that no being can have a substantial property which God does not have, or that those substantial properties which all creatures have must be substantial properties of being as such. It is not that the only substantial properties in contingent things are those which God has. His point is that the substantial properties of all beings — transcendental properties — are such because they are properties of God's own Being. The reason for this is that contingent being as such is similar to God, but the specific and determinate forms of being are not similar to God insofar as they are specific and determinate forms of being, precisely because they are specific and determinate forms of being, whereas God is Being itself purely and simply.

Justice vs. Goodness

Boethius's closing remark in *Quomodo Substantiae* regards justice. If all created things are good in virtue of their essences, are not all things just in virtue of their essences? His response is that they are not:

> According to this reasoning, then, ought not all things be just, since He who willed them is justice itself? This is not so either. For being good refers to essence, being just, to action. But in Him being and acting are the same: and therefore being good is the same as being just. But for us being is not the same as acting: we are not simple. Therefore being good is not the same for us as being just, but being is the same for all of us in virtue of our essence. Therefore all things are good, but not also just. Moreover, good is a genus, but just is a species, and this species does not apply to all. Therefore some things are just, others are something else, but all things are good.[121]

---

121. *Quomodo,* 162–74: "Secundum hanc igitur rationem cuncta oportet esse iusta,

His object here is (1) to issue a precaution to those who would make exemplarity the sole cause of things' goodness, and (2) to make a distinction in contingent things' goodness.

The first point is a Boethian parry to a possible objection to his implicit doctrine of exemplarity. For if the good is a substantial property of all things because it is one of God's properties, then it seems to follow that all of God's properties have to be substantial properties of all things. *Omne agens agit sibi simile.* As such, it might seem to follow that created things are like God in all respects. But this is not the case. For some of God's properties pertain to His simplicity: to the fact that His Essence is His Existence. "But in Him being and acting are the same: and therefore being good is the same as being just" (167–68).[122] And these are not properties that He can communicate to His creatures, because they are not simple: their essences are not their existences. "But for us being is not the same as acting: we are not simple" (168–69). God is, for instance, substantially just, but created things are not.

There are two conclusions to be drawn here: (1) that exemplarity does not entail the identity of God and creation; and (2) although exemplarity is a cause of things' goodness it cannot be the only one. As for the first conclusion, which is the more important one, it is one with which Boethius qualifies God's exemplarity: a doctrine of exemplarity must allow for the ontological distinction between God and creation. This is a point that Boethius has already implicitly made,[123] and it is a problematic point. For since God's Being is His acting, it might seem to follow that his creatures are His Being, because his creating is His Being. That this is not so can be seen from the fact that creation does not have all of the properties God does, and that it does not have those properties which it does share with God in the same way in which God has them. God is simple, and creatures are not; God's goodness is justice, but creatures' goodness is not. Hence the fact that the modalities of God's goodness and creatures goodness differ — "Moreover, good is a genus, but just is a species, and this species does not apply to all"

---

quoniam ipse iustus est qui ea esse voluit? Ne hoc quidem. Nam bonum esse essentiam iustum vero esse actum respicit. Idem autem est in eo esse quod agere; idem igitur bonum esse quod iustum. Nobis vero non est idem esse quod agere; non enim simplices sumus. Non est igitur nobis idem bonis esse quod iustis, sed idem nobis esse omnibus in eo quod sumus. Bona igitur omnia sunt, non etiam iusta. Amplius bonum quidem generale est, iustum vero speciale nec species descendit in omnia. Idcirco alia quidem iusta alia aliud omnia bona."

122. This is a point which Boethius makes in his axioms. Cf. *Quomodo*, VII, 45–46: "Omne simplex esse suum et id quod est unum habet."

123. It is the explicit reason why he claims that things cannot be similar to God. Cf. *Quomodo*, 128–35: "Idcirco enim licet in eo quod sint bona sint, non sunt tamen similia primo bono, quoniam non quoquo modo sint res ipsum esse earum bonum est... [sed] illud enim quoquo modo sit bonum est in eo quod est."

(168–69) — demonstrates that exemplarity does not entail the identity of God and creation, as does the fact that God has properties which creatures do not — God is simple and creatures are not (167–69). The converse is also true. For the ontological distinction between God and creation implies that the modalities of God's goodness and creation's goodness must differ.

The second conclusion is a corollary of the first one. For if the modalities of God's and creatures' common properties differ, then there must be an ontological difference between God and creation. This difference is that God is simple but creatures are not. But the fact that creatures are not simple proves that they cannot be the cause of their own existences, as we saw in the third and fourth sections of the *exitus*. If this is so, then they cannot have the properties they do simply because they are the properties of being as such. Hence, composite things cannot be good simply because goodness is a property of being. This means that they cannot be good simply because God is their exemplary cause. For they do not exist because God is their exemplary cause. They exist because God is their efficient cause. As such, they must also be good because God is their efficient cause.

The second point of the passage, which is given in passing, is that things' own goodness is in some sense also acquired after their creation: for goodness is also something which refers to things' activities. This would seem to be a closing nod at created things' *reditus*.

The Good in the *Quomodo Substantiae*

Having seen the solution to the problem of the good, what is one to make of it? Why are things substantially good? Boethius's answer has three principal parts. Firstly, it claims that things' existences are good because they are willed by God and like God, although this does not mean that their goodness is unconditional, or like God's in all ways. Secondly, it claims that things' indeterminate essence (*ipsum esse*) is good because it is created by God and like Him, in some way, although again it is not unconditionally good. Thirdly — and primarily — it claims that particular things are substantially good because they actuate the indeterminate essence of all created things: because they have real relations with *ipsum esse*. This third point has a proviso. Boethius specifies that things can actualize *ipsum esse* if and only if they are created by God. For it is in virtue of God's creating something that it "derives from the good" and is not "apart" from it. There is, of course, also a fourth point: that things' can be good in virtue of their actions, just.

Now, leaving the fourth point aside — for it is indeed an aside — the heart of the complex solution is the third point, and it is a synthesis of the two definitions of the good with which Boethius introduced his problem in his opening syllogism: namely, a relational definition and a substantial one. For the third point makes two real relations and complex things' essences the cause of their goodness. Boethius shows that complex things must have a real relation with *ipsum esse* in order to be substantially good—for it is through that real relation that they actualize their good indeterminate essence. But things' real relations with *ipsum esse* are contingent upon their having real relations with God. For it is through their real relations with God that they exist. This clearly means that the cause of things' substantial goodness includes both a real relation and their substances, just as Boethius's opening syllogism requires. As the second part of his *exitus* requires, then, the real relation is the cause of created things' existences, and their being substantially good does not entail either that their essence is the cause of their existence or that their essence is God's own. Hence Boethius's solution satisfies the conditions he outlined in the first two parts of his argument.

This main part of the solution has two subordinate points. For Boethius also claims that *ipsum esse* and things' existences *per se* are good. These subordinate points are clearly an integral part of Boethius's argument. For he could not very well prove that things are substantially good—good, that is, in virtue of their substances—without proving that things' substances are good. Moreover, they show that Boethius holds that the good is a transcendental property of being.

As for his definition of *ipsum esse*'s and created things' existences goodness, Boethius shows that it is not merely a logical relation to the Good, as Geiger claims, or that its cause is not simply that they are willed by God, as Aquinas claims. Rather, he claims that they are intrinsically good because God is their exemplary cause as well as being their efficient cause. This can be inferred from the fourth part of his argument, but is almost explicit in the last part, where Boethius seems to overcome his reluctance and explicitly shows that he believes exemplarity to be a cause of created things' goodness.

As for the good's being a transcendental property of being, it follows from the fact that Boethius holds that *ipsum esse* and things' existences are good. For if he holds that *ipsum esse* and existence *per se* are good, then he must also hold that goodness is a property of all things: those which exist in the proper sense of the word (particular things and God) and those which do not (*ipsum esse* and things' existences *per se*), those which are created (particular things, *ipsum esse*, and things' existences) and those which are not created (God). But if goodness is a property of all things, then it must be a property of being as such. The fact that goodness is a transcendental property of being, in his view, stems from the fact that it is one of God's substantial properties. We saw this in the last part of his argument, where he claims that goodness can be a "substantial" property of being because it is one of God's properties. His point is that created being is intrinsically good because it is like God. This point is very important. For it is what allows Boethius to solve the problem of the one and the many, since it furnishes a common transcendent cause for the goodness of all things: a One which is the cause of the many.

The fact that the good is a transcendental property of being, however, does not imply that all things are substantially good. For Boethius distinguishes the good *qua* transcendental property of being from things' substantial goodness. He does not claim that either things' existences *per se* or *ipsum esse* are substantially good, although he claims that both are *per se* good. Rather, his claim is that only actually existing things which have good existences and which actuate their good essences are substantially good.

This distinction is important for our purposes: it shows that Boethius distinguishes the goodness of existing things' *components* from things' actual goodness. This clearly means that he does distinguish things' essences from their existences, and things' existences *per se* from their actual existences. It also shows why he held that things' substantial goodness requires two real relations. For if things' existences *per se* are only transcendentally good, then actual things' substantial goodness must require more than just that real relation between things and God, whereby existence *per se* is bestowed upon them. It must require a second real relation: one which things have with *ipsum esse*. The same thing holds for *ipsum esse*. As such, things must have two real relations in order to be substantially good.

The distinction, however, also shows that Boethius simply cannot have held that existing things are substantially good simply because they are willed by God. For although one could argue (perhaps) that he holds that things are transcendentally good because they are willed by God, the fact that they are transcendentally good does not prove that they are substantially so for Boethius. The distinction confirms our interpretation of Boethius's argument.

Chapter 12

THE *CONSOLATIO PHILOSOPHIAE*

The *Consolatio* is at once a simpler work than the *Quomodo* and one which is far more complex. It is a simpler work, because Boethius does not force his interpreters to furnish the reasoning which justifies the various points he makes in it, as he does in the *Quomodo*.[1] The *Consolatio* is not pithy. Its complexity, on the other hand, derives from its manifold object. For unlike the *Quomodo*, whose sole point is to explain why things are substantially good, the *Consolatio* deals with a number of different topics: the nature of man's happiness, the nature of divine intelligence,[2] the necessity of future contingents,[3] the causes and nature of evil,[4] the difference between chance and providence,[5] and so forth.

The variety of its topics is what makes the *Consolatio* the rich work it is. But it is also what makes determining Boethius's position on any one of the topics which he discusses in the work difficult. For although none of the *Consolatio*'s claims on any topic is *per se* ambiguous, the overall scheme of the work has been taken to be. And this would seem to make for some ambiguity with regards to the claims themselves, and consequently to Boethius's treatment of his topics. For a work's object determines the import of its claims. This point clearly has bearing on our work. For our intent is to outline the *Consolatio*'s doctrine of the good, insofar as it is the key to determining Boethius's doctrine of participation.

There would seem to be two basic ways in which to interpret the *Consolatio*'s claims. One can hold that: (1) they are not related to a

---

1. In the *Quomodo* Boethius openly claims that he "relies" upon his readers' intelligence to furnish the arguments for his points. Cf. *Quomodo*, 53–55: "Sufficiunt igitur quae praemisimus; a prudente vero rationis interprete suis unumquodque aptabitur argumentis." In the *Consolatio*, on the other hand, he does no such thing.
2. *Consolatio*, V, 5–6.
3. *Consolatio*, V, 3–4.
4. Cf. e.g., *Consolatio*, I, 4 and *Consolatio* IV, 1–6.
5. Cf. e.g., *Consolatio*, V, 1, 23–24: "Quis enim coercente in ordinem cuncta deo locus esse ullus temeritati reliquus potest? Nam nihil ex nihilo exsistere vera sententia est cui nemo umquam veterum refragatus est, quamquam illi non de operante principio, sed de materiali subiecto hoc omnium de natura rationum quasi quoddam iecerint fundamentum."

single basic point, which is the object of the work as a whole; or (2) that they are related to a single point, which is the object of the work as a whole. On the prior position, one must hold that the *Consolatio* is a *pastiche* of unrelated arguments, and consequently that none of its arguments can complement another. Now, if this were so, then the only thing that one would need to do in order to determine Boethius's position on any one of the topics which he discusses in the *Consolatio* is to analyze the argument which he presents on that topic. Thus, to understand what he means by chance one would only need to analyze the second chapter of the fifth book of the *Consolatio,* where Boethius deals with the matter specifically. Since each of the *Consolatio*'s arguments is rather clear, then, determining Boethius's position on any one of the topics he discusses in the work would not seem to be problematic at all.

If one believes the *Consolatio* as a whole to have a coherent point, on the other hand, the picture changes. For in this latter case determining Boethius's position on any one of the topics which he discusses in the work — such as his view on chance — would not only entail understanding his specific treatment of that topic. It would also entail understanding how that topic is related to the work's primary object, and how his various points on other topics are related to it. Hence, in order to understand what Boethius means by chance, would not just require understanding how he deals with the matter in the second chapter of the fifth book of the *Consolatio,* but also what chance has to do with both the *Consolatio*'s main point and, say, the second book's allegory of fortune. For if the *Consolatio*'s various points are related, then to draw one's interpretation of Boethius's treatment of a specific topic from one of the points he makes with regards to that topic to the exclusion of others, is clearly to draw an interpretation from an insufficient source. In this second case, as such, one must determine both the *Consolatio*'s object and the relations between its various claims in order to delineate Boethius's position on any one of the topics he does discuss in the work.

Which of these two methods should one use, then? The question here is rhetorical. For the premise of the former of these methods would seem to be faulty. The simple fact of the matter is that since Boethius deals with each of his topics in different places throughout the *Consolatio,*[6]

---

6. Boethius's technical discussion of chance, for example, is in the *Consolatio*'s fifth book (V, 2), but he introduces the topic in the first book (I, 6) where Lady Philosophy explicitly asks Boethius whether he believes the universe to be governed by chance or by God; this contrast is then drawn out in his allegory of fortune in the second book, and so forth; his technical discussion of the relation between freedom and predetermination

the work cannot be a *pastiche* of unrelated arguments. Modern scholarship tends to agree with this point.[7] This clearly also means that one cannot determine Boethius's position on any one of the topics which he discusses in the *Consolatio* simply by analyzing one of his claims with regards to that topic.[8]

The fact that *Consolatio*'s object plays a role in the meaning of its many arguments is one of the causes of the many different interpretations that one can find of the work. For the specific point of the *Consolatio* as a whole is a matter of dispute.[9] The natural con-

---

is again to be found in the fifth book (V, 3), but he introduces the problem in the first book (I, 5m) where he points out that the entire universe is guided by God's laws with the exception of man; the problem of evil emerges in the first book (I, 4) but is clearly the source of Boethius's discussion of freedom and predetermination, for if there were no freedom, God would be the cause of evil (IV, 1).

7. Cf. H. F. Steward and E. K. Rand, introduction to the Boethius, *The Theological Tractates and the Consolation of Philosophy*, p. xii: "The *Consolatio* is not, as has been maintained, a mere patchwork of translations from Aristotle and the Neoplatonists. Rather it is the supreme essay of one who throughout his life had found his highest solace in the dry light of reason. His chief source of refreshment, in the dungeon to which his beloved library had not accompanied him, was a memory well stocked with the poetry and thought of former days. The development of the argument is anything but Neoplatonic; it is all his own." See also Varvis, pp. 25 ff.

The point here is connected with the debate regarding the Christianity of the *Consolatio*, as Colin Starnes points out. Cf. Colin J. Starnes, "Boethius and the Development of Christian Humanism: the Theology of the *Consolatio*," in *Congresso Internazionale di Studi Boeziani*, p. 27: "The history of its interpretation falls into two periods. First throughout the Middle Ages, the *Consolation* was generally, though not universally, regarded as a thoroughly Christian work.... In modern times, on the other hand, from the Renaissance to the present, the contrary view has prevailed." The difference between the early interpretations of the *Consolatio* and the modern ones, Starnes points out then, is that the latter are 'literal,' whereas the former are 'spiritual' readings of the work. For he claims that a literal reading of the text elicits a pagan interpretation, whereas a spiritual reading reveals Boethius's Christianity. Cf. Starnes, p. 29: "Indeed, in the whole history of the controversy over the nature of the *Consolation* it is probably no exaggeration to say that those who have had an eye to the letter of the text are just those who have regarded it as a pagan work. And with this criterion in mind, their judgement about the pagan character of the work can scarcely be faulted! However, it remains a question as to whether the spirit of the work can be understood to be Christian even though the letter is not." The point here would seem to be that if one does not look for the inherent unity of the work, it could seem to be pagan, but if one reads the work with its object in mind its Christianity is more than clear. Obertello makes a similar point. Cf. Obertello, introduction to Boezio, *Consolazione della filosofia* (Milan: Rusconi, 1996) pp. 6–7: "È qui che più aspramente viene contestata l'affermazione di cui sopra, poiché si obietta che, in realtà, tutto il discorso filosofico di Boezio, anziché avere fattezze e andamento illuminati, sia pure riflessamente... è invece di fatto null'altro che un *collage* di concetti e addirittura di passi tolti di peso da una miriade di testi di autori pagani, conservando — come sarebbe a ciò consequenziale — l'impianto dei valori propri della cultura e della visione pagana." In the lines that follow, Obertello defends both the unity of the work and its Christianity.

8. Cf. Obertello, *Dintorni*, p. 41: "I punti qualificanti del pensiero boeziano, almeno quali ci sono proposti nel *De consolatione*, sono ben noti, e già molte volte sono stati ripresentati dalla critica contemporanea. Nella maggior parte dei casi, però, non s'è tenuto conto di un elemento chiave, tanto importante quanto il loro significato intrinseco: la loro coerenza all'interno di un insieme organico di dottrine, che ne costituisce il quadro di riferimento obbligato."

9. We saw that it is generally held that the *Consolatio* is an *itinerarium mentis in*

sequence of this is that there is no scholarly consensus with regards to any of Boethius's positions on any of the topics he presents in the work.¹⁰

This problem is, however, not the only or even the main source of the lack of scholarly consensus with regards to the *Consolatio*. For despite the fact that scholars generally accept that the work has a coherent point, most scholarly interpretations of its many points seem to disregard the *Consolatio*'s coherence.¹¹ That is, scholars tend to do one of two things when they examine the content of the *Consolatio*: (1) focus on one or another of the work's points on any given topic, analyze it, comment on it, and claim that their interpretation of that point delineates Boethius's position on that topic; or (2) summarize each of the *Consolatio*'s various points without attempting to show how they are related, or the underlying metaphysical doctrine that they delineate.¹²

Barrett's analysis of the *Consolatio* is a good illustration of the latter approach. It is divided into three parts. In the first part, she gives a summary of the content of each of the work's five books.¹³ In the second part, which deals with the *Consolatio*'s "philosophical background" she identifies some of the philosophical sources of its doctrines.¹⁴ In the third part, she analyzes Boethius's view of eternity as it is to be found in the fifth book and contrasts it with other classical notions of eternity and perpetuity in order to defend Boethius's Christianity.¹⁵ Crocco does

---

Deum, but that the details of its account are a matter of dispute. For there is no consensus as to what goal the *itinerarium* is directed (what Boethius's *Deus* is), as to the metaphysics in which the *itinerarium* is cast (some scholars contend that the work's metaphysics is wholly Stoic, some contend it is wholly Aristotelian, others contend that it is Neoplatonic, and so forth), or as to what branch of philosophy the work is to be ascribed — some scholars contend that the *itinerarium* is ethical, some contend that it is metaphysical, and so forth. Cf. pp. 10ff. in the second chapter.

10. That is, it would seem to justify the various claims we saw in the first chapter of our work: i.e., that the work is wholly Stoic, wholly Aristotelian, completely Neoplatonic, and so forth; that its procedure is ethical, metaphysical, and so forth. Cf. footnotes 5–12 in chapter two.

11. Cf. footnotes 7–8 above.

12. A third method has recently been used to determine the content of the *Consolatio*: analyzing its poems. This is Reiss's method. Cf. Reiss, chapter V, pp. 103–30. What makes Reiss's interpretation interesting is that it can and does account for the basic continuity of the work and for the work's basic points. The problem with the method is that the bulk of Boethius's arguments in defense of his points lies in the prose section of his text. Hence although analyzing the *Consolatio*'s poetry does indeed give one the chance to grasp the main lines of the work, it does not give one the chance to show how Boethius backs his points. As such, Reiss's method is not the best one to determine the philosophical content of the *Consolatio*.

13. Barrett, chapter VII, pp. 75–101.
14. Barrett, chapter VIII, pp. 102–22.
15. Barrett, chapter IX, pp. 123–38.

something similar in his analysis of the *Consolatio*.[16] It is divided into two main parts: in the first part he summarizes the content of each of the work's five books.[17] In the second part he defends Boethius's Christianity.[18] Ghisalberti's analysis of the third book of the *Consolatio*, on the other hand, is a good example of the former approach. For its intent is to analyze the *Consolatio*'s *itinerarium* through its third book alone.[19]

The same thing holds for scholarly interpretation of the *Consolatio*'s doctrine of the good. For in this case too, scholars tend either to focus on one or another of the work's definitions of the good, or to summarize Boethius's various points concerning man's good without showing how they are related. Chadwick's analysis of the *Consolatio* is a good illustration of the latter approach. His comment on the work summarizes its principal definitions of the good and identifies some of their possible philosophical sources, but does not indicate how these principal definitions are related, or what the good really is in the work itself. Thus, Chadwick tells us that the second book's doctrine of the good is largely Stoic,[20] whereas in the third[21] and fourth[22] books the doctrines of the good are largely Platonic. But he does not explain how these different doctrines of the good are related. Nor does he advance any hypothesis which might explain why Boethius does delineate three different doctrines of the good which happen to be "Stoic" and "Platonic" respectively.

Obertello's analyses of the *Consolatio*'s doctrine of the good, on the other hand, are a good illustration of the prior approach. For in both his introduction to the *Consolatio*[23] and his sketch of Boethius's

---

16. Antonio Crocco, *Introduzione a Boezio* (Naples: Liguori, 1975) pp. 80–163.
17. Crocco, chapter III, pp. 80–145.
18. Crocco, chapter IV, pp. 147–63.
19. Ghisalberti, "L'Ascesa boeziana a Dio nel libro III della *Consolatio*," pp. 183–92.
20. Chadwick, *Consolations*, 229: "Accordingly, the second book and the first sections of the third operate with Stoic themes in which comfort is discovered by reconciling oneself to a world of determined inevitability."
21. Chadwick, *Consolations*, p. 236: "Only the perfect good can be at the summit of the hierarchy of goods. By 'God,' therefore, we mean the perfection of both goodness and happiness and goodness is of the same essence of happiness.... For Boethius' Platonic ontology this is a demonstration with mathematical force, carrying a corollary that a perfectly happy man participates in the being of God and in this sense can be said to become a god."
22. Chadwick, *Consolations*, p. 240: "Much of the philosophical argument in the first sections of the fourth book hangs on Plato's *Gorgias*."
23. Obertello, intro. *Consolazione*, pp. 5–24. The introduction's intent is to defend Boethius's Christianity, and Obertello shows that Boethius's *itinerarium* is from transitory good things to God, the *Summum Bonum*, which is the point of the work's third book. What Obertello does not discuss is the fourth book's definition of man's 'good' or the second book's primary definition.

metaphysics[24] he draws his interpretation of its doctrine of the good solely from the third book.[25]

Now, our intent is not to show if or why scholarly interpretation of the *Consolatio* misinterprets the work, or how it is lacking. Our object is to delineate the *Consolatio*'s doctrine of the good, and to point out that if it is conceded that the *Consolatio* is a coherent work — that is, that its various points do complement each other — then one must also concede: (1) that we cannot define that doctrine simply by analyzing one of work's definitions of the good, and (2) that we cannot grasp the import of its doctrine if we list the various points Boethius does make with regards to the good in the *Consolatio* without showing how they are related. The latter point clearly calls us to show how the various points which he does make with regards to the good are related to the object of the work as a whole. This is what we will attempt to do.

Our analysis of the *Consolatio*'s doctrine of the good will as such be divided into four parts. In the first part we will briefly delineate the *Consolatio*'s object and its structure: Boethius's treatment of man's 'good.' In the second part, we will analyze his primary three definitions of the 'good' — the "Stoic" definition and the two "Platonic" ones, to use Chadwick's terminology — which are to be found in the *Consolatio*'s first and second, the third, and the fourth books respectively. In the third part we will analyze the relation between freedom and providence; in the last part, we will delineate Boethius's doctrine of the 'good.'

The *Consolatio*'s Object and Structure

The *Consolatio*, as we saw in chapter two, is an *itinerarium mentis in Deum*: an account of man's *reditus*.[26] Its intent is to console a beleaguered Boethius, who was bereft of all that he held dear, by showing him that he can obtain true happiness despite everything he lost and

---

24. Cf. Obertello, *Dintorni*, pp. 41–66. Obertello's point here is to delineate Boethius's doctrine of the good — the main lines of his cosmology — by analyzing the *De Trinitate*, the *Quomodo*, and those parts of the *Consolatio* which are most like the *Quomodo*. The parts of the *Consolatio* which are most similar to the *Quomodo* are to be found mainly in the third book, insofar as it makes use of a doctrine of participation to define the good. Hence he does not analyze the second or fourth books' definitions of the good or discuss the relation between the *Consolatio*'s different definitions of the good.

25. This is not true of Obertello's interpretation of the *Consolatio* in *Severino Boezio*. For in that work he gives a fine analysis of the work's structure, although he does not delineate its notion of the good.

26. Cf., e.g., Chadwick, *Boethius*, p. 11: "The essential shape of the *Consolation* is a Neoplatonic thesis that the imperfections of this world are allowed to facilitate the return of the soul to its origin in God." See also Gastaldelli, p. 51: "L'opera appare nel suo insieme... [come] un *itinerarium mentis in Deum*," and Crocco, p. 144, "La *Consolatio*, di cui rileviamo ancora una volta le precise caratteristiche di un *itinerarium mentis in Deum*."

how he can do so.[27] Its main object is to define man's final cause or perfection: his 'good.'[28]

Boethius's definition of that 'good' has three main parts. In the first and second books he claims that it lies in man's self-sufficiency,[29] which is man's possessing his intellect,[30] the noblest part of his soul, and in his mastering his need for extrinsic goods.[31] In the third book, after having analyzed why those things which man commonly believes to be his 'good' — or, to be precise, which he believes to be the means with which to attain his self-sufficiency that is, wealth, power, honor, fame, and pleasure[32] — are insufficient, since self-sufficiency can by definition lack nothing, and none of those things man believes to be his 'good' lacks nothing,[33] he claims that there is only one true Good, i.e., God, "the good other than whom nothing better can be conceived" (III, 10, 26),[34] which is the source and sum total of all good things, and that man's 'good' lies in his participating in that Good.[35] Finally in the fourth book, he claims that man's 'good' is his reward for his good activities.[36]

---

27. Lady Philosophy's first express intention is to "cure" Boethius of his despair. Cf. *Consolatio*, I, 2, 1-2: " 'Sed medicinae,' " inquit, 'tempus est quam querelae.' "

28. Cf. *Consolatio*, III, 1, 15-20: "Sed quod tu te audiendi cupidum dicis, quanto ardore flagrares, si quonam te ducere aggrediamur agnosceres...ad veram...felicitatem, quam tuus quoque somniat animus, sed occupato ad imagines visu ipsam illam non potest intueri."

29. Cf., e.g., *Consolatio*, II, 4, 72-84: "Quid igitur o mortales extra petitis intra vos positam felicitatem? Error vos inscitiaque confundit. Ostendam breviter tibi summae cardinem felicitatis. Estne aliquid tibi te ipso pretiosius? Nihil inquies. Igitur si tui compos fueris, possidebis quod nec tu amittere umquam velis nec fortuna possit auferre. Atque ut agnoscas in his fortuitis rebus beatitudinem constare non posse, sic collige. Si beatitudo est summum naturae bonum ratione degentis nec est summum bonum quod eripi ullo modo potest, quoniam praecellit id quod nequeat auferri, manifestum est quoniam ad beatitudinem percipiendam fortunae instabilitas adspirare non possit." Cf. I, 4m, 1ff.

30. Cf., e.g., *Consolatio*, I, 3, 43-49: "Qui si quando contra nos aciem struens valentior incubuerit, nostra quidem dux copias suas in arcem contrahit, illi vero circa diripiendas inutiles sarcinulas occupantur. At nos desuper inridemus vilissima rerum quaeque rapientes securi totius furiosi tumultus eoque vallo muniti quo grassanti stultitiae adspirare fas non sit."

31. Cf., e.g., *Consolatio*, II, 5, 85ff.

32. Cf. *Consolatio*, III, 1-8. The first eight chapters of the third book show how what man commonly interprets to be his 'good' — fame, honor, and so forth — does not afford him true happiness.

33. Cf. *Consolatio*, III, 9, 4ff.

34. Our English citations of the *Consolatio* will be drawn from the Steward, Rand, and Tester translation.

35. Cf., e.g., *Consolatio*, III, 11, 22-24: " 'Omne quod bonum est boni participatione bonum esse concedis an minime?' 'Ita est.' " *Consolatio*, III, 10, 83-90: "Nam quoniam beatitudinis adeptione fiunt homines beati, beatitudo vero est ipsa divinitas, divinitatis adeptione beatos fieri manifestum est: sed uti iustitiae adeptione iusti, sapientiae sapientes fiunt, ita divinitatem adeptos deos fieri simili ratione necesse est. Omnis igitur beatus deus, sed natura quidem unus; participatione vero nihil prohibet esse quam plurimos."

36. Cf., e.g., *Consolatio*, IV, 3, 4-14: "Rerum etenim quae geruntur illud propter quod unaquaeque res geritur, eiusdem rei praemium esse non iniuria videri potest, uti currendi in stadio propter quam curritur iacet praemium corona. Sed beatitudinem esse idem ip-

For man's virtuous behavior is both his possession of himself,[37] and his becoming a god,[38] where one supposes such a claim to mean man's participating in God.[39] The main point of the *Consolatio* must as such be to delineate the intrinsic and extrinsic causes of man's perfection.

There is, however, a second problem which plays a prominent role in the work: the cause and nature of evil. This too is in line with the work's being a consolation. For Boethius was *unjustly* bereft of all he held dear,[40] and wants to understand: how it is possible for evil to exist at all,[41] and if it is possible for it to defeat the good.[42]

In Boethius's treatment, the problem of evil is closely linked to the problem of the 'good.' For its cause is a misinterpretation of the 'good'[43] — of one's final cause and the means with which to obtain it[44] — and its effect is a corruption of its cause's nature,[45] and being.[46] Evil, he concludes as such, is a *privatio boni,* in the full sense of the

---

sum bonum propter quod omnia geruntur ostendimus. Est igitur humanis actibus ipsum bonum veluti praemium commune propositum. Atqui hoc a bonis non potest separari neque enim bonus ultra iure vocabitur qui careat bono; quare probos mores sua praemia non relinquunt."

37. The point is made negatively, for Boethius claims that the good man's reward is reflected in an opposite manner in the evil man's punishment (*Consolatio*, IV, 3, 33–36) and the punishment of evil men is their loss of their humanity. See *Consolatio*, IV, 3, 44–50: "Omne namque quod sit unum esse ipsumque unum bonum esse paulo ante didicisti, cui consequens est ut omne quod sit id etiam bonum esse videatur. Hoc igitur modo quidquid a bono deficit esse desistit; quo fit ut mali desinant esse quod fuerant, sed fuisse homines adhuc ipsa humani corporis reliqua species ostentat." This clearly means that the good man's reward is his possession of his humanity.

38. Cf., e.g., *Consolatio*, IV, 3, 21–31: "Postremo cum omne praemium idcirco appetatur quoniam bonum esse creditur, quis boni compotem praemii iudicet expertem? At cuius praemii? Omnium pulcherrimi maximique. Memento etenim corollarii illius quod paulo ante praecipuum dedi ac sic collige: cum ipsum bonum beatitudo sit, bonos omnes eo ipso quod boni sint fieri beatos liquet. Sed qui beati sint deos esse convenit. Est igitur praemium bonorum quod nullus deterat dies, nullius minuat potestas, nullius fuscet improbitas, deos fieri."

39. Lady Philosophy herself allows us to make this deduction. For the corollary she refers to in the passage quoted ("Memento etenim corollarii illius quod paulo ante praecipuum dedi") is that men become gods by participating in God, who is transcendent. Cf. *Consolatio*, III, 10, 80–90.

40. Cf. *Consolatio*, I, 4 where Boethius gives an account of the reasons for his imprisonment.

41. Cf. *Consolatio*, I, 4.

42. Cf. *Consolatio*, IV, 1.

43. Cf., e.g., *Consolatio*, III, 3, 4–6: "Et ad verum bonum naturalis ducit intentio et ab eodem multiplex error abducit."

44. Cf., e.g., *Consolatio*, IV, 2, 63–66: "Sed summum bonum, quod aeque malis bonisque propositum, boni quidem naturali officio virtutum petunt, mali vero variam per cupiditatem, quod adipiscendi boni naturale officium non est, idem ipsum conantur adipisci."

45. See footnote 37.

46. Cf. *Consolatio*, IV, 2, 104–12: "Nam qui mali sunt eos malos esse non abnuo; sed eosdem esse pure atque simpliciter nego. Nam uti cadaver hominem mortuum dixeris, simpliciter vero hominem appellare non possis, ita vitiosos malos quidem esse concesserim,

word. For it is by definition its cause's not attaining its end, and it strips its cause of its ontological goodness.[47]

Herein lies the solution to one of Boethius's problems regarding evil. For power is by definition the means to obtain an end. All of creation,[48] man included,[49] Boethius points out then, seeks to obtain its good: to become fully actualized. As evil arises both from man's misinterpretation of his 'good' and from his acquisition of 'false goods' it must be the antithesis of his actualization.[50] This is why it corrupts the evil-doer's nature and being.

What is more important is that since evil actions corrupt a person's nature and being, they must also strip the evil-doer of that which is to be actualized by his acquisition of the good: his own being and humanity.[51] What follows is that evil must not only be the antithesis of one's actualization, it must also be the antithesis of the power to obtain the good.[52] It must therefore by definition be the lack of power.[53] As such, it cannot defeat the Good, by definition.[54]

There is, however, a deeper problem to solve here. Granted that evil acts make the evil-doer powerless with regards to his own good, does the very fact that evil doers exist not demonstrate that man has power over God? After all, since God exists and is Good, any evil act must be contrary to His will. If this is so, however, and if man can commit evil acts, then he must be able to do things which are contrary to God's will. It therefore seems to follow that man has power over God. What ensues is a paradox. If evil exists, then God cannot be omnipotent.[55]

---

sed esse absolute nequeam confiteri. Est enim quod ordinem retinet servatque naturam; quod vero ab hac deficit, esse etiam, quod in sua natura situm est, derelinquit."

47. Cf. *Consolatio*, IV, 3, 56–69 where Boethius draws a list of the effects of man's evil activities: the plunderer becomes like a wolf; the irate person becomes like a lion; the fearful person becomes like a deer. — and concludes that: "Ita fit ut qui probitate deserta homo esse desierit."

48. Cf. e.g., *Consolatio*, I, 6, 24ff., III, 2m, and IV, 2.

49. Cf. *Consolatio*, III, 2, 13–14: "Est enim mentibus hominum veri boni naturaliter inserta cupiditas." See also III, 3, 1–5: "Vos quoque, o terrena animalia, tenui licet imagine vestrum tamen principium somniatis verumque illum beatitudinis finem licet minime perspicaci qualicumque tamen cogitatione prospicitis eoque vos et ad verum bonum naturalis ducit intentio."

50. Cf. *Consolatio*, IV, 2, 33–44.

51. Cf. *Consolatio*, IV, 3, 67–69: "Ita fit ut qui probitate deserta homo esse desierit, cum in divinam condicionem transire non possit, vertatur in beluam."

52. Cf. *Consolatio*, IV, 2, 5ff.

53. Cf. *Consolatio*, IV, 2, 115–20: "Possunt enim mala quae minime valerent, si in bonorum efficientia manere potuissent. Quae possibilitas eos evidentius nihil posse demonstrat. Nam si, uti paulo ante collegimus, malum nihil est, cum mala tantummodo possint, nihil posse improbos liquet."

54. Boethius's comment on this point is very similar to the *Gorgias*'s. For he draws the same conclusion that Plato did: that the wicked are happier when they are punished than they are when they are not. Cf. *Consolatio*, IV, 4.

55. Cf. *Consolatio*, IV, 1, 14–19: "Nam imperante florenteque nequitia virtus non

But this is impossible. The alternative is no less palatable: if God must be omnipotent, and if evil acts do exist, then God Himself must be the cause of the evil acts.[56] But this too is impossible. God can do nothing evil by definition,[57] since an evil is contrary to His will. How, then Boethius asks himself, can God and evil co-exist?

> If there is a God, whence comes evil? But whence good, if there is not? (I, 4, 105–6)[58]

Boethius's response to this problem lies in affirming the freedom of man's will and in delineating the reasons why providence — divine knowledge — and freedom can co-exist. He explains that free will is a necessary attribute of rational beings.[59] For one cannot think without judging, and judgement presupposes free will.[60] Thus since man is a rational being, God must have created him with a free will.[61] But if man has free will, he must be the cause of his own actions, and consequently God cannot be. Man's free will, Boethius indicates however, does not exclude providence: God's direction of the universe. For God is omniscient,[62] and His knowledge of the universe is *providence*.[63] What this

---

solum praemiis caret, verum etiam sceleratorum pedibus subiecta calcatur et in locum facinorum supplicia luit. Quare fieri in regno scientis omnia, potentis omnia sed bona tantummodo volentis dei nemo satis potest nec admirari nec conqueri."

56. Cf. *Consolatio*, V, 3, 81ff.

57. *Consolatio*, III, 12, 79–80: " 'Num igitur deus facere malum potest?' 'Minime,' inquam."

58. *Consolatio*, IV, 1, 9–12: "Sed ea ipsa est vel maxima nostri causa maeroris, quod, cum rerum bonus rector exsistat, vel esse omnino mala possint vel impunita praetereant."

59. *Consolatio*, V, 2 5–6: " 'Est,' inquit, 'neque enim fuerit ulla rationalis natura quin eidem libertas adsit arbitrii.' "

60. *Consolatio*, V, 2, 5–12: " 'Est,' inquit, 'neque enim fuerit ulla rationalis natura quin eidem libertas adsit arbitrii.' 'Nam quod ratione uti naturaliter potest id habet iudicium quo quidque discernat; per se igitur fugienda optandave dinoscit. Quod vero quis optandum esse iudicat petit; refugit vero quod aestimat esse fugiendum. Quare quibus in ipsis inest ratio, inest etiam volendi nolendique libertas.' " In the lines that ensue he explains that there is a hierarchy of freedom among rational beings, for 'heavenly divine substances' are absolutely free, where man can become a slave of his own vices.

61. Boethius first makes this point in the first book of the *Consolatio*: I, 5m 25–27: "Omnia certo fine gubernans / Hominum solos respuis actus / Merito rector cohibere modo."

62. Boethius's solution to the problem of reconciling divine foreknowledge and freedom is an ingenious one. He firstly shows that knowledge need not be the cause of an event (*Consolatio*, V, 4), and then he shows that divine foreknowledge is not foreknowledge at all. For God is eternal, as opposed to perpetual, and does not exist in time: His being is *tota simul* (*Consolatio*, V, 6, 5–31). As He does not exist in time, His acts cannot exist in time. Therefore, His knowing cannot exist in time. His knowledge of events cannot as such be foreknowledge. Rather it is knowledge which is simultaneous with events (V, 6, 59ff.).

63. Cf. *Consolatio*, IV, 6, 27–28: "Qui modus cum in ipsa divinae intelligentiae puritate conspicitur, providentia nominatur." *Consolatio*, V, 6, 69–72: "Unde non praevidentia sed providentia potius dicitur, quod porro ad rebus infimis constituta quasi ab excelso rerum cacumine cuncta prospiciat." Boethius distinguishes providence from fate: the prior is God's governance as seen from the divine perspective; the latter is God's governance as present in contingent things. The relation between providence and fate is similar to the relation in

means is that man's free actions do not limit God's power. To do so, they would have to occur outside the range of His knowledge. It means that there are some acts within the province of God's power which do not have God as their efficient cause, or in other words, that God is omnipotent even though rational beings have free will.

As this is true of man's activity in general, so too is it true of his evil acts. Evil is caused by those beings who have free will and who act against both God's will and their own natures. But it does not limit God's power or providence.[64] For all free acts, even those which are evil, occur within providence. Thus, Boethius points out that God can and does care for all things (even those who have free will) by directing them towards their proper ends and by excluding from His kingdom those things which have forsaken their ends.[65] Thus, if evil does limit something, it is only its cause: for it debases the evil-doer.

Boethius's treatment of evil is clearly a corollary of his definition of man's good. For in his definition, man's good is at once his self-sufficiency — his complete realization — and his real relation with the Highest Good. He defines evil, on the other hand, as man's negating both his own goodness and his relation with the highest good. What is more important is that together with his definition of man's good, his definition of evil delineates and solves the two basic metaphysical problems which man's acquisition of the good implies. For if one wants to explain why the good is man's final cause, he must explain both: (1) how a being can become and (2) how becoming can be the act of both the becomer's passive and active potency in the case of rational beings. Man's attaining his final cause, after all, entails his becoming, and he has the choice as to whether to become or not.

As for the first problem, there is something paradoxical about actualization. For to be actualized a being must become itself: it must attain its own final cause. Its actualization must be its own perfection, its own activity, or its own self-sufficiency, to use Boethius's term. The problem is that that activity, perfection, or self-sufficiency cannot stem

---

St. Augustine's thought between a *verbum mentis* and a product which is similar to it. Cf. on this latter point *Consolatio*, IV, 6, 44ff. As for St. Augustine, see *In Ioh. Evangelium Tractatus*, I.

64. Cf. *Consolatio*, III, 12, 56–60: " 'Nihil est igitur quod naturam servans deo contraire conetur.' 'Nihil,' inquam. 'Quod si conetur,' ait, 'num tandem proficiet quidquam adversus eum quem iure beatitudinis potentissimum esse concessimus?' 'Prorsus,' inquam, 'nihil valeret.' "

65. Cf. *Consolatio*, IV, 6, 199–204: "Hoc tantum perspexisse sufficiat, quod naturarum omnium proditor deus idem ad bonum dirigens cuncta disponat, dumque ea quae protulit in sui similitudinem retinere festinat, malum omne de reipublicae suae terminis per fatalis seriem necessitatis eliminet."

from the being to be actualized. For if a being is to be actualized, it must be in potency to what it is to be, and what is in potency cannot actualize itself with regards to that to which it is in potency. Hence that act whereby a being is actualized must be the act of a being other than the one to be actualized. *Quidquid movetur ab alio movetur.*

There ensues a series of apparent paradoxes. Firstly, if a being's actuality is its own activity, then it would not seem possible for that activity to be the activity of something other than the actualized being. But if a being is actualized by something other than itself, then its actuality must also be the activity of something other than itself. This is ostensibly contradictory, for *omne agens agit sibi simile.*

Secondly, a being's perfection is its self-sufficiency, to use Boethius's term. The act whereby that being is actualized, on the other hand, is the act of something other than itself, and upon which the actualized being depends in order to be actualized. What follows is that a being's self-sufficiency entails its dependence upon a being other than itself. But this too seems to be a contradiction in terms.

Thirdly, the very fact that a being can be actualized by something other than itself seems to be contradictory. For a being's perfection is its complete possession of its own essence. Now, if that possession takes place through a being's possessing the activity of something other than itself, then a being's possession of its own essence must take place through its possession of something other than itself. There are two reasons why this is problematic: (1) it is not clear how a being can come to possess something other than itself; and (2) it is not clear how a being's possession of something other than itself can cause or entail its possession of its own essence.

The second point is the most paradoxical. For if a being can be actualized by something whose essence is other than its own, then its actualization must be both its possession of its own essence and its possession of an essence other than its own. But this is contradictory. It seems to imply that the actualized being's essence is the essence of the being which actualizes it. After all, if something becomes itself completely when it possesses itself, and if it possesses itself when it possesses something other than itself, then it seems to follow that something's possession of itself is its possession of what is other than itself. But if something's possession of itself is tantamount to its possession of what is other than itself, then it seems to follow that the possessor is identical to what it comes to possess. But this is not possible. A being which is actualized cannot be identical to what actualizes it, since a being which is actualized is in potency before it is actualized, whereas what actualizes it cannot be. How, then, can a being become actualized, if by that term one means that it becomes perfected or that it possesses itself more fully, if its actualization entails its possession of something other than itself?

It is precisely problems such as these that Boethius attempts to solve with his threefold definition of man's 'good.' His first definition of the good is intrinsic. It defines man's good in terms of his nature and as his complete possession of that nature. His second definition of the good defines it in terms of its efficient cause: God. His third definition is an attempt to solve the apparent discrepancy between these causes. It is to delineate the reasons why man's good can (and must) at once be his participating in God even though it is his complete possession of his nature.

Free will introduces another variable to the problem of actualization. There is also something paradoxical about man's search for what he does not have and which will actualize him. For it does not seem possible for man to be actualized by something which he obtains through his own free activity. A being's free activity is that activity which stems from his actuality, and no being can be potential to that to which he is actual. On the other hand, it does also not seem possible for man to be actualized by something which he does not obtain at least in part through his free will. For since man is rational, his free will must play a part in his actualization. What we have here, as such, is another paradox, which would seem to be the metaphysical variation of the problem of *docta ignorantia*. For it is not at all clear how one is to reconcile free will with actualization. As a result, it seems impossible for man to be actualized at all. And yet, a complete account of the causes of man's happiness must solve this problem. Man's free will must play a part in his actualization. Were it not to, there would be no evil. Boethius's analysis of the problem of evil, and his attempt to reconcile freedom and providence, are his attempt to solve this second problem.

The *Consolatio* is thus an intricate metaphysical account of the causes of man's perfection. Boethius's object in it is to define and solve the primary and most difficult problems which the perfection of contingent things poses: to define the relation between the immanent and transcendent causes of that perfection, with all of the problems that this presents.

The Good

Boethius's treatment of the good is ascensional, and has three main parts. In the first part (book II) he defines man's happiness, or 'good,'

The *Consolatio Philosophiae* 199

and shows how it is not to be attained; in the second part (book III) he clarifies his definition of the 'good' and explains how it is to be attained; in the third part (book IV) he solves an apparent paradox which arises from his definition of the means with which man is to attain his 'good.' For Boethius claims that the means through which man attains his 'good' is God, and that the end which God affords man is his self-sufficiency. And it is odd to claim that God affords man self-sufficiency since self-sufficiency is by definition that state in which a being is not dependent upon anything other than itself.

Man's 'Good' and His False Goods

Man's 'good,' his happiness, is his self-sufficiency, or perfection: his complete possession of himself:

> Why then do you mortals look outside for happiness when it is really to be found within yourselves? Error and ignorance confuse you. Let me briefly show you on what the greatest happiness really turns. Is there anything more precious to you than yourself? Nothing, you will agree. If therefore you are in possession of yourself (*tui compos*), you will possess that which you will never wish to lose, and which fortune cannot take away from you. (II, 4, 72–77)[66]

For man's 'good' is his perfect state: it is that state in which he lacks nothing,[67] and therefore cannot be affected by things other than himself.[68] Consequently, it is that state which cannot be taken away from him who possesses it.[69] Indeed, Boethius claims that if one were to be able to strip man of his 'good,' it would not be his highest good at all.[70]

How, then, does one attain that good? For it is clear that it is not

---

66. Cf., e.g., *Consolatio*, I, 4m.
67. Cf., e.g., *Consolatio*, III, 2, 5–12: "Id autem est bonum quo quis adepto nihil ulterius desiderare queat. Quod quidem est omnium summum bonorum cunctaque intra se bona continens, cui si quid aforet summum esse non posset, quoniam relinqueretur extrinsecus quod posset optari. Liquet igitur esse beatitudinem statum bonorum omnium congregatione perfectum." See also *Consolatio*, III, 3, 24–26: " 'Qui vero eget aliquo, non est usquequaque sibi ipse sufficiens?' 'Minime,' inquam."
68. See footnotes 29 and 30.
69. Cf. *Consolatio*, e.g., I, 5, 17–20: "An ignoras illam tuae civitatis antiquissimam legem, qua sanctum est ei ius exulare non esse quisquis in ea sedem fundare maluerit? Nam qui vallo eius ac munimine continetur, nullus metus est ne exul esse mereatur. At quisquis eam inhabitare velle desierit, pariter desinit etiam mereri."
70. Cf. *Consolatio*, e.g., II, 4, 79–82: "Beatitudo est summum naturae bonum ratione degentis nec est summum bonum quod eripi ullo modo potest, quoniam praecellit id quod nequeat auferri."

something which man possesses by nature, else we would all already be self-sufficient. By that very reason it is also clear that self-sufficiency cannot be something which man gives himself, or whose efficient cause is man. For if man is not self-sufficient by nature, then he must be only potentially self-sufficient by nature. But that which is only potentially self-sufficient by nature cannot be the efficient cause of its own self-sufficiency. *Actiones non progrediuntur nisi ab existente in actu secundum quod est in actu.* The cause of man's self-sufficiency must be something other than himself. What, then, is that cause, and what is the nature of the relation that exists between man and it?

Boethius begins his examination of the cause of man's 'good,' or self-sufficiency, by listing all of those things which are commonly thought to confer it: wealth, fame, honor, and so forth. His list is not an original one.[71] The specific differences of the things he does list, then, are: (1) that they are all things which man can obtain through his own free activity, and (2) that they do not afford man his 'good.' He tells us that wealth cannot confer man's 'good' because it does not make men self-sufficient.[72] Wealth does not make man the master of himself: "riches cannot get rid of avarice, for it is insatiable" (II, 6, 56–57). For as good as material things are by nature, they cannot make men good since they can never truly belong to him.[73] They cannot truly belong to him because they cannot communicate their goodness to him.[74] And they cannot communicate their goodness to man because man's 'good' is of a different kind from theirs.[75] This, he claims, is proven by the fact that wealth does not make man good. After all, a person's 'good'

---

71. Chadwick claims the list is Stoic. Cf. Chadwick, *Boethius: the Consolations,* p. 232: "the first sections of the third book recapitulate the Stoic arguments of the type predominant in the second book. Men seek happiness in external things: in riches, power, fame, pleasure, family ties, above all in friendship, which is a matter not of luck but of moral virtue." It could, however, very well be Aristotelian. For Aristotle's *Nicomachean Ethics* has a similar list (1.41, 1095a 18–27), as Barrett points out, pp. 107–8: "And there are many signs in the book that the writer knows Aristotle well: the discussions as to the *'Summum Bonum'* recall parts of the *Nicomachean Ethics.*"

72. *Consolatio,* III, 3, 28–30: "Opes igitur nihilo indigentem sufficientemque sibi facere nequeunt et hoc erat quod promittere videbantur." Cf. *Consolatio,* II, 5, 63ff., III, 3, 41ff.

73. *Consolatio,* II, 5, 6–7: "Divitiaene vel vestrae vel sui natura pretiosae sunt?" *Consolatio,* II, 5, 31–40: "An vos agrorum pulchritudo delectat? Quidni? Est enim pulcherrimi operis pulchra portio. Sic quondam sereni maris facie gaudemus; sic caelum sidera lunam solemque miramur. Num te horum aliquid attingit? Num audes alicuius talium splendore gloriari? An vernis floribus ipse distingueris aut tua in aestivos fructus intumescit ubertas? Quid inanibus gaudiis raperis? Quid externa bona pro tuis amplexaris? Numquam tua faciet esse fortuna quae a te natura rerum fecit aliena."

74. *Consolatio,* II, 5, 53–58: "Ex quibus omnibus nihil horum quae tu in tuis conputas bonis tuum esse bonum liquido monstratur. Quibus si nihil inest appetendae pulchritudinis, quid est quod vel amissis doleas vel laeteris retentis? Quod si natura pulchra sunt, quid id tua refert?"

75. *Consolatio,* II, 5, 70–93.

cannot harm its possessor.[76] But wealth can.[77] Thus, neither wealth, nor any material thing at all, can be man's 'good.'

The same thing holds for power. Power does not make man any more self-sufficient than wealth does.[78] And that not only because man's power over creation[79] and other men is illusory.[80] The main reason why man's power over other men is illusory in Boethius's view is that it does not give him power over himself. Power does not produce self-mastery.[81] It cannot, as such, make man good. This is, Boethius points out, also proven by experience. For were power to produce self-mastery, no evil men could hold office,[82] which is clearly contrary to experience. What this means, of course, is that power cannot be man's 'good.'

Nor can fame and glory be man's 'good.' For they cannot make man either self-sufficient[83] or good. Indeed, they can be stripped from man,[84] are limited in space and time,[85] and above all add nothing to a man's self-sufficiency, even if his fame and glory are deserved.[86]

But if wealth and power, fame and glory cannot be man's 'good,' Boethius concludes, nothing in this world can be man's 'good.' For there is nothing in this world that can make him self-sufficient or perfect.[87]

Out of all of which we may gather this in sum, that these things which can neither provide those goods they promise nor are per-

---

76. *Consolatio*, II, 5, 94–95: "Ego vero nego ullum esse bonum quod noceat habenti."
77. *Consolatio*, II, 5, 96–97: "Atqui divitiae possidentibus persaepe nocuerunt." See also *Consolatio*, III, 2.
78. *Consolatio*, III, 5, 5–7: "O praeclara potentia quae ne ad conservationem quidem sui satis efficax invenitur!"
79. *Consolatio*, II, 6, 13ff.
80. *Consolatio*, II, 6, 37–39: "Ullamne igitur eius hominis potentiam putas, qui quod ipse in alio potest, ne id in se alter valeat efficere non possit?" See also *Consolatio*, III, 4, 35ff.
81. *Consolatio*, II, 6, 57–61: "Nec potestas sui compotem fecerit quem vitiosae libidines insolubilibus adstrictum retinent catenis, et collata improbis dignitas non modo non efficit dignos, sed prodit potius et ostentat indignos."
82. *Consolatio*, II, 6, 40–46: "Ad haec si ipsis dignitatibus ac potestatibus inesset aliquid naturalis ac proprii boni, numquam pessimis provenirent. Neque enim sibi solent adversa sociari; natura respuit ut contraria quaeque iungantur. Ita cum pessimis plerumque dignitatibus fungi dubium non sit, illud etiam liquet natura sui bona non esse quae se pessimis haerere patiantur." See also *Consolatio*, III, 4, 2–4.
83. *Consolatio*, III, 8, 6–8: "Dignitatibus fulgere velis? Danti supplicabis et qui praeire ceteros honore cupis, poscendi humilitate vilesces." Cf. also, *Consolatio* II, 7, 64ff.
84. Cf. *Consolatio*, II, 7, 63ff.
85. Cf. *Consolatio*, II, 7, 46ff.
86. *Consolatio*, III, 6, 8–11: "Quae si etiam meritis conquisita sit, quid tamen sapientis adiecerit conscientiae qui bonum suum non populari rumore sed conscientiae veritate metitur?"
87. *Consolatio*, II, 4, 79–84: "Si beatitudo est summum naturae bonum ratione degentis nec est summum bonum quod eripi ullo modo potest, quoniam praecellit id quod nequeat auferri, manifestum est quoniam ad beatitudinem percipiendam fortunae instabilitas adspirare non possit."

fect by amassing all goods, neither lead to happiness like so many roads, nor themselves make men happy (III, 8, 31–35).

The Reductio Ad Unum *of the False Goods and the True 'Good'*

The reason Boethius gives for man's not being able to obtain his 'good' — that which truly makes him self-sufficient — by acquiring what the world has to offer is that the world just offers partial images, or imperfect versions of man's true 'good':

> These things, therefore, seem to give mortals images of the true good, or certain imperfect goods, but they cannot confer the true and perfect good. (III, 9, 92–94)

Man's true 'good' is what can truly make him self-sufficient, and true self-sufficiency cannot be distinguished from true power.[88] Nor can it be distinguished from what is truly worthy of respect,[89] or from what should be renowned.[90] Thus, Boethius concludes, 'power,' 'self-sufficiency,' 'glory,' and 'honor' must differ only insofar as they are the many names which man gives his 'good.' For in reality they all denote one and the same thing:

> And this too is necessary according to those same arguments, that the *names* of sufficiency, power, fame, respect, and pleasure are different, but their *substance* differs in no respect. (III, 9, 42–44)

What this means is that man could not secure his own happiness, even if he were able to secure the world's 'goods.' For, Boethius continues, the true cause of his self-sufficiency cannot be attained through what only confers a piece of it.[91] The true good has no parts.[92] Hence man can at best only gain a false image of his 'good' when he acquires them:

> Now, this, which is one and simple in its nature, man's perversity splits up, and while he tries to obtain a part of it, though in fact it has no parts, he gains neither a portion of it, for there are no

---

88. *Consolatio*, III, 9, 13–19.
89. *Consolatio*, III, 9, 19–23.
90. *Consolatio*, III, 9, 26–36.
91. *Consolatio*, III, 9, 71–73: "In his igitur quae singula quaedam expetendorum praestare creduntur, beatitudo nullo modo vestiganda est."
92. *Consolatio*, III, 10, 112–17: "Si haec omnia beatitudinis membra forent, a se quoque invicem discreparent. Haec est enim partium natura ut unum corpus diversa componant. Atqui haec omnia idem esse monstrata sunt; minime igitur membra sunt. Alioquin ex uno membro beatitudo videbitur esse coniuncta — quod fieri nequit."

portions, nor the thing itself, which he is not in the least trying to get. (III, 9, 45–49)

The implications here are clear: (1) since man's good is a single thing, there can only be one true cause of man's self-sufficiency, or perfection, and (2) that the cause of man's perfection is nothing this world can offer. For the one cause of man's 'good' must itself be everything which it causes man to be when he attains his 'good.'[93] Thus, since man's good is at once his self-sufficiency, his power, his being worthy of respect, that cause must itself be self-sufficient, powerful, worthy of respect, and so forth, and there is nothing in this world that is truly self-sufficient, powerful, and worthy of respect, at once. These are Boethius's own conclusions.[94] There is, he claims, one true cause of man's self-sufficiency, the Good itself, God, who is man's final cause, because He is Self-caused, who can confer self-sufficiency because He is Self-sufficient, and who is happiness, because he is the Good.[95]

That the Good exists, Boethius continues, is proven by the fact that there are imperfect versions of it. For the imperfect presupposes the existence of the perfect thing it imitates.[96] Nor can there be any doubt that the true Good is God, the Creator of all things. For God is that 'of which nothing better can be thought,'[97] and there would be something better than He, were He not the Good Itself. Indeed, Boethius points out that if God were not the Good, He could not be the Creator of all things.[98]

As God is the Good, He must also be the final cause of all things: Happiness. Indeed, Boethius claims that if God were not Happiness,

---

93. Cf. *Consolatio*, II, 6, 49ff.
94. Cf. *Consolatio*, III, 9, 80–91: " 'Nam nisi fallor ea vera est et perfecta felicitas quae sufficientem, potentem, reverendum, celebrem laetumque perficiat. Atque ut me interius animadvertisse cognoscas, quae unum horum, quoniam idem cuncta sunt, veraciter praestare potest hanc esse plenam beatitudinem sine ambiguitate cognosco.'... 'Essene aliquid in his mortalibus caducisque rebus putas quod huiusmodi statum possit afferre?' 'Minime,' inquam, 'puto idque a te, nihil ut amplius desideretur, ostensum est.' "
95. *Consolatio*, III, 10, 43–62: "Ne hunc rerum omnium patrem illud summum bonum quo plenus esse perhibetur vel extrinsecus accepisse vel ita naturaliter habere praesumas, quasi habentis dei habitaeque beatitudinis diversam cogites esse substantiam. Nam si extrinsecus acceptum putes, praestantius id quod dederit ab eo quod acceperit existimare possis. Sed hunc esse rerum omnium praecellentissimum dignissime confitemur. Quod si natura quidem inest, sed est ratione diversum, cum de rerum principe loquamur deo, fingat qui potest: quis haec diversa coniunxerit?... Omnino enim nullius rei natura suo principio melior poterit exsistere, quare quod omnium principium sit, id etiam sui substantia summum esse bonum verissima ratione concluserim."
96. *Consolatio*, III, 10, 1–22.
97. *Consolatio*, III, 10, 25–27: "Nam cum nihil deus melius excogitari queat, id quo melius nihil est bonum esse quis dubitet?"
98. *Consolatio*, III, 10, 27–30: "Ita vero bonum esse deum ratio demonstrat, ut perfectum quoque in eo bonum esse convincat. Nam ni tale sit, rerum omnium princeps esse non poterit."

He could not be 'that of which nothing better can be thought' since His 'good' — His final cause — would have to be something other than He.[99] But this is absurd. For if God's 'good' were something other than Himself, then that 'good' would have to be the highest good. If it were the highest good, however, then God would not be the Creator of all things. God is the Creator of all things insofar as He is the Good. Worse yet, if God's 'good' were something other than He, there could be no highest good at all.[100] But this is manifestly not so, because there are imperfect goods. God must therefore be both the Good and Happiness:

> But we have concluded that both God and happiness are the highest good, so that that must be the highest happiness which is the highest divinity. (III, 10, 77-78)

As God is the Good and Happiness, He alone can be the cause of man's happiness. Thus, Boethius claims that man acquires his 'good' by participating in God, and that by participating in God, he becomes like God, who is Happiness itself:

> For since men are made happy by the acquisition of happiness, but happiness is itself divinity, it is obvious that they are made happy by the acquisition of divinity. But as by the acquisition of justice they become just, or by the acquisition of wisdom wise, so by the same argument they must, when they have acquired divinity, become gods. Therefore every happy man is a god, though by nature God is one only: but nothing prevents there being as many as you like by participation. (III, 10, 83-90)[101]

What he means by this is that God is the efficient cause of man's happiness. For He alone can confer that 'good' which is at once man's self-sufficiency, his power, his pleasure, that in him which is worthy of respect, and so forth, since He alone is all-powerful, self-sufficient, happiness, and worthy of respect. God alone can make man perfect:

> "Have we not shown," said she, "that those things which are sought by many are not true and perfect goods for this reason, because they are different from one another; and since each one lacks the others none can confer the full and absolute good; but

---

99. *Consolatio*, III, 10, 70-78.
100. *Consolatio*, III, 10, 54-58.
101. Cf. *Consolatio*, III, 11, 22-24: " 'Sed omne quod bonum est boni participatione bonum esse concedis an minime?' 'Ita est.' " *Consolatio*, III, 12, 86-91: "Etenim paulo ante beatitudine incipiens eam summum bonum esse dicebas quam in summo deo sitam loquebare. Ipsum quoque deum summum esse bonum plenamque beatitudinem disserebas; ex quo neminem beatum fore nisi qui pariter deus esset quasi munusculum dabas."

the true good is only produced when they are gathered as it were into one form which as efficient cause makes that which is sufficiency the same as power, respect, fame and pleasure; but unless all are one and the same, they possess nothing to justify their inclusion among those things which we should seek." "That has been demonstrated," I said, "and it cannot by any means be doubted." (III, 11, 8–18)

The Paradox of Means and End

There seems to be a bit of a discrepancy here. For the claim that man's happiness is at once his self-sufficiency and his participating in God seems contradictory. After all, if man's 'good' is his participating in God — that is, if God is the efficient cause of man's 'good' — then man's 'good' must be his dependence upon God.[102] And if man's 'good' is his dependence upon God, it sounds contradictory to claim that it is his self-sufficiency. Self-sufficiency is by definition that state in which one does not depend upon anything.

There is a related contradiction. For if man's 'good' is his perfection, and if his perfection is his possessing his own essence completely,[103] then it makes no sense to claim that his perfection is his 'acquisition' of something which is other than himself: God. After all, if man is not God, then his participating in God — his "acquiring God" — cannot be his acquiring himself: his actualizing his own nature. As such, it sounds contradictory to claim that man's happiness is his perfection, if that perfection is his participation in God. Or must we believe that Boethius holds that man is God? After all, if man is God, then his possessing himself can take place through his possessing God, or his participating in Him.

The point here is that claiming that perfection is or ensues from a real relation is paradoxical. For if what a thing possesses substantially it possesses in and of itself, then it would not seem possible for a real relation to be the cause of a being's possessing something substantially.

---

102. Cf. *Consolatio*, III, 12, 56–64: " 'Nihil est igitur quod naturam servans deo contraire conetur.' 'Nihil,' inquam. 'Quod si conetur,' ait, 'num tandem proficiet quidquam adversus eum quem iure beatitudinis potentissimum esse concessimus?' 'Prorsus,' inquam, 'nihil valeret.' 'Non est igitur aliquid quod summo huic bono vel velit vel possit obsistere.' 'Non,' inquam, 'arbitror.' 'Est igitur summum,' inquit, 'bonum quod regit cuncta fortiter suaviterque disponit.'
103. *Consolatio*, III, 2, 5–12: "Id autem est bonum quo quis adepto nihil ulterius desiderare queat. Quod quidem est omnium summum bonorum cunctaque intra se bona continens, cui si quid aforet summum esse non posset, quoniam relinqueretur extrinsecus quod posset optari. Liquet igitur esse beatitudinem statum bonorum omnium congregatione perfectum." See also *Consolatio*, III, 3, 24–26: " 'Qui vero eget aliquo, non est usquequaque sibi ipse sufficiens?' 'Minime,' inquam."

And yet this is precisely what Boethius's claim that God is the efficient cause of man's happiness implies. For happiness is man's substantial possession of himself. If its efficient cause is God, however, then it must also be a real relation. What, then, is man's happiness and how is it caused?

Boethius's solution to his paradoxes does not involve the ontological identity of man and God. The passage in which he claims that man's happiness is his participating in God shows as much. For in it he explicitly states that there is only one God by nature:

> Therefore every happy man is a god, though by nature God is one only. (III, 10, 89)

But if there is only one God by nature, and if God is by nature self-sufficient — as He must be in order to be man's 'good' — then nothing which seeks its self-sufficiency can be God. But man seeks his self-sufficiency. It stands to reason that he cannot be God.

Nor does his solution claim that man's perfection is his subsumption of God's Being, his deification, where by deification we mean man's ontological acquisition of God's nature. For Boethius explicitly states that that is impossible:

> For such is the form of the divine substance that it does not slip away into external things, nor does it receive anything external into itself, but as Parmenides says of it:
>
> > Like the body of a sphere well-rounded on all sides,
>
> it turns the moving circle of the universe while it keeps itself unmoved. (III, 12, 102–7)

Boethius's solution lies in showing that man's perfection is nothing other than his acquisition of the good because goodness is one of his substantial properties. For as this is so, goodness must also be his final cause. Thus man must approach (and attain) his final cause when he acquires the good. But man cannot give himself that good which he does not possess, precisely because he does not possess it. Hence his acquisition of the good must be, or entail, his real relation with what possesses what he does not. That is the alternative.

He clarifies this point by delineating the relation between being and unity. Every existing thing is a unity. For things come to exist when they acquire unity and cease to be when they lose it.[104] Unity, as such, is a

---

104. *Consolatio*, III, 11, 28–30: "Omne quod est tam diu manere atque subsistere quam diu sit unum, sed interire atque dissolvi pariter atque unum destiterit."

substantial property of all things. The fact of the matter is, however, that it is also something which all things desire. For all things strive by nature to preserve their unity,[105] and in so doing they demonstrate their natural desire for unity itself.[106]

Things' natural desire for unity is their natural desire for their own perfection. For if things desire unity, they must be able to acquire unity. Nothing can desire what it already has.[107] But if things can acquire unity, they must be capable of becoming. Things' desire for unity must therefore be their desire to become. But when things do become they do not acquire essences other than their own: all things must retain their natures in order to be.[108] They become when they come to possess their natures more completely. Things' desire for unity must as such be their desire to possess their natures more completely. But when things possess their natures, they attain their final cause: they are perfected. Things' desire for unity must be their desire for perfection.

As things' desire for unity is their desire for perfection, their acquisition of unity must be their perfection. That is, since unity is a substantial property of all things, things' acquisition of unity must be their acquisition of being. But beings' acquisition of being must be their acquisition of their "own being" — of that being for which they have the potential. For beings must retain their natures in order to be. But things' acquisition of "their own being" is their perfection. Thus, things' acquisition of unity must be their perfection.

To apply the point to man, Boethius tells us that man's happiness too is an acquisition of unity. For happiness is his acquisition of that which unifies self-sufficiency, power, pleasure, worthiness of respect and so forth.[109] But man's happiness is by definition his self-sufficiency, or per-

---

105. *Consolatio*, III, 11, 42–48: " 'Estne igitur,' inquit, 'quod in quantum naturaliter agat relicta subsistendi appetentia venire ad interitum corruptionemque desideret?' 'Si animalia,' inquam, 'considerem quae habent aliquam volendi nolendique naturam, nihil invenio quod nullis extra cogentibus abiciant manendi intentionem et ad interitum sponte festinent." Boethius gives many examples to back this point.

106. *Consolatio*, III, 11, 104–8: " 'Quod autem,' inquit, 'subsistere ac permanere petit, id unum esse desiderat; hoc enim sublato ne esse quidem cuiquam permanebit.' 'Verum est,' inquam. 'Omnia igitur,' inquit, 'unum desiderant.' "

107. Cf. *Consolatio*, III, 3, 23–24: " 'Eget vero,' inquit, 'eo quod quisque desiderat?' 'Eget.' " See also *Consolatio*, III, 2, 5ff.

108. *Consolatio*, IV, 2, 110–11: "Est enim quod ordinem retinet servatque naturam."

109. *Consolatio*, III, 11, 8–21: " 'Nonne,' inquit, 'monstravimus ea quae appetuntur pluribus idcirco vera perfectaque bona non esse quoniam a se invicem discreparent cumque alteri abesset alterum, plenum absolutumque bonum afferre non posse? Tum autem verum bonum fieri cum in unam veluti formam atque efficientiam colliguntur, ut quae sufficientia est, eadem sit potentia, reverentia, claritas atque iucunditas, nisi vero unum atque idem omnia sint, nihil habere quo inter expetenda numerentur?' 'Demonstratum,' inquam, 'nec dubitari ullo modo potest.' 'Quae igitur cum discrepant minime bona sunt, cum vero unum esse coeperint, bona fiunt; nonne haec ut bona sint, unitatis fieri adeptione contingit?' 'Ita,' inquam, 'videtur.' "

fection: his complete possession of his own nature.[110] What we have, as such, is that man's acquisition of unity must be his self-sufficiency, or perfection: what allows him to possess his own nature. Man's acquiring unity is his becoming.

The fact of the matter is, however, that the efficient cause of both the universe's[111] and man's[112] acquisition of unity is God. And in all acts of efficient causality *actio est in passo*. Hence God confers unity upon things as it is received by that upon which He confers it. That unity God confers must be similar to His own. For *omne agens agit sibi simile*.[113] Thus, things must acquire unity by receiving that unity which God bestows upon them, and which makes them like Him. The point can be stated more simply by saying that things receive unity insofar as they participate in God.

As this is true of all things, so too it must be true of man. Man must therefore acquire unity through God's efficient causality — when he receives it from God — and by receiving it, he must become like God. Or to put it simply, man acquires unity by participating in God. What we have, as such, is the apparently contradictory conclusion that man possesses himself (or his own nature) by participating in God.

The point, Boethius specifies, is applicable to the good. For unity and goodness are the same thing.[114] This means that the good is both a substantial property of all things[115] and their final cause.[116] Indeed, it means that the good is things' final cause because it is one of their substantial properties. For if the good is a substantial property of all things, things' being must be good, and consequently their perfection must be good. Thus, all things must desire the good because they desire

---

110. This is why Boethius claims that none of the 'goods' man can acquire in this world is his good. For none give him self-mastery. Cf., e.g., *Consolatio*, II, 6, 53–61.

111. Cf. *Consolatio*, III, 12, 15–26: "Mundus hic ex tam diversis contrariisque partibus in unam formam minime convenisset, nisi unus esset qui tam diversa coniungeret. Coniuncta vero naturarum ipsa diversitas invicem discors dissociaret atque divelleret, nisi unus esset qui quod nexuit contineret. Non tam vero certus naturae ordo procederet nec tam dispositos motus locis, temporibus, efficientia, spatiis, qualitatibus explicarent, nisi unus esset qui has mutationum varietates manens ipse disponeret. Hoc quidquid est quo condita manent atque agitantur, usitato cunctis vocabulo deum nomino."

112. See footnote 109.

113. Cf. *Consolatio*, II, 6, 53–54: "Agit enim cuiusque rei natura quod proprium est."

114. *Consolatio* III, 11, 24–26: "Oportet igitur idem esse unum atque bonum simile ratione concedas; eadem namque substantia est eorum quorum naturaliter non est diversus effectus." Cf also *Consolatio*, III, 11, 108–9: "Sed unum id ipsum monstravimus esse quod bonum."

115. *Consolatio* IV, 3, 44–47: "Omne namque quod sit unum esse ipsumque unum bonum esse paulo ante didicisti, cui consequens est ut omne quod sit id etiam bonum esse videatur."

116. *Consolatio* III, 11, 110–12: "Cuncta igitur bonum petunt, quod quidem ita describas licet: ipsum bonum esse quod desideretur ab omnibus."

their perfection. But if the good is things' perfection, then things must become perfected when they acquire the good. Boethius makes this point implicitly when he demonstrates that worldly goods are not man's 'good.' For if he believes that wealth, power, fame and glory cannot make man self-sufficient insofar as they do not make men good, by the converse he must believe that what does make man self-sufficient must also make him good.[117] But man's self-sufficiency is his perfection. Thus, his acquisition of the good must be his perfection.

The point here is not one which Boethius only makes negatively. He explicitly states that good men become good by acquiring the good,[118] and that their being good is the perfection of their natures. For, he claims, the good which men acquire cannot be separated from good men. If one were to be able to separate a good man from his goodness, that man could not be considered good.[119] And that good is his happiness:

Since the good itself is happiness, it is clear that all good men are made happy for this reason, that they are good. (IV, 3, 28–29)

The fact of the matter is, however, that the efficient cause of man's acquiring the good is God. For God is the Good and Happiness, and He alone can confer them. God confers them when man receives that which God bestows upon him through His efficient causality, and thereby becomes like God. That is, God confers goodness when man participates in Him. It follows that it is not at all contradictory to claim that man's final cause is at once his participating in God and his own self-sufficiency. For man's participating in God is what allows him to acquire goodness, and the goodness man acquires is the perfection of his nature.[120] Man's 'good,' as such, is his real relation with God.

---

117. See footnotes 76, 82.
118. *Consolatio* IV, 2, 35-37: " 'Sed certum est adeptione boni bonos fieri.' 'Certum.' 'Adipiscuntur igitur boni quod appetunt?' 'Sic videtur.' "
119. See footnote 36.
120. That Boethius holds that the good man acquires through his participation in God to be the perfection of man's nature can best be seen through what he considers the effects of man's evil actions. For evil actions strip man of his humanity — "Quare versi in malitiam humanam quoque amisere naturam" (IV, 3, 50–51) — and of his being — "Est enim quod ordinem retinet servatque naturam; quod vero ab hac deficit, esse etiam, quod in sua natura situm est, derelinquit" (IV, 2, 110–12). Now, if evil is the contrary of the good, as Boethius himself tells us it is — "Nam cum bonum malumque contraria sint" (IV, 2, 6–7) — then their effects must be contrary to one another — "Nam cum bonum malumque item poenae atque praemium adversa fronte dissideant, quae in boni praemio videmus accedere eadem necesse est in mali poena contraria parte respondeant" (IV, 3, 33–36). Thus, if evil strips man of his humanity and his being, then the good must be the perfection of his humanity and being.

Freedom and God

There is one last point which we must clarify: man's role in his actuation. For man is not completely passive with regards to the Good in Boethius's metaphysics. He has free will. Boethius's claim is that if he were completely passive with regards to the Good, there would be no explaining the existence of evil in this world.[121]

One would expect Boethius to claim that man's role in his actuation is indirect: that it is his assenting to God, following God's command, seconding God's ordering of the universe, or something along these lines. There are at least two reasons for this. The first is his claim that God is the efficient cause of man's 'good,' or that man's good is his participating in God. For if God is the direct cause of man's actuation, then man cannot be, since he is not God. The second reason, on the other hand, is that *actiones non progrediuntur nisi ab existente in actu secundum quod est in actu*. What is potential cannot actuate itself insofar as it is potential. But man must only potentially possess that good which he seeks. Hence it cannot be possible for him to acquire that good through his own free activity. But his acquiring that good is his actuation. It follows that man cannot actuate himself.

Boethius is more than aware of this. It is the reason why his search for man's 'good' leads him to examine worldly goods. For if man seeks his 'good,' the cause of his good must be something other than himself. It is also what makes him reject 'material goods' as the possible causes of man's 'good.' For what causes man to be good must itself be what it causes man to become. This is why Boethius points out both that the goodness of material things is of a different kind from man's,[122] and that it cannot truly belong to man.[123]

The problem is that Boethius would seem to claim exactly the opposite of what one would expect of him to. He seems to maintain that man's actuation is the direct result of his own free activity. This can be seen in his claim that one of the reasons why good men are more powerful that evil men is that they obtain the good through the "natural function of their virtues," whereas evil men try to obtain it through their "fluctuating desire,"[124] and do not succeed:

---

121. *Consolatio*, V, 3, 81ff.
122. *Consolatio*, II, 5, 53–58.
123. *Consolatio*, II, 5, 6–7, 31–40.
124. *Consolatio*, IV, 2, 62–66: "Sed summum bonum, quod aeque malis bonisque propositum, boni quidem naturali officio virtutum petunt, mali vero variam per cupiditatem, quod adipiscendi boni naturale officium non est, idem ipsum conantur adipisci." See also *Consolatio*, IV, 2, 39–42: "Cum igitur utrique [both good men and evil men] bonum petant, sed hi quidem adipiscantur, illi vero minime, num dubium est bonos quidem potentes esse, qui vero mali sunt imbecillos?"

> And it is in this matter that the strength of good men is outstandingly clear. For just as you would judge him most powerful in walking who, proceeding on foot, was able to reach a place so distant that no further passable place lay before his step, so you are bound to judge him most powerful who attains the end of all things desirable, beyond which is nothing. (IV, 2, 86–91)

For if man does become good through the "natural function of his virtues," and if his becoming good is his actuation, it seems to follow that man causes his own actuation. That activity whereby man actuates himself, then, must be free. For if evil men do exist, man must have the choice as to whether attain his 'good' through his "virtues" or through his "desire." Boethius therefore seems to be claiming that man's actuation is the direct result of his own free activity, or (conversely) that man is the direct moving cause of his actuation.

The same thing can be seen in Boethius's assertion that goodness is man's "reward" for his good actions and cannot, as such, be taken away from him.[125] His claim is that the only goods which can be taken away from man are those which are given to him by someone other than himself. But the converse of this is that man must give himself that goodness which cannot be taken away from him:

> But should a man rejoice in what he received from someone else, some other man or even he who gave it would be able to take it away. But since his goodness confers on each man his reward, he will only lack it when he has ceased to be good. (IV, 2, 17–21)

But if man gives himself goodness, then once again Boethius seems to be claiming that man is the moving cause of his own actuation.

To make matters worse, in the lines that follow the passage above Boethius seems to claim that the good which man gives himself is his participation in God:

> But what reward? The greatest and fairest of all: for remember that corollary which I gave you a little time ago as an excellent present, and conclude this: since the good itself is happiness it is clear that all good men are made happy for this reason, that they are good. But those who are happy, it is agreed, are gods; and therefore that is the reward of men which no time can lessen, no man's power diminish, no man's wickedness obscure, to become gods. (IV, 2, 24–29)

---

125. *Consolatio*, IV, 3, 9–11.

What we have, as such, is that Boethius would seem to claim not only that man is the moving cause of his own actuation, but also that he is the moving cause of his own participating in God.

There is clearly something paradoxical about these passages. For if Boethius is indeed claiming in them that man is the direct or moving cause of his own goodness, then he is not only claiming something which contradicts his own definition of the cause of man's goodness — for he claims that God is the efficient cause of man's goodness. He is also claiming something which he considers metaphysically impossible. For if man were the moving cause of his participating in God, as the third passage above would seem to suggest, then not only would it have to be possible for a finite being to produce a relation with an infinite one, it would also have to be possible for man to change God. That is, if man is finite,[126] as his own search for the good shows, and if God is infinite,[127] and if again Boethius's claim here is that man himself is the moving cause of his participating in God, then that claim must imply that a finite being is capable of producing its own relation with an infinite one. If man is the moving cause of his participating in God, on the other hand, then he must also be capable of changing God. For in order to be the moving cause of his participating in God, he would have to cause God to be the efficient cause of his own actuation, since Boethius construes man's participating in God as his receiving God's efficient causality. Both are points which Boethius himself will not concede. He not only claims that there is no bridging the finite and the infinite,[128] but also claims that God is the unmovable mover of all things.[129] How, then, are we to interpret Boethius's claims? What does Boethius believe man's role in his actuation to be?

The key to solving this paradox is Boethius's own definition of the "natural function of man's virtues." All things seek the good by nature.[130] Their search for the good, that is, is not voluntary but is an action which is consequent upon their natures.[131] Man is no exception

---

126. Cf. *Consolatio*, IV, 2, 124–26: " 'Est igitur,' inquit, 'aliquis qui omnia posse homines putet?' 'Nisi quis insaniat, nemo.' "

127. Cf. Boethius's definition of God's Being as *tota simul*. *Consolatio*, V, 6, 9–11: "Aeternitas igitur est interminabilis vitae tota simul et perfecta possessio."

128. *Consolatio*, II, 7, 59–61: "Etenim finitis ad se invicem fuerit quaedam, infiniti vero atque finiti nulla umquam poterit esse collatio."

129. *Consolatio*, III, 12, 102–8.

130. *Consolatio*, III, 11, 110–12: "Cuncta igitur bonum petunt, quod quidem ita describas licet: ipsum bonum esse quod desideretur ab omnibus."

131. *Consolatio*, III, 11, 89–97: "Nam ne in animalibus quidem manendi amor ex animae voluntatibus, verum ex naturae principiis venit. Nam saepe mortem cogentibus causis quam natura reformidat voluntas amplectitur, contraque illud quo solo mortalium rerum

to this. For he too has an inborn desire for the good,[132] and his nature too almost "compels" him to seek the good.[133] The fact of the matter is, however, that it is God who made things' natures and infused them with the need to search for the good.[134] It follows that whatever acts in accordance with its own nature follows God's command, or ordering of the universe.[135]

> "There is therefore nothing," she said, "which while remaining true to its nature would try to go against God?" "Nothing," I said. (III, 12, 56–57)

This holds for man as well. But if what acts in accordance with its nature follows God's command, then the "natural function of man's virtue" must be to follow God's command or His ordering of the universe.

There ensues a paradox. For it would not seem possible for man at once to be both a free agent and one all of whose acts are commanded or ordered by God. But Boethius's own point cannot but lead to this conclusion. For if a free act is by definition one which originates in the agent, and if every agent must act in conformity with its own nature — *omne agens agit sibi simile*[136] — then every free act must conform with the agent's nature. The problem is that Boethius claims that one's acting in accordance with his nature is following God's command. Thus, it seems to follow that every free act must be ordered by God, and that is a contradiction in terms. To make matters worse, it implies that God is responsible for evil. God's causality precedes man's activity, after all. God makes man. Thus if God makes man, and if man must act in accordance with his nature, God himself must be the principal cause of

---

durat diurnitas gignendi opus, quod natura semper appetit, interdum coercet voluntas. Adeo haec sui caritas non ex animali motione sed ex naturali intentione procedit." The point is specifically applicable to things' desire for unity, but since Boethius himself tells us that unity and goodness are the same thing — *bonum et unum convertuntur* — it can be applied to the good.

132. *Consolatio*, III, 2, 13–14: "Est enim mentibus hominum veri boni naturaliter inserta cupiditas." See also *Consolatio*, III, 3, 5ff.

133. *Consolatio*, IV, 2, 75–79: "Vide enim quanta vitiosorum hominum pateat infirmitas qui ne *ad hoc quidem pervenire queunt ad quod eos naturalis ducit ac paene compellit intentio*. Et quid si hoc *tam magno ac paene invicto praeeuntis naturae* desererentur auxilio." [The italics are mine.] See also *Consolatio*, III, 3, 1–6.

134. *Consolatio*, III, 11, 97–100: "Dedit enim providentia creatis a se rebus hanc vel maximam manendi causam ut quoad possunt naturaliter manere desiderent." The point here regards unity, but *unum et bonum convertuntur*. Cf. IV, 6, 86ff.

135. *Consolatio*, III, 12, 47–55: " 'Cum deus,' inquit, 'omnia bonitatis clavo gubernare iure credatur eademque omnia sicuti docui ad bonum naturali intentione festinent, num dubitari potest quin voluntaria regantur seque ad disponentis nutum veluti convenientia contemperataque rectori sponte convertant?' 'Ita,' inquam, 'necesse est; nec beatum regimen esse videretur, si quidem detrectantium iugum foret, non obtemperantium salus.' "

136. Cf. *Consolatio*, II, 6, 53–54.

man's activities, including the evil ones. Can this be? How is freedom possible in God's creation?

Boethius's response to this specific problem is to distinguish freedom of the will from true freedom. Every rational being, he points out, must have free will because he must determine whether or not to pursue, or to avoid, things in accordance with his understanding of them.[137] This does not, however, mean either that all rational beings are free, or that all of their acts are free. For if a free act is one which originates in a being's own nature, a free act must conform to a being's nature. The fact of the matter is, however, that rational beings can act in a way which is contrary to their natures, precisely because they have free wills.[138] This leads to what seems to be a contradictory conclusion: that a rational being's free acts of will can cause unfree acts.[139]

Boethius's point is that the paradox of freedom and predetermination has a false premise which derives from the ambiguity of the word 'freedom.' For 'freedom' is both that property of the will which makes it self-determining, and that property of man's being which ensues from his conforming to his own nature,[140] and it might seem to follow that the one is produced by the other, or that both refer to the same thing. The fact of the matter is, however, that if freedom in the latter sense were to ensue from freedom of the will, then man would necessarily be predestined. For freedom thus defined is also a necessary result of God's own activity.

What one must do, as such, is distinguish the two meanings of the word 'freedom.' For *freedom* in the ontological sense is not the necessary result of one's *free* act of will. The whole point of the freedom of the will is that it accounts for the fact that rational beings need not act in conformity with their natures. What one must do, in other words, is distinguish freedom of the will from true freedom. Freedom of the will is one's choice as to whether follow his nature or not. True freedom, on the other hand, results from one's acting in conformity with his nature and is by definition one's following God:

---

137. *Consolatio*, V, 2, 5–12: " 'Est,' inquit, 'neque enim fuerit ulla rationalis natura quin eidem libertas adsit arbitrii.' 'Nam quod ratione uti naturaliter potest id habet iudicium quo quidque discernat; per se igitur fugienda optandave dinoscit. Quod vero quis optandum esse iudicat petit; refugit vero quod aestimat esse fugiendum. Quare quibus in ipsis inest ratio, inest etiam volendi nolendique libertas.' "

138. Cf. e.g., *Consolatio*, III, 11, 91–96: "Nam saepe mortem cogentibus causis quam natura reformidat voluntas amplectitur, contraque illud quo solo mortalium rerum durat diurnitas gignendi opus, quod natura semper appetit, interdum coercet voluntas."

139. *Consolatio*, V, 2, 16–21: "Humanas vero animas liberiores quidem esse necesse est cum se in mentis divinae speculatione conservant, minus vero cum dilabuntur ad corpora, minusque etiam, cum terrenis artubus colligantur. Extrema vero est servitus, cum vitiis deditae rationis propriae possessione ceciderunt."

140. Cf., e.g., *Consolatio*, I, 5, 9ff.

"There is one ruler, one king," who delights in associating with his subjects, not in driving them out; to be guided by his hand and obey his justice is true freedom. (I, 5, 12–15)[141]

Freedom in the former sense is what accounts for the existence of evil. For if a rational being can act in a way which does not conform with his nature, and if his acting in conformity with his nature is seconding God's ordering of the universe, then his not acting in conformity with his nature must by definition be evil. God is the Good, any act which does not conform with His will must by definition be evil. Freedom in the latter sense, on the other hand, is the perfection of the agent. For if a free act is one which originates in the agent, and if the perfection of every agent is acting in complete conformity with its nature, then true freedom must be the agent's perfection. This clearly means that the agent's perfection is his following God's command. For freedom is also following God's command.

To get back to our initial point, if man's acting in accordance with the "natural function of his virtues" is following God's command, then man cannot be the moving cause of his actuation or perfection. For since God is the efficient cause of man's desire for the good — that is, since man desires the good by nature, and God is the cause of his nature — God alone can be the moving cause of the fulfillment of man's desire: his actuation or perfection.[142] This is logical. As we saw in the previous section, an object of desire can be one of two things: the efficient cause and term of an act of desire, or the term of an act of desire which originates in the desirer. If an object is the efficient cause of something's desire, however, then the desirer cannot possibly be the moving cause of his obtaining that object. An object can be the cause of one's desire if and only if the desirer is passive or receptive with respect to it. *Actio est in passo.* But if the desirer is passive, or receptive, with regards to an object, his possession of that object can only be potential: reception is the act of what is in potency insofar as it is in potency. But what is in potency with respect to a given object cannot obtain that object through its free acts. *Actiones non progrediuntur nisi ab existente in actu secundum quod est in actu.* If this is so, then the object of desire must be the moving cause of the desirer's possession of itself. *Tertium non datur.* As such, if God is the moving cause of man's desire for the good, then He must be the cause of man's obtaining the good.

---

141. Cf. *Consolatio,* V, 2, 16ff.
142. *Consolatio,* IV, 6, 199–201: "Hoc tantum perspexisse sufficiat, quod naturarum omnium proditor deus idem ad bonum dirigens cuncta disponat."

Boethius himself claims as much. He states that all of the movement, change, and progress in the universe is caused by God,[143] as is the change, movement, and progress in man's life specifically.[144] But things acquire their perfection through their change, movement, or progress. Thus all things are perfected by God. In this sense, Boethius claims that God directs all things to Himself,[145] not only by providing each one with the means necessary to stay true to its own nature,[146] but also by binding all of the creatures who are like Him to Himself.[147]

> *You* then bring forth, with the same bases, lesser living souls,
> And giving them light chariots fitting their heavenly nature,
> Broadcast them in the heavens and on earth, and by your
>   bounteous law,
> Make them, turned towards you, with returning fire come back.
> Grant, Father, to my mind to rise to your majestic seat,
> Grant me to wander by the source of good, grant light to see,
> To fix the clear sight of my mind on you.
> Disperse the clouding heaviness of this earthly mass
> And Flash forth in your brightness. For to the blessed, *you*
> Are clear serenity, and quiet rest: to see *you* is their goal,
> And you, alone and same,
> Are their beginning, driver, leader, pathway, end. (III, 9, 18–28)

What then are we to make of the passages in which Boethius seems to claim that man attains his good through his own free activity? The point here clearly calls us to distinguish between the causes of man's perfection. Boethius's main claim is the God is the efficient cause of man's happiness. But this does not mean that man plays no role at all in his acquisition of his perfection. For, he points out, the presupposition of God's perfecting man is man's acting in accordance with the "natural

---

143. *Consolatio*, IV, 6, 22–25: "Omnium generatio rerum cunctusque mutabilium naturarum progressus et quidquid aliquo movetur modo, causas, ordinem, formas ex divinae mentis stabilitate sortitur." See also *Consolatio*, III, 12, 24–26: "Hoc quidquid est quo condita manent atque agitantur, usitato cunctis vocabulo deum nomino."
144. *Consolatio*, IV, 6, 86–89: "Haec actus etiam fortunasque hominum indissolubili causarum conexione constringit, quae cum ab immobilis providentiae proficiscatur exordiis, ipsas quoque immutabiles esse necesse est."
145. Cf. *Consolatio*, V, 2, 27–29: "Quae tamen ille ab aeterno cuncta prospiciens providentiae cernit intuitus et suis quaeque meritis praedestinata disponit."
146. Cf. *Consolatio*, IV, 6, 109ff. where Boethius gives specific examples of the way in which God through Providence disposes things for men in order for them to be able to reach the good.
147. *Consolatio*, IV, 6, 200–204: "Naturarum omnium proditor deus idem ad bonum dirigens cuncta disponat, dumque ea quae protulit in sui similitudinem retinere festinat, malum omne de reipublicae suae terminis per fatalis seriem necessitatis eliminet."

function of his virtues," and that precisely because man's will is free.[148] God's kingdom could not be a happy one, he indicates, if things were made members of it against their wills.[149] The reasoning behind this claim is clear. If the perfection of every being is its complete possession of its nature, then the perfection of rational beings must include the perfection of their wills, and the perfection of their wills must be their acting in conformity with their natures. The fact of the matter is that no being who has free will can be forced to act in conformity with his nature precisely because he has free will. Hence, rational beings must choose to conform with their natures in order to be perfected by God.

Boethius makes this point negatively. He shows that those rational beings who do not act in accordance with their natures do not attain their good precisely because they do not act in accordance with their natures:

> For see how plainly great is the weakness of corrupt men, who cannot attain even to that towards which their natural inclination draws and almost compels them. And what would it be like if they were deprived of this great and almost invincible aid, of nature leading the way? And consider also how great is the impotence that grips wicked men. For those things they seek as rewards, which they cannot acquire and possess, are not trifles of playthings; they fail in what concerns the very sum and summit of things, nor do the wretches achieve the performance of that for which alone they spend days and nights striving; and it is in this matter that the strength of good men is outstandingly clear. (IV, 2, 75–86)

Nor is this all he claims. He adds that those men who do not act in conformity with their natures also "lose" their being,[150] and their humanity as a result of their so doing:

> Whatever falls from goodness, ceases to be; wherefore evil men cease to be what they were — but that they were men till now their still surviving form of the human body shows — and therefore by turning to wickedness they have by the same act lost their human nature. But since only goodness can raise anyone above mankind, it follows necessarily that wickedness thrusts down be-

---

148. *Consolatio*, I, 5m, 25–27: "Omnia certo fine gubernans / Hominum solos respuis actus / Merito rector cohibere modo."
149. See footnote 260.
150. *Consolatio*, IV, 2, 110–13.

neath deserving the name of men those whom it has cast down from the human condition. (IV, 3, 48–54)

But if by choosing to not act in conformity with one's nature one fails to attain his happiness and loses his nature, then by the converse it follows that man must choose to act in conformity with his nature in order to be perfected by God. He must, in other words, act in accordance with the "natural function of his virtues." This clearly means that man does play a role in his own actuation. As this is so, his attaining the good must in part result from his own activity. Hence Boethius's claim that man acquires the good through his own activity. Man's role is not, however, a direct one: man does not actuate himself. Man's role is to assent to God's providence. It is in this sense that Boethius claims that 'goodness' is a reward for one's good actions, a reward which one loses when he ceases to be good:

> Surely you know the ancient and fundamental law of your city, by which it is ordained that it is not right to exile one who has chosen to dwell there? No one who is settled within her walls and fortification need ever fear banishment: but whoever ceases to desire to live there has thereby ceased to deserve to do so. (I, 5, 15–20)

It is in this sense in which he claims that goodness is the effect of one's acting in accordance with the "natural function of his virtues."

It will also be noticed that Boethius never claims that man is the moving cause of his own actuation. The point of those passages in which he would seem to claim that man is the moving cause of his actuation is rather to indicate that man's virtuous activity is a prerequisite of his being actuated by God, or that man is the instrumental cause of his perfection. This can even be seen in the most suspicious of the passages we quoted above. For in it Boethius claims that man is *made* happy if he is good, where the accent at this point is to be placed on the *made*:

> But what reward? The greatest and fairest of all: for remember that corollary which I gave you a little time ago as an excellent present, and conclude this: since the good itself is happiness it is clear that all good men are made happy for this reason, that they are good. But those who are happy, it is agreed, are gods; and therefore that is the reward of men which no time can lessen, no man's power diminish, no man's wickedness obscure, to become gods. (IV, 2, 24–29)

The *Consolatio's Reditus*

The *Consolatio*'s definition of the *reditus*, has two principal parts. Primarily, Boethius claims that man's perfection is his acquisition of goodness which takes place through his real relation with God: by participating in Him. For since God is the Good, things can only receive goodness when they receive His activity: when they are guided by providence. This reception of goodness is their perfection, in Boethius's view, because goodness is a substantial property of all things. For this implies that things receive being when they receive goodness. But things' reception of being is their becoming, and their becoming is their actualizing their natures: their perfection. Things' perfection is therefore their reception of God's efficient causality.

There is a twist to this, however. There are some beings who have a choice as to whether be actualized by God or not: rational beings. Rational beings, Boethius points out, have free wills, and can as such be perfected by God if and only if they choose to act in conformity with their own natures. For, he claims, it is only when their actions conform with their natures that they actualize or possess those natures, and it is only when they actualize or possess their natures that they can be actualized by God. What does not exist in the true sense of the word cannot be perfected. To put the point in other terms, it is only when rational beings actualize their own natures that they are substantially good, and it is only when they are substantially good that they can be actualized by the goodness which God bestows upon them through His providence. Hence rational beings must be the instrumental causes of their perfection.

Boethius's account of man's *reditus* mirrors his account of the *exitus* of good things and like his *exitus* it is a reconciliation of the substantial and teleological definitions of the good. Boethius's account of the *exitus* calls for two real relations: one with God and one with *ipsum esse*. The first real relation affords things' existence and the second accounts for their acquisition of a determinate mode of existence: an essence. His claim in the *Quomodo* is that things must have a real relation with God in order to be able to actualize their good essence, and that it is only when they actualize their good essence that they are substantially good. His account of the *reditus,* on the other hand, calls for things to actualize their good essences in order to be perfected by God's efficient causality: by their real relations with God. Thus things must receive God's efficient causality and actuate their essences in order to be, and they must actualize their essences and receive God's efficient causality in order to be perfected. Just as Boethius holds that God's causal efficiency is the prerequisite of things' being able to actuate their essences and exist, in other words, he holds that things' actualizing their essences is the prerequisite of their being perfected. In the *exitus,* therefore, God's causal efficiency is the prerequisite of a being's actuating its essence, whereas a being's actualizing its essence is the prerequisite of its being actualized by God's causal efficiency — providence — in the *reditus.*

Boethius's account of the *exitus* is also an attempt to synthesize the two classical definitions of the good: to show that the good is at once a real relation and a substantial property of being. The *Quomodo* demonstrates that goodness is a substantial property of created things because it is a real relation. For things are substantially good because they are created by God and actuate their essence. Their actuating their essence, Boethius explains then, is contingent upon their having a real relation with Him who is the Good. For it is only if things' own existences are real relations with God that they can actuate their good essences through real relations. Thus, things' substantial goodness must be contingent upon the good's being a real relation. We find something similar in the *Consolatio*'s *reditus.* In it Boethius shows that the good is a real relation because it is a substantial property of being: he claims that the good is a real relation because it is a substantial property of both beings who become and of that being who actualizes them: God. For things' actualization — their attaining their 'good' — is contingent upon both their being substantially good, and upon their real relations with Him who is the Good. The point here, in other words, is that the Good can be things' final cause if and only if things are substantially good and if they are actualized by what is the substantially good being *par excellence.*

Boethius makes points explicitly. He proves that things must be actualized by what is substantially the Good by showing that worldly 'goods' cannot actualize men insofar as no material thing makes man good; he proves that things must be substantially good in order for the Good to be their final cause by showing both (1) that those rational beings who do not choose to conform with their natures cannot be actualized by God, and (2) that the good is things' final cause insofar as it is one of their substantial properties.

Boethius's attempt to reconcile the two definitions of the good is deliberate, and it is in the *Consolatio* that one can find its root. In it he claims that the good is a substantial property and a real relation for all created things, because created things are likenesses of God in whose simple nature the Good is at once His Beginning, His Being, and His

End. God is the principle of all things and happiness. Created beings cannot share in this simplicity. They are not their own origins or their perfection: their origin and perfection is something other than they. Their goodness must as such be their real relations with their cause — those real relations whereby they are actuated and perfected — and is their substantial goodness because they actuate it. Creation's goodness is a moving image of what is simple in God:

> For this present nature of unmoving life that infinite motion of temporal things imitates, and since it cannot fully represent and equal it, it falls from immobility into motion, it shrinks from the simplicity of that present into the infinite quantity of the future and the past and, since it cannot possess at once the whole fullness of its life, in this very respect, that it in some way never ceases to be, it seems to emulate to some degree which it cannot fully express, by binding itself to the sort of present of this brief and fleeting moment, a present which since it wears a kind of likeness of that permanent present, grants to whatsoever things it touches that they should seem to be. But since it could not be permanent, it seized on the infinite journeying of time, and in that way became such that it should continue by going on a life the fullness of which it could not embrace by being permanent. (V, 6, 40–56)

Part Four

PARTICIPATION

If participation is the means whereby Boethius explains why complex things are good—if it is the cause of the goodness of complex things—then participation must mean two different things in his metaphysics. For Boethius claims that complex things are good for two different reasons. In the *Quomodo Substantiae* he claims that they are substantially good: that they are good in virtue of their essences. In the *Consolatio Philosophiae*, on the other hand, he claims that they become good when they acquire the good and that their acquisition of the good is their perfection.

Now, these two causes of complex things' goodness cannot clearly be the same. For if things are substantially good—if they are good in virtue of their essences—then they must be good insofar as they are. After all, complex things are what they are because they actuate an essence. Complex things are not, however, perfect simply because they are. Perfection is something which complex things acquire after they come to be. As such, that acquisition of the good whereby complex things become perfect cannot be their acquisition of that substantial goodness which is necessary for them to exist. Thus, the causes of complex things' acquiring goodness and of their being substantially good must differ. But according to Boethius participation is the cause of both things. Participation must therefore mean two different things for Boethius.

Participation in the first sense must explain why beings are: it must be the cause of their existences. For if things are substantially good because they are good in virtue of their essences, then whatever causes a being to be substantially good must cause that being to possess, or actuate, an essence. But whatever causes a being to possess an essence must also cause that being to exist, if its possession is ontological, as it must be if a being's possession of an essence is the cause of its substantial goodness. For an essence is a determinate mode of existing, and nothing can cause something to possess a determinate mode of existing if it does not cause that something to exist. But participation is the cause of things' substantial goodness. Hence participation must be the cause of things' existences.

Participation in the second sense is the cause of a being's perfection. For if beings are substantially good, their acquisition of goodness must be their perfection. After all, if goodness is a substantial property of being, then something must acquire being when it acquires goodness. Boethius points this out.[1] But when an existing thing acquires being, it cannot undergo substantial change, else its acquisition of being would not be *its* acquisition of being at all. It is once again Boethius who points this out.[2] But if a complex thing does not undergo substantial change when it acquires being, it cannot acquire being other than its own. Beings must actuate their own potential when they become. When a being actualizes its own potential it is perfected. If participation is the cause of existing things' acquisition of goodness, as such, it must be the cause of existing things' perfection.

Now, in the *Consolatio Philosophiae* Boethius explicitly claims that participation is the cause of contingent things' perfection; in the *Quomodo Substantiae,* on the other hand, he delineates that doctrine of participation which accounts for the existences of contingent things. The latter doctrine is the more difficult and controversial of the two. For the *Quomodo Substantiae* is simply a more abstruse text than the *Consolatio* is. This does not, however, mean that the *Consolatio*'s doctrine of participation is simple.

In this part we will finally draw out Boethius's doctrine of participation. Since participation means two different things in Boethian metaphysics, the part will have two chapters. In the first chapter we will delineate the *Quomodo Substantiae*'s doctrine; in the second we will draw out the *Consolatio Philosophiae*'s doctrine of participation. In the final section we will review the doctrine as a whole.

---

1. *Consolatio*, III, 10, 8ff.
2. *Consolatio*, IV, 2, 110–11: "Est enim quod ordinem retinet servatque naturam."

Chapter 13

THE *QUOMODO SUBSTANTIAE*

The *Quomodo Substantiae* has two main parts. The first half of the work is a "summula"[1] of seven metaphysical axioms which Boethius claims are the "bounds and rules according to which he will develop all that follows."[2] With these axioms he will determine how things are "substantially good without being God." The second half, on the other hand, is his definition of the cause of things' substantial goodness. Now, there is some dispute as to whether the two parts of the work are coherent. For the "rules and bounds" which Boethius outlines in the first part of his work do not seem to be those which he uses in the second part of the work.[3] This is especially evident to those readers whose intent is to determine Boethius's doctrine of participation. For the metaphysical "summula" contains two axioms which concern participation, the second of which clearly claims that participation is the cause of complex things' existences:

> Omne quod est participat eo quod est esse ut sit; alio vero participat ut aliquid sit. Ac per hoc id quod est participat eo quod est esse ut sit; est vero ut participet alio quolibet. (VI, 41–44)

One would thus expect participation to play a crucial role in Boethius's definition of the cause of things' substantial goodness. After all, whatever causes something to be substantially good must cause it to exist. The fact of the matter is, however, that this is apparently not the case. For Boethius's definition of the cause of the substantial goodness of complex things simply contains no positive reference to participation at all. The two times he does mention participation in the second part

---

1. The term "summula" is Maioli's. Cf. Maioli, 14.
2. *Quomodo,* 14–17: "Ut igitur in mathematica fieri solet ceterisque etiam disciplinis, praeposui terminos regulasque quibus cuncta quae sequuntur efficiam."
3. McInerny's comments on Brosch's approach to the *Quomodo*'s axioms is very telling on this point. Cf. McInerny, p. 177: "In what, given his approach, amounts to real daring, Brosch decides to examine the body of the tractate before looking at the axioms as such."

of his work he seems to dismiss it as a possible cause of things' substantial goodness. This apparent discrepancy in the text seems to call one to choose whether he believes Boethius's true doctrine of participation to be the one which is to be found in the first half of the text or in the second half.[4]

It was to obviate this problem that we began our analysis of Boethius's notion of participation with the second half of the work. For the truth of the matter is that there is no real discrepancy in the text at all. The reason why Boethius can claim that complex things are good in virtue of their essences without being God, we saw, is that he believes that their essences cannot cause their existences or their own becoming determinate in particular things. What this means is that both things' existences and their actuating their essences require an extrinsic cause. But if the cause of complex things' existences and of their actuating an essence is something other than themselves, then both complex things' existences and their actuating an essence must be real relations. To be precise, that cause must be participation. Hence Boethius's solution does use a doctrine of participation.

As such, we will begin our reconstruction of the first meaning of participation in Boethius's metaphysics by reviewing the conclusion of our analysis of the *Quomodo Substantiae*'s definition of the cause of things' substantial goodness. We will then turn to the axioms. Our analysis of the axioms will have two objects and three parts. The objects are: (1) to understand the main tenets of the metaphysics which Boethius delineates in them, and (2) to show how the cause of things' substantial goodness as it is delineated in the second half of the work follows the "rules and bounds" which Boethius sets out in the axioms. We will begin that analysis by reviewing the most important contemporary interpretations of them; then we will set forth our own interpretation of the axioms by examining each of them; finally we will compare the metaphysics of the first and second parts of the *Quomodo*, and delineate its doctrine of participation.

The *Quomodo* and the Causes of Complex Things' Substantial Goodness

Boethius's problem in the *Quomodo*, as we saw, is to show that complex things are good in virtue of their essences but are not God. Things' substantial goodness is problematic because it seems to imply that com-

---

4. This is one of the causes of scholarly dissent with regards to the *Quomodo* itself, as we saw in the first chapter. See p. 5ff.

plex things are the causes of their own existences. After all, if all existing things are substantially good, as Boethius himself claims they are,[5] then whatever causes complex things to exist must also cause them to be good. If this is so, however, then by the converse, the cause of complex things' goodness must be the cause of their existences. What seems to follow is that complex things' essences have to be the cause of their existences. For complex things' essences are the cause of their goodness.[6] The fact of the matter is, however, that complex things' essences cannot be the cause of their existences. For if they were, then complex things would have to be God: God alone is the cause of His existence. And this is precisely the conclusion which Boethius is trying to avoid. Hence he has to show how complex things' essences can be the cause of their goodness without being the cause of their existences. The heart of his solution is to distinguish the formal and efficient causes of things' being and goodness.

Boethius's claim is that complex things are substantially good because they actuate — are determinations of — their essence (*ipsum esse*) which is good. The reason why this does not imply that complex things are God, he points out, is that composite things' essences (*ipsum esse*): (1) cannot be identical to their existences and (2) cannot be the moving or efficient causes of their existences. The first case is only God's. God is *id quod est esse*: Being itself. It cannot, however, apply to anything which comes into existence. For Being itself cannot come to be. Thus whatsoever comes to exist cannot be Being itself. But complex things come to be. As such, their essences cannot be Being. Nor can their essences be their existences.

Boethius makes the point in a slightly different way. He firstly shows that essence and existence must be distinct in all complex things. Were they not to be, he claims, then complex things' various properties would have to be identical to each other.[7] But this is clearly impossible. Thus, all beings other than God are complex.[8] The conclusion here is foregone: no being other than God can be his essence, and no essence other than God's can be or cause existence.

This leaves us with the second point: that complex things' essences cannot be the moving or efficient causes of their existences. Boethius's claim is that if complex things' essences were the efficient causes of their

---

5. *Quomodo*, 56–60.
6. Hence, Boethius claims that his problem is to understand how things are substantially good without being substantial goods as can be seen from the work's title: "*Quomodo substantiae in eo quod sint bonae sint cum non sint substantialia bona.*"
7. *Quomodo*, 100–108.
8. *Quomodo*, 117–19: "Quae quoniam non sunt simplicia, nec esse omnino poterant, nisi ea id quod solum bonum est esse voluisset."

existences, there could be no "things" at all.[9] That is, things' essences would have to subsist if they were to cause particular things to exist. But the essences of complex things cannot be subsisting things. Were they to be, they could not be essences. Thus, complex things' essences cannot be the efficient causes of their existences.

Boethius's point is clearly that we have to distinguish the efficient and the formal causes of complex things' substantial goodness. When we claim that complex things are good in virtue of their essences, we are not claiming that their essences are the efficient causes of their goodness. They cannot be. We are claiming that they are the formal causes of their goodness.

Now, if the essences of complex things cannot be the efficient causes of their existences, then two things follow: (1) the efficient cause of the existences of complex things must be something other than they; and (2) the efficient cause of complex things' actuating their essences must be something other than they. The first point is obvious. The second point, on the other hand, is a corollary of the first. For if the essences of complex things cannot be the efficient causes of their existences, then they cannot be the efficient causes of complex things' having a determinate mode of existence. But things have a determinate mode of existence when they actuate an essence. As such, the essences of complex things cannot be the efficient cause of complex things' actuating an essence. This means that the efficient cause of complex things' actuating an essence must be something other than both they and their essences. But if the efficient cause of both the existences of complex things and of their actuating an essence must be something other than they and their essences, then both the existences of complex things and their actuating an essence must be caused by real relations. *Actio est in passo* for all acts of efficient causality after all. This implies that composite things must have two real relations in order to exist: the first one is the cause of their existence; the second one is the cause of their actuating their essences — i.e., their being a determination of *ipsum esse*.

What we have here is the backbone of Boethius's solution. For there are only three steps left to take in order to prove that things are substantially good and not God: (1) apply the distinction between the formal and efficient causes of complex things' existences to the problem; (2) show that complex things' essences are their formal causes; and (3) prove that complex things' essences are good.

Boethius's first step is to prove that goodness is a transcendental property of being: that *ens et bonum convertuntur*. His claim is that

---

9. *Quomodo*, 111–15.

both complex things' existences[10] and the indeterminate essence of all things (*ipsum esse*)[11] must be good because they are created by God, who is the Good. This leaves us with the second point. For the fact that both the existences and essences (*ipsum esse*) of complex things are transcendentally good does not mean that complex things themselves are substantially good. In order for complex things to be substantially good, their essence (*ipsum esse*) must be the formal cause of their goodness. Hence, Boethius claims that complex things must "derive from the good (*ipsum esse*) and not be apart from it,"[12] if they are to be substantially good. His point is that complex things must have a real relation with *ipsum esse* in order to be substantially good. After all, *ipsum esse* must at once be what causes them to be good, and be other than they. This real relation has a presupposition, however. For Boethius's claim is that things cannot "derive from the good" unless their existences are efficiently caused by God.[13] The reasoning behind his point is clear. Complex things cannot actuate an essence if they do not exist. But as *ipsum esse* cannot be the efficient cause of the existences of complex things, it cannot be the efficient cause of their having a determinate mode of existence. As such, it cannot be the efficient cause of the goodness of complex things. It follows that in order for things' essences to be their formal causes, God must be their efficient cause.

What we see here is the application of the distinction between the efficient and formal causes of things' goodness. Boethius's conclusion, as such, is that things' substantial goodness is efficiently caused by God and is formally caused by their essences; this is to say that things can be substantially good only if they have two real relations: the first is in God and confers existence upon them; the second is in their good essences (*ipsum esse*) and causes them to actuate their good essences.[14]

Now, if Boethius's definition of the cause of things' substantial goodness abides by the *rules and bounds* which he delineates in his axioms, then one should expect his axioms to claim that things' existences are

---

10. See footnote 8 above.
11. *Quomodo*, 124–27: "Sed ipsum esse omnium rerum ex eo fluxit quod est primum bonum et quod bonum tale est ut recte dicatur in eo quod est esse bonum. Ipsum igitur eorum esse bonum est; tunc enim in eo."
12. *Quomodo*, 140–50.
13. *Quomodo*, 143–46.
14. *Quomodo*, 128–40: "Qua in re soluta quaestio est. Idcirco enim licet in eo quod sint bona sint, non sunt tamen similia primo bono, quoniam non quoquo modo sint res ipsum esse earum bonum est, sed quoniam non potest esse ipsum esse rerum, nisi a primo esse defluxerit, id est bono; idcirco ipsum esse bonum est nec est simile ei a quo est. Illud enim quoquo modo sit bonum est in eo quod est; non enim aliud est praeterquam bonum. Hoc autem nisi ab illo esset, bonum fortasse esse posset, sed bonum in eo quod est esse non posset. Tunc enim participaret forsitan bono; ipsum vero esse quod non haberent a bono, bonum habere non possent."

caused by two acts of participation: the first is in God and is what confers existence upon things; the second is in their essences and is what causes them to be specific things.

The *Quomodo*'s Axioms: Interpretations

Boethius's axioms are intentionally elliptical.[15] For in them he sets forth what seem to be the basic principles of being[16] without explaining either what he means by them or what he means by the two main terms with which he expounds these principles: *esse* and *id quod est*. Indeed, he says quite explicitly that he is relying upon the intelligence of his interpreter to understand what he means by both:

> These preliminaries are enough then for our purpose. The intelligent interpreter will supply arguments appropriate to each point. (53–55)[17]

This abstruseness has engendered a myriad of interpretations of the meanings of both the terms and of the principles.[18] Pierre Duhem claims that *id quod est* "is the concrete really existing thing which exists as the product of the union of matter and form" whereas *esse* is its essence: the "form which all individual things of the same species have in common."[19] His point is that the distinction Boethius draws between these terms is between the particular instance of a universal and the universal itself. Cornelio Fabro concurs that *id quod est* means the concrete par-

---

15. My use of "intentional" is intentional. Boethius himself says he wants to be obscure. Cf. *Quomodo*, 8–14: "Hebdomadas vero ego mihi ipse commentor potiusque ad memoriam meam speculata conservo quam cuiquam participo quorum lascivia ac petulantia nihil a ioco risuque patitur esse seiunctum. Prohinc tu ne sis obscuritatibus brevitatis adversus, quae cum sint arcani fida custodia tum id habent commodi, quod cum his solis qui digni sunt conloquuntur."
16. This is in keeping with the mathematical model Boethius says he is going to follow. Cf. *Quomodo*, 14–17: "Ut igitur in mathematica fieri solet ceterisque etiam disciplinis praeposui terminos regulasque quibus cuncta quae sequuntur efficiam."
17. *Quomodo*, 53–55: "Sufficiunt igitur quae praemisimus; a prudente vero rationis interprete suis unumquodque aptabitur argumentis."
18. This debate has been going on for at least eleven centuries. Scholars have discovered commentaries on the *Quomodo* which date back to the ninth century. Cf. "Der Kommentar des Johannes Scottus su den *Opuscola Sacra* des Boethius," in *Johannes Scotus*, ed. E. K. Rand (Munich: Quellen und Untersuchungen zur lateinischen Philologie des Mittelalters, 1906) pp. 28–80.
19. Pierre Duhem, *Le Système du Monde: Histoire des doctrines cosmologiques de Platon à Copernic* (Paris: Librairie Scientifique Hermann, 1913) p. 289: "Le *id quod est*, c'est la chose concrète et réellement existante que produit l'union de la matière et de la forme; l'*esse*, l'essence, c'est la forme commune à toutes le choses individuelles de même espèce, telle la gravité, forme spécifique commune à tous les corps graves."

ticular,[20] but he believes *esse* to mean either a substantial form in the Aristotelian sense (*ipsum esse*), or an accidental form (*aliquid esse*).[21] Varvis claims that *esse* is a Platonic form.[22] Viktor Schurr takes another position yet. For although he concurs that *esse* can mean essence in Boethius's lexicon, he contends that can also mean existence, or *actus essendi*.[23] Pierre Hadot maintains that *esse* is to be understood Neoplatonically as meaning pure indeterminate activity (*agir pur*), and that *id quod est* is the limitation of the *esse* in a concrete thing, which exists according to a certain form. Hence, he holds that the distinction between *esse* and *id quod est* is between pure being without determination and being determined by a form, which he says can also be called the distinction between existence and substance.[24] Chadwick agrees that the work is Neoplatonic[25] and states rather laconically that the distinction between *esse* and *id quod est* is "between simple being (*esse*) and existence (*id quod est*)."[26] Finally, Steward, Rand, and Tester, the translators of the Loeb volume of Boethius's theological tractates, translate *id quod est* either literally as the "thing that is," the "particular thing," or they take *id quod est* as "existence" and *esse* as "existence," "being," "simple being," or "absolute being."[27] Nor is the discussion limited to the meanings of the terms and principles, for scholars have also debated whether the distinction between these terms is merely conceptual or real, and so on.

The main source of contention among scholars is the meaning of *esse* and its variants: *ipsum esse* and *aliquid esse*. For interpreters generally concede that *id quod est* means a particular existing thing,[28] although they do not agree upon what Boethius means by a particular existing

---

20. Fabro, *Nozione*, p. 99: "Da buon aristotelico, Boezio osserva che solo il concreto, l'*id quod est*, esiste: l'astratto invece, l'*esse*, ancora da solo non esiste, e che solo il concreto, che esiste di fatto, può arricchirsi di altre determinazioni."

21. Fabro, *Nozione*, p. 103: "Adunque le due partecipazioni dell'*id quod est*, prima all'*ipsum esse* e poi all'*esse aliquid*, vanno intese come partecipazione l'una alla forma sostanziale e l'altra alle forme accidentali."

22. Varvis, p. 48: "That which is, then, participates in being through its form. And here Boethius refers to a Platonic "form," the metaphysical constituent of existence." He backs the point by quoting Gilson's *History of Christian Philosophy*.

23. Viktor Schurr, *Die Trinitätslehre des Boëthius im Lichte der skythischen Kontroversien* (Paderborn: Schöningh, 1935) pp. 33–34 and 44.

24. Pierre Hadot, *Distinction*, p. 150: "Nous retrouvons la même opposition entre l'*esse* et *quod est* dans la distinction, également traditionnelle, entre existence et substance, *hyparchis* et *ousia*, et nous retrouvons ici encore Marius Victorinus et son correspondant, l'Arien Candidus."

25. Cf. Chadwick, *Consolations*, p. 203: "The third tractate, dedicated to John the deacon, is the most technical and obviously Neoplatonic of the five opuscola."

26. Chadwick, *Consolations*, p. 209.

27. Boethius, *The Theological Tractates and The Consolation of Philosophy*.

28. One of the exceptions here is Gangolf Schrimpf, who holds that *id quod est* means essence: "Wesen des Dinges." Cf. Schrimpt, pp. 3–35.

thing: that is, whether he believes particular things to be material, concrete, simple, consubstantial with God, and so forth. For the specific meaning of *id quod est* is in part determined by the meaning of *esse*, and the meaning of *esse* is the source of scholarly dissent.

Now, there are four basic positions with regards to the meaning of *esse*. For scholarly opinion is split between those who interpret *esse* to mean essence, and those who interpret *esse* to mean existence. Each of these two camps is, in turn, split. For some of those scholars who hold that it means essence believe Boethius to claim that things' essences are the cause of their existences, while others hold that Boethius does not believe things' essences to be the cause of their existences. Some of those scholars who believe *esse* to mean existence, on the other hand, believe Boethius to hold that contingent things are consubstantial with God. Others, on the other hand, claim that Boethius does not believe contingent things to be consubstantial with God. Let us analyze each of these positions.

St. Thomas and the Thomists: Actus Essendi *vs.* Essentia

St. Thomas wrote a commentary on the *Quomodo*. This is in itself rather strange, given the thirteenth century's general lack of interest in the text.[29] What is stranger yet is the intra-Thomistic dispute as to whether his interpretation is faithful to Boethius's text. Aquinas's methodology and position are simply stated. *In de Hebdomadibus* is a straight-forward logico-linguistic and metaphysical analysis of the text. It is one of those rare texts in which St. Thomas does not call upon *auctoritates* to back his interpretation.[30] His interpretation of the meaning of the axioms' main terms is as follows: *ipsum esse* is an abstract universal. It means 'being' in the abstract sense: being which becomes determinate in particular things through particular substantial forms.[31] It is the most universal of all concepts, insofar as it can participate in nothing.[32] *Esse,* as such, means a particular thing's

---

29. Cf. Pandolfi, p. 36: "C'è da ripetere che il Commento tomista è opera quasi unica per il XIII secolo, perché i *magistri* dell'epoca si disinteressarono quasi tutti all'ostica 'pubblicazione' boeziana."

30. Pandolfi and Fabro both remark on this fact. Cf., e.g., Pandolfi, p. 36: "Particolare anch'esso raro (per la consueta metodologia tomista), va avanti da solo, senza protezione di *auctoritates,* senza citazioni (tranne qualche iniziale riferimento scritturistico, e qualche citazione da Aristotele quasi 'automatica': 'Bonum est id quod omnia appetunt')."

31. *In de Hebdomadibus*, II: "Circa ens autem consideratur ipsum esse quasi quiddam commune et indeterminatum, quod quidem dupliciter determinatur, uno modo ex parte subiecti quod esse habet, alio modo ex parte praedicati utpote cum dicimus de homine vel de quacumque alia re, non quidem quod sit simpliciter, sed quod sit aliquid puta album vel nigrum."

32. *In de Hebdomadibus*, II: "Similiter autem nec potest aliquid participare per modum quo particulare participat universale; sic enim etiam ea quae in abstracto dicuntur partici-

"being." *Id quod est,* on the other hand, means an existing thing, *id quod in se ipso subsistit:* the *subiectum essendi,*[33] or more simply yet, *ens.*[34] The gist of Aquinas's interpretation is that Boethius's axioms are an analysis of the *components* of being and of the relations between them.

There is no disputing that this is precisely what Boethius is doing. What can and has been disputed by both Thomists and non-Thomists alike is the precise meaning which St. Thomas attributes to Boethius's *esse,* and his view of the relations between being's components. Now, 'being' as far as Aquinas is concerned means *actus essendi:* the act of being. Thus, the distinction between *ipsum esse* and *id quod est* in his view is at once the distinction between 'existence,' or the act of being abstractly taken, and particular determinate acts of existence which are determined by their *supposita,*[35] and between a thing's act of being and its *suppositum.*[36] For things can be of two sorts: they can be simple or composite. If they are simple, then their existing must be their *suppositum.*[37] If they are composite, on the other hand, then there must be a real distinction between things' acts of existing and their *supposita.*[38] That is, their existences can neither be what they are, nor can they cause their existences. Hence, in order for composite things

---

pare aliquid possunt sicut albedo colorem, sed ipsum esse est communissimum, unde ipsum quidem participatur in aliis, non autem participat aliquid aliud."

33. *In de Hebdomadibus,* II: "Id quod est significatur sicut subiectum essendi."
34. *In de Hebdomadibus,* II: "Id quod est sive ens, quamvis sit communissimum, tamen concretive dicitur, et ideo participat ipsum esse."
35. *In de Hebdomadibus,* II: "Ipsum esse non significatur sicut subiectum essendi,... sed id quod est significatur sicut subiectum essendi... ita possumus dicere quod ens sive id quod est sit in quantum participat actum essendi. Et hoc est quod dicit quod *ipsum esse nondum est* quia non attribuitur sibi esse sicut subiecto essendi, sed *id quod est, accepta essendi forma,* scilicet suscipiendo ipsum actum essendi, *est atque consistit,* id est in se ipso subsistit."
36. *In de Hebdomadibus,* II: "Deinde cum dicit: *Omni composito* etc., ponit conceptiones de composito et simplici, quae pertinent ad rationem unius, et est considerandum quod ea quae supra dicta sunt de diversitate ipsius esse et eius quod est, est secundum ipsas intentiones. Hic ostendit quomodo applicetur ad res; et primo ostendit hoc in compositis, secundo in simplicibus."
37. *In de Hebdomadibus,* II: "Id autem solum erit vere simplex quod non participat esse, non quidem inhaerens sed subsistens. Hoc autem non potest esse nisi unum, quia, si ipsum esse nihil aliud habet admixtum praeter id quod est esse, ut dictum est, impossibile est id quod est ipsum esse multiplicari per aliquid diversificans, et, quia nihil aliud praeter se habet adiunctum, consequens est quod nullius accidentis sit susceptivum. Hoc autem simplex, unum et sublime est ipse Deus."
38. *In de Hebdomadibus,* II: "Est ergo primo considerandum quod sicut esse et quod est differunt secundum intentiones, ita in compositis differunt realiter. Quod quidem manifestum est ex praemissis. Dictum est enim supra quod ipsum esse neque participat aliquid ut eius ratio constituatur ex multis, neque habet aliquid extrinsecum admixtum ut sit in eo compositio accidentalis; et ideo ipsum esse non est compositum; res ergo composita non est suum esse; et ideo dicit quod in *omni composito aliud est* esse ens et *aliud* ipsum compositum quod est participando *ipsum esse.*"

to exist, they must participate in simple being, God,[39] who is the Act of Existing Itself.[40]

This is precisely what scholars claim Boethius is not doing. For *esse*, they claim, does not mean *actus essendi* in Boethius's lexicon. It means essence. Hence one must not look for the distinction between essence and existence in the text. Thus, Roland-Gosselin claims that:

> Il nous paraît donc certain que Boèce ne parle jamais de l'existence distincte de l'essence.[41]

Boethius's distinction, he claims, derives from Themistius's interpretation of Aristotle's distinction between primary and secondary substances. Themistius distinguished ὕδωρ from ὕδατι εἶναι: this specific concretely existing water, and the abstract essence of water. Boethius makes that *distinction* his own. Thus, the distinction between *id quod est* and *esse* must be the distinction between a primary substance and a secondary substance, or the distinction between a particular example of a concretely existing thing and its form or cause. After all, in the *De Trinitate* he claims that "omne namque *esse ex forma* est."[42] Hence, like Aristotle, he must believe that forms are the causes of things.

Although *esse* can mean existence in some of Boethius's works, Brosch adds, it does not mean existence in the *Quomodo*:

> Trotz der Dunkelheiten, die das Axiom mit sich bringt, können wir uns nicht ganz der Ansicht von Bruder anschließen, der das *Esse* als Dasein und das *id quod est* als "jedes durch eine individuelle Wesenheit bestimmte Einzelding" deutet, und zwar als folgenden Gründen: Erstens wurde das *Esse* in den theologischen Schriften nie als Dasein gebraucht; warum sollte es gerade in diesem Axiom so verstanden werden, da es doch ausdrücklich zur Lösung des Inhaltes dienen soll?[43]

Indeed, both *esse* and *id quod est* mean essence, and the distinction between them is that the former means essence in a universal way, whereas the latter means a particular thing's essence:

> Das '*Esse* ohne Beifügung' hatte dort die Bedeutung von spezifischer Wesenheit oder, gebrauchen wir den boethianischen Aus-

---

39. *In de Hebdomadibus*, II: "Nam aliquid est simpliciter per hoc quod *participat* ipso *esse*."
40. See footnote 37.
41. M.-D. Roland-Gosselin, *Le De Ente et Essentia de Saint Thomas d'Aquin* (Paris: Bibliothèque Thomiste, 1926) p. 145.
42. *De Trinitate* 2, 19–21.
43. Brosch, p. 67.

druck, 'substantieller Wesenheit.' *Id quod est* ist die Gesamtwesenheit, oder wir können sie auch 'konkrete Wesenheit' nennen.[44]

Fabro agrees that St. Thomas's interpretation of *esse* reads something into the text[45] and claims that his commentary is an exposition of his own thought rather than Boethius's.[46] *Esse* does not mean existence for Boethius. It means essence. Boethius's concept of essence, he explains then, is Aristotelian, but St. Thomas's interpretation of it is not:

> L'umanità non esiste per sé, da sola, ma negli uomini singoli... fin qui sembra ci si muova nell'aristotelismo più ortodosso che attribuisce la sussistenza ai soli individui singolari e il carattere di *ens* in senso forte alle sole sostanze (prime) e non agli accidenti. Eppure un piccolo inciso finale ci avverte che l'*esse essentiae* di Aristotele è superato: infatti ciò che Boezio rende con raffinata perizia con *"essendi forma,"* diventa per San Tommaso l'*"ipse actus essendi."*[47]

Boethius's distinction between *esse* and *id quod est*, he adds, is logical, whereas Aquinas's is metaphysical.[48] Boethius's real problem, in his view, regards the tension between essence in the abstract sense and essence in concrete things, but St. Thomas transforms it into a distinction between modes of predicating being and modes of being itself.[49] Fabro's point is that we must not look for the distinction between essence and existence in the *Quomodo*. For *esse* simply does not mean existence in Boethius's lexicon.

Maioli adds his voice to the lot. He claims that St. Thomas's reading of the *Quomodo*'s axioms is anachronistic. For the distinction between

---

44. Brosch, p. 65.
45. Fabro, *Nozione*, p. 28: "S. Tommaso nel Commento, è essenziale notarlo fin d'ora, introduce un nuovo uso della nozione di partecipazione, quello fra gli stessi astratti... che non solo è estranea al testo di Boezio, ma ripugnante allo spirito del medesimo, secondo il quale l'astratto ha la proprietà di essere partecipato, ma non può partecipare; ma S. Tommaso è stato costretto a farvi quell'aggiunta per quella nozione di *esse* da lui assunta fin dall'inizio."
46. Fabro, *Nozione*, p. 25, "Le implicazioni dottrinali seguono l'una all'altra in modo serrato, senz'alcun riferimento d'ordine storico, onde è il pensiero personale dell'Aquinate che qui viene espresso."
47. Cornelio Fabro, *Partecipazione e causalità secondo S. Tommaso d'Aquino* (Turin: Società Editrice Internazionale, 1960) p. 205.
48. Fabro, *Nozione*, p. 26: "Le preoccupazioni di ordine logico che sentiva Boezio nel porre il problema della bontà nelle creature sono diventate per S. Tommaso di ordine metafisico e lo indirizzano verso una serie di considerazioni che toccano la struttura intima dell'essere finito, come essere."
49. Fabro, *Causalità*, p. 206: "La tensione di concreto e astratto denunziata da Boezio sul piano logico-semantico, si trasforma nel commento tomista in una considerazione universale della predicazione dell'essere e dei modi principali dell'essere fino all'*esse purum* ch'è Dio, discendendo poi alle forme pure o intelligenze fino alle sostanze materiali."

essence and existence arose after Boethius wrote the text. Indeed, Aquinas came to know the distinction between essence and existence from Avicenna. Hence Aquinas's reading of the text is mistaken:

> È certo che Tommaso legge e commenta le formule del *De Hebdomadibus* boeziano ed usa la sua terminologia (in particolare la coppia 'quod est' e 'esse') alla luce di una teoria che storicamente gli derivava da Avicenna. Non si può quindi interpretare *esse* nel senso di *actus essendi*, atto contingente di essere e di esistere, contrapposto al *quod est,* inteso a sua volta come essenza possibile.[50]

Today it is McInerny alone, it seems, who sides with St. Thomas.[51] Cunningham puts it quite succinctly:

> No Boethian scholar today would deny that the primary meaning for this *esse* and *quod est* is the difference between an abstract nature and its concrete supposit. No Boethian scholar, I say, who is not a neoplatonist. Some of these would try to read the First Hypostasis into the Boethian *esse,* and the Second into his *ens*; they simply ignore the obvious reading.[52]

Obertello

Cunningham's remark brings us to Obertello, whose first reading of the text is frankly very Neoplatonic. Obertello defends St. Thomas's interpretation of the principal terms of the *Quomodo*'s axioms. *Esse* means *actus essendi* in Boethius's lexicon. Aquinas, he tells us, was the work's most brilliant interpreter.[53] The reason critics do not see this is that they believe Aquinas's application of the distinction between essence and existence to the Boethian text to be an anachronism, insofar as they believe that distinction to have been first drawn by Avicenna. In Obertello's opinion, however, there is nothing farther from the truth. He claims that we can find the distinction between essence and existence in Porphyry, that Boethius picked it up from Porphyry, and that the *Quomodo* is the very text through which the distinction was transmitted to the Middle Ages:

---

50. Maioli, p. 19.
51. McInerny, p. 249: "The thesis of this book is that Boethius taught what Thomas said he taught and that the Thomistic commentaries on Boethius are without question the best commentaries ever written on the tractates."
52. Francis A. Cunningham, S.J., *Essence and Existence in Thomism: A Mental vs. the "Real Distinction"* (Lanham, Md.: University Press of America, 1988) p. 97.
53. Obertello, *Boezio,* p. 651.

The *Quomodo Substantiae* 237

> L'opera... trasmise al Medioevo la distinzione tra l'Essere, agire puro e trascendente ogni forma, e l'Esistente, soggetto che riceve una forma determinata dell'essere, affermando la derivazione immediata dell'essere degli Esistenti dall'Essere primo.[54]

What is more to the point, Obertello claims that it is possible that the source of St. Thomas's own technical formulation of the distinction is Boethius's text. For Aquinas's formulation is remarkably like Porphyry's (and Boethius's) own.[55] What this means is that Aquinas's interpretation of the main terms of the *Quomodo*'s axioms is not only not anachronistic, it is correct.

This does not, however, mean that St. Thomas's interpretation of the text is entirely correct, Obertello warns his readers, for its terms do not mean precisely the same thing for Boethius and St. Thomas. Mediaeval readers were original thinkers and reinterpreted classical terminology and thought.[56]

What then do the *Quomodo*'s terms mean? Obertello claims that we must locate the axiom's sources in order to understand them. Those sources are the Neoplatonists Victorinus and Porphyry, or more precisely their distinction between Being Itself and its subsequent hypostases:

> L'opposizione tra *id quod est* ed *esse* si ritrova nella distinzione egualmente tradizionale, tra ὕπαρξις e οὐσία (sussistenza ed essenza) presente anch'essa in Vittorino e nel suo corrispondente l'ariano Candido. La ὕπαρξις è per entrambi puro essere: "existentia ipsum esse est et solum esse et non in alio esse aut subiectum alterius," è cioè sostanza. La sostanza, poi, è ciò che è qualificato: come dice Candido, "substantia autem non esse solum habet, sed et quale aliquid esse." Analogamente Vittorino: "substantiam autem, subiectum, cum his omnibus quae sunt accidentia in ipsa inseparabiliter existentibus." La sussistenza corrisponde all'essere

---

54. Obertello, *Boezio*, p. 646.
55. Obertello, *Boezio*, p. 652: "Ciò non toglie che, nella sua formulazione tecnica, San Tommaso riprenda largamente i termini porfiriani e boeziani, e che egli sia solito esprimerla, servendosi delle stesse espressioni di Boezio, come distinzione tra *id quod est* e *esse*."
56. Obertello, *Boezio*, p, 652: "Nel contesto tomistico, tuttavia, non è possibile attribuire a queste ed altre espressioni, riprese dai classici, l'identico significato che hanno negli originali. Non è il caso di ricordare ancora una volta l'indipendenza e l'originalità mentale dei maggiori rappresentanti della Scolastica (sempre tuttavia misurata su di un costante rispetto della verità interiore dei testi), nell'utilizzare le 'auctoritates' anche più venerabili e universalmente accettate, il loro assorbente si direbbe esclusivo interesse per lo spirito a preferenza e al di là della lettera."

puro, la sostanza all'esistenza. La sussistenza dunque è propria di Dio. Essa designa l'Essere puro.[57]

We are thus to interpret Boethius's *ipsum esse* as meaning Being itself: Pure Being as it exists prior to any hypostatization:

> L'Essere è ciò che vi è di più originale e più universale, ciò che è libero da ogni forma. L'Essere è dunque agire puro, non limitato né da un soggetto né da un oggetto. Ogni forma, ogni determinazione intelligibile appare come effetto dell'atto d'essere originario e fondante, e non può che essere posteriore all'Essere perché introduce una composizione. Vi sono, in sintesi, due modi d'essere: l'Essere trascendente che è superiore a ogni forma, e l'essere che deriva da esso. All'infuori dell'Essere assoluto non vi sono che forme di essere determinate che corrispondono a soggetti determinati. È questa, sostanzialmente...la dottrina di Boezio. L'Essere primo trascende ogni forma. Esso non è ancora, cioè non è ancora sostanza...è infatti anteriore alla sostanza, poiché è la loro causa.[58]

Esse thus means the act of being in particular things. The act of being, Obertello clarifies then, means two things. It is what causes things to exist:

> L'*esse* può anche venir denominato *essendi forma,* in quanto è causa e ragione di essere. Non si può propriamente dire che, come tale l'*esse* esista (o meglio, che esista in maniera determinata); esso è ciò per cui tramite e in virtù del quale una qualche realtà "est atque subsistit."[59]

And it is that which makes particular things what they are. It is their form of existence:

> *Esse* sembrerebbe così usato primariamente nel senso di "forma"; è la forma dell'essere in virtù della quale il tutto esiste ed è quello che è. L'*esse* è tutto ciò che costituisce una cosa nel suo essere particolare (*id quod est*).[60]

Id quod est, on the other hand is a particular subsistent thing:

> *Id quod est* è preso come il soggetto dell'essere; di conseguenza può venir tradotto con: 'ciò che è.' Esso indica l'intera realtà di

---

57. Obertello, *Boezio,* p. 643.
58. Obertello, *Boezio,* p. 644.
59. Obertello, *Boezio,* p. 647.
60. Obertello, *Boezio,* p. 638.

un essere concretamente esistente: include la materia, la forma, e l'essere, e la collezione di accidenti che costituisce l'essere individuale.[61]

It exists because it receives *esse:*

L'id quod est è l'esistente. Esso è e sussiste, cioè diviene sostanza, nel momento in cui riceve una forma del suo essere.[62]

It is composite, Obertello tells us, because it becomes when it acquires being:

Id quod est significa 'ciò che è' o, con un termine parallelo 'l'esistente.' La sua nozione implica la composizione tra un soggetto e le forme che esso riceve. Esso è, ossia l'essere gli si aggiunge secondo una forma determinata *(forma essendi)*: diviene allora una sostanza, sussiste.[63]

Its acquisition of being, then, seems to take place through two acts of participation. For *id quod est* exists and has a determinate form. Its first participation is in being and is what confers existence upon it. The second one, on the other hand, is in "something else" and gives its existence a determinate form:

Partecipa dunque insieme all'essere, nella misura in cui è, e a qualche cosa d'altro dall'essere nella misura in cui è secondo una certa forma. L'esistente si può così definire 'soggetto che è qualche cosa.'[64]

It is in Obertello's interpretation of the meaning of *esse* that we see the difference between his view of Boethius's axioms and St. Thomas's. Obertello's Boethius is an emanationist.[65] St. Thomas's Boethius definitely is not. Obertello would seem to recant a bit, however. For after having claimed that *ipsum esse* is the First Being — l'Essere primo — he claims that one must not think that Boethius believes *ipsum esse*

---

61. Obertello, *Boezio*, p. 638.
62. Obertello, *Boezio*, p. 644.
63. Obertello, *Boezio*, p. 644.
64. Obertello, *Boezio*, p. 639.
65. Obertello's interpretation in his first work is very similar to Hadot's. Cf. Pierre Hadot, *Porphyre et Victorinus* (Paris: Études Augustiniennes, 1968) p. 495: "Nous reconnaissons en effet dans l'*esse*, tel que le décrit Boèce, des traits qui correspondent à l'einai porphyrien. Il ne participe à rien et ne se mêle à rien, il est donc *esse solum*, ni sujet ni prédicat. Il 'n'est pas encore,' c'est-à-dire qu'il n'est pas encore substance. Au contraire l'étant participe à l'être pour être, c'est-à-dire pour subsister, et l'étant subsiste, est substance, lorsqu'une forme particulière vient s'ajouter à l'être, pour le déterminer... D'autre part, l'être des choses a découlé de l'être divin."

to be *Ipsum Esse Subsistens*. For Boethius's *Esse* is not God, but the *quality of being*:

> Si noti però che Boezio, quando parla dell'*esse* in sé e per sé, non intende parlare dell'*ipsum Esse subsistens* degli Scolastici, ma della *qualità dell'essere*. La qualità astratta dell'essere non è ancora, dice Boezio, proprio perché, in senso stretto, è soltanto l'individuo concreto.[66]

This last remark casts a shadow on his interpretation. For if Boethius's distinction between *esse* and *id quod est* is one which derives from Porphyry and Victorinus, as Obertello insists it does, and if Porphyry's and Victorinus's distinction is between Primordial Being and its subsequent hypostatizations, Boethius's distinction must call for *ipsum esse* to be the First Being. Obertello's own account shows as much:

> È questa, sostanzialmente... la dottrina di Boezio. L'Essere primo trascende ogni forma. Esso non è ancora, cioè non è ancora sostanza... è infatti anteriore alla sostanza, poiché è la loro causa.[67]

If this is so, then it is not altogether clear how *ipsum esse* can just mean a "quality of being."[68]

Esse *Qua Essence*

The debate among scholars who believe *esse* to mean essence concerns two points: (1) the cause of *id quod est*'s existence and (2) the meaning of *forma* in Boethius's lexicon. The two points are related. For Boethius claims in the *De Trinitate* that *"omne namque esse ex forma est,"*[69] and this statement, along with the *Quomodo*'s parallel *id quod est "accepta essendi forma est atque subsistit,"* has led several scholars to claim that Boethius's *esse* is the cause of *id quod est*'s existence. Others counter their claim and maintain that this interpretation is based upon a misunderstanding of Boethius's notion of *forma*. For although *esse* does mean essence in Boethius's lexicon, and although Boethius does believe that the cause of *id quod est*'s existence is a form, it is a mistake to conclude that Boethius claims that contingent things' essences are the cause of their existences thereby. For that "Form" which causes a particular thing's *esse* is not the particular things' own form. Others

---

66. Obertello, *Boezio*, p. 650.
67. Obertello, *Boezio*, p. 644.
68. Obertello's second interpretation of the *Quomodo* is significantly different from his first precisely because he completes his recantation in it. Cf. Obertello, *Dintorni*, pp. 158ff.
69. *De Trinitate*, 20–21.

yet, claim that the mistake in the interpretation which claims that *esse* is the cause of *id quod est*'s existence is that it misunderstands the meaning of *ipsum esse*. For the latter term is ambiguous. Let us briefly see each of these positions.

Bruno Maioli's interpretation of the axioms is a good example of the first position. His reading is based upon the *De Trinitate*:

> La nostra convinzione è che il significato base di *esse* (sostanzialmente costante negli *Opuscola*) sia quello di "struttura che fa essere": *forma essendi*. Il postulato base di tutta la metafisica boeziana è la tesi del *De Trinitate: omne esse ex forma est*.[70]

Esse, he tells us, means form or essence, although he admits that it also implies existence.[71] Now, things' being is never abstract, indeterminate, or undifferentiated. Things are always specific kinds of things. As *esse* is the "structure which makes things be" it too must be determinate:

> In forza di questa costitutiva correlazione alla forma, e in quanto ogni forma è una forma determinata e determinante l'essere dell'esistente, l'*esse* boeziano non è l'essere nel senso depotenziato di essere astratto, universale indeterminato, indifferenziato.[72]

Esse as such must also mean essence in Boethius's lexicon: that which causes a determinate modality of being.[73] Every essence, or form, is a *forma essendi*.[74]

Now, since *esse* is the cause of things' being — *omne esse ex forma est* — it must be the cause of both things' existence and their having a specific kind of existence. That is, *esse* must be both a principle of determination and of being:

---

70. Maioli, p. 24.
71. Maioli, p. 26: "L'*esse* boeziano...connota e significa la struttura ontologica sostanziale dell'*id quod est*; e contemporaneamente implica l'esserci, l'essere al mondo, l'atto di essere.... È naturale che Boezio, nel suo tipico platonismo aristotelizzante, privilegi l'*esse* nel suo aspetto formale-strutturale, più che esistenziale; consideri l'*esse* da un punto di vista prevalentemente essenzialistico; ma sarebbe impoverirne il ricco significato ridurlo al ruolo di pura essenza possibile, che attenda il suo atto di essere."
72. Maioli, p. 25.
73. Maioli, p. 25: "*Esse* è sempre essere qualche cosa o qualche cosa d'altro: essere questo o quello, non a livello di pura individualità numerica, ma — stante la natura primariamente formale dell'*esse* — a livello di essenza o natura o proprietà: a livello di 'esser tale' o tal'altro: essere uomo, animale, essere buono, essere bianco, ecc.; anche se 'l'esser tale' sia sempre l'esser tale di un concreto esistente." See also p. 28: "*Esse* significa invece il 'ciò per cui' (quo est) quella realtà 'che è ed esiste': il principio costituente l'esistente, la struttura formale — sostanziale — che determina quella realtà ad essere ed a esser tale: è l'essenza o natura considerata in se stessa, prescindendo dalle proprietà accidentali che la individualizzano; è la natura astratta del soggetto concreto."
74. Maioli, p. 30: "Ogni forma è a suo modo *forma essendi*: in senso primario e fondante 'forma essendi' è forma specifica: l'uomo è quello che è per l'umanità."

> La forma dà contemporaneamente l'essere e l'essere tale: è principio ontologico strutturale ed esistenziale insieme: non fa semplicemente essere, ma fa essere facendo essere tale o tal'altro.... Poiché non è possibile che esista un qualche cosa che non sia determinato... ciò che è principio di determinazione è anche principio dell'essere: principio di determinazione ontologico è la forma, quindi anche l'essere, oltreché l'esser tale, deriva dalla forma. La forma fa essere determinando e informando la materia, costituendo così l'*id quod est*: per cui il concreto esistente, in forza del suo *esse* o forma, non soltanto è quello che è, un qualche cosa di determinato, ma anche di esistente nel mondo: *est atque consistit*.[75]

This does not, however, mean that *esse* exists in the strict sense of the word for Boethius. For it does not. Only *id quod est* exists in the strict sense of the word:

> L'*id quod est* "*est atque consistit*," ciò non si può propriamente dire dell'*esse*: "*ipsum esse nondum est*," ove l'"*est*" va inteso nel senso forte di esservi, esistere, essere una realtà del mondo, concretamente esistere: tutto ciò è prerogativa dell'*id quod est*.[76]

Esse is what causes *id quod est* to exist when it informs matter:

> Mentre l'*esse* non si può dire che in sé e per sé propriamente esista (*nondum est*), ma esiste soltanto come forma informante una materia, "est *atque consistit*" soltanto l'*id quod est*, una volta ricevuta (*accepta*) attraverso l'atto creativo-partecipativo la propria *forma essendi*, cioè il proprio *esse*.[77]

Id *quod est* exists and is a specific thing insofar as it receives determinate being from *esse*.[78]

There seems to be a contradiction in Maioli's claim. For if *esse* means form, then it is difficult to explain why Boethius claims that "*omne namque esse ex forma est.*" For if *esse* and *forma* mean the same thing, then the statement above seems to be to the effect that *esse* is its own cause: "*omne namque esse ex esse est.*" But since *esse* does not exist

---

75. Maioli, pp. 25–26.
76. Maioli, p. 29.
77. Maioli, p. 30.
78. Maioli, p. 32: "Occorre chiarire bene il senso della 'partecipatio' di cui qui si tratta, per capire poi il perché l'*esse* 'nullo modo aliquo participat.' La *susceptio* ribadisce la passività dell'ente creato e finito di fronte alla prima, fondante e costituente, partecipazione all'*esse* o *forma essendi*, in forza della quale 'est atque consistit.' "

in its own right, as Maioli himself notes, the statement must also mean *"nondum est ex nondum est,"* which is, of course, a true statement. But it is a rather strange principle if it is meant to explain why things exist.[79]

This point, among other things, has led Claudio Micaelli to claim that there is a basic mistake in those interpretations of Boethius's axioms which identify *esse* and *forma*. His claim is that *forma* in Boethius's lexicon does not necessarily mean εἶδος in the Aristotelian sense: a form which is immanent in particular composite things and is the cause of their being. For Boethius's *De Trinitate* distinguishes the *Forma* from an *imago*.[80] Both are forms.[81] But the *forma* is the transcendent Form *par excellence*, God, and *imagines* are the immanent forms of particular complex things:

> Non è il caso di riassumere il vasto e complesso dibattito volto a chiarire il valore dell'espressione *forma essendi:* ci limiteremo ad osservare che il problema di fondo è quello di stabilire se la *forma* di cui parla è da intendersi come Forma trascendente o come forma immanente, equiparabile, in qualche misura all'*eidos* aristotelica. Nel *De Trinitate* il pensiero di Boezio appare molto chiaro, operando una netta distinzione tra la forma *quae vere forma neque imago est* e le *imagines,* che sono abusivamente chiamate forme, ma che non possono realmente essere considerate tali in quanto immanenti ad un sostrato materiale.[82]

Now, given the two meanings of *forma,* Micaelli continues, the formula *"omne namque esse ex forma est"* must mean that there are two causes of things' existence: their immanent forms and God:

> Il principio secondo il quale *omne esse ex forma est* si deve intendere, pertanto, in un duplice senso: il primo è quello che vede in Dio la Forma suprema, il principio *ex quo omnium esse proficiscitur*; il secondo è quello che vede la forma immanente come causa prossima dell'essere corporeo.[83]

---

79. McInerny points this out too. Cf. McInerny pp. 171 and 197.
80. *De Trinitate* II, 17–21: "In divinis intellectualiter versari oportebit neque diduci ad imaginationes, sed potius ipsam inspicere formam quae vere forma neque imago est et quae esse ipsum est et ex qua esse est. Omne namque esse ex forma est."
81. Micaelli claims that this distinction is Platonic. Micaelli, p. 106: "È fuori di ogni dubbio, peraltro, che la contrapposizione di *forma* a *imago,* intese rispettivamente come forma trascendente e come forma immanente, corrisponda ad uno schema concettuale di origine platonica."
82. Micaelli, p. 105.
83. Micaelli, p. 107.

This point is important, he tells us, for if we do not make this distinction, we risk identifying God with *ipsum esse*,[84] and this is simply not what Boethius does,[85] even though some of his commentators do.[86]

Lambert De Rijk points out that there is a second mistake in scholars' belief that the *Quomodo*'s axioms claim that things' essences are the cause of their existences. For just as *forma* is an ambiguous term in Boethius's metaphysics, so too is *ipsum esse*: it can mean both things' essence *per se* or God. What this means is that the cause of *id quod est*'s existence is not things' essences, or not merely so, but must also be God.

De Rijk claims that Boethius's distinction between *esse* and *id quod est* is nothing more than the distinction between a material substrate[87] and the form of being taken in itself:

> La formule fameuse... qui établit la distinction entre "être" (*esse*) et "ce qui est" (*id quod est*) ne fait rien d'autre que souligner la différence entre la forme d'être (*forma essendi*) prise en soi (c.à.d. sans le substrat qu'implique (je ne dis pas: *inclut*) chaque verbe comme désignant une forme non-subsistante) d'une part, et le substrat (*ens* = "ce qui est") de l'autre.[88]

The *Quomodo*'s seven metaphysical axioms specify how we are to understand that distinction. Boethius tells us that *ipsum esse* and *quod est* differ as the "material meaning" of notions does from their "formal meaning": that is, as "mankind," or "humanity" do from "this man."[89] His second important step is to distinguish things' forms in themselves from things' forms as they are to be found in a substrate. This distinction plays a key role in Boethius's solution to the problem of things' substantial goodness in De Rijk's view.[90] Boethius's third

---

84. Micaelli, p. 112: "Da questa posizione, tuttavia, si genera una frattura insanabile tra il *De Trinitate*, nel quale Dio è definito come *Forma*, e come *ipsum esse*, e il *De hebdomadibus*, nel quale la forma apparirebbe legata al concetto di essere composto."

85. See Micaelli, p. 115: "È con espressioni analoghe che Boezio, nel *De hebdomadibus*, respinge l'ipotesi panteista come *nefas*."

86. Micaelli, p. 113: "Di questa incongruenza non sembra aver tenuto conto, invece, G. Schrimpf, che sostiene l'identità tra Dio e *ipsum esse* nel secondo assioma del *De Hebdomadibus*. Una tale identificazione potrebbe avere un fondamento coerente in una metafisica di tipo eriugeniano."

87. Lambert M. De Rijk, "Boèce logicien et philosophe," in Luca Obertello, *Atti del Congresso Internazionale di studi boeziani*, p. 151: "'Ce qui est,' prise dans sa nature concrète et matérielle, peut fonctionner comme substrat de quelque chose d'autre."

88. De Rijk, p. 151.

89. De Rijk, p. 151: "Ensuite Boèce parle de la différence entre le signifié matériel des notions (comme '*homo*,' '*albedum*') et leur signifié formel (comme '*humanitas*,' '*albedo*'). Le dernier n'est rien d'autre que l'essence formelle (homme en tant que tel (ou: humanité) prise sans le substrat materiel; le premier est l'homme pris concrètement, avec le substrat = *id quod est* (*homo*)."

90. De Rijk, p. 152: "Ici Boèce met en lumière la différence importante entre la forme prise en soi ('homme,' 'humanité'; 'blanc,' 'blancheur') et cette même forme en tant que

step is to explain how *id quod est* comes to be. He does this through "three theses which define the real nature of participation."[91] In order to understand the first of these theses, the author continues, we must understand what *ipsum esse* means in the *Quomodo*. His point is clear. For since the sixth axiom claims that things are insofar as they participate in "eo quod est esse," the meaning of *esse* must determine the nature of participation.

Ipsum esse is an ambiguous term in the *Quomodo*. In most cases it means an immanent form of being. The fact of the matter is, however, that it also means God:

> Il faut remarquer cependant que l'expression peut se rapporter à celui qui est l'*Etre en Soi,* l'Etre Pur aussi bien que à l'être pris en tant tel des choses périssables.[92]

> Partout où Boèce parle de "ce qui est" (*id quod est*), la formule *ipsum esse* désigne la forme d'être immanente... Deux fois seulement l'expression se rapporte à Dieu (IPSUM ESSE).[93]

This means that although Boethius's claim that things are insofar as they participate in *"eo quod est esse"* might seem to mean that they exist insofar as they participate in their own forms — or that their essences are the cause of their beings — this interpretation cannot be altogether correct. For *ipsum esse* also means God. Indeed, the real point of that claim is that complex things must participate in God in order to exist, or that God is the cause of their existence:

> Il y a là une ambiguité fondamentale d'ordre sémantique, qui d'ailleurs a son pendant métaphysique dans la doctrine de la participation. En effet l'être pris en soi (*ipsum esse*) des choses périssables est une participation à l'Etre en Soi (IPSUM ESSE). Ainsi *l'ipsum esse* des choses n'est que la forme d'être (*forma essendi*) prise comme *immanente* dans les choses, tandis que l'IPSUM ESSE est la Forme d'être Transcendente ou plutôt la Transcendence Elle-même.[94]

As De Rijk points out, Boethius cannot have held that complex things' essences are the causes of their existences purely and simply. Were he to

---

présente dans un substrat. Cette distinction devait jouer le rôle decisif dans la solution donnée par Boèce de la question principale de son traité."

91. Re Rijk, p. 152.
92. De Rijk, p. 154.
93. De Rijk, p. 154.
94. De Rijk, p. 154.

have done so, then he would also have to have held that God *"nondum est,"* and that is simply ridiculous.⁹⁵

De Rijk concludes by showing that properly speaking *id quod est* has two causes: an immanent cause and a transcendental cause. Both are important. For if *id quod est* were not to have an immanent cause, it could not property said to be; if it were not to have a transcendental cause, on the other hand, it could not exist at all:

> Ce qui compte dans l'argumentation de Boèce, c'est surtout la différence (sémantique et ontologique à la fois) entre la forme immanente et la Forme Transcendente. L'immanence (= non-transcendence) de la forme participée assure l'être...a chose périssable, lequel est tout...fait différent de l'Etre absolu et parfait dans lequel toutes les propriétés...coincident aussi bien que l'essence et l'existence. D'autre part, le caractère d'essence formelle qu'a la forme immanente elle aussi, fait que l'être (participé) en tant qu'être (en tant que *ipsum esse*) est *essentiellement* (*substantialiter*) bon ("un bien participé," bien entendu).⁹⁶

The *Quomodo*'s Axioms

The *Quomodo* has nine axioms altogether. In the first one Boethius delineates his notion of an axiom. The last one[97] concerns the relation between a being's nature and its final cause and is the premise of the syllogism whereby Boethius proves that things are substantially good insofar as they seek the good.[98] The central seven axioms, on the other hand, delineate: (1) the components of beings, (2) the nature of the relations between these components, (3) the cause of complex things' existences, (4) the different types of entities: simple and complex beings. It is clearly the central seven axioms in which we are presently interested.

Rather than reading the axioms with an eye to criticizing what has been said about them, however, I prefer to comment on them without presupposing an interpretation, in order to deduce what they — and their terms — mean from them directly. This means, of course, reading

---

95. De Rijk, p. 155: "Comment pourrait-on dire de Dieu (à propos de l'Axiome II) qu'il n'est pas encore (*nondum est*)?"

96. De Rijk, p. 155.

97. *Quomodo* IX, 49–52: "Omnis diversitas discors, similitudo vero appetenda est; et quod appetit aliud, tale ipsum esse naturaliter ostenditur quale est illud hoc ipsum quod appetit."

98. *Quomodo*, 56–60: "Ea quae sunt bona sunt; tenet enim communis sententia doctorum omne quod est ad bonum tendere, omne autem tendit ad simile. Quae igitur ad bonum tendunt bona ipsa sunt."

them in the original and having a lot of patience. But it is the only way to get to Boethius's own thought rather than that of his interpreters.

The first axiom is Boethius's methodological prelude, for in it he defines what he means by an axiom:

> Communis animi conceptio est enuntiatio quam quisque probat auditam. Harum duplex modus est. Nam una ita communis est, ut omnium sit hominum, veluti si hanc proponas: "Si duobus aequalibus aequalia auferas, quae relinquantur aequalia esse," nullus id intellegens neget. Alia vero est doctorum tantum, quae tamen ex talibus communibus animi conceptionibus venit, ut est: "Quae incorporalia sunt, in loco non esse," et cetera; quae non vulgus sed docti comprobant. (I, 18–27)

An axiom is a statement to which one must give his immediate assent, and can be of two types. All people can understand the first type, whereas only the learned can understand the second type. An example of the first type, he says, is the statement: "If equal quantities are subtracted from equal quantities there result equal remainders." He uses the statement, "Things which are incorporeal are not in space," on the other hand, to illustrate the second type. These types of principles, he adds, do not differ because they belong to different classes. Rather, they belong to the same class.

The second example, which is more than just a vague anticipation of Kant's analytic *a priori* judgments, supplies the key to understanding Boethius's conception of an axiom. It shows that it is a statement in which *predicatum est de ratione subiecti*. Thus, if a person understands the terms, he cannot but understand the axiom. As such, axioms call for immediate assent, insofar as they state what the concepts of their terms imply. Conversely, if axioms state what the concepts of their terms imply, then they must be explicitations of the concepts of their terms. That is, if an axiom is a statement in which the *predicatum est de ratione subiecti*, the *predicatum* itself must tell us something about the *subiectum*. It follows, then, that axioms can also be used to determine the nature of the *subiectum*.

This helps to clarify two things: (1) Boethius's distinction between the two types of axioms; and (2) how to read his own axioms. For if it is true that understanding an axiom depends upon understanding its terms, then the difference between those axioms which are intelligible to all people, and those which are not, must lie in their types of terms. Hence, universally intelligible axioms must contain terms that are universally known, whereas the terms in those axioms which can be understood only by the learned must not be universally understood.

As for Boethius's own axioms, on the other hand, if they are no exception to his rule, then they must be self-evident for those people who understand his terms. For those who do not, on the other hand, understanding the predicates attributed to the terms must allow them to clarify the meanings of the terms themselves. This gives us our program. If we do not immediately understand the axioms or their terms, we must understand the relations between the terms and their predicates, insofar as they must be the keys to understanding the meanings of the axioms themselves.

Having defined what he means by an axiom, Boethius turns to his doctrine of being, and begins his exposition of the main tenets of his metaphysics by distinguishing *id quod est* and *esse*:

> Diversum est esse et id quod est; ipsum enim esse nondum est, at vero quod est accepta essendi forma est atque consistit. (II, 26–30)

To this distinction he adds that *esse* itself "is not yet," while *id quod est* is and subsists "once it has received the *forma essendi*."

Here is where the problems begin. Firstly, it is not clear what to make of the primary terms in the axiom. For if we interpret them literally as meaning "being/to be" and "that which is" we run into trouble with the first of these terms. A literal interpretation of the axiom's first distinction would seem to contrast a generic act or essence (secondary substance) and a particular instance of that act or essence (substance) — "To be/being and that which is are different" — but it is not altogether clear how to reconcile this with the qualification that "To be/being itself is not yet." For not only does the qualification "To be/being itself is not yet" seem to be contradictory, it also seems to contradict both the interpretation of the first distinction we gave above and the very fact of Boethius's distinguishing "to be/being" from "that which is." How can *id quod est* be a particular instance of what is not? And yet that is precisely what a literal reading of the text seems to imply. For *id quod est* seems to be a particular instance of *esse,* and *esse* is "not yet." Moreover, does not the very fact of distinguishing two things presuppose that both exist? After all, distinguishing something from nothing merely reaffirms the existence of what is distinguished from nothing and thus does not distinguish it from anything at all. Does not Boethius's distinguishing *esse* from *id quod est* presuppose that both exist, then? And if this is so, does not his denying existence to "being/to be" contradict his distinguishing it from "that which is?"

Since Boethius was a keen logician we can neither suppose that he did not understand the contradictions implicit in predicating *nondum* of *ipsum esse* after having distinguished it from *id quod est,* nor believe that he was intentionally contradicting himself thereby. We must therefore assume that there is a noncontradictory way of interpreting what *esse* means. But this must mean either that the relation between *esse* and *id quod est* which we supposed to be the correct one in the reading above is mistaken, or that a literal interpretation of *esse* is incorrect. In either case, we need more information to solve the problem.

If the problem with the first term in the axiom is that it would seem to contradict its predicate, the problem with the second term is that it is not clear what to make of Boethius's account of its constitution. For the axiom tells us how *id quod est* becomes what it is only by introducing a third undefined term: *"forma essendi."* Nor is this the only other difficulty. For the axiom does not specify how *esse* and the *forma essendi* relate: whether they refer to the same thing or not. This is clearly also true of *id quod est*'s relation to *esse*. For a first reading of the axioms suggests that they stand as a particular instance does to a generic act or essence. But this is only a supposition at this point. For the axiom itself merely contrasts its two primary terms and does not specify how they relate. This means that we do not know if *esse* and *id quod est* refer to a single entity or to different entities.

What Boethius seems to have done, as such, is set up a three-part problem. For there are three things which an adequate interpretation of the axiom must determine: (1) the proper meanings of its terms; (2) how *id quod est* is constituted; and (3) how the axiom's primary terms are related to one another. These problems are related in the way pointed out by Boethius's preliminary axiom. For one cannot completely solve the first problem unless he solves the second and third problems, insofar as the second and third specify the meanings of the predicates of the second axiom's terms. That is, we cannot determine the proper meanings of either *ipsum esse* or *id quod est* without understanding how *id quod est* is constituted and how *id quod est* relates to *ipsum esse*. Nor, as we shall see, can one solve the second problem without solving the third: i.e., we cannot understand how *id quod est* is constituted without establishing how *id quod est* and *ipsum esse* are related.

The sequence of the axioms that follow this first metaphysical one seems to indicate that this set-up is intentional. For the third and fourth axioms give one the means with which to derive the preliminary and problematic meanings of the second axiom's primary terms; the fifth and sixth axioms have to do with the constitution of *id quod est,* and they give the means with which to solve the problems posed by the third and fourth axioms; and the seventh and eighth axioms deal directly with the relations between *esse* and *id quod est*. It is only once one has analyzed all seven metaphysical axioms that he can fully grasp the meanings of the their terms and of the metaphysics that they delineate. Let us follow what would seem to be Boethius's own order.

The next axiom regards participation, and it sheds light on the meaning of *id quod est*:

> Quod est participare aliquo potest, sed ipsum esse nullo modo aliquo participat. Fit enim participatio cum aliquid iam est; est autem aliquid, cum esse susciperit. (III, 31–34)

Id quod est can participate in something, while *ipsum esse* cannot. There is a double qualification to this, though. For as a condition to participation Boethius adds that the participant already be something (*cum aliquid iam est*) and specifies that in order for something to be, it must acquire *esse* (*cum esse susciperit*).

Since Boethius attributes two properties to what can participate in something — existence (*est*) and determinacy (*aliquid est*) — we can immediately infer two things about *id quod est* from the fact that it can participate in something: it must exist and be something determinate. If it is something determinate, however, then it must be a finite thing. Therefore, I think it is safe to concur with Duhem, Roland-Gosselin, Fabro, Maioli, De Rijk, and so forth, and deduce that *id quod est* means a particular existing thing,[99] although I do not understand how they can infer that this implies that *id quod est*'s being is a union of matter and form without reading something into the text or limiting the meaning of its terms.

From the fact that *ipsum esse* cannot participate in anything — *ipsum esse nullo modo participat* — we can deduce that it must neither exist as something determinate nor acquire *esse*. The next axiom confirms this. For in it Boethius states that *id quod est* can possess something other than what it itself is while *ipsum esse* can possess nothing admixed to it other than itself:

> Id quod est habere aliquid praeterquam quod ipsum est potest; ipsum vero esse nihil aliud praeter se habet admixtum. (IV, 35–38)

That is, if *ipsum esse* can possess no "admixture" of anything other than itself, then it surely cannot acquire something. If it cannot acquire something, then it cannot acquire *esse*. But acquiring *esse* is what constitutes a particular or determinate thing. Therefore, *ipsum esse* cannot itself be or become a particular or determinate thing. It follows that it must be indeterminate being.

---

99. This clearly means that I cannot concur with Schrimpf, who claims that *id quod est* means essence. Cf. footnote 28 in this chapter.

The third and fourth axioms furnish the preliminary meanings of the second axiom's two primary terms: *ipsum esse* means indeterminate being, and *id quod est* means a particular-determinate-existing thing. These preliminary meanings are, however, problematic. For if *id quod est* is a particular existing finite thing and *ipsum esse* indeterminate being, then we have ascertained that they mean precisely what we thought they could not mean. And this leads straight back into the lion's den. For if *ipsum esse* does mean "indeterminate being that cannot become a particular or determinate thing," then why does Boethius specify that *"ipsum esse nondum est"* in the second axiom? If *ipsum esse* is "not yet," then it would seem to have to become. After all, *nondum* does not mean *never* or *cannot*. It means "not yet." And "not yet" seems to imply "will." The problem is that what becomes acquires *esse* — *"quod est accepta essendi forma est atque consistit"* — and Boethius tells us that what acquires *esse* exists as a determinate thing — *"est autem aliquid cum esse susciperit."* Thus, if *ipsum esse* "*nondum* est," it apparently must be able to acquire being and become determinate in order to exist. But this is precisely what he tells us *ipsum esse* cannot do. For *ipsum esse* cannot acquire anything. *"Ipsum vero esse nihil aliud praeter se habet admixtum."* How, then, can *ipsum esse* both not yet be, and thus need to become determinate in order to exist, and not be something which can become determinate?

In truth, we can only solve this problem by establishing both what the relations between *ipsum esse* and *id quod est* are and how *id quod est* is constituted. For the solution to the problem above is to claim that *ipsum esse* exists and becomes determinate in something other than itself. But determinate existing being, as we have seen, is *id quod est*. It would seem to follow that *ipsum esse* exists and becomes determinate in *id quod est*, or conversely that *id quod est* is the actuation and determination of *ipsum esse*. The point is understanding how this is to be conceived.

The first and most obvious solution is that of equating *ipsum esse* with that *esse* which the third axioms tells us *id quod est* must acquire in order to exist: *"est autem aliquid cum esse susciperit."* For if *ipsum esse* becomes determinate in *id quod est*, then since *id quod est* itself becomes a determinate thing only insofar as it acquires *esse*, *ipsum esse* would seem to be the very *esse* which Boethius says *id quod est* receives when it becomes a determinate thing. Thus, it seems logical to infer that *ipsum esse* is *id quod est*'s essence. As we have seen, many scholars make this deduction.[100] For what makes a particular thing

---

100. Maioli, Duhem, Roland-Gosselin, and Fabro all hold that *ipsum esse* and the *esse*

what it is is its essence. Moreover, since Boethius claims that *id quod est* is *"aliquid, cum esse susciperit,"* he seems to be claiming that *ipsum esse* is an essence which causes *id quod est*'s existence and as such that it is a secondary substance, or form in the true Aristotelian sense, as again we have seen scholars maintain.[101]

This particular solution, however, is not feasible. For it would have it that *ipsum esse* is simultaneously what becomes determinate in *id quod est* and the cause of the *id quod est*'s determinacy. This cannot be. For if *ipsum esse* does indeed become determinate in *id quod est*, then the *esse* in *id quod est* cannot be *ipsum esse*, insofar as *ipsum esse* is indeterminate. But the determinate *esse* in *id quod est* is its essence (or substance), as is indeed corroborated by the axiom that follows the one which gave rise to these problems. For in it Boethius explicitly states that *id quod est*'s essence (or substance) is the determinate *esse* that exists in it:

> Diversum est tantum esse aliquid et esse aliquid in eo quod est; illic enim accidens hic substantia significatur. (V, 38–40)[102]

If this is so, however, then *ipsum esse* cannot be *id quod est*'s essence (or substance). But if *ipsum esse* is not *id quod est*'s substance, then it cannot be the cause of *id quod est*'s determinacy. For *id quod est*'s essence (or substance) is the cause of its determinacy and *ipsum esse* is not *id quod est*'s essence (or substance). As such, if *ipsum esse* does indeed become determinate in *id quod est*, it cannot be the *esse* which *id quod est* acquires in order to become determinate.[103]

---

existing things receive are to be identified, and as such that *esse* is things' essence. See footnotes 41–50; 70–78.

101. Maioli, Duhem, Roland-Gosselin, and Fabro all hold that *ipsum esse* is a secondary substance. See footnotes 41–50; 70–78.

102. Roughly translated this axiom states: "Merely to be something and to be something in that which is are different; the prior is an accident, the latter signifies substance."

Given this definition, I think it clear that substance for Boethius, at least in this tractate, does not mean what it meant, say, for St. Thomas — "A thing to which it belongs to exist not in a subject," or "That which has a quiddity to which it belongs to exist not in another" (*Contra Gentiles*, I, 25 §10) — but rather essence. I will therefore treat substance and essence as equivalent terms.

103. There is clearly a parallel problem with this interpretation: the cause of *id quod est*'s existence. For *ipsum esse* cannot be both that which exists in *id quod est* and the cause of *id quod est*'s existence. There are two basic reasons for this: (1) *ipsum esse* cannot cause things' existence; (2) *ipsum esse* cannot at once be what does not exist yet and what exists in *id quod est*. As for the first point, *ipsum esse* would have to exist in order to cause *id quod est*'s existence. But this is not possible since the second axiom tells us that *ipsum esse nondum est*, and Boethius tells us in his solution to the problem of complex things' substantial goodness that a non-existent essence cannot cause existence. Cf. *Quomodo*, 111–17. As for the second point, if *ipsum esse nondum est*, it cannot be what exists in *id quod est*. For what exists in *id quod est* must exist. We will deal with this problem in the pages to come.

One can of course respond that what Boethius intends by claiming that *ipsum esse* is the cause of *id quod est*'s existence and determinacy is not that *ipsum esse* itself is the cause of *id quod est*'s determination or existence, but that *aliquid esse* is, and that *aliquid esse* is a determination of *ipsum esse*. This may be true. The problem with this response, however, is that it contradicts the premise which led to it — that is, that *ipsum esse* and the *esse* which *id quod est* acquires in order to become a determinate thing are one and the same — and begs the question, thus forcing one to introduce a principle of individuation which the text itself does not mention. For the response simply cannot explain why *ipsum esse* becomes *aliquid esse* without a principle of individuation and the text does not provide one.[104] Thus, *ipsum esse* cannot be the *esse* which existing things acquire in order to be and be determinate.

Now, if *ipsum esse* cannot be the *esse* which *id quod est* acquires in order to become determinate, then the deduction which scholars draw from the inference that it is — that is, that *ipsum esse* is the cause of *id quod est*'s existence — must also be mistaken. What can be made of our paradox, then? For if *ipsum esse* is not the *esse* which causes *id quod est* to become a determinate thing, then it would not seem possible for *ipsum esse* to become determinate in *id quod est*. If *ipsum esse* does not become determinate in *id quod est*, however, then it would not seem possible for *ipsum esse* to become determinate at all. After all, *id quod est* is determinate being. If this is so, then how can *ipsum esse* not "be yet"?

The way out of this mess lays in correcting the error that gave rise to the interpretation that *ipsum esse* means a secondary substance in the Aristotelian sense in the first place: thinking that *ipsum esse*'s becoming determinate in *id quod est* makes it the efficient cause of *id quod est*'s own determinacy — that is, that x's becoming determinate in y makes x the efficient cause of y. This is a logical mistake. For the fact that humanity — i.e., an indeterminate universal — is determinate in me, does not mean that I am who I am because of my humanity, and Boethius was aware of this. For in his next axiom, where he addresses the problem of *id quod est*'s constitution, he says that it is due to its participation, and not to its substance, or to *ipsum esse*:

> Omne quod est participat eo quod est esse ut sit; alio vero participat ut aliquid sit. Ac per hoc id quod est participat eo quod est esse ut sit; est vero ut participet alio quolibet. (VI, 41–44)

---

104. This seems to be the reason for which those scholars who do think that *esse* means substance purely and simply introduce matter into the picture.

The axiom, then, distinguishes two acts of participation on the part of "everything that is": one in "that which/He who is being," which confers its existence (*ut sit*), and one in "something else," which makes it be something (*ut aliquid sit*). By the first participation, he then specifies, *id quod est* exists, and it exists in order to participate in something else.

Let us proceed with order. *Quod est*'s first participation is in God, as the next axiom will confirm — for He who is *esse* cannot but be the being in which *esse* is *quod est* — and gives it its existence;[105] the second participation is in something other than God and gives it determinacy, i.e., makes it something. What this means is that Boethius is affirming precisely the opposite of what scholars like Maioli and Fabro have held. For by stating that *id quod est* is because it participates in God, Boethius is specifically denying that a being's essence is the cause of its existence, and is thereby avoiding the logical fallacy we saw above. As such, even if *ipsum esse* were the same *esse* that *id quod est* acquires in order to exist — or be something determinate — it could not be the efficient cause of *id quod est,* unless of course it were God. And in the latter case it would be rather difficult to explain how God could *nondum est,* if He is *Id quod est esse,* as indeed this axiom states He is.[106]

The next thing which we must determine is how this dual participation is to be understood. There are two possible interpretations, it seems: either both acts of participation are substantial, or only one is. By the former, a thing participates in God in order to exist, and it participates in what seems to be a universal *ante rem* (an *indeterminate essence*) in order to become something determinate. By the latter, a thing's first participation is substantial, and its second participation is accidental. Hence only the first participation determines what *id quod est* is.

The importance of ascertaining which of these cases is the correct one consists in the fact that the meaning of *esse* depends upon how one

---

105. The point is rather paradoxical. For by Boethius's own account, participation presupposes the existence of the participant. I think it is rather clear, however, that participation in this context refers to creation — and thus that the type of participation this axiom is dealing with must be distinguished from the one described in the third axiom.

106. Maioli's position on this specific axiom is that *id quod est esse* is *ipsum esse*. Cf. Maioli, p. 32: "La *susceptio* ribadisce la passività dell'ente creato e finito di fronte alla prima, fondante e costituente, partecipazione all'*esse* o *forma essendi* in forza della quale 'est atque consistit.' Che la *susceptio* o *acceptio* dell'*esse* sia la prima e costituente partecipazione è riconfermato — pena una palese contraddizione — dall'assioma VI." Now, if *id quod est esse* were *ipsum esse*, and if *ipsum esse* were to be that very *ipsum esse* of which the second axiom speaks, then the second axiom and the sixth axiom would contradict one another. For the *esse* in this sixth axiom "est," whereas the *esse* in the second axiom "*nondum est.*" I take this to mean that *id quod est esse* cannot mean the second axiom's *ipsum esse*. Boethius was too good a logician to have contradicted himself this openly. We will deal with this point further on.

understands *id quod est* to be constituted. For since the third axiom tells us that a thing is insofar as it acquires *esse,* then since participation is what makes it be, we must infer that participation is what gives it *esse.* If this is so, however, then the nature of participation must determine the meaning of *esse.*

On the first reading *esse* can either be what a thing acquires from its participation in God or what it acquires through its participation in a "something else." Thus, since the prior is a participation in pure actuality — *id quod est esse* — and is what gives a being its actuality — the act of being (*ut sit*) — *esse* must mean existence. On the other hand, since by the latter participation *id quod est* becomes something determinate (*aliquid sit*) — and I take it that by something (*aliquid*) Boethius means a thing of a certain kind, a human being, a cat, a dog, etc. — it must be a participation in something which qualifies a being substantially, or which determines the modality of its existence. But an essence is what determines the modality of things' existences. Hence the second participation must be in an essence — a universal *ante rem,* it seems — and it must confer an essence upon that which participates in it. If this is so, then *esse* must also mean essence: that through which *id quod est* has a determinate mode of existence. This is corroborated by Boethius's own definition of essence (or substance). For he claims that it is *"esse aliquid in eo quod est."*

We must qualify this. For if the second participation makes *id quod est* become a determinate thing, that in which it participates in order to become a determinate thing must become determinate and actual in it. As such, there must be a difference between that in which *id quod est* participates in order to become something determinate and *id quod est*'s own actualization of that which makes it be a determinate thing. — There must be a difference between Fido and dogginess. — If this is so, however, then there must be something which specifies the universal in which *id quod est* participates in order for it to become actual and determinate in *id quod est* itself. This is the very problem we were dealing with above. Boethius's solution to it, on this reading, is to make *id quod est*'s determination a secondary participation, one, that is, which presupposes its participation in God. Indeed, he says that *id quod est* can participate in what makes it a determinate thing only once it is given existence: *"id quod est participat eo quod est esse ut sit; est vero ut participet alio quolibet."* If this is so, however, then the first participation must determine the modality of the second. Namely, it must determine how a universal becomes determinate and actual in a particular thing. Existence, therefore, must be a principle of individuation as well as one of actuation. This would seem to account for Boethius's saying that something is and subsists once it has received a *essendi forma* in the second axiom: "*Quod est accepta essendi forma est atque consistit.*" For if existence is both a principle of individuation and of actuation, it is not merely an *actus essendi*: something which actuates. It is also what determines how and what that *actus* will be: an *essendi forma*.

On the second reading, on the other hand, *esse* must mean the act of existence. For on the second reading only *id quod est*'s first act of participation — its participation in God — is substantial, and that first act of participation confers existence upon it. This too must be qualified. For if *id quod est* is a determinate thing — its essence is "*aliquid esse in eo quod est*" — and if it becomes determinate through its reception of esse — "*est autem aliquid cum esse susciperit*" — then since *esse* means existence, existence itself must also be the cause of its determinacy. As such, Boethius's elusive *essendi forma* must be a principle of determination, rather than individuation, as well as a principle of actuation.

Now, both interpretations of the sixth axiom have their appeal and both seem to have textual support. As far as the latter is concerned, it is not only difficult to understand how a thing can exist without being something, but the conclusion of the sixth axiom would also make it seem that Boethius himself thought as much. For the conclusion of the sixth axiom claims that: "*(id quod est) est vero ut participet alio quolibet.*" This would seem to imply that *id quod est* exists in the proper sense of the term after it has participated in God. Moreover, the third axiom which specifically deals with accidental participation, specifies that this can take place once something is: "*Fit enim participatio cum aliquid iam est.*" But *id quod est*'s first participation undeniably gives it existence — actuality. Hence *id quod est*'s second participation would seem to be accidental. Finally, since Boethius's distinction between substance and accidents in the fourth axiom specifies that the difference between them consists in the fact that the former inheres in *id quod est* while the latter do not, and since again *id quod est* exists once it has participated in God, it seems to follow that anything in which *id quod est* participates after the first participation cannot but be accidental. As such, the second of the interpretations would seem to be the only viable one.

This second reading has a lot of backing. Fabro,[107] Maioli,[108] and

---

107. Cf., e.g., Fabro, *Nozione*, p. 103: "Adunque le due partecipazioni dell'*id quod est*, prima all'*ipsum esse* e poi all'*esse aliquid* vanno intese come partecipazione l'una alla forma sostanziale e l'altra alle forme accidentali."

108. Maioli, pp. 32-33: "Boezio distingue tra una prima e seconda partecipazione da

Aquinas,[109] for instance, all claim that the second participation is accidental.

The former reading also has its support. For although it is difficult to understand how something can exist without being something, it is also true that this critique of the first interpretation of the sixth axiom presupposes that there be a temporal lapse between *id quod est*'s two acts of participation. The fact of the matter is, however, that it is not only not necessary for there to be a temporal lapse between the two acts of participation — if a child is both created and procreated, there are two causes of his existence, two acts of participation if you will, but one need not precede the other temporally — but the text does not claim that there is. For the sixth axiom does not claim that a thing exists "after" it has participated in God. Nor does it vaguely suggest that there is a temporal lapse between *id quod est*'s two acts of participation. It merely states that it participates in God in order to exist, that it participates in something else in order to be determinate and that the second participation presupposes the first insofar as *id quod est* must participate in God in order to participate in something else. Now, if there need not be a temporal lapse between *id quod est*'s two acts of participation, then the priority of the first participation need not necessarily imply its exclusivity in the constitution of a particular thing. Hence, the first of the arguments above does not refute the first of the two possible interpretations of the sixth axiom. Nor, however, do the second and third arguments and for the very same reason. For although it is true that the third axiom deals with accidental participation and states that it takes place once *id quod est* exists, it is not said that *id quod est* does exist after its first participation. Lastly, if it is not necessarily said that *id quod est* is constituted by its first participation alone, then it is also not necessary for its "subsequent" acts of participation to be accidental. Indeed, it is not said that the second participation takes place "after" the first at all. The two acts of participation could be simultaneous, and their succession only a logical one.

This second reading also has scholarly backing. Obertello and

---

parte dell'*id quod est*. La prima, che è una *susceptio* o *acceptio* piuttosto che una vera partecipazione, è quella fondante e costituente, cioè sostanziale: la partecipazione all 'eo quod est esse ut sit,' in forza di cui è ed è quello che è. La seconda è quella complementare o accidentale, in quanto appunto gli accidenti sono modi di essere secondari: 'alio vero participat ut aliquid sit.' ... Ed è naturale: la partecipazione accidentale è possibile a condizione che sussista già il supposto a cui inerisca la proprietà partecipata: sussista già l'*id quod est* nella sua struttura sostanziale."

109. *In de hebdomadibus* II, "Dicit quod ad hoc quod aliquid *sit* simpliciter subiectum *participat* ipsum *esse*, sed ad hoc quod *sit aliquid*, oportet quod participet aliquo *alio*, sicut homo ad hoc quod sit albus participat non solum esse substantiale sed etiam albedinem."

Hadot, for instance, both interpret the sixth axiom along similar lines.[110]

As I see it, the matter hinges on *id quod est*'s determinacy. *Id quod est* is something determinate: *est aliquid*, as Boethius specifically says in the third axiom, when it *"suscipit esse."* Now, if the second interpretation we gave of the sixth axiom were the correct one — i.e., if *id quod est* were only constituted by its participation in God — then *id quod est*'s first participation would have to give it its determinacy, as we said above. Namely, the first participation would have to give it the *esse* whereby it is *aliquid*. If the first participation were to bestow the *esse* whereby *id quod est* "aliquid est," however, then Boethius would not have stated that *id quod est* participates in God in order to be — *ut sit* — in order to specify that it participates in something else in order to become something — *ut aliquid sit*. He would very simply have stated that *id quod est* participates in God *"ut aliquid sit."* Since he did not I take it that he did not believe *id quod est* to be *aliquid* through its participation in God.

Moreover, had Boethius's intention been to claim that *id quod est "est aliquid"* because it participates in God, then his distinction between what makes *id quod est* exist (*ut sit*) and what makes it determinate (*aliquid sit*) would not be a distinction at all. For the first participation would already have made it determinate: *aliquid*. But if there were no distinction between the causes of *id quod est*'s existence (*ut sit*) and its determinacy (*ut aliquid sit*), then Boethius's claim that *id quod est* **"alio** participet" in order to be determinate — as opposed to its participating in *id quod est esse* in order to exist — would flatly contradict his intention. If this is so, then I think it is rather clear that both participations must be substantial.

The point is also corroborated by the fifth axiom. For in it Boethius states that *id quod est*'s essence is *"aliquid* esse in eo quod est," rather than *"esse* in eo quod est." Now, if *id quod est*'s second participation were just accidental, then *id quod est*'s essence could not be *"aliquid esse* in eo quod est" very simply because Boethius tells us that *id quod est* just is — "est" — through its first participation and it is *ex hypothesi*

---

110. Obertello, *Boezio*, p. 648: "La specificazione è introdotta da un elemento diverso dall'essere, così che la progressiva determinazione della cosa concreta può essere descritta in questi termini: dapprima vi è l'essere-in-generale. Non ancora determinato; 'ciò che è' partecipa di questo essere-in-generale, per essere; ma per essere 'qualche cosa' (ossia una realtà determinata) deve partecipare ad un principio che lo determini: 'ac per hoc id quod est participat eo quod est esse, ut sit; est vero, ut participet alio quolibet." Hadot also reads the sixth axiom as claiming that *id quod est*'s two participations are substantial. Cf. Pierre Hadot, "Forma essendi. Interprétation philologique et interprétation philosophique d'une formule de Boèce," in *Les Etudes Classiques*, XXXVIII, 1970, pp. 143–56.

that the only the first participation is substantial. The fact of the matter is, however, that Boethius does not claim that *id quod est*'s essence is "*esse* in eo quod est." He tells us that it is "*aliquid esse* in eo quod est." As such, both acts of participation must be substantial. For it is through the second participation that *id quod est* "aliquid est."

Now, if *id quod est* is what it is because it acquires *esse*, as the third axiom tells us (*"est autem aliquid, cum esse susciperit"*), then *esse* must be what *id quod est* acquires in order to be. But *id quod est* is constituted by two acts of participation: the first one is in God and is the one through which it acquires its existence; the second one is in an essence — a universal *ante rem* — and is the one through which it acquires a determinate mode of being. As such, since *esse* must mean either existence (= actualization) or the determination of a universal essence in *id quod est* (= determinate being) or an essence.

We are now, finally, in a position to deal with *ipsum esse*. For if *ipsum esse* is indeterminate being — the universal of which *id quod est* is a particular instance — then it can be either what is made determinate and actual in *id quod est* through its second participation — that in which *id quod est* participates in order to be something determinate — or it can be that in which *id quod est* participates in its first act of participation: that in which it participates in order to exist. In the prior case, it would mean an indeterminate and unactuated essence: that is, things' own essence insofar as it is indeterminate and unactuated. This would explain why Boethius claims that it *"nondum est."* For a universal *ante rem* does not exist in itself. In the latter case, on the other hand, *ipsum esse* would mean pure actuality as opposed to the determinate actuality of *id quod est*. *Ipsum esse*, as such, can mean either pure potentiality or pure actuality.

We must distinguish these two possibilities before we decide which of them is the correct one, or if both are correct. If we do not, we run the risk of concluding either that Boethius believes that God is not yet, or that he believes that a universal (things' indeterminate essence) is purely actual. After all, if *ipsum esse* were to mean both God and a universal *ante rem* indiscriminately, then since universals do not exist in the strict sense of the word — the second axiom clearly states that *ipsum esse* *"nondum est"* — God would also not exist in the strict sense of the word: He would "not be yet." Alternatively, if *ipsum esse* were to mean both God and things' indeterminate essences indiscriminately, then since God is pure actuality — *id quod est esse* as the sixth axiom claims — things' indeterminate essences would have to be pure actuality. Both of these conclusions are absurd, and both contradict Boethius's distinction between those things in which *id quod est* participates in order to exist and be determinate in the sixth axiom.

Both of these conclusions are absurd, we were saying, for if God were not to exist "yet," the cause of things' existences would not exist "yet." After all, "omne quod est" participates in *"id quod est esse ut sit."* Thus, if God were not to "be yet," things could not be at all. But this cannot be the case and Boethius was more than aware of the fact. That is why he claims that the cause of things' existences is *"id quod est esse"*: the existing thing which is being.[111] But if the cause of things' existences exists, then it cannot "not be yet." One of two conclusions follows: either (1) Boethius is contradicting himself when he claims that *ipsum esse "nondum est"*; or (2) *ipsum esse* cannot mean both God and a universal essence indiscriminately. Boethius was too good a metaphysician to claim the former. Hence we cannot accept the first of these options. As such, *ipsum esse* cannot mean both God and a universal *ante rem* indiscriminately.

If *id quod est*'s indeterminate essence were pure actuality, on the other hand, then not only could it not *nondum est,* as the second axiom claims, but it could not be *id quod est*'s essence: the essence of a particular determinate thing which comes to be. For if *id quod est*'s indeterminate essence were pure actuality, then it could not be a particular determinate essence: *aliquid.* If something is both particular and determinate (*aliquid*), then it cannot be pure actuality. But *id quod est*'s essence must be determinate, insofar as *id quod est* is particular and determinate. Boethius claims that it is *"aliquid* in eo quod est esse." Hence, were *id quod est*'s indeterminate essence to be God, then there could be no *id quod est*: a particular determinate thing. But this too is clearly contrary to what Boethius claims. As such, we once again have a choice: either Boethius was contradicting himself when he claimed that *id quod est* is a particular determinate thing, or he did not hold that *ipsum esse* means both God and *id quod est*'s indeterminate essence. Since the former of these options is untenable, then *ipsum esse* cannot mean both God and a universal *ante rem* indiscriminately.

What is more important than either of the arguments above is that both the claim that God is "not yet" and the claim that things' inde-

---

111. Boethius makes this point explicitly in his definition of the cause of complex things' substantial goodness. See *Quomodo*, 111–19: "Quod si nihil omnino aliud essent nisi bona neque gravia neque colorata neque spatii dimensione distenta nec ulla in eis qualitas esset, nisi tantum bona essent, tunc non res sed rerum viderentur esse principium nec potius viderentur, sed videretur; unum enim solumque est huiusmodi, quod tantum bonum aliudque nihil sit. Quae quoniam non sunt simplicia, nec esse omnino poterant, nisi ea id quod solum bonum est esse voluisset."

terminate essences are pure actuality contradict Boethius's distinction between those things in which *id quod est* participates in order to exist and be determinate. For Boethius explicitly claims that *id quod est esse* is not that in which *id quod est* participates in order to be *aliquid*:

> Omne quod est participat eo quod est esse ut sit; *alio* vero participat ut aliquid sit. Ac per hoc id quod est participat eo quod est esse ut sit; est vero ut participet *alio* quolibet. (VI, 41–44)

Now, if Boethius himself tells us that that in which *id quod est* participates in order to exist and that in which it participates in order to be something are different, then he clearly cannot have identified things' indeterminate essences and God. For that in which *id quod est* participates in order to exist is *id quod est esse:* pure actuality or God. That in which it participates in order to be something determinate, on the other hand, is a universal *ante rem:* its indeterminate essence. Hence if we were to claim, as some scholars do,[112] that *ipsum esse* means God and things' indeterminate essences indiscriminately, then we would be claiming something which Boethius does not.[113]

This distinction between things' indeterminate essence and God is corroborated by Boethius's seventh axiom where he claims that in every simple being 'what it is' (its essence) and that it is (its actuality) are one:

> Omne simplex esse suum et id quod est unum habet. (VII, 45–46)[114]

Now, if *ipsum esse* were *ex hypothesi* to mean both that in which non-simple *ea quae sunt* participate in order to exist and that in which they participate in order to be determinate things — were *ipsum esse* to mean both God and a universal *ante rem* indiscriminately — then the cause of things' existences (and determination) would have to be

---

112. The scholars I have in mind are Hadot, Obertello, and Schrimpf. See footnotes 53–68 above.
113. This point is corroborated by De Rijk's reading of the axioms. See footnotes 88–96.
114. This passage combined with Boethius's infamous *nondum* would also seem to make Hadot's interpretation dubious. For if *ipsum esse* were God — *agir pur* as Hadot puts it — then by the *nondum* clause it would seem that God Himself would have to acquire *esse* in order to be. But *ipsum esse* cannot itself acquire *esse* for as we saw in the axiom above, *ipsum vero esse nihil aliud praeter se habet admixtum*. Hence *ipsum esse* cannot become determinate in itself. If it cannot become determinate in itself, however, it cannot be *Ipsum Esse Subsistens*, for in *Ipsum Esse Subsistens*, "*esse et id quod est unum habet.*"

As a final note, there is a difference between saying that "*ipsum esse* non est," and that "*ipsum esse* nondum est." Had Boethius said that "*ipsum esse* non est," this would have been in keeping with the Neoplatonic tradition of negative affirmation, and *ipsum esse* could have been construed to mean *Ipsum Esse Subsistens*. As matters stand, I find Hadot's interpretation very difficult to reconcile with the text.

one with *ea quae sunt*. For the cause of things' existences is *id quod est esse* according to the sixth axiom, and the seventh axiom tells us that *id quod est esse* is a simple being. The problem is that if *ea quae sunt* were one with that in which they participate in order to exist, and if that in which they participate were both God and a universal *ante rem* indiscriminately, then God could not be simple and *ea quae sunt* could not exist.

The first point is obvious. God could not be simple if He were *ea quae sunt*'s indeterminate essence. For if He were *ea quae sunt*'s indeterminate essence, then *ea quae sunt* would have to be His existences. If they were His existences, He could not be *Id quod est esse*. This is absurd. The second point shows this even more strongly. For if *ipsum esse* were God and a universal *ante rem* indiscriminately, then *ipsum esse* thus conceived would have to be one with its determinations: *ea quae sunt*. After all, "*omne simplex esse suum et id quod est unum habet.*" But this is absurd. For if the purely actual universal *ante rem* were one with *ea quae sunt*, then *ea quae sunt* could not acquire existence. For the third axiom states that *ipsum esse* cannot participate in anything — "*ipsum esse nullo modo aliquo participat*" — and the fourth axiom states that it cannot have anything added to itself — "*ipsum esse vero nihil aliud praeter se habet admixtum.*" Thus, if *ea quae sunt* were one with *ipsum esse*, they would not be capable of participating in anything or of receiving anything. The fact of the matter is, however, that the third axiom also tells us that *ea quae sunt* are because they receive being — "*est autem aliquid, cum esse susciperit*" — and the sixth axiom tells us that they are because they participate in *id quod est esse*: "*Omne quod est participat eo quod est esse ut sit.*" As such, if *ea quae sunt* were to be one with *ipsum esse*, then they could not exist. This is manifestly absurd. Hence, *ipsum esse* cannot mean both God and a universal *ante rem* indiscriminately.

The seventh axiom thus proves that Boethius cannot have held that *ipsum esse* is both that in which *id quod est* participates in order to exist and that in which it participates in order to become something determinate. Were God "not to be yet," then since His essence is His existence, He would not be at all: for His actuality would have "to be not yet," since *omne simple esse suum et id quod est unum*. But if God were not to be yet, there would be nothing in which a particular thing participates in order to be. Thus, it would not be at all. But the text does affirm that particular things are, and that they participate in God. Therefore, God must be simple. If God is simple, however, then He cannot "not be yet." Having made this distinction, I think it is rather clear that *ipsum esse* means the universal essence of things before it is made determinate in *id quod est:* a universal *ante rem.* That is the alternative. That is, if *ipsum esse* cannot mean God — that in which things participate in order to exist — then it must mean that in which they participate in order to become determinate kinds of things. But that, we have said, is a universal *ante rem.*[115]

Boethius's next axiom completes and summarizes his circle, which began with the distinction between a universal *ante rem* (a thing's indeterminate essence) and its determination in a particular existing thing, characterized both of the terms, and explained that a particular thing is constituted through a dual participation in God and in a universal *ante rem.* The first participation, he specified, gives it existence, which is also a principle of individuation, while the second makes the thing an actualization and determination of the universal itself. For the conclusion of this circle is that there is a triple distinction to be made for every created being, in virtue of its creation. The first is between the mere fact of its existence and its actualizing an essence; the second is between its existing as the actualization of an essence and the essence it actualizes; the third is between the determinate essence in it, and the universal in which it participates in order to acquire a determinate essence. That is, one must distinguish its essence from its existence:

Omni composito aliud est esse, aliud ipsum est (VIII, 47–48).

In every composite being, its essence and what it itself is are different.[116]

The Axiom's Metaphysics and Doctrine of Participation

Now that we have analyzed the *Quomodo*'s axioms and determined the meanings of their primary terms, we can finally delineate the main lines of their metaphysics. Boethius's claim is that there are two types of beings in the universe: simple beings and composite beings. A simple being exists necessarily: its essence is the cause of its existence because

---

115. I take *"id quod est"* in this case not to mean a particular thing, for a simple thing cannot have a particular existence, insofar as a particular existence necessarily differs from other particular existences of beings of a similar nature. If it is not the only being of its kind, however, then it cannot be identical with its essence. And the axiom states that it is. I therefore think it is to be interpreted as actuality. For *id quod est* has two principal attributes: actuality and determinacy. The latter derives from its participating in something. Since simple being does not participate in anything, I would think it difficult to ascribe it to simple being. Therefore, I think that only actuality can be ascribed to simple being. As such I think *id quod est* in this context means actuality purely and simply.

116. This axiom proves that *esse* can mean essence or substance for Boethius, because it makes no sense to distinguish a thing's existence from its existence. That is, since *"ipsum est"* clearly refers to a being's actuality, its existence, if *esse* in this context were also to refer to a being's actuality, Boethius's distinguishing these terms would be a contradiction.

it is identical to its essence (which is tantamount to claiming that its essence is existence): *omne simplex esse suum et id quod est unum habet*. There is one such being, God: *Id quod est esse*.[117] All beings other than God are composite.[118] Their essences are not their existences — *omni composito aliud est esse, aliud ipsum est* — and cannot cause their existences. A composite thing's essence cannot cause its existence for two reasons. Firstly, a composite thing is not identical to its essence: *diversum est esse et id quod est*. Thus, even if its essence were to exist in its own right, the composite thing itself would not necessarily exist. The fact of the matter is, however, that a composite thing's essence does not exist in its own right — *ipsum esse nondum est*. As such, it cannot cause existence. Nor is existence something which is added to a composite thing's essence in order to form an existent composite thing: *id quod est*. Composite things' essences are not substrates.[119] *Ipsum esse nullo modo aliquo participat* and cannot have anything added to it: *ipsum vero esse nihil aliud praeter se habet admixtum*. A complex thing's essence becomes actual in a complex determinate thing — *id quod est* — by 'informing' it: by determining the modality of its existence. In its actual state a complex thing's essence is a determinate mode of being: it is *esse aliquid in eo quod est*. It informs *id quod est* when *id quod est* participates in it: *alio vero participat ut aliquid sit*. *Id quod est*, however, must have an efficient cause in order to be able to participate in its essence. For *id quod est* is not existence itself (only God is) and its essence cannot be its moving cause or efficient cause. That efficient cause, then, is the one simple being in the universe: *Id quod est esse*. All complex things exist, as such, because they participate in God: *omne quod est participat eo quod est esse ut sit*. By participating in God *id quod est* exists and is an individual thing: *est atque subsistit accepta essendi forma*. God, however, is not the cause of its determinate mode of existing: God is not its formal cause. *Alio vero participat ut aliquid sit*. Its essence is the cause of its determinate mode of existing: its formal cause. Once *id quod est* participates in God, it participates in *ipsum esse* and becomes a determinate thing: *est aliquid cum esse susceperit*. *Ac per hoc id quod est participat eo quod est esse ut sit; est vero ut participet alio quolibet*.

The doctrine of participation which they axioms delineate is a doc-

---

117. Cf. *De Trinitate*, II, 29–31: "Sed divina substantia sine materia forma est atque ideo unum et est id quod est."
118. Cf. *De Trinitate*, II, 31: "Reliqua enim non sunt id quod sunt."
119. Cf. *De Trinitate*, II, 43: "Formae vero subiectae esse non possunt." See also *De Trinitate*, II, 48–51: "Forma vero quae est sine materia non poterit esse subiectum nec vero inesse materiae, neque enim esset forma sed imago."

trine of dual participation. Complex things are constituted by: (1) their participation in God, which bestows an individual existence upon them; and (2) their participation in a universal *ante rem* whereby they become things of specific kinds. Boethius's claim is that God is their efficient cause and that their essences are their formal causes.

This is precisely what Boethius claims in his solution to the problem of composite things' substantial goodness. For the backbone of his solution is that complex things are substantially good insofar as: (1) their existence is efficiently caused by God — that is, their existence is a real relation with God, for *actio est in passo*; and (2) their existence is formally caused by their essences (*ipsum esse*) — which Boethius claims is good because it is created by God — because they have a real relation with *ipsum esse*, through which they actuate *ipsum esse*.

The order of this two-fold participation in Boethius's axioms and in his definition of the cause of complex things' substantial goodness is also the same. For in the axioms Boethius claims that composite things must participate in God in order to participate in something other than God and be something:

> Omne quod est participat eo quod est esse ut sit; alio vero participat ut aliquid sit. Ac per hoc id quod est participat eo quod est esse ut sit; est vero ut participet alio quolibet. (VI, 41–44)

The same thing holds for complex things' participating in *ipsum esse* in order to be substantially good. For Boethius explicitly claims that things could not be substantially good if their existences were not created by God. For were their existences not created by God, they "would be apart from the good and could not derive from it."[120]

Sed Contra

Now, our interpretation of Boethius's doctrine of participation is different from those which other scholars propose. This is a direct result of two factors: (1) the difference between our interpretation of the meaning of the axioms' primary terms and the interpretations which other scholars propose; and (2) the fact that that most scholars do not consider the two parts of the *Quomodo* to be congruent. As we saw in

---

120. *Quomodo*, 140–50: "Igitur sublato ab his bono primo mente et cogitatione, ista licet essent bona, tamen in eo quod essent bona esse non possent, et quoniam actu non potuere exsistere, nisi illud ea quod vere bonum est produxisset, idcirco et esse eorum bonum est et non est simile substantiali bono id quod ab eo fluxit; et nisi ab eo fluxissent, licet essent bona, tamen in eo quod sunt bona esse non possent, quoniam et praeter bonum et non ex bono essent, cum illud ipsum bonum primum [est] et ipsum esse sit et ipsum bonum et ipsum esse bonum."

our first and eleventh chapters, most scholars do not believe Boethius's definition of complex things' substantial goodness to make use of a doctrine of participation. We must as such respond to the primary interpretations of the *Quomodo* itself before proceeding.

We saw that some scholars claim that *ipsum esse* means a secondary substance in the Aristotelian sense, and as such that *ipsum esse* is the moving cause of *id quod est*'s existence. Those scholars who interpret *ipsum esse* in this way clearly have to interpret Boethius's doctrine of participation as claiming that complex things participate in their indeterminate essences both in order to exist and to be determinate things. Thus, Maioli, to cite one example, claims that *id quod est*'s two participations are substantial and accidental respectively, and that *id quod est*'s first participation is in *ipsum esse* rather than in God:

> Boezio distingue tra una prima e seconda partecipazione da parte dell'*id quod est*. La prima, che è una *susceptio* o *acceptio* piuttosto che una vera partecipazione, è quella fondante e costituente, cioè sostanziale: la partecipazione all'"eo quod est esse ut sit," in forza di cui è ed è quello che è. La seconda è quella complementare o accidentale, in quanto appunto gli accidenti sono modi di essere secondari: "alio vero participat ut aliquid sit." ... Ed è naturale: la partecipazione accidentale è possibile a condizione che sussista già il supposto a cui inerisca la proprietà partecipata: sussista già l'*id quod est* nella sua struttura sostanziale.[121]

This leads him to claim that Boethius does not make composite things' ontological dependence upon God explicit in the axioms:

> La dipendenza ontologica [dell'essere finito] non è esplicitata negli assiomi, ma nel seguito del testo.[122]

Now, the main problem with his interpretation, and those similar to it — i.e., those which interpret *ipsum esse* to be the moving cause of *id quod est*'s existence — is that Boethius does not claim that *omne quod est* participates in *ipsum esse* — i.e., in their essences — in order to exist. He claims that *omne quod est* participates in *id quod est esse* in order to exist. And from what we saw above, *id quod est esse* cannot possibly mean things' essences for Boethius.

Moreover, Maioli's interpretation — and those similar to it — does not explain how Boethius can have held that *ipsum esse* — which he explicitly claims *nondum est* — can cause something to exist. This is

---

121. Maioli, pp. 32–33.
122. Maioli, p. 15.

problematic because Boethius himself claims that a non-existent thing cannot be the cause of anything's existence.[123]

One could of course object that Boethius does not claim in the axioms that an existing thing must have an existent cause no matter what he claims in the second half of the work. After all, his claim in the sixth axiom is that all existing things must participate in *id quod est esse* in order to exist, and it is not said that *id quod est esse* is an existing thing. For if *omne quod est* must participate in *id quod est esse ut sit*, then whatever exists must participate in *id quod est esse ut sit*, including *id quod est esse*, if it does indeed exist in the full sense of the word. But it is impossible for *id quod est esse* to participate in itself, no matter what one chooses to interpret *id quod esse* to mean *Petit principium*. To be precise, it is no more possible for *id quod est esse* to participate in itself if one takes *id quod est esse* to mean things' indeterminate essences than it is if one believes *id quod est esse* to mean God. For things' indeterminate essences cannot participate in anything: *ipsum esse nullo modo aliquo participat*. Nor can God participate in anything. God is simple. But if *id quod est esse* cannot participate in itself, and if *omne quod est* must participate in *id quod est esse* to exist, then *id quod est esse* cannot exist. Therefore, Boethius's claim in the sixth axiom cannot be that existing things have an existent cause.

The main source of the problem here is clearly *omne*. Now, were that *omne* to be a universal term in the sixth axiom, then we would indeed have a problem. The fact of the matter is, however, that it cannot be a universal term. It cannot include simple beings. The seventh axiom makes this more than clear. For it claims that a simple being is its own cause insofar as it is identical to its essence.

Omne simplex esse suum et id quod est unum habet. (VII, 45–46)

But if a simple being is the cause of its own existence, then the cause of a simple being's existence cannot be participation. Nothing can participate in itself: not even a simple being. As such, the *omne* in the first proposition of the sixth axiom cannot include simple beings. The proposition, therefore, must mean that "all beings other than simple ones" participate in *id quod est esse* in order to exist. All beings which are not simple, however, are composite. Hence the proposition must

---

123. *Quomodo*, 111–19: "Quod si nihil omnino aliud essent nisi bona neque gravia neque colorata neque spatii dimensione distenta nec ulla in eis qualitas esset, nisi tantum bona essent, tunc non res sed rerum viderentur esse principium nec potius viderentur, sed videretur; unum enim solumque est huiusmodi, quod tantum bonum aliudque nihil sit. Quae quoniam non sunt simplicia, nec esse omnino poterant, nisi ea id quod solum bonum est esse voluisset."

read *"omne compositum"* must participate in *id quod est esse ut sit*. This is half of the solution to the problem above.

The other half is a corollary of the first. For if *omne* need not include all beings, then it is not at all said that *id quod est esse* cannot be an existing thing: i.e., that *id quod est esse* needs to participate in itself in order to exist. The fact of the matter is, then, that *omne* cannot include *id quod est esse*. *Id quod est esse* is the simple being. For that being in whom *id quod est* is one with *esse* — *omne simplex esse suum et id quod est unum habet* — is *id quod est esse*. What we have is that the proposition must mean: *omne compositum participat esse simplici ut sit,* or *omne compositum participat Deo ut sit.* Hence our point stands, as does our interpretation of the axioms' doctrine of participation.

There is another group of scholars, we saw, who claim that *Ipsum Esse* means Pure Being and that *esse* means a determination of pure Being. Obertello holds this view:

> L'Essere primo trascende ogni forma. Esso non è ancora, cioè non è ancora sostanza — come la sussistenza pura presso Damascio —: è anteriore alla sostanza e all'esistente, poiché è la loro causa.[124]

Accordingly, he interprets participation to mean *Ipsum Esse*'s hypostatization which takes place through a series of determinations:

> La specificazione è introdotta da un elemento diverso dall'essere, così che la progressiva determinazione della cosa concreta può essere descritta in questi termini: dapprima vi è l'essere-in-generale, non ancora determinato; ciò che è partecipa di questo essere-in-generale, per essere; ma, per essere 'qualchecosa' (ossia una realtà determinata), deve partecipare anche a un principio che lo determini.[125]

Now, there are two main problems with this interpretation. Both have to do with the identification of *ipsum esse* as God. For this identification is as foreign to Boethius's thought as is its corollary: that a non-existent thing is the cause of complex things' existences. The first point is one which we addressed while we were analyzing the axioms. If *Ipsum Esse* in Boethius's metaphysics were Pure Being which becomes determinate in *ea quae sunt,* then God would both have to be "not yet"

---

124. Obertello, *Boezio,* p. 644.
125. Obertello, *Boezio,* p. 648.

and to admit determinations. After all, Boethius claims that *ipsum esse nondum est*. Obertello is well aware of this implication, as his claim that: "L'Essere primo trascende ogni forma. Esso non è ancora, cioè non è ancora sostanza" demonstrates. The problem is that this is not what Boethius claims. For were God not to exist yet, He could not be a simple being. But this violates both the sixth and seventh axioms. Moreover, the third and fourth axioms explicitly claim that *ipsum esse* cannot be a substrate. Hence the identification of *ipsum esse* as God also violates these axioms.

There is another basic problem here. For if God were "not yet," then a non-existing thing would have to be the cause of things' existences. The second problem with Obertello's interpretation, as such, is similar to the one which arises in the "essentialist" interpretation of *esse*. And as we responded to the "essentialists," this is simply not what Boethius claims. Hence our interpretation of the meaning of the axioms' terms and of their doctrine of participation stands.

Aquinas's interpretation of the terms in Boethius's axioms also differs from ours. He holds that *esse* means the act of existence. Hence, he claims that *id quod est*'s first participation is in *Ipsum Esse Subsistens,* which in Aquinas's language means God, and is that participation through which *id quod est* comes to exist. This is something which we too claim. The difference between his interpretation and ours is that we do not claim that *esse* only means existence — it can also mean essence — and Aquinas does.

This difference naturally shows up in Aquinas's interpretation of Boethius's doctrine of participation. For where we claimed that both *id quod est*'s participation in God and its participation in "aliud" (= *ipsum esse*) are substantial — and thus that *esse* must mean both existence and essence in the axioms — Aquinas seems to claim that only *id quod est*'s first participation is substantial. His claim is — or rather seems to be — that the second participation is accidental:

> Dicit quod ad hoc quod aliquid *sit* simpliciter subiectum *participat* ipsum esse, sed ad hoc quod sit *aliquid,* oportet quod participet aliquo *alio,* sicut homo ad hoc quod sit albus participat non solum esse substantiale sed etiam albedinem.[126]

The passage here is a bit ambiguous, and is made that much more so by what follows:

---

126. Aquinas, *In de Hebdomadibus,* II.

Est autem haec differentia quod primo oportet ut intelligatur aliquid esse simpliciter, et postea quod sit aliquid, et hoc patet ex praemissis. Nam aliquid est simpliciter per hoc quod *participat* ipso *esse*; sed quando iam *est,* scilicet per participationem ipsius esse, restat *ut participet* quocumque *alio* ad hoc scilicet quod sit aliquid.[127]

The first passage's example suggests that St. Thomas held that *id quod est*'s second participation is accidental, for he claims that men do not only participate in substantial being — where one supposes substantial being to be what *id quod est* acquires through its participation in *id quod est esse* — but also in whiteness — where whiteness, one assumes, is an accidental property which *id quod est* acquires through its second participation. This is how some scholars have interpreted the claim.[128]

Now, if Aquinas does indeed claim that the second participation is accidental — the second passage casts some doubt on the matter — it was not necessary for him to have done so. For in his analysis of participation, which is prompted by the third axiom, St. Thomas claims both: (1) that participation takes place when "particular things receive what pertains to another universally" — and thus that Socrates participates in humanity — and (2) that effects participate in their causes.[129] This is precisely what we interpreted *id quod est*'s second participation to be. That is, our claim can be interpreted to mean either that through its second participation *id quod est* participates in its formal cause — and hence that it is the participation of an effect in its cause much in the same way in which its first participation is — or that through its second participation *id quod est* participates in its essence, or receives in a particular way what pertains to another universally. Hence Aquinas could well have interpreted the sixth axiom as we did.

De Rijk's and Micaelli's interpretation of the axioms seem to be the most similar to ours. For they both claim that Boethius holds that

---

127. Aquinas, *In de Hebdomadibus,* II.
128. Cf., e.g., Fabro, *Nozione,* p. 103: "Adunque le due partecipazioni dell'*id quod est,* prima all'*ipsum esse* e poi all'*esse aliquid,* vanno intese come partecipazione l'una alla forma sostanziale e l'altra alle forme accidentali; per la partecipazione alla forma sostanziale, da cui ha il suo modo di essere, la creatura è detta partecipare a Dio: a S. Tommaso basta indicare il fatto." See also McInerny, p. 208.
129. I am referring to the first and third meanings Aquinas attributes to participation. Cf. *In de hebdomadibus,* II. "Est autem participare quasi partem capere. Et ideo quando aliquid particulariter recipit id quod ad alterum pertinet universaliter, dicitur participare illud, sicut homo dicitur participare animal quia non habet rationem animalis secundum totam communitatem; et eadem ratione Socrates participat hominem... Et similiter etiam effectus dicitur participare suam causam, et praecipue quando non adaequat virtutem suae causae, puta si dicamus quod aer participat lucem solis quia non recipit eam in claritate qua est in sole."

id quod est has both an immanent and a transcendent cause.[130] The problem is that they do not discuss participation.

Universals *Ante Rem*

There is one last matter to clear up regarding the *Quomodo*'s notion of participation before we turn to the *Consolatio*. Our claim is that *id quod est*'s second participation is in a universal *ante rem*. This is what the sixth axiom suggests. For if *id quod est* becomes *aliquid* through its second participation, and if its essence is the *"esse aliquid"* in it, then its second participation must give it its essence. If its second participation gives it its essence, however, then since every effect is similar to its cause, it must be in an indeterminate essence, or a universal *ante rem*. Now, the term 'universal *ante rem*' is clearly not Boethius's own. It is Aquinas's. One might wonder, as such, whether we are ourselves reading something into the text by claiming that the second participation is in a universal *ante rem*.

This may be. However, the second half of the *Quomodo* corroborates our interpretation. For that *ipsum esse* from which Boethius claims *id quod est* "derives," and "from which it cannot be apart," can only be its essence.[131] And what is more to the point, Boethius also claims that that essence is "in God" prior to its actuation in *id quod est*,[132] and means by that both: (1) that it does not exist in the proper sense of the word, and (2) that it is not God. If this is so, that is if *ipsum esse* does not exist *per se* — if it is indeterminate — and if it is what becomes actual in *id quod est,* then it must be a universal *ante rem*. And if it is the formal cause of *id quod est*'s goodness, then *id quod est* must participate in it.

Nor is it the only confirmation. Our interpretation is also substantiated by that infamous chapter two of the *De Trinitate* which has prompted so many scholars to claim that Boethian metaphysics is Aristotelian.[133] That second chapter deals with forms: different types of

---

130. See footnotes, 81–96.
131. *Quomodo,* 140–50: "Igitur sublato ab his bono primo mente et cogitatione, ista licet essent bona, tamen in eo quod essent bona esse non possent, et quoniam actu non potuere exsistere, nisi illud ea quod vere bonum est produxisset, idcirco et esse eorum bonum est et non est simile substantiali bono id quod ab eo fluxit; et nisi ab eo fluxissent, licet essent bona, tamen in eo quod sunt bona esse non possent, quoniam et praeter bonum et non ex bono essent, cum illud ipsum bonum primum [est] et ipsum esse sit et ipsum bonum et ipsum esse bonum."
132. *Quomodo,* 124–27: "Sed ipsum esse omnium rerum ex eo fluxit quod est primum bonum et quod bonum tale est ut recte dicatur in eo quod est esse bonum. Ipsum igitur eorum esse bonum est; tunc enim in eo."
133. A closer look at the chapter shows that Boethius does not believe things' forms to

existing forms and their hierarchy. Boethius claims that God is pure form: He is what He is.[134] God is the summit of the hierarchy of forms. There are then those forms which do not exist in their own right. These forms, he claims, are also pure. For they are not substrates, and cannot be material in any way.[135] That fact of the matter is, however, that these immaterial forms do not exist in their own right. Rather, Boethius adds, they are the formal causes of composite material things,[136] and material things, in his view, are the bottom rung in the hierarchy of forms. For existing things are images of the pure immaterial forms.[137] Indeed, Boethius claims that calling material things 'forms' is a mistake, because they are really just images.[138]

What we see here are universals *ante rem*. For Boethius's "pure forms" — the middle tier in the hierarchy of forms — are the archetypes of material things, and they do not exist in their own right.[139] They are the forms which "precede" existing particular things, and are their formal causes. But they are also what Boethius calls *ipsum esse* in the *Quomodo:* they *nondum sunt* and are what make *id quod est aliquid.*

---

be their efficient causes. His claim is that statues are not what they are because of their matter, but because of their forms; that bronze is not what it is because of prime matter but that *omne namque esse ex forma est.* Cf. *De Trinitate* 20ff. Now, I simply do not see an efficient cause in the examples. Bronze is not the efficient cause of a statue, the sculptor is. The same thing holds for all other things. Hence, *omne namque esse ex forma* does not mean that a form is the efficient cause of particular things' existences. It means that things' essences derive from a form.

134. *De Trinitate*, 29–31: "Sed divina substantia sine materia forma est atque ideo unum et est id quod est."

135. *De Trinitate*, 44–51: "Nam quod ceterae formae subiectae accidentibus sunt ut humanitas, non ita accidentia suscipit eo quod ipsa est, sed eo quod materia ei subiecta est; dum enim materia subiecta humanitati suscipit quodlibet accidens, ipsa hoc suscipere videtur humanitas. Forma vero quae est sine materia non poterit esse subiectum nec vero inesse materiae, neque enim esset forma sed imago."

136. *De Trinitate*, 51–53: "Ex his enim formis quae praeter materiam sunt, istae formae venerunt quae sunt in materia et corpus efficiunt."

137. *De Trinitate*, 53–56: "Nam ceteras quae in corporibus sunt abutimur formas vocantes, dum imagines sint. Adsimilantur enim formis his quae non sunt in materia constitutae."

138. The *Consolatio* also confirms this. Cf., e.g., *Consolatio*, IV, 6, 43–51: "Ordo namque fatalis ex providentiae simplicitate procedit. Sicut enim artifex faciendae rei formam mente praecipiens movet operis effectum, et quod simpliciter praesentarieque prospexerat, per temporales ordines ducit, ita deus providentiae quidem singulariter stabiliterque facienda disponit, fato vero haec ipsa quae disposuit multipliciter ac temporaliter administrat." See also *Consolatio*, IV, 6, 22ff.

139. Maioli suggests that they exist in the Divine Word. Cf. p. 45: "Vi sono poi delle forme archetipo, divine e trascendenti il mondo sensibile e che si identificano con il Verbo divino: anch'esse, in quanto forme pure 'sine materia,' non possono inerire nella materia né essere in alcun senso sostrato di accidenti. Ad immagini di esse Dio ha ordinato e informato la materia indeterminata e caotica dando origine alla cosmogenesi, come Boezio canta nel celebre metro 9 del III libro del *De Consolatione.*" Maioli's point is well taken. I find it difficult, however, to reconcile with his interpretation of *esse.*

They are, in other words, the "aliud" in which *id quod est* participates in order to be *aliquid*.

Another important confirmation of our interpretation is to be found in the *De Fide Catholica,* or to be precise in Boethius's critique of the monophysite heresy. The monophysite heresy held that Christ was not a human being — or that He was only God — and is, of course, contrary to the doctrine of the Council of Chalcedon. Now, it is not Chalcedonian Christology that interests us here. That is a theological matter. What is important is Boethius's formulation of cause of his dissent with the monophysite Eutychus. For the formulation tells us how Boethius believed a human being to be constituted. What Boethius claims, then, it that Eutychus's doctrine is false because it holds Christ was:

> God alone, and that the human body which Christ put on had not come *by participation in human substance.*[140]

What this claim implies, of course, is that in order to be fully human, Christ must have participated in the "human substance," that is in the essence of humanity, since essence and substance are equivalent terms in Boethius's metaphysics. As this holds for Christ, then, so too must it hold for any other being who is human. What we have, as such, is that in order to be fully human one must participate in the essence of humanity.

But the essence of humanity, the "human substance," does not exist *per se*. As Boethius points out in the *De Trinitate,* it is an immaterial form, which is the formal cause of composite material things, but does not exist in its own right. *Nondum est.* The "human substance" is thus a *universal ante rem*.

---

140. *De Fide Catholica,* 208–15: "Sed huic tam sanae atque veracissime fidei exstiterant multi qui diversa garrirent et praeter alios Nestorius et Eutyches repertores haereseos exstiterunt, quorum unus hominem solum, alter *deum solum putavit asserere nec humanum corpus Christus induerat de humanae substantiae participatione venisse.*" [The italics are mine and indicate the passage we quoted in the text.]

Chapter 14

THE *CONSOLATIO PHILOSOPHIAE*

The 'good' with which the *Consolatio* deals is man's perfection — his final cause — and Boethius explicitly claims that man obtains that 'good' by participating in God.[1] Accordingly, participation cannot mean in the *Consolatio* what it does in the *Quomodo*. For in the *Quomodo* participation is the cause of contingent things' being and substantial goodness. Consequently, I cannot in principle agree with those scholars who use the *Consolatio*'s doctrine of participation to elucidate the *Quomodo*'s doctrine of participation, and vice versa.[2] What, then, does participation mean in this second work?

What is unquestionable is that participation is the heart of the *Consolatio*'s metaphysics:

---

1. Cf., e.g., *Consolatio*, III, 11, 22–24: " 'Omne quod bonum est boni participatione bonum esse concedis an minime?' 'Ita est.' " See also *Consolatio*, III, 10, 83–90: "Nam quoniam beatitudinis adeptione fiunt homines beati, beatitudo vero est ipsa divinitas, divinitatis adeptione beatos fieri manifestum est: sed uti iustitiae adeptione iusti, sapientiae sapientes fiunt, ita divinitatem adeptos deos fieri ratione necesse est. Omnis igitur beatus deus, sed natura quidem unus; participatione vero nihil prohibet esse quam plurimos."

2. Cf., e.g., Obertello, *Dintorni*, pp. 53–55. This is not to say that the *Consolatio* does not presuppose contingent things' substantial participation, or that its remarks on contingent things' participation are not similar to the *Quomodo*'s. This is not true. Cf. e.g., *Consolatio*, III, 11, 22–24: " 'Omne quod bonum est boni participatione bonum esse concedis an minime?' 'Ita est.' " It is to say that using the *Consolatio*'s comments on contingent things' participation to corroborate one's interpretation of the *Quomodo*'s doctrine of participation is to simplify the latter and to misinterpret the former. For although it is certainly true that Boethius's doctrine in the *Quomodo* claims that contingent things are substantially good because they participate in the good — which is what the above remark in the *Consolatio* claims — it is careful to distinguish that good in which complex things participate in order to exist and that good in which complex things participate in order to have good essences. And again, although the *Consolatio* does claim that complex things are good because they participate in the good, Boethius distinguishes their substantial participation in the good — that participation whereby goodness becomes one of their substantial properties — and that participation in the good whereby they are perfected. And more than not so, its remarks on participation regard the latter rather than the former. This is also true of the passage quoted above, as can be seen from the lines that precede it. Cf. *Consolatio*, III, 11, 15–21. To make a long story short, I do not mean to claim that it is wrong to use the *Consolatio*'s doctrine of participation to corroborate one's interpretation of the *Quomodo*'s doctrine. My claim is that it is simplistic to do so if one does not bear the doctrine in its entirety in mind.

It is at the core of the *Consolation*. Both references to participation occur within the main argument of Book III, which develops the argument for the goodness of God and leads to the questions of his providence.[3]

But as the passage above suggests, one can only grasp the full scope of Boethius's view of participation by viewing its role in the *Consolatio* as a whole. For although Boethius does explicitly claim that men attain their 'good' by participating in God, what he believes that to mean and entail is only clear in light of: (1) his definition of man's 'good'; (2) his delineation of the false means of attaining that 'good'; (3) his view of Providence; and (4) his explication of man's own role in his becoming 'good.' The *Consolatio* is not as abstruse a work as the *Quomodo* is, but it is certainly a complex one. Here again, as such, we must begin our reconstruction of Boethius's doctrine of participation by reviewing his doctrine of the 'good.' This chapter will, as such, have two principal parts.

The *Consolatio* and the Causes of Complex Things' Perfection

The *Consolatio*'s principal problem, as we saw, is determining how man can simultaneously be and not be the cause of his perfection.[4] This problem admits of two formulations. For man is both a contingent and a rational being. Generally speaking, explaining how contingent beings are perfected entails explaining how some given thing's perfection can be caused by something other than itself. This is difficult. For a being's perfection is by definition its possession or actuation of its own nature. If a contingent being's perfection is caused by something other than itself, however, then its perfection must be its reception of the perfecter's activity. What one must do in order to explain how contingent beings are perfected, as such, is to solve what looks like a contradiction: that a being's possession of its nature is its reception of the activity of what is other than itself.

The tempting way to solve the apparent contradiction is to claim that the perfecter's being is the perfected being: to claim that they share one and the same nature, or something of this sort. But this is not a viable way of doing so. For the reason why the apparent contradiction arises in the first place is that the being to be perfected must be other

---

3. Varvis, p. 46.
4. Cf., e.g., *Consolatio*, I, 5m, 25ff.

than what perfects it, if it is to be perfected at all. *Quidquid movetur ab alio movetur.* How, then, does one avoid the contradiction?

This is what Boethius must explain. The heart of his solution is to distinguish the efficient and formal causes of contingent things' perfection. It is to claim that God is the efficient cause of the perfection of all contingent things, but that the formal causes of the perfection of all contingent things are their own natures.

The perfection of rational beings presents a special instance of the paradox implicit in the perfection of contingent things. Simply stated, rational beings must be free.[5] For they must be the moving causes of their own acts. Were they not free, God would be the efficient cause of evil,[6] and that is simply impossible. God cannot be both the efficient cause of evil and God.[7] Now, if rational beings are the moving causes of their own acts, then it seems necessary for them to be the moving causes of their own perfection. For perfection is either an act or the result of an act, and a free rational being, it seems, must be the moving cause of all of his own acts. The fact of the matter is, however, that a contingent rational being cannot be the moving cause of his own perfection. Those rational beings who desire their perfection — and there is no seeking perfection if one does not desire it — cannot be perfect. They could not desire their perfection if they were.[8] But imperfect beings cause imperfect acts and perfection does not result from imperfect acts.[9] That is, a being who seeks his perfection cannot as yet possess or have actuated his nature completely. But *actiones non progrediuntur nisi ab existente in actu secundum quod est in actu.* Hence, a being whose possession of his nature is incomplete can only express his nature incompletely in his acts. But the incomplete expression of one's nature cannot cause the complete possession of that nature. Thus, a contingent rational being cannot be the moving cause of his perfection. Therefore, something other than the contingent rational being must be the efficient cause of his perfection. That is the alternative. *Quidquid movetur ab alio movetur.* There ensues the apparent contradiction that a rational being must be the cause of his perfection if he is free, and that he cannot be the cause of his perfection if he is contingent.

---

5. *Consolatio*, V, 2, 5–12.
6. Cf. *Consolatio*, V, 3, 81ff.
7. *Consolatio*, III, 12, 79–80.
8. Cf. *Consolatio*, III, 3, 23–24.
9. Cf. *Consolatio*, III, 10, 9–19: "Omne enim quod inperfectum esse dicitur, id inminutione perfecti inperfectum esse perhibetur. Quo fit, ut si in quolibet genere inperfectum quid esse videatur, in eo perfectum quoque aliquid esse necesse sit. Etenim perfectione sublata, unde illud quod inperfectum perhibetur exstiterit ne fingi quidem potest. Neque enim ab deminutis inconsummatisque natura rerum coepit exordium, sed ab integris absolutisque procedens in haec extrema atque effeta dilabitur."

There is clearly something paradoxical about this. For if a being's perfection is its complete possession of its nature, then a rational being's perfection must entail his complete possession of his freedom. Rational beings are by nature free. But it seems contradictory to claim that a rational being's freedom is the effect of an act which originates in something other than himself. After all, a free act is one which originates in the agent, and no cause can produce an effect which is contrary to itself.[10] But if it is contradictory to claim that a rational being's freedom results from its reception of another being's act, then it must be contradictory to claim that a rational being's perfection results from his reception of another being's act. A being's perfection cannot entail the negation of his nature,[11] and the negation of a rational being's freedom must be the negation of his nature. Can a rational being truly be perfected by something other than himself? It seems not. The fact of the matter is, however, that a contingent rational being can only be perfected by something other than himself, since he cannot by definition perfect himself. What this means, of course, is that if a complex rational being cannot be perfected by something other than himself, he cannot become perfect at all. How, then, can rational beings obtain their good?

This is what Boethius must explain.[12] The heart of his solution, once again, is to distinguish the efficient and formal — efficient and instrumental — causes of a rational being's perfection. It is to claim that God can be the efficient cause of a rational being's perfection if and only if that rational being's own free acts conform to his nature. It is to claim that God is the efficient cause of a rational being's perfection if the rational being himself is its instrumental cause.

Contingent Beings' Perfection

Boethius's claim is that contingent beings attain their perfection through Providence. For God is the efficient cause of the existence of all things in the universe,[13] and of all motion and change in the universe.[14] That

---

10. Cf. *Consolatio*, II, 6, 43–44: "Neque enim sibi solent adversa sociari; natura respuit ut contraria quaeque iungantur."
11. *Consolatio*, IV, 2, 110–11.
12. Cf. *Consolatio*, I, 6. When Philosophy questions Boethius in order to ascertain the cause of his depression, she explicitly asks him: (1) if the universe is governed by chance or not, (2) who governs the universe, and (3) how He does so. Boethius replies to the first question correctly. The universe is not governed by chance. God, he claims then in answer to the second question, is the governor of the universe. But he cannot answer the third question. This, then, is the problem to which the work as a whole sets out to respond. "Iam scio," says Philosophy, "morbi tui aliam vel maximam causam."
13. *Consolatio*, IV, 6, 43–51.
14. *Consolatio*, IV, 6, 22–30: "Omnium generatio rerum cunctusque mutabilium naturarum progressus et quidquid aliquo movetur modo, causas, ordinem, formas ex divinae mentis stabilitate sortitur." See also *Consolatio*, III, 12, 24–26: "Hoc quidquid est quo con-

this is so can be seen if we analyze the proximate cause of the perfection of contingent beings. Contingent things become perfect when they actualize their natures completely. They actualize their natures completely, Boethius points out, when they acquire unity and goodness.[15] For since unity and goodness are substantial properties of being,[16] things must acquire being when they acquire unity and goodness. But when things acquire being they are actualized. This, Boethius claims, is why unity and the good are things' final cause.[17] Now, contingent things acquire unity and goodness when unity and goodness are bestowed upon them,[18] and they are bestowed upon them by God,[19] who is Unity itself and the Good.[20] God is the efficient cause of contingent things' perfection.

God is not, however, the formal cause of contingent beings' perfection. For every being must retain its nature in order to be,[21] and were God the formal cause of the perfection of contingent things, contingent things could not retain their natures when they are perfected. Were God the formal cause of contingent things' perfection, as such, they could not be perfected at all.

But how can God not be the formal cause of the perfection of contingent things if He is the efficient cause of their perfection? There is something paradoxical about this. For if every effect is similar to its cause, then it stands to reason that an efficient cause must be the formal cause of its effect. Is that not why *omne agens agit sibi simile*? Is

---

dita manent atque agitantur, usitato cunctis vocabulo deum nomino." See also *Consolatio*, IV, 6, 83ff.

15. *Consolatio*, III, 11, 8–21: " 'Nonne,' inquit, 'monstravimus ea quae appetuntur pluribus idcirco vera perfectaque bona non esse quoniam a se invicem discreparent cumque alteri abesset alterum, plenum absolutumque bonum afferre non posse? Tum autem verum bonum fieri cum in unam veluti formam atque efficientiam colligitur, ut quae sufficientia est, eadem sit potentia, reverentia, claritas atque iucunditas, nisi vero unum atque idem omnia sint, nihil habere quo inter expetenda numerentur?' 'Demonstratum,' inquam, 'nec dubitari ullo modo potest.' 'Quae igitur cum discrepant minime bona sunt, cum vero unum esse coeperint, bona fiunt; nonne haec ut bona sint, unitatis fieri adeptione contingit? 'Ita,' inquam, 'videtur.' "

16. *Consolatio*, III, 11, 24–26: "Omne quod est tam diu manere atque subsistere quam diu sit unum, sed interire atque dissolvi pariter atque unum destiterit." The same thing holds for the good insofar as goodness and unity are one. Cf. *Consolatio* III, 11, 27–30 and 108–10: "Sed unum id ipsum monstravimus esse quod bonum."

17. Cf., e.g., *Consolatio* III, 11, 110–12.

18. *Consolatio*, III, 11, 23–24.

19. Cf., e.g., *Consolatio*, III, 12, 15–26: "Mundus hic ex tam diversis contrariisue partibus in unam formam minime convenisset, nisi unus esset qui tam diversa coniungeret. Coniuncta vero naturarum ipsa diversitas invicem discors dissociaret atque divelleret, nisi unus esset qui quod nexuit contineret. Non tam vero certus naturae ordo procederet nec tam dispositos motus locis, temporibus, efficientia, spatiis, qualitatibus explicarent, nisi unus esset qui has mutationem varietates manens ipse disponeret. Hoc quidquid est quo condita manent atque agitantur, usitato cunctis vocabulo deum nomino."

20. *Consolatio*, III, 10, 43–62.

21. *Consolatio*, IV, 2, 110–11.

it not why Boethius claims that God is the efficient cause of contingent things' perfection: namely, (1) because their perfection is constituted by their acquisition of unity and goodness; (2) because the efficient cause of one's acquisition of a given property must possess that property;[22] and (3) because God alone is both Unity and the Good?[23] How can God not be the formal cause of contingent things' perfection, if their perfection is their acquisition of unity and goodness and if God Himself is Unity and the Good?

The source of this paradox is a false premise. The fact that every effect must be similar to its cause cannot mean that an effect is its cause. But that is precisely what it would have to mean if God were the formal cause of creatures' perfection. After all, God is simple: His Form and *id quod est* are one, as Boethius puts it in the *De Trinitate*.[24] Thus, if God were the formal cause of the perfection of contingent things, then contingent things would have to become God when they are perfected: *ea quae sunt* would have to be one with God's Form. But this is impossible, as Boethius himself notes. For there is only one being who is God by nature,[25] since God does not diffuse his essence *ad extra* and cannot be receptive.[26] Hence contingent things cannot become God when they are perfected. What this means is that God cannot be the formal cause of their perfection.

The mistake in the premise above is that it confuses a thing's formal and exemplary causes. When one claims that *omne agens agit sibi simile,* or that every effect is similar to its cause, he is not claiming that every agent is the formal cause of effects—else no acts could have effects. What that claim means is that every agent is the exemplary cause of his effects. And there is a difference between these two things. A sculptor is the exemplary cause of his statues. For since *actiones non progrediuntur nisi ab existente in actu secundum quod est in actu,* an agent's actuality is reflected in his acts. Is that not why Phidias's statues

---

22. This is why Boethius claims that material things cannot be man's 'good.' Cf., e.g., *Consolatio,* II, 5, 95ff. and *Consolatio* II, 6, 40ff.

23. Cf. *Consolatio,* II, 6, 53–54. This is why Boethius claims that none of the 'goods' man can acquire in this world is his good. For none make him good. Cf., e.g., *Consolatio,* II, 5, 53–58: "Ex quibus omnibus nihil horum quae tu in tuis conputas bonis tuum esse bonum liquido monstratur. Quibus si nihil inest appetendae pulchritudinis, quid est quod vel amissis doleas vel laeteris retentis? Quod si natura pulchra sunt, quid id tua refert?"

24. Cf. *De Trinitate,* II, 29–31: "Sed divina substantia sine materia forma est atque ideo unum et est id quod est."

25. Cf. *Consolatio,* III, 10, 88–90: "Omnis igitur beatus deus, sed natura quidem unus; participatione vero nihil prohibet esse quam plurimos."

26. *Consolatio,* III, 12, 102–8: "Ea est enim divinae forma substantiae ut neque in externa dilabitur nec in se externum aliquid ipsa suscipiat, sed, sicut de ea Parmenides ait: 'Πάντοθεν εὐκύκλου σφαίρης ἐναλίγκιον ὄγκῳ' rerum orbem mobilem rotat, dum se immobilem ipsa conservat."

are so different from Rodin's? But the fact that an agent's actuality is reflected in his acts does not make the agent himself the formal cause of his the effects of his acts. Rodin wasn't the formal cause of his statues, else *The Hand of God* would speak.

The point clearly holds for contingent things' perfection. We must therefore distinguish the formal and efficient causes of contingent things' perfection. As such, that God is the efficient cause of the perfection of contingent things makes Him the exemplary cause of their perfection. But it does not make Him the formal cause of their perfection.

Now, Boethius was more than aware of the difference between formal and exemplary causes. For although he explicitly states that God is the exemplary cause of man's perfection,[27] he also indicates that God cannot be the formal cause of his perfection. His claim is that God moves all things through Providence and that Providence is Divine Intelligence: that knowledge and power which disposes all things in accordance with their own natures.[28] Providence is the enactment of God's Ideas,[29] and God's Ideas are contingent things' natures:

> The whole development of changeable natures and whatever is moved (*movetur*) are given their causes, order and forms by the stability of the divine mind. That mind, firmly placed in the citadel of its own simplicity of nature, established the manner in which all things behave. (IV, 6, 22–27)[30]

What this means is that we must distinguish between the formal and efficient causes of the perfection of contingent things. God, the unmoved mover, is its efficient cause.[31] But things' own natures are their formal causes. For things' natures are the formal cause of Providence itself: God directs nature by enacting his Ideas in it, and God's Ideas are the natures of contingent things.

This clearly means that it is not contradictory to affirm that the perfection of complex things is at once their possession of their own natures and their reception of God's causal efficiency. Hence the paradox of the perfection of contingent things is solved.

---

27. Cf., e.g., *Consolatio*, III, 10, 83–88.
28. *Consolatio*, IV, 6, 27–28: "Qui modus cum in ipsa divinae intelligentiae puritate conspicitur, providentia nominatur."
29. See footnote 14.
30. Cf. *Consolatio*, III, 9m, 1ff.
31. Cf. *Consolatio*, I, 6, 8–11: " 'Atqui,' inquam, 'nullo existimaverim modo ut fortuita temeritate tam certa moveantur, verum operi suo conditorem praesidere deum scio nec umquam fuerit dies qui me ab hac sententiae veritate depellat.' " See also *Consolatio*, III, 12, 15–26.

Rational Beings' Perfection

The distinction between the formal and efficient causes of the perfection of contingent things is much more pronounced in contingent rational beings. For the formal and efficient causes of contingent rational beings' perfection are not only logically distinct — distinct, that is, *in mente Dei* — they are also (in a sense) distinct *in re*. Rational beings have the choice as to whether or not to live in accordance with their natures. Rational beings are free. Since a being must retain its nature in order to be perfected, however, a rational being's choice as to whether or not live in accordance with his nature has bearing upon his perfection: it determines whether or not he can be perfected. A being can be perfected if and only if it actualizes its nature, after all. Rational beings are therefore not only the instrumental causes of their actualizing their natures once they exist, they are also the instrumental causes of their perfection.

This does not, however, make them either the efficient or the formal causes of their perfection. For only God can be the efficient cause of the perfection of a contingent thing. Moreover, although a rational being is the instrumental cause of his actualizing his nature, he is not his own formal cause, else there could not be other rational beings who share his same nature. Boethius thus claims that contingent rational beings' perfection has three distinct causes: God, their formal causes, and contingent things' own free wills.

Man is a rational being and must as such be free.[32] For rational beings must be able to choose what they will or will not pursue.[33] Now, all contingent beings desire their perfection by nature.[34] That desire is placed in their natures by God Himself.[35] In non-rational beings that desire causes an involuntary motion: their involuntary acceptance of God's will and their involuntary actualization of their own natures.[36] In rational beings, however, things are slightly different. For although

---

32. *Consolatio*, V, 2, 5–6.
33. *Consolatio*, V, 2, 7–12.
34. *Consolatio*, III, 11, 110–12.
35. *Consolatio*, III, 11, 97–100: "Dedit enim providentia creatis a se rebus hanc vel maximam manendi causam ut quoad possunt naturaliter manere desiderent." See *Consolatio*, III, 11, 118ff.
36. *Consolatio*, III, 11, 89–97: "Nam ne in animalibus quidem manendi amor ex animae voluntatibus, verum ex naturae principiis venit. Nam saepe mortem cogentibus causis quam natura reformidat voluntas amplectitur, contraque illud quo solo mortalium rerum durat diurnitas gignendi opus, quod natura semper appetit, interdum coercet voluntas. Adeo haec sui caritas non ex animali motione sed ex naturali intentione procedit." The point is specifically applicable to things' desire for unity, but since Boethius himself tells us that unity and goodness are the same thing — *bonum et unum convertuntur* — it can be applied to the good.

they also have a natural desire for perfection,[37] and although their natures too "almost compel" them to seek the good,[38] they cannot do so without their consent.

Man's natural desire for perfection is a vague awareness of his end and of the means to attain that end.[39] The problem is that his awareness is not knowledge of his end or of the means to attain that end,[40] and man, unlike non-rational beings, must understand what his end is in order to pursue it.[41] Rational beings are rational precisely because their understanding must precede their acts. The fact of the matter is, however, that nothing can force man to understand the true nature of his end, and nothing can do his understanding for him. Man's intellect is not completely passive.[42] Those things which man understands do not impress themselves upon his mind, as the Stoics claimed.[43] Nor does man's nature force him to understand himself, or any other thing, properly.[44] Man's free will therefore also plays a part in his understanding. This implies two things. Firstly, it implies that man does not actualize (or possess) his own nature involuntarily—once he exists, that is. For it is when man understands things that he actualizes his nature. Man is a rational animal, after all,[45] and Boethius tells us that it is in his knowing himself that he acquires his nobility.[46] Secondly, and consequently, it implies that man's pursuit of his end cannot be coerced, but must be preceded by a real effort on his part to understand what his end is and how it is to be attained. Man's free will must therefore play a role in his own actualization.

Now, since both man's pursuit of his end and his actualization of his own nature are voluntary, man must play an active role in his own perfection. Boethius illustrates these points both negatively and positively: by showing both how man can be the cause of his own undoing and how he can be instrumental in his own perfection.

Man's pursuit of his end can go awry, Boethius claims, if he misunderstands the true nature of the end which he desires by nature.[47]

---

37. *Consolatio*, III, 2, 13–14; III, 3, 5ff.
38. *Consolatio*, IV, 2, 75–79: "Vide enim quanta vitiosorum hominum pateat infirmitas qui ne *ad hoc quidem pervenire queunt ad quod eos naturalis ducit ac paene compellit intentio. Et quid si hoc tam magno ac paene invicto praeeuntis naturae* desererentur auxilio." [The italics are mine.] See also *Consolatio*, III, 3, 1–6.
39. *Consolatio*, III, 3, 1–5.
40. Cf. *Consolatio*, III, 8, 45–49.
41. *Consolatio*, V, 2, 9–11.
42. *Consolatio*, V, 4, 115–20.
43. Cf. *Consolatio*, V, 4m, 1ff.
44. *Consolatio* V, 2, 16ff.
45. *Consolatio*, I, 6, 35ff.
46. *Consolatio*, II, 5, 85ff.
47. *Consolatio*, III, 3, 5–8.

This happens when he chooses to seek a portion of what he desires by nature[48] — wealth, honor, power, and so forth — in the belief that he can secure his end through his own free acts.[49] The fact of the matter is, Boethius specifies, that man loses his nature when he misinterprets his end and pursues 'false goods.'[50] For man's pursuit of his good goes awry precisely because he does not attempt to understand his true nature.[51] The effect of man's pursuit of the wrong good, Boethius concludes, is that he cannot be perfected. For the man who pursues the wrong end ceases to be,[52] and nothing can be perfected if it does not exist:

> In this way, then, whatever falls from goodness, ceases to be; wherefore evil men cease to be what they were — but that they were men till now their still surviving form of the human body shows — and therefore by turning to wickedness have by the same act lost their human nature. But since only goodness can raise anyone above mankind, it follows necessarily that wickedness thrusts down beneath deserving the name of men those whom it has cast down from the human condition... So he who having left goodness aside has ceased to be a man, since he cannot pass over into the divine state, turns into a beast. (IV, 3, 47–69)

If, on the other hand, man acts in conformity with his nature, he actualizes his nature and is therefore also perfected:

> But see what eternal law ordains. Suppose you have conformed your mind to better things: there is no need of a judge to confer rewards, you have yourself joined yourself to more excellent things. (IV, 3, 100–103)

For when man is true to his nature he is also true to God. All things by nature follow God's will,[53] and whatever acts in accordance with God's will is perfected by God. Whatever follows God's will is guided by Providence, and whatever is guided by Providence is perfected by it:

> He, when he has looked out from the lofty watch-tower of his providence, sees what is fitting for each individual, and arranges what he knows is fitting. (IV, 6, 121–23)

---

48. *Consolatio*, III, 9, 45–49.
49. Cf. *Consolatio* IV, 2, 62–66.
50. *Consolatio*, IV, 3, 50–51: "Quare versi in malitiam humanam quoque amisere naturam." See also *Consolatio*, IV, 2, 97–101: "An scientes volentesque bonum deserunt, ad vitia deflectunt? Sed hoc modo non solum potentes esse sed omnino esse desinunt. Nam qui communem omnium quae sunt finem relinquunt, pariter quoque esse desistunt."
51. Cf., e.g., *Consolatio*, II, 5, 73ff.
52. *Consolatio*, IV, 2, 110–12.
53. *Consolatio*, III, 12, 47–57.

When man actualizes his nature, as such, he becomes like God,[54] and when he is like God he is at once everything he was meant to be — for man was made in God's image[55] — and happy.[56]

This does not mean that man is the efficient cause of his perfection, for God is.[57] Nor does it mean that man is the formal cause of his perfection, for his nature is, and that nature is bestowed upon him by God. It means that he is the instrumental cause of his perfection when he chooses to actualize his nature.

What we have here is the key to solving the paradox of man's perfection: i.e., the fact that he is a free being whose perfection originates in something other than himself. The solution consists in distinguishing between what is within the scope of a contingent rational being's freedom and what is not. For what is not within the scope of the freedom of a contingent rational being cannot limit his freedom.

Now, all free acts presuppose a judgment.[58] This means that no act which is not preceded by a judgment can be free. A contingent rational being's choice of what end to pursue can be free, as such, because it is preceded by his judgment that that end is worthy of pursuit.[59] Furthermore, since the ends a contingent rational being pursues determine how his nature is actualized in him,[60] then by extrapolation a contingent rational being's actualization also is within the scope of his freedom. This is the reason why Boethius claims that men can become beasts.[61] What is not within the scope of a contingent rational being's freedom, on the other hand, is the choice to exist, or to have a specific nature. For his being and his having a given nature cannot be preceded by his own judgment. As such, neither the efficient nor the formal causes of his perfection can be within the scope of a contingent rational being's freedom. For the cause of a being's perfection is contingent upon its nature, and a contingent rational being cannot choose his nature. If this is so, however, then neither of these things can limit his freedom. Hence it is no more contradictory to claim that the efficient and formal

---

54. *Consolatio*, IV, 6, 199–204.
55. *Consolatio*, II, 5, 72–79: "Sic rerum versa condicio est ut divinum merito rationis animal non aliter sibi splendere nisi inanimatae supellectilis possessione videatur? Et alia quidem suis contenta sunt; vos autem deo mente consimiles ab rebus infimis excellentis naturae ornamenta captatis nec intellegitis quantum conditori vestro faciatis iniuriam. Ille genus humanum terrenis omnibus praestare voluit."
56. *Consolatio*, III, 10, 83–90.
57. *Consolatio*, III, 11, 9–18.
58. *Consolatio*, V. 2, 5–9.
59. *Consolatio*, V, 2, 9–11.
60. *Consolatio*, IV, 2–3.
61. *Consolatio*, IV, 3.

causes of a contingent rational being's existence are something other than the contingent rational being himself, than it is to claim that the efficient and formal causes of his perfection are something other than the rational being himself. For a rational contingent being is not free to choose to give itself existence any more than it is to choose how its existence is perfected.

This is Boethius's own solution. His claim is that both a rational being's nature and his perfection are bestowed upon him by Providence,[62] but that Providence itself is in some sense consequent upon a rational being's own free acts. For these free acts determine who the rational being has become, and it is who the rational being has become that determines both whether or not he can be perfected, and what he requires in order to be perfected. Thus:

> To some providence metes out a fitting mixture of good and ill fortune according to the quality of their minds: some it vexes, lest they run to excess with long prosperity; others it allows to be troubled with hardships, that the virtues of their minds may be strengthened by the use and practice of patience. Some are over afraid of what they can bear, others are over contemptuous of what they can not — these it leads with harsh treatment to test themselves. Some have bought a name respected in the word at the price of a glorious death; others by remaining unbeaten by their torments have shown the rest of men an example, that virtue is unconquered by evils. And there is no doubting how rightly and in what good order these things are done, and how much in accord with the good of those to whom they come. (IV, 6, 147–59)

What this solution implies is that there are three causes of rational beings' perfection: an efficient cause, a formal cause, and an instrumental cause. The instrumental cause is the rational being himself. The formal cause is the rational beings' nature, or God's Idea. The efficient cause is God Himself.

Participation in the *Consolatio*

We are finally in a position to determine what participation means in the *Consolatio*. Participation is the means whereby contingent things become good:

---

62. *Consolatio*, IV, 6, 22–27.

> Everything that is good is good by participation in the good. (III, 11, 22–23).

But things' being good is their own perfection. For Boethius's claim is that contingent things' acquisition of goodness is their acquisition of being — *ens et bonum convertuntur* — and contingent things' acquisition of being is their perfection. Thus, participation is the means whereby contingent things are perfected. Nor is it any participation at all which is contingent things' perfection. For the passage above explicitly claims that the cause of the perfection of contingent things is their participation in the good: "Everything that is good is good *by participation in the good.*" But Boethius claims that God is the Good. We must therefore assume that the perfection of contingent things is their participation in God. As such, the *Consolatio*'s main claim regarding participation is that contingent things' participation in God is the cause of their perfection.

What does this mean? Generally speaking, Boethius's account of the *reditus* claims that Providence is the cause of the perfection of contingent things. Providence, he specifies, is both the formal and the efficient cause of contingent things' perfection. For (1) God moves all things in the universe through Providence; (2) Providence itself is God's knowledge; and (3) God's knowledge is contingent things' forms. What this means is that the perfection of contingent things is their reception of Providence, and that their reception of Providence is their reception of the formal and efficient causes of their perfection. But the cause of the perfection of contingent things is also their participation in God, as we saw above. Now, if Boethius claims both that contingent things' participation in God is the cause of their perfection and that the cause of contingent things' perfection is their reception of Providence, then it follows that contingent things' reception of Providence must be their participating in God.

Although Boethius does not explicitly claim it, we can therefore suppose that the single act of participation through which contingent things are perfected is logically speaking two different acts of participation through which contingent things receive their natures and their actuality respectively. For if contingent things' participating in God is their reception of Providence, and if Providence is both the efficient and the formal cause of their perfection, then participation too must be both the efficient and the formal cause of their perfection. The deduction here also follows from Boethius's own logical distinction between the causes of contingent things' perfection. For his claim is that although the efficient cause of contingent things' perfection is God Himself, the formal causes of their perfection are not God Himself, but His Ideas of contingent things.[63]

That things' reception of their actuality and their reception of their formal causes can be thought of as participation follows from the fact that contingent things cannot be identical to either the formal or the efficient causes of their perfection. After all, contingent things — or at least material ones[64] — do not have their own individual forms. What this means is that contingent things cannot be identical to their forms — God's Ideas — even when they are perfect. If they are not identical to their forms — God's Ideas — however, and if they nonetheless acquire the modality of their perfection from them, then they must participate in them in order to be perfect.

As for things' goodness (or their actuality), on the other hand, it too cannot be identical to its cause. For that cause is God Himself and, as we have seen, Boethius holds that contingent things cannot be God. Nonetheless, contingent things must receive His goodness in order to become perfect. But if things receive God's goodness when they are perfected and are not God, then they must participate in God in order to be perfected. "Everything that is good is good by participation in the good." Hence, contingent things' perfection must be caused by two logically distinct acts of participation. Their participation in God and their participation in His Ideas.

Our inferences are confirmed by Boethius's definition of the cause of man's perfection. Boethius's claim is that man is perfected: (1) when he "preserves his nature" (IV, 2, 111), or is good (IV, 3, 46) and (2) when he "conforms his mind to better things" (IV, 4, 101). These two things are in reality one and the same thing. For man is "good" when he "preserves his nature" — *ens et bonum convertuntur* — and he "preserves his nature" when he "conforms his mind to better things." Man's nature is rational, after all. Both of these things take place, Boethius tells us then, when man "joins himself to more excellent things" (IV, 4, 104), or makes his the Pythagorean motto: ἕπου Θεῷ.[65] For although man is the instrumental cause of his perfection, he is neither its efficient nor its formal cause. Man is perfected when he assents to Providence,

---

63. *Consolatio*, IV, 6, 43–51: "Ordo namque fatalis ex providentiae simplicitate procedit. Sicut enim artifex faciendae rei formam mente praecipiens movet operis effectum, et quod simpliciter praesentarieque prospexerat, per temporales ordines ducit, ita deus providentiae quidem singulariter stabiliterque facienda disponit, fato vero haec ipsa quae disposuit multipliciter ac temporaliter administrat."

64. Cf. *Consolatio*, IV, 6, 82–86: "Ea series caelum ac sidera movet, elementa in se invicem temperat et alterna commmutatione transformat; eadem nascentia occidentiaque omnia per similes fetuum seminumque renovat progressus."

65. *Consolatio*, I, 4, 143–44.

and it is Providence that furnishes the formal and efficient causes of his perfection. Boethius thus specifies that God is the efficient cause of the perfection of all things — He "directs all things towards the good" (IV, 6, 200–201) — and that He bestows their formal causes on them: He gives them their "causes, order, and forms" (IV, 2, 24). Hence, man's perfection must have a double cause and that double cause is furnished by Providence.

The fact of the matter is, however, that Boethius also tells us that participation — man's participating in God — is the cause of man's perfection:

> For since men are made happy by the acquisition of happiness, but happiness is itself divinity, it is obvious that they are made happy by the acquisition of divinity. But as by the acquisition of justice they become just, or by the acquisition of wisdom wise, so by the same argument they must, when they have acquired divinity, become gods. Therefore every happy man is a god, though by nature God is one only: but nothing prevents there being as many as you like by participation. (III, 10, 83–90)

If this is so, however, and if man's perfection has a double cause — a formal and an efficient cause — then his participating in God must furnish both the formal and the efficient causes of his perfection. But God Himself cannot be the formal cause of man's perfection, as we saw above, else man would be God when he is perfected, and that is simply not what Boethius claims either in the passage at hand or elsewhere in the *Consolatio*. Hence, the formal cause of man's perfection must be other than God. But man must acquire this cause when he participates in God. For the passage above claims that man's happiness — or perfection — is his participating in God. As such, man must acquire the formal cause of his perfection by participating at once in something which is not God and in God. But as the *Quomodo* shows, what is not God but is in God are God's Ideas.[66] Hence man's perfection must be his participating in God and in God's Ideas. "Everything good is good by participation in the good."

The *Consolatio*'s doctrine of participation is therefore dual. It claims (1) that things must participate in God in order to acquire their actuality, and (2) that they must participate in His ideas in order to acquire the modality of their actuality: their essences. It is as such similar to the *Quomodo*'s doctrine of participation. For the *Quomodo*'s doctrine

---

66. *Quomodo*, 124–27: "Sed ipsum esse omnium rerum ex eo fluxit quod est primum bonum et quod bonum tale est ut recte dicatur in eo quod est esse bonum. Ipsum igitur eorum esse bonum est; tunc enim in eo."

claims that contingent things participate in God (*id quod est esse*) and in their indeterminate essences (*aliud*) in order to exist (*ut sit*) and be specific things (*ut aliquid sit*). The difference between these doctrines is that the *Consolatio*'s doctrine presupposes the existence of the contingent things which participate in God and in His Ideas in order to be perfected, whereas the *Quomodo*'s doctrine of participation accounts for the existence of contingent things by claiming that their existence is caused by their participating in God and in His Ideas.

Now, it may be objected that our interpretation of the *Consolatio*'s passage regarding man's participation in God is simply mistaken. For the passage claims that God Himself is the formal cause of man's happiness. That is, just as wisdom is the formal cause of one's being wise, and justice is the cause one's being just, so too must God be the formal cause of man's beatitude. As such, what Boethius is describing in this passage is not man's 'natural perfection' but his 'supernatural perfection.' If this is so, however, then we cannot infer either that man's natural perfection takes place through participation, or that that participation must be two-fold. For the premise of our inference is that that perfection which is caused by Providence — i.e., man's natural perfection — is that very same perfection whose cause is defined in the passage regarding participation, and that premise is mistaken.

This may be true. The passage at hand may concern man's 'supernatural perfection' since Boethius himself seems to claim that goodness does perfect man supernaturally:

> Only goodness can raise anyone above mankind. (IV, 3, 50–51)

But the passage need not mean that man is supernaturally perfected when he participates in God. To be precise, it need not mean that exclusively. There are two main reasons for this. The first is that Boethius himself claims that the beatitude which man acquires by participating in God is 'his' goodness:

> We have shown that happiness is the good itself... But this cannot be separated from good men — for he will no longer rightly be called good who lacks goodness. (IV, 3, 8–14)

He tells us that man can lose that goodness only when *he* ceases to be good:

> But since his goodness confers on each man his reward, he will only lack it when he has ceased to be good. (IV, 3, 19–21)

What this seems to imply is that the goodness which man acquires by participating in God is his 'natural' perfection. For that goodness is an integral part of man himself. Our point is corroborated by Boethius's claim that the goodness which is man's happiness is "directly opposite" to the wretchedness which is man's evil.[67] For the wretchedness which is man's evil is the loss of his nature.[68] It would seem to follow that the goodness which is man's happiness is the actualization of his nature.

The second reason why the beatitude which Boethius describes in the passage regarding participation is most probably man's 'natural perfection' is that Boethius himself claims that man's nature is God-like.[69] Now, if man's nature is God-like, then the actualization of his nature must make him God-like. As such, man's natural perfection must be what the passage on participation calls 'being a god.' Hence our point stands.

---

67. *Consolatio*, III, 3, 33–36: "Nam cum bonum malumque item poenae atquae praemium adversa fronte dissideant, quae in boni praemio videmus accedere eadem necesse est in mali poena contraria parte respondeant."
68. *Consolatio*, III, 3, 50–51.
69. *Consolatio*, II, 6, 73–79: "Sic rerum versa condicio est ut divinum merito rationis animal non aliter sibi splendere nisi inanimatae supellectilis possessione videatur? Et alia quidem suis contenta sunt: vos autem deo mente consimiles ab rebus infimis excellentis naturae ornamenta captatis nec intellegentis quantum conditori vestro faciatis iniuriam. Ille genus humanum terrenis omnibus praestare voluit."

Part Five

CONCLUSION

Boethius's doctrine of participation is substantial and dual. It is the means whereby he explains both why complex things exist and how they attain their perfection. For participation is the means whereby Boethius explains why complex things are good, and goodness is both a substantial property of all things and their final cause. Participation is as such the means whereby Boethius defines both complex things' *exitus* and *reditus*.

The duality runs deeper than that. For in Boethius's metaphysics both that participation which accounts for the *exitus* of complex things and that participation which accounts for their *reditus* are two-fold. His claim in the *Quomodo* is that complex things are constituted by their participation in both God and in a universal *ante rem*:

> Omne quod est participat eo quod est esse ut sit; alio vero participat ut aliquid sit. Ac per hoc id quod est participat eo quod est esse ut sit; est vero ut participet alio quolibet. (VI, 41–44)

This claim is mirrored by his definition of the cause of complex things' substantial goodness in that same work. For in his view complex things are substantially good insofar as they have real relations with both God and their good essences.[1] In the *Consolatio,* on the other hand, Boethius claims that complex things attain their perfection when they participate in both God's Ideas and in God Himself. For God is the efficient cause of the perfection of contingent things and His ideas are the formal cause of contingent things' perfection.[2] Contingent things' perfection,

---

1. *Quomodo,* 140–50: "Igitur sublato ab his bono primo mente et cogitatione, ista licet essent bona, tamen in eo quod essent bona esse non possent, et quoniam actu non potuere exsistere, nisi illud ea quod vere bonum est produxisset, idcirco et esse eorum bonum est et non est simile substantiali bono id quod ab eo fluxit; et nisi ab eo fluxissent, licet essent bona, tamen in eo quod sunt bona esse non possent, quoniam et praeter bonum et non ex bono essent, cum illud ipsum bonum primum [est] et ipsum esse sit et ipsum bonum et ipsum esse bonum."

2. *Consolatio,* IV, 6, 22–30: "Omnium generatio rerum cunctusque mutabilium naturarum progressus et quidquid aliquo movetur modo, causas, ordinem, formas ex divinae

in other words, is afforded by Providence and Providence is both God's governance of the universe and His knowledge of it.[3]

Man's perfection, or happiness, illustrates most clearly the two-fold nature of that participation whereby complex things attain their perfection. For since man is a rational being he has the choice as to whether or not actuate (or follow) his own nature. His actuating his nature is the prerequisite of his perfection. If man does not actuate his nature, Boethius tells us, he ceases to exist, and what does not exist cannot be perfected.[4] This does not mean that man is the efficient cause of his actualizing his nature or of his perfection. Boethius's claim is that man actuates his nature when he follows God and that his following God is his allowing Providence to guide him.[5] Nor does it mean that man is the formal cause of his perfection. For his nature or God's Ideas are. It means that man is the instrumental cause of his own perfection. But the very fact that man is the instrumental cause of his perfection (the fact, that is, that man must choose to actuate his nature in order to be perfected) shows that one must distinguish the formal and efficient causes of his perfection. That is, it shows that man must participate in both his nature and in God in order to be perfected. It is for this reason that Boethius tells us that man's perfection is both his participating in God[6] and his complete possession of his nature.[7]

This latter duality, the duality, that is, of both that participation which accounts for contingent things' existence and that participation which affords their perfection, is the most distinctive characteristic of the Boethian doctrine of participation and differs in the case of contingent things' *exitus* and *reditus*. For in his account of the *exitus* Boethius claims that contingent things' participation in their essences — their be-

---

mentis stabilitate sortitur." See also *Consolatio*, III, 12, 24–26: "Hoc quidquid est quo condita manent atque agitantur, usitato cunctis vocabulo deum nomino."

3. *Consolatio*, IV, 6, 43–51: "Ordo namque fatalis ex providentiae simplicitate procedit. Sicut enim artifex faciendae rei formam mente praecipiens movet operis effectum, et quod simpliciter praesentarieque prospexerat, per temporales ordines ducit, ita deus providentiae quidem singulariter stabiliterque facienda disponit, fato vero haec ipsa quae disposuit multipliciter ac temporaliter administrat."

4. *Consolatio*, IV, 3, 50–54: "Quare versi in malitiam humanam quoque amisere naturam. Sed cum ultra homines quemque provehere sola probitas possit, necesse est ut quos ab humana condicione deiecit, infra hominis meritum detrudat improbitas." See also *Consolatio*, IV, 2, 97–101: "An scientes volentesque bonum deserunt, ad vitia deflectunt? Sed hoc modo non solum potentes esse sed omnino esse desinunt. Nam qui communem omnium quae sunt finem relinquunt, pariter quoque esse desistunt."

5. *Consolatio*, I, 4, 143.

6. *Consolatio*, III, 10, 83–90: "Nam quoniam beatitudinis adeptione fiunt homines beati, beatitudo vero est ipsa divinitas, divinitatis adeptione beatos fieri manifestum est: sed uti iustitiae adeptione iusti, sapientiae sapientes fiunt, ita divinitatem adeptos deos fieri simili ratione necesse est. Omnis igitur beatus deus, sed natura quidem unus; participatione vero nihil prohibet esse quam plurimos."

7. Cf. *Consolatio*, IV, 2–3.

coming specific things — is contingent upon their participating in God. In his account of the *reditus*, on the other hand, he claims that contingent things must actuate their natures (or participate in them) in order to be able to participate in God and attain their perfection.

The proximate cause of Boethius's doctrine of two-fold participation is his attempt to reconcile the two classical definitions of the good.[8] God, Boethius tells us in the *Consolatio*, is substantially Good because He is identical to His essence, which is the Good, and because He is His final cause.[9] God, in other words, is simple[10] and what that means is: (1) that God's essence is His existence, or that His formal cause is His existence,[11] and (2) that His formal cause is His final cause. This is clearly not the case with complex things. For although complex things are also substantially good: (1) they are not identical to their essences precisely because they are complex things,[12] i.e., they are not identical to either their formal causes or to their final causes; and (2) their essences do not cause them to exist because they are complex,[13] i.e., their formal causes are not their existences or the moving or efficient causes of their existences. What this means is clearly that complex things must participate in both their essences and in God in order to be substantially good. This is precisely what Boethius claims in the *Quomodo*. It also means that complex things must participate in both their essences and in God in order to attain their perfection. This is precisely what Boethius claims in the *Consolatio*.

Now, one may wonder whether Boethius's doctrine of participation scheme is simply too complicated. For making complex things' existences contingent upon their actualizing their essences and making their actualizing their essences contingent upon their real relations with God sounds a trifle outlandish. So too does making contingent things' perfection contingent upon their participating in God and making their participation in God contingent upon their actualizing their natures. Boethius's point, however, is very important. Although there is in reality only one cause of things' existences (and perfection) — God — logically speaking that one cause must be two distinct causes of their existences

---

8. Cf. *Quomodo*, 56–61: "Quaestio vero huiusmodi est. Ea quae sunt bona sunt; tenet enim communis sententia doctorum omne quod est ad bonum tendere, omne autem tendit ad simile. Quae igitur ad bonum tendunt bona ipsa sunt."
9. *Consolatio*, III, 10, 43ff.
10. *Quomodo*, VII, 45–46: "Omne simplex esse suum et id quod est unum habet."
11. *De Trinitate*, II, 29–31: "Sed divina substantia sine materia forma est atque ideo unum et est id quod est."
12. *Quomodo*, VIII, 47–48: "Omni composito aliud est esse, aliud ipsum est."
13. *Quomodo*, 117–19: "Quae quoniam non sunt simplicia, nec esse omnino poterant, nisi ea id quod solum bonum est esse voluisset."

(and perfection): God and His Ideas. For although God is the efficient cause of things' existences (and perfection), He cannot be the formal cause of their existences (or perfection). The formal cause of contingent things' existences (and perfection) must as such be something other than God.

The fact of the matter is, however, that complex things cannot be identical to their formal causes, else complex things would not be complex.[14] Hence, they must participate in their formal causes both in order to exist and in order to be perfect. But so too must they participate in God in order to exist and attain their perfection. As such, the cause of contingent things' existences and perfection must be two acts of participation: their participation in their formal causes and their participation in God.

Now, the formal cause of a complex thing cannot be an existing thing. Hence complex things' formal causes cannot be the efficient causes of complex things' coming to possess determinate modes of existence.[15] Nor can the efficient cause of complex things' coming to possess determinate modes of existence be the complex things themselves. *Petit principium.* What is more important yet, complex things cannot exist without possessing a determinate mode of existence. What this means is that the efficient cause of complex things' participating in their formal causes must be the efficient cause of their existence. It follows that complex things' actualizing their essences is contingent upon their having an efficient cause of their existence. Thus, complex things' existences are contingent upon their actualizing their essences, and their actualizing their essences is contingent upon their real relations with God, which is precisely what Boethius claims in the *Quomodo:*

> Omne quod est participat eo quod est esse ut sit; alio vero participat ut aliquid sit. Ac per hoc id quod est participat eo quod est esse ut sit; est vero ut participet alio quolibet. (VI, 41–44)

So too, however, is the perfection of complex things contingent upon their actualizing their essences and their actualizing their essences is contingent upon God's efficient causality. Boethius claims as much in the *Consolatio:*

> The whole development of changeable natures and whatever is moved (*movetur*) are given their causes, order and forms by the stability of the divine mind. That mind, firmly placed in the citadel

---

14. *Quomodo,* VIII, 47–48: "Omni composito aliud est esse, aliud ipsum est."
15. Cf. *Quomodo,* 100–117.

Conclusion 295

of its own simplicity of nature, established the manner in which all things behave. (IV, 6, 22–27)

But things' perfection presupposes their existence, and their existence presupposes that they have already actuated their essences. Hence the inversion of the order of the two acts of participation whereby complex things are perfected, that is, the fact that Boethius makes complex things' participation in God contingent upon their participating in their natures in the case of their perfection. This inversion is especially necessary for rational complex beings, insofar as they are the instrumental causes of their perfection.

There is one last point to be made: although the two causes of contingent things' existences (and perfection) are logically distinct they cannot be so in reality. For if they were, complex things would have to be simple at some point — or existing complex things would have to be able to acquire substantial properties other than their own — and that is impossible. It is perhaps best to see the point more closely.

Just as complex things cannot be the efficient causes of their existences, they cannot be their own formal causes. That is, just as I cannot cause myself to exist, I cannot be the cause of my being a human being. For there are beings other than I who are human, and I am not they. Even supposing that I were to exist and not be human I could not become human through my own activity. For firstly something cannot acquire substantial properties after it has come to exist and not be annihilated. Secondly, nothing can cause itself to be what it itself is not actually or supereminently. Thus, I would have to be human actually or supereminently in order to be capable of causing myself to become human. The first case is impossible. It begs the principle. But so too is the second. For only God is supereminently human and nothing which comes to exist is God. Hence, I cannot be the cause of my own humanity. No complex thing can be its own formal cause. Thus, just as the efficient cause of the existence of every complex thing must be something other than the complex thing which comes to exist, so too must the formal cause of every complex thing be something other than the complex thing.

Now God cannot be the formal cause of complex things. For God is existence itself and not a specific mode of existing. That is, if all effects are similar to their causes, a real relation with God cannot confer the specific modality of being which a complex thing must have in order to be what it is. For God is not that specific mode of being which He confers upon complex things. This means that although complex things must have real relations with God in order to exist, they cannot acquire their specific mode of existence through their real relations with God directly. I am not human because of my real relation to God, else God would have to be human. Hence, that real relation which makes specific beings what they are must be a real relation to something other than God.

Nor can a complex thing's formal cause be an existing thing. For if it were there could be no complex things at all. That is, if a complex thing's formal cause were an existing thing, it would have to be either a complex thing or a simple thing. If it were a complex thing, however, then it too would have to have a formal cause other than itself. For complex things are not identical to their formal causes.[16] If its formal cause were something other than itself, then that cause too would have to be either a simple thing or a composite thing. If it were a composite thing, then it too would have to have a formal cause other than itself. The point, as such, is that if the formal causes of complex things were composite things we would have an infinite regress of formal causes. This clearly means that the formal causes of complex things cannot be complex things. Nor, however, can they be simple things. For if the formal causes of complex things were simple, they could not be the formal causes of complex things.[17] But if the formal causes of complex things cannot be complex things or simple things, they cannot be existing things. As such, Boethius claims that the formal causes of complex things are universals *ante rem*: God's Ideas.

Now, if the formal and efficient causes of complex things are distinct, then the acts whereby they are bestowed upon complex things must be distinct. Hence, Boethius's two-fold participation. This, in essence, is the reason why Boethius insists upon distinguishing the act of participation through which complex things acquire existence and the act of participation through which they acquire an essence. For the acts are logically distinct. His point is that although something's being a specific thing is contingent upon that very act through which it is made, its formal and efficient causes — its essence and its existence — are logically distinct causes of its being a specific thing. This is important. For it shows that complex things' formal causes are not God, and proves that Boethius was not an emanationist.

We must take one last step. For if the formal causes of complex things do not exist, then they cannot be the efficient causes of complex things' possessing them. What this means is that the efficient cause of complex things' actuating a form — or of their participating in their

---

16. See footnote 14.
17. Cf. *Quomodo*, 100–117.

essences — must be something other than that form. But the cause of complex things' actuating a form must be the cause of their existence. For a complex thing's existence is a determinate mode of existence and that determinate mode of existence is the actualization of that complex thing's form. Hence, complex things' participating in their essences cannot be other than their participating in God. Thus, although we must distinguish things' participating in God and their participating in their forms, these two acts of participation cannot be distinct in *re*. This is why Boethius claims that contingent things' participating in their essences is contingent upon their participating in God. This claim must be qualified. For it defines that participation whereby complex things come to exist. Their perfection is another matter. It too is their participating in God, but it presupposes that they exist and that they already actuate their natures. Hence, Boethius's claim that complex things' participation in God is contingent upon their actuating their natures when that participation is their *reditus*.

Therefore, as cryptic and awkward as Boethius's doctrine of participation seems, it is a viable way of accounting for the *exitus* and *reditus* of complex things. And that is precisely its intent.

BIBLIOGRAPHY

Boethius. *The Theological Tractates and The Consolation of Philosophy* (with an English translation). Ed. H. F. Steward, E. K. Rand, and S. J. Tester. Cambridge: Harvard University Press, 1973.
Boezio. *La Consolazione della Filosofia.* Ed. Luca Obertello. Milan: Rusconi, 1996.
Boezio. *Gli opuscoli teologici.* Catania: Centro di Studi e di Arte e Letteratura Cristiana Antica, 1947.

Other Literature Consulted

Adamo, L. "Boezio e Mario Vittorino traduttori e interpreti dell'*Isagoge* di Porfirio." *Rivista critica di storia della filosofia* 22 (1967) 141–64.
Aertsen, J. A. "The Convertability of Being and Good in St. Thomas Aquinas." *The New Scholasticism* 59 (1985) 449–70.
Alfonsi, L. "Problemi Filosofici della *Consolatio* Boeziana." *Rivista Critica di Filosofia Neoscolastica* 35 (1943) 323–28.
Amerio, R. "Probabile fonte della nozione boeziana di eternità." *Filosofia* 1 (1950) 21–39.
Aristotelis Opera, Oxonii. *Scriptorum Classicorum Bibliotheca Oxoniensis*; *Metaphysics.* Ed. R. McKeon. New York: Random House, 1941. Ed. C. Kirwan. Oxford: Clarendon Press, 1971. *Nicomachean Ethics,* Ed. T. Irwin. Indianapolis: Hackett, 1985.
Astell, A. W. *Job, Boethius, and Epic Truth.* Ithaca: Cornell University Press, 1994.
Baltes, M. "Gott, Welt, Mensch in der *Consolatio philosophiae* des Boethius." *Vigiliae Christianae* 34 (1980) 313–40.
Bardy, G. "Boèce." *Le Christianisme et l'Occident Barbare.* Paris: Les Editions du Cerf (1945) 265–319.
Bark, W. "Boethius' Fourth Tractate, the So-called *De Fide Catholica.*" *Harvard Theological Review* 39 (1946) 55–69.
Barnes, J. "Boethius and the Study of Logic." In *Boethius: His Life, Thought, and Influence.* Ed. Margaret Gibson. Pp. 73–89. Oxford: Blackwell, 1981.
Barrett, H. M. *Boethius: Some Aspects of his Times and Work.* New York: Russell & Russell, 1966.
Becker-Freiseng, A. *Die Vorgeschichte des philosophischen Terminus 'contingens': eine Untersuchung über die Bedeutung von 'contingere' bei Boethius.* Heidelberg: Selbstverlag, 1938.
Bidez, J. "Boèce et Porphyre." *Comptes Rendus de l'Academie des Inscriptions et des Belles Lettres* (1922) 346–50.

———. "Boèce et Porphyre." *Revue belge de philologie et d'histoire* 1 (1923) 189–201.
Bolton, D. K. "Remigian commentaries on the *Consolation of Philosophy* and Their Sources." *Traditio* 33 (1977) 33–78.
Bonnaud, R. "L'éducation scientifique de Boèce." *Speculum* 4 (1929) 199–206.
Bragard, R. "L'harmonie des sphères selon Boèce." *Speculum* 4 (1929) 206–13.
Brosch, H. J. *Der Seinsbegriff bei Boethius. Mit besonderer Berücksichtigung der Beziehung von Sosein und Dasein.* Innsbruck: Felizian Rauch, 1931.
Bruder, K. *Die Philosophischen Elemente in den Opuscola Sacra des Boethius.* Leipzig: Meiner, 1928.
Brunner, F. "Providence et liberté." *Revue de Théologie et de Philosophie* 26 (1976) 12–24.
Bruno, L. "La tradizione platonica del *De Consolatione Philosophae* di Boezio." *Giornale Italiano di Filologia* 15 (1962) 257–58.
Carton, R. "Le Christianisme et l'Augustinisme de Boèce." *Revue de Philosophie* 1 (1930) 573–659.
Chadwick, H. Introduction to *Boethius: His Life, Thought, and Influence.* Ed. Margaret Gibson. Pp. 1–14. Oxford: Basil Blackwell, 1981.
———. *Boethius: The Consolations of Music, Logic, Theology, and Philosophy.* Oxford: Clarendon Press, 1981.
———. "Theta on Philosophy's Dress in Boethius' *Consolatio.*" *Medium Aevum* (1980) 302–21.
———. *The Early Church.* London: Penguin, 1967.
Collins, J. "Progress and Problems in the Reassessment of Boethius." *The Modern Schoolman* 23 (1945–46) 19–58.
Cooper, L. A. *A Concordance of Boethius.* Cambridge, Mass.: Mediaeval Academy of America, 1928.
Coster, C. H., and Patch, H. R. "Procopius and Boethius." *Speculum* 23 (1948) 284–87.
Courcelle, P. *La Consolation de Philosophie dans la tradition littéraire: Antecedents et posterité de Boèce.* Paris: Études Augustiniennes, 1967.
———. *Les lettres grecques en Occident: De Macrobe à Cassiodore.* Paris: De Boccard, 1948.
———. "Etude Critique sur les Commentaires de Boèce (IX–XV siècles)." *Archives d'histoire doctrinale et littèraire du Moyen Age* 13 (1939) 5–140.
———. "Boèce et l'école d'Alexandrie." *Mélanges de l'école française de Rome* 52 (1935) 185–223.
Crabbe, A. M. "Anamnesis and Mythology in the *De Consolatione Philosophiae.*" *Congresso Internazionale di Studi Boeziani.* Rome: Herder (1981) 311–26.
Crämer-Rugenberg, F. *Die Substanzmetaphysic des Boethius in den opuscula sacra.* Diss. Cologne, 1967.
Crocco, A. *Introduzione a Boezio.* Naples: Liguori, 1975.
Crouse, R. "The Doctrine of Creation in Boethius: The *Hebdomadibus* and the *Consolatio. Studia Patristica* 17 (1982) 417–21.
Cunningham, F. A., S.J. *Essence and Existence in Thomism: A Mental vs. the "Real Distinction,"* Lanham, Md.: University Press of America, 1988.
Degli Innocenti, M. "Nota al *De Hebdomadibus* di Boezio." *Divus Thomas* 42 (1939) 397–99.

De Rijk, L. M. "Boece logicien et philosophe: Ses positions sémantiques et sa métaphysique de l'être." Pp. 141–56. *Atti del Congresso Internazionale di Studi Boeziani*. Rome: Herder, 1981.
De Vogel, C. "Amor quo caelum regitur." *Vivarium* 1 (1963) 2–34.
———. "Boethiana." *Vivarium* 9 (1971) 49–66; and *Vivarium* 10 (1972) 1–40.
———. "The Problem of Philosophy and Christian Faith in Boethius' *Consolatio*." In *Romanitas et Christianitas, Studia J. H. Waszink Oblata*. Pp. 357–70. Amsterdam: North Holland Pub. (1973).
Duhem, P. *Le System du Monde*. Paris: Librairie Scientifique Hermann, 1913.
Fabro, C. *La nozione metafisica di partecipazione secondo S. Tommaso d'Aquino*. Turin: Società Editrice Italiana, 1950.
———. *Partecipazione e causalità secondo S. Tommaso d'Aquino*. Turin: Società Editrice Internazionale, 1960.
Fay, C. "Boethius's Theory of Goodness and Being." In *Readings in Ancient and Medieval Philosophy*. Ed. James Collins. Pp. 164–72. Westminster, Md.: Newman, 1960, 164–72.
Fuhrmann, M., and J. Gruber, eds. *Boethius: Wege der Forschung*. Darmstadt: Wissenschaftlichen Buchgesellschaft, 1984.
Gastaldelli, F. *Boezio*. Rome: Edizioni Liturgiche, 1974.
Geiger, L. B. *La Participation dans la Philosophie de S. Thomas d'Aquin*. Paris: Librairie Philosophique J. Vrin, 1941.
Ghisalberti, A. "L'Ascesa boeziana a Dio nel libro III della *Consolatio*." Pp. 183–92. *Atti del Congresso Internazionale di Studi Boeziani*. Rome: Herder, 1981.
Gibson M., ed. *Boethius: His Life, Thought, and Influence*. Ed. Margaret Gibson. Oxford: Basil Blackwell, 1981.
Gruber, J. *Kommentar zu Boethius Consolatio Philosophiae*. Berlin: De Gruyter, 1978.
Hadot, P. "Dieu comme acte d'être dans le néoplatonisme." In *Dieu et l'être*. Paris: Études Augustiniennes, 1978.
———. "Forma essendi: Interprétation philologique et interprétation philosophique d'une formule de Boèce." *Les Etudes Classiques* 38 (1970) 143–56.
———. *Porphyre et Victorinus*. Paris: Études Augustiniennes, 1968.
"La distinction de l'être et de l'étant dans le *De Hebdomadibus* de Boèce." *Miscellanea Medievalia* 2. Pp. 147–53. Berlin: De Gruyter, 1963.
Knowles, D. *The Evolution of Mediaeval Thought*. New York: Image, 1962.
MacDonald, S. "Boethius's Claim That All Substances Are Good." *Archif für die Geschichte der Philosophie* 27 (1988) 245–79.
Magee, J. *Boethius on Signification and Mind*. Leiden: E. J. Brill, 1989.
Maioli, B. *Teoria dell'essere e dell'esistente e classificazione delle scienze in M. S. Boezio*. Rome: Bulzoni, 1978.
Mayer, F. *A History of Ancient and Medieval Philosophy*. New York: American Book Company, 1950.
McInerny, R. *Boethius and Aquinas*. Washington, D.C.: Catholic University of America Press, 1990.
———. "Boethius and St. Thomas Aquinas." *Rivista di filosofia neoscolastica* 66 (1974) 219–45.
Micaelli, C. *Studi sui trattati teologici di Boezio*. Naples: D'Auria, 1988.
———. *Dio nel pensiero di Boezio*. Naples: D'Auria, 1995.

Milani, M. *Boezio: l'Ultimo degli Antichi.* Milan: Camunia, 1994.
Nitzsch, F. *Das System des Boethius und die ihm zugeschriebene theologischen Schriften: eine kritische Untersuchung.* Berlin: Verlag von Wiegandt und Grieben, 1860.
Obertello, L. *Boezio e Dintorni: Ricerche sulla Cultura Altomedievale.* Florence: Nardini, 1989.
———. "Boezio." *Dizionario degli scrittori greci e latini.* Pp. 329–41. Settimo Torinese: Marzorati Editore, 1988.
———. "Boezio e il Neoplatonismo Cristiano. Gli Orientamenti Attuali della Critica." *Cultura e Storia* 22 (1983) 95–103.
———. *Severino Boezio.* Genoa: Accademia Ligure di Scienze e Lettere, 1974.
Obertello, L., ed. *Atti del Congresso Internazionale di Studi Boeziani.* Rome: Herder, 1981.
Pandolfi, C. Introduction to Tommaso d'Aquino, *L'essere e la partecipazione: Commento al libro di Boezio de Hebdomadibus.* Bologna: Edizioni Studio Domenicano, 1995.
Patch, H. R. *The Tradition of Boethius: A Study of His Importance in Medieval Culture.* Oxford and New York: Oxford University Press, 1935.
Rand, E. K. *Boethius: The First of the Scholastics and Founders of the Middle Ages.* New York: Dover, 1957.
Rapisarda, E. *La crisi spirituale di Boezio.* Catania: Letteratura Cristiana Antica, 1947.
———. *Gli opuscoli teologici.* Catania: Letteratura Cristiana Antica, 1947.
Reiss, E. *Boethius.* Boston: Twayne, 1982.
Roland-Gosselin, M.-D. *Le de ente et essentia de S. Thomas d'Aquin.* Le Saulchoir: Bibliothèque Thomiste, 1926.
Schrimpf, G. *Die Axiomenschrift des Boethius (de Hebdomadibus) als philosophisches Lehrbuch des Mittelalters.* Leiden: E. J. Brill, 1966.
Schurr, V. *Die Trinitätslehre des Boëthius im Lichte der skythischen Kontroversien.* Paderborn: Schöningh, 1935.
Sciuto F. "Il dualismo della *Consolatio* di Boezio." *Acta Philologica* 3 (1964) 361–71.
Shiel, J. "Boethius and Eudemius." *Vivarium* 12 (1974) 14–17.
———. "Boethius the Hellenist." In *History Today* 14 (1964) 478–86.
———. "Boethius and Andronicus of Rhodes." *Vigiliae Christianae* 11 (1957) 179–85.
Silk, E. T. "Boethius' Consolation as a Sequel to Augustine's *Dialogues* and *Soliloquia.*" *Harvard Theological Review* 32 (1939) 19–39.
Silvestre, H. "Le commentaire inédit de Jean Scot Erigène au mètre IX du Livre III du *De consolatione Philosophiae.*" *Revue d'histoire ecclésiastique* 47 (1952) 44–122.
Starnes, C. J. "Boethius and the Development of Christian Humanism: The Theology of the *Consolatio.*" In *Congresso Internazionale di Studi Boeziani.* Pp. 27–38. Rome: Herder, 1981.
Sulowski, F. S. "Les Sources du *De Consolatione Philosophiae* de Boèce." *Sophia* 25 (1957) 76–85.
———. "The Sources of Boethius' *De Consolatione Philosophiae.*" *Sophia* 29 (1961) 67–94.

Te Velde, R. A. *Participation and Substantiality in Thomas Aquinas*. Leiden: E. J. Brill, 1996.
Thomae de Aquino Sancti. Opera, Rome, Typographia Polyglotta. *S. Thomae Aquinatis Doctoris Angelici Opera Omnia iussu impensaque Leoni XIII P. M. edita*, 1882–19–; *Expositio libri Boetii de Hebdomadibus*, ed. C. Pandolfi, Bologna: Edizioni Studio Domenicano, 1995; *Super Boetium De Trinitate*, ed. G. Mazzotta, Messina: Rubettino, 1996; ed. R. E. Brennan, St. Louis: Herder, 1946.
Tränkle, H. "Ist die *Philosophiae Consolatio* des Boethius zum vorgesehenen Abschluss gelangt?" *Vigiliae Christianae* 31 (1977) 148–56.
———. "Philologische Bemerkungen zum Boethiusprozess." In *Romanitas et Christianitas, Studia J. H. Waszink Oblata*. Pp. 329–39. Amsterdam: North Holland Pub., 1973.
Troncarelli, F. *Tradizioni Perdute*. Padua: Antenore, 1981.
Usener, H. *Anecdoton Holderi: Ein Beitrag zur Geschichte Roms in Ostgothischer Zeit*. Bonn: Universitäts-Buchdrückerei, 1877.
Vann, G. *The Wisdom of Boethius*. Oxford: *The Aquinas Papers*, 1952.
Varvis, S. *The "Consolation" of Boethius: An Analytical Inquiry into His Intellectual Processes and Goals*. San Francisco: Mellen Research University Press, 1991.
Wallis, R. T. *Neoplatonism*. New York: Scribners, 1972.
Weinberger, W. *Anicii Manlii Severini Boethii philosophiae consolationis libri quinque. Rudolfi Peiperi atque Georgii Schepssii copiis et Augusti Engelbrechti studiis usus ad fidem codicum recensuit Guglielmus Weinberger*, Corpus Scriptorum Ecclesiasticorum Latinorum 67. Vienna: Hölder-Pichler-Tempsky, 1938.
White, A. "Boethius in the Mediaeval Quadrivium." In *Boethius: His Life, Thought, and Influence*. Ed. Margaret Gibson. Pp. 162–205. Oxford: Blackwell, 1981.
Whittaker, T. *The Neoplatonists*. Cambridge: Cambridge University Press, 1928.
Wiltshire, S. F. "Boethius and the Summum Bonum." *The Classical Journal* 67 (1972) 216–20.
Wippel, J. F. "Thomas Aquinas and Participation." In *Studies in Medieval Philosophy*. Pp. 117–58. Washington, D.C.: Catholic University of America Press, 1984.
Wurm, K. *Substanz und Qualität*. Berlin: De Gruyter, 1973.

INDEX

Aquinas, 6, 7, 8, 18, 27, 45, 62, 83, 106, 120, 121, 122, 124, 125, 126, 141, 170, 178, 184, 232, 233, 235–37, 257, 269, 270–71
Aristotle, xiv, 1, 11, 12, 19, 22, 24, 25, 27, 32–34, 36, 39, 41, 43, 55, 83, 85, 100, 105, 140, 141, 156, 157, 188, 200, 234
Augustine, 12, 32, 43, 196

Barnes, Jonathan, 26
Barrett, Helen M., 10, 189, 200
Brosch, Hermann Josef, 9, 225, 234, 235

Chadwick, Henry, 10, 11, 12, 16, 25, 26, 127–30, 178, 190–91, 200, 231
Consolatio, Christianity of, 10
Courcelle, Pierre, 12, 23

De Fide Catholica, 2, 28, 273
De Rijk, Lambert M., 244, 246, 250, 261, 270
De Trinitate, 2, 9, 19, 23, 25, 26, 28, 29, 157, 191, 234, 240, 241, 243, 244, 264, 271, 272, 279, 293
Duhem, Pierre, 230, 250, 251, 252

Evil, 193, 196
 and God, 194, 196, 210, 213, 215, 276
 as privation of being, 194, 196, 201, 218, 285
Exemplarity, 57, 79, 166, 172, 178, 182, 279
 as opposed to formal causality, 280

Fabro, Cornelio, 125, 230, 231, 232, 235, 250, 251, 252, 254, 256, 270

Forma essendi, 19, 239, 241, 242, 243, 244, 245, 248, 249, 254
 as principle of determination, 256
 as principle of individuation, 256
Freedom
 ontological vs. freedom of the will, 214, 282
 and Providence, 195, 210, 281

Gastaldelli, Ferruccio, 11, 12, 129, 130, 191
Geiger, L. B., 8, 18, 120, 122–24, 126, 130, 166, 184
Ghisalberti, Alessandro, 11, 190
Good, 51
 Aristotle and the, 32
 as cause of desire, 51
 definition of, 113
 Final and Efficient Cause of goodness, 204
 final cause because substantial property, 44, 57, 208, 220
 formal and efficient causes of complex things' substantial goodness, 227, 280, 281
 man as instrumental cause of, 217, 284
 as object of a free act of will, 51
 as object of passive potency, 53
 as real relation, 49, 51
 as real relation and object of a free act of will, 110
 as substantial property and cause of desire, 82, 96, 111, 206
 as substantial property and object of free act of desire, 76, 79, 165, 229, 166

305

Good (*continued*)
  as substantial property and real relation, 77, 89, 96, 114, 142, 144, 146, 184, 207, 220
  transcendental as opposed to a substantial property of being, 184

Hadot, Pierre, 18, 133, 231, 239, 258, 261

Id quod est, 230
  and Aquinas, 233
  concrete particular, 230
  ens, 233
  as essence, 234
  existence, 231
  interpretational problems, 231
  limitation of *esse*, 231
  and Porphyry, 240
  primary substance, 234, 242
  and Victorinus, 237
Ideas (Platonic), 26
  divine ideas, 170, 271, 273, 280, 287, 291, 292, 294, 296
Individuation, 253, 255, 256, 263
Infinite, and the finite, 212
Ipsum esse
  ambiguous term meaning both God and form, 245
  Aquinas on meaning of, 232
  ambiguous term meaning both God and form, 245
  cannot be cause of complex things' existence, 252
  cannot be secondary substance, 253
  cannot mean God, 259, 268
  as essence, 230, 235, 241
  indeterminate being, 251
  is not God, 167
  meaning of, 259
  as pure activity, 231, 236
  as secondary substance, 234, 266
  as substantial form, 231
  universal ante rem, 272

Maioli, Bruno, 5, 7, 8, 18, 19, 23, 27, 225, 235, 236, 241, 242, 250, 251, 252, 254, 256, 266, 272

McInerny, Ralph, 6, 37, 122, 124, 125, 225, 236, 243, 270
Micaelli, Claudio, 27, 243, 270

Obertello, Luca, 1, 20, 21, 22, 23, 24, 25, 27, 130–38, 154, 188, 190, 191, 236–40 , 257, 258, 261, 268, 269, 274

Pandolfi, Carmelo, 5, 40, 125, 138–41, 147, 148, 232
Perfection, as acquisition of self though other, 284
Plato, 11, 22, 25, 32, 34, 45, 55, 140, 141, 190, 194
Porphyry, 16, 18, 22, 24, 26, 236, 237, 240
Proclus, 12
Providence, 12, 186, 191, 195, 196, 198, 218, 219, 220, 275, 280, 283, 285, 286
  and fate, 24, 195
  and freedom, 285
  and formal cause of complex things, 279, 280, 283, 286, 288

Quomodo, apparent discrepancy of two parts, 6, 145, 225

Rapisarda, Emanuele, 16, 23, 27, 29
Real relations
  acquisition of self through other, 57, 85, 197, 205, 277
  cannot be caused by real relater, 58, 205
Roland-Gosselin, M.-D., 234, 250, 251, 252

Starnes, Colin J., 188
Substance, as essence, 120

te Velde, Rudi A., 7, 74, 125, 126, 146
Themistius, 18, 234

Varvis, S., 10, 23, 188, 231, 275
Victorinus, 18, 231, 237, 239, 240

www.ingramcontent.com/pod-product-compliance
Lightning Source LLC
Chambersburg PA
CBHW021354290426
44108CB00010B/242